✗20

Tourism Imaginaries

TOURISM IMAGINARIES
Anthropological Approaches

Edited by

Noel B. Salazar and Nelson H. H. Graburn

berghahn
NEW YORK · OXFORD
www.berghahnbooks.com

Published in 2014 by

Berghahn Books

www.berghahnbooks.com

Library of Congress Cataloging-in-Publication Data

Tourism imaginaries : anthropological approaches / edited by Noel B. Salazar
and Nelson H. H. Graburn.
    pages cm.
Includes bibliographical references and index.
ISBN 978-1-78238-367-3 (hardback : alk. paper) – ISBN 978-1-78238-368-0
(ebook)
    1. Tourism—Anthropological aspects. I. Salazar, Noel B., 1973–

G155.A1T5919 2014
306.4'819—dc23

2013041903

British Library Cataloguing in Publication Data

A catalogue record for this book is available from the British Library

Printed on acid-free paper

ISBN: 978-1-78238-367-3 hardback
ISBN: 978-1-78238-368-0 ebook

To those who dare to dream

"The shortest distance between a human being and truth is a story."
Anthony de Mello

Contents

List of Illustrations   ix

Acknowledgments   xi

Introduction. Toward an Anthropology of Tourism Imaginaries   1
     Noel B. Salazar and Nelson H. H. Graburn

Part I. Imaginaries of Peoples

1. Toward Symmetric Treatment of Imaginaries: Nudity and Payment in Tourism to Papua's "Treehouse People"   31
     Rupert Stasch

2. Scorn or Idealization? Tourism Imaginaries, Exoticization, and Ambivalence in Emberá Indigenous Tourism   57
     Dimitrios Theodossopoulos

3. Deriding Demand: Indigenous Imaginaries in Tourism   80
     Alexis Celeste Bunten

4. Myth Management in Tourism's Imaginariums: Tales from Southwest China and Beyond   103
     Margaret Byrne Swain

5. Tourism Moral Imaginaries and the Making of Community   125
     João Afonso Baptista

Part II. Imaginaries of Places

6. The Imaginaire Dialectic and the Refashioning of Pietrelcina   147
     Michael A. Di Giovine

7. Temporal Fragmentation: Cambodian Tales   172
     Federica Ferraris

8. The Imagined Nation: The Mystery of the Endurance of
   the Colonial Imaginary in Postcolonial Times   194
   Paula Mota Santos

9. Belize Ephemera, Affect, and Emergent Imaginaries   220
   Kenneth Little

10. Envisioning the Dutch Serengeti: An Exploration of
    Touristic Imaginings of the Wild in the Netherlands   242
    Anke Tonnaer

Afterword. Locating Imaginaries in the Anthropology of Tourism 260
   Naomi Leite

Notes on Contributors   279

Index   283

Illustrations

Figure 0.1. Hosts "gazing" at guests in an ethnic village in southwest China (Copyright: N. Salazar).   14

Figure 0.2. Cleaning up Kuta Beach, Bali (Copyright: N. Salazar).   20

Figure 1.1. Korowai lands in Papua (Copyright: R. Stasch).   33

Figure 1.2. Members of a German tour group photographing the house of Saxip Bumxai (Copyright: R. Stasch).   34

Figure 1.3. A film crew enacting a desire to "be like them," after completing their film shoot (Copyright: R. Stasch).   43

Figure 2.1. Emberá men waiting for the arrival of the tourists (Copyright: D. Theodossopoulos).   59

Figure 2.2. Emberá children learning how to type on the anthropologist's computer (Copyright: D. Theodossopoulos).   61

Figure 2.3. Emberá child looking at the arriving tourists (Copyright: D. Theodossopoulos).   69

Figure 4.1. Sani vendor dressing up tourists at the Ashima rock, Shilin Park (Copyright: M. Swain).   113

Figure 4.2. Destroying Sani village of Wukeshu in Shilin for tourism development (Copyright: W. Swain).   120

Figure 5.1. Workshop in Canhane (Copyright: J. Baptista).   138

Figure 6.1. Recreation of Pio's childhood home in Pietrelcina (Copyright: M. Di Giovine).   160

Figure 6.2. Scene from Marko Ivan Rupnik's fresco cycle (Copyright: M. Di Giovine).   160

Figure 8.1. Portugal dos Pequenitos (Source: Fundação Bissaya
    Barreto/Portugal dos Pequenitos; Copyright: L. Salt & P. Santos).   200

Figure 8.2. Original entrance (top) and present-day entrance
    (bottom) (Copyright: P. Santos).   203

Figure 8.3. Angola's original Padrão dos Descobrimentos (left)
    and present-day inscription (right) (Copyright: P. Santos).   204

Figure 8.4. Depiction of African male human figures (Copyright:
    P. Santos).   206

Figure 9.1. Lighthouse beer coaster (Copyright: K. Little).   221

Acknowledgments

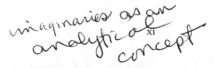

This edited volume is the result of the fortuitous coming together of tourism scholars on both sides of the Atlantic Ocean who had been working on similar issues and who were developing remarkably similar conceptual frameworks. In December 2007, the French sociologist Bertrand Réau met American-based anthropologist Nelson Graburn at the conference "Tourism and Indigenous People/Minorities in Multi-cultural Societies" in the Xishuangbanna Dai Autonomous Region, Yunnan, China. Striking up discussions about their research, they discovered many common interests in the study of tourism and hoped to meet again. When Graburn took up his part-time position the following year as senior professor at the International Institute of Culture, Tourism and Development, at London Metropolitan University, Réau invited him to speak in Lyon and at the École des Hautes Études en Sciences Sociales (EHESS) in Paris in October 2008. Réau introduced Graburn to geographer Maria Gravari-Barbas, director of the Institute of Advanced Studies and Research on Tourism (IREST) at the University of Paris 1 Pantheon-Sorbonne, and they discussed mutual interests and possible cooperation between their research groups.

Around the time Réau and Graburn were meeting in China, Belgian anthropologist Noel Salazar was wrapping up his dissertation on tour guiding practices and narratives. Partly inspired by his former training as a psychologist, he was applying the concept of imaginaries (developed in the French academic tradition as *imaginaires*) to tourism in order to explain the fundamental elements on which guiding discourses are based. He successfully defended his dissertation at the University of Pennsylvania in May 2008 and immediately started working on a postdoctoral project at the University of Leuven (Belgium) in which he further explored the usefulness of imaginaries as an analytical concept. This work resulted in the monograph *Envisioning Eden: Mobilizing Imaginaries in Tourism and Beyond* (2010, Berghahn Books). Having been in touch with Graburn and various members of the Tourism

Studies Working Group at the University of California–Berkeley for many years, Salazar decided to attend the June 2009 workshop in Paris entitled "The Heritage Industry and the Tourist Imagination," co-organized by the Berkeley group and the Sorbonne équipe. It was here and at the ensuing international conference on "Tourist Imaginaries/Imaginaires Touristiques" in 2011 in Berkeley that the idea for this volume was fleshed out.

The editors of this book would like to express their gratitude to all the contributors, and particularly to Naomi Leite, author of the afterword, who was founder of the Tourism Studies Working Group at Berkeley but who was brought into this book project long after its inception. We also express our gratitude to Maria Gravari-Barbas for her hospitality and for her enthusiasm in stimulating our project. We are grateful to the two anonymous readers for their critical and eager feedback. Finally, we thank Marion Berghahn and the staff at Berghahn Books for their advice and patience during the production of this book.

Noel B. Salazar   Nelson H. H. Graburn
Brussels   Berkeley

Summer of 2013

Introduction

Toward an Anthropology of Tourism Imaginaries

Noel B. Salazar and Nelson H. H. Graburn

As with many other activities—reading novels, playing games, watching movies, telling stories, daydreaming, etc.—tourism involves the human capacity to imagine or to enter into the imaginings of others. Stories, images, and desires, running the gamut from essentialized, mythologized, and exoticized imaginaries of Otherness to more realistic frames of reference, often function as the motor setting tourism in motion (Amirou 1995). Marketers eagerly rely on them to represent and sell dreams of the world's limitless destinations, activities, types of accommodation, and peoples to discover and experience. Seductive images and discourses about peoples and places are so predominant that without them there probably would be little tourism, if any at all (Salazar 2010a). It is, indeed, hard to think of tourism without imaginaries or "fantasies."[1] Some of these can be very specific: tourism imaginaries about the Pacific, for example, distinguish a masculinized Melanesia from a feminized Polynesia (Stephen 1999).

In this edited volume, we conceptualize imaginaries as socially transmitted representational assemblages that interact with people's personal imaginings and that are used as meaning-making and world-shaping devices (Salazar 2012). Imaginaries are "implicit schemas of interpretation, rather than explicit ideologies" (Strauss 2006: 329). They are often structured by dichotomies, sometimes difficult to discern in practice, that represent the world in paradigmatically linked binominals: nature-culture, here-there, male-female, inside-outside, and local-global (cf. Barthes 1972 and his concept of "mythologies"; Durand 1999).[2] The turning into tourism products of the everyday, the alternative, the intangible, and that which has not yet been memorialized in guidebooks and official histories is a response to the

1

increasing demand for experiential tourism, often based on processes of temporal and spatial Othering (cf. Fabian 2002). This offers those participating in tourism the opportunity to move from (more passively) lived imagining, which is self-enclosed and concentrated on the imaginaries themselves, to (more actively) experienced imagining, which is directed and intentional (Kunz 1946).

Studying imaginaries seems as daunting as it is exciting (Sneath et al. 2009; Strauss 2006). By their very nature, imaginaries remain intangible, so the only way to study them is by focusing on the multiple conduits through which they pass and become visible in the form of images and discourses (see below). Through a combination of historical and ethnographic methods, it is possible to assess how imaginary activities, subjects, social relations, and so forth are materialized, enacted, and inculcated. Thus, although the precise workings of imaginaries are hidden from view, the operating logic can be inferred from its visible manifestations and from what people say and do. Tourism imaginaries in particular become tangible when they are incarnated in institutions, from archaeological sites, museums, and monuments to hotels, media, and cultural productions (Wynn 2007: 21). In order to understand how tourism's foundational imaginaries circulate and perpetuate themselves, we need theoretical frameworks that allow a comprehensive study of inner dynamics that transcend the unproductive binary opposition between the economic global and the cultural local. Anthropology may give us some important clues here (Salazar 2010a; Skinner and Theodossopoulos 2011).

While the imagination plays an essential role in tourism, ranging from the role of fantasy to imaginative play (e.g., film-induced tourism), this volume focuses specifically on tourism imaginaries of peoples and places. Where do tourism imaginaries come from? How and why are they circulated across the globe? What material impact do they have on people's lives? This edited volume illustrates ethnographically how a critical analysis of tourism imaginaries offers a powerful deconstruction device of ideological, political, and sociocultural stereotypes and clichés. The various contributors pay particular attention to how personal imaginings of tourists, "locals," and tourism intermediaries interact with and are influenced by institutionally grounded imaginaries implying power, hierarchy, and hegemony. In this introduction, we offer a broad overview of anthropological takes on tourism imaginaries. This helps to frame the other chapters in which the multiple links between tourism and the imagination are discussed, illustrating the overlapping but conflicting ways in which imaginaries drive tourists, host societies, and tourism service providers alike.

CONCEPTUALIZING IMAGINARIES

Scholars from a wide array of disciplines have given attention to the imagination (Brann 1991; Kearney 1998). As Claudia Strauss (2006) points out,
imaginaries have been conceptualized as a culture's ethos or a society's
shared, unifying core conceptions (Castoriadis 1987), as fantasies or illusions created in response to a psychological need (Lacan 1977), and as cultural models or widely shared implicit cognitive schemas (Anderson 1991;
Taylor 2004). Most conceptualizations have been developed in the fields of
continental philosophy (the phenomenological and hermeneutic legacies of
Merleau-Ponty, Husserl, and Heidegger), psychoanalysis (including arche-
typal and transpersonal psychology), poststructuralism (especially Deleuze),
the social sciences (Latour and the literature on enchantment), visual studies (Mitchell), analytical philosophy (the philosophy of mind and of aesthetics), and, increasingly, the intersection of these various approaches and the
neurosciences (Roth 2007). The imaginary is both seen as a function of producing meanings and as the product of this function (Ricoeur 1994).

Imaginaries are "complex systems of presumption—patterns of forgetfulness and attentiveness—that enter subjective experience as the expectation
that things will make sense generally (i.e., in terms not wholly idiosyncratic)"
(Vogler 2002: 625). Although culturally shaped imaginaries influence collective behavior, they are not necessarily an acknowledged part of public
discourse or coterminous with implicit or covert culture. They are building
"upon implicit understandings that underlie and make possible common
practices" (Gaonkar 2002: 4). While imaginaries are alienating when they
take on an institutional(ized) life of their own (e.g., in religion or politics)
(Castoriadis 1987: 108, 132), in the end the agents who imagine are individuals, not societies. However, the strength and power of imaginaries, as
opposed to personal imaginings, lies in the fact that they are widely shared
by people and that they increasingly circulate across the globe. Imaginaries exist "by virtue of representation or implicit understandings, even when
they acquire immense institutional force; and they are the means by which
individuals understand their identities and their place in the world" (Gaonkar 2002: 4). Shared imaginaries can be "about other people, as with the
nineteenth- and early twentieth-century European imagining of African
peoples as cannibals. They can be about other places, as with the British
colonial idea of 'the tropics' as steaming hot year round, disease ridden, and
somewhat dangerous" (J. Adams 2004: 295).

Some scholars have pointed to the similarity between "myths"—traditional explanatory stories (often of a sacred nature)—and tourism imaginar-

ies (Hennig 2002; Selwyn 1996). Echtner and Prasad (2003), for example, identify three recurring myths in tourism to developing countries: the myth of the unchanged, the myth of the unrestrained, and the myth of the uncivilized. Modern myths—nature, the noble savage, art, individual freedom and self-realization, equality, and paradise—all have special significance for and are manifested in the social practices of tourism (Hennig 2002). As Brann reminds us, such myths are "systemic public illusions, spontaneous or manipulated by the image-makers" (1991: 546). Various imaginaries combine to offer a program of travels that legitimizes some of the daydreams of traveling individuals. Dann (1976) distinguishes two basic characteristics underlying all tourist imaginings. On the one hand, there is the overcoming of monotony, anomie, and meaninglessness of everyday life with more satisfying experiences—escapism and the desire for exoticism or difference.[3] On the other hand, there is the boosting of personality—ego-enhancement, leading to the accumulation of symbolic capital. Such desires, once again, are not simply internalized wishes, but, rather, part of widely shared imaginaries that are articulated through constellations of social practice and media (Crouch et al. 2005).

For Said (1994), geographic imaginaries refer, literally, to how spaces are imagined, how meanings are ascribed to physical spaces (such that they are perceived, represented, and interpreted in particular ways), how knowledge about these places is produced, and how these representations make various courses of action possible. Tourist ways of "seeing" places often differ from other representations because places are being fashioned in the image of tourism (Hughes 1992). The Caribbean as "tropical nature," for example, is mobilized through a range of tourism imaginaries and practices (Sheller 2004: 17). The past is being reworked by naming, designating, and historicizing landscapes to enhance their tourism appeal (Bacchilega 2007; Gold and Gold 1995). Some have argued that "to remake the world imaginatively" is "our most specifically human mission" (Brann 1991: 774). Who represents what, whom, and how are critical and often contested issues for sociocultural insiders as well as outsiders (K. M. Adams 2004; Morgan and Pritchard 1998; Mowforth and Munt 2008). There are important bonds between imaginative geographies and imagined communities, as peoples and places are constructed in both the imaginative and the material sense (Anderson 1991; Gregory 1994).

In the words of Hollinshead, "This immense imaginary power to invent iconic traditions afresh or to manufacture felt authenticities amounts to the 'fantasmatics' of global tourism image-making, rhetoric mongering, and discourse articulations, *viz.* the very craft by which not only knowledge but life-style and life-space is created" (1998: 75). The challenge, then, is to study not only how the existing power relations and inequalities that characterize circulating tourism imaginaries are maintained, reproduced, and reinforced, but also how they are challenged, contested, and transformed (Edensor 1998). While various facets of imaginaries within tourism are studied by cultural geography, cultural studies, and critical tourism studies scholars, this task in particular is being taken up by anthropologists (Leite and Graburn 2009).

ANTHROPOLOGICAL TAKES ON TOURISM IMAGINARIES

The pioneer anthropologist E. B. Tylor (1889) and his contemporaries divided the human characteristic of culture into "mental culture" and "material culture," both of which display patterns representative of certain groups, whether communities, "tribes," or even nations. While this early culture concept stressed shared continuities rather than innovation and cultural change, the core importance of shared understandings and behaviors can be applied to two of the most important features in the study of tourism: (tangible and intangible) heritage and imaginaries. Through time, anthropologists have become specialists in the study of cultural images and representations, whether these are part of a group's self-image or whether they are held up for the consumption of others, and particularly when they are dialectically co-constructed by insiders and outsiders, often through the agency of mediators or brokers (including anthropologists). Research on such inside-outside views is the basis of the study of ethnicity and ethnic boundaries (Barth 1969). One special kind of "co-construction" is the ethnographic portrait of a culture, brought about through the collaboration of an anthropologist and his or her informants or collaborators (Wagner 1975).

Indeed, anthropologists are in a special position to both understand and criticize sociocultural imaginaries. Anthropologists study people's views of themselves and of outsiders, and those of outsiders adjacent to the communities studied.[4] They are often responsible, through their writings, for creating "outsider" views of previously marginalized societies. Some anthropologists have been professionally active in promulgating and controlling tourism imaginaries in their roles as professional tour guides—Bruner (1989) in Indonesia, Guldin (1989) in China, Little (2004) in Guatemala, Bunten (2008) in Alaska, Di Giovine (2008) in Italy and Cambodia, and D. Picard (2011) on the island of Reunion—or as authors of writings about places that have become destinations (Graburn 2003). Kaspin (1997), Salazar (2013), and others have pointed out that anthropologists have been respected as authenticators of information and imaginaries about exotic places, even though the ethnographic works chosen or cited may be passé and their theories obsolete. Tourism marketers borrow from traditional ethnology an ontological and essentialist vision of exotic cultures, conceived as static entities with clearly defined characteristics (Thomas 1994). Ideas of old-style colonial anthropology—objectifying, reifying, homogenizing, and naturalizing peoples—are widely used by a variety of tourism shareholders, staking claims of identity and cultural belonging on strong notions of place and locality (Hall and Tucker 2004).

But the allure of anthropological knowledge is current, even if anthropologists themselves experienced a "crisis of representation" (Marcus and Fischer 1986) or reflexively pointed out that most of their work was dated (Fabian 2002). In Graburn's (2013) experiences of fieldwork among the Canadian Inuit since 1959, he has often noted that the anthropologist is the "authority on the spot," who rather than just asking questions of the locals spends far more time answering questions about the "outside world" for the locals, and sometimes about the locals for other outside visitors, such as census takers, schoolteachers, or doctors. Theodossopoulos (this volume) makes the very same point: the Emberá of Panama expect him to inform them about the national cultures of the tourists (from England, France, or Italy) in the same way that the local Panamanians and tourists expect him to be the authority on the indigenous Emberá.

Anthropologists have been looking at tourism in relation to colonialism and neo- and postcolonialism (Nash 1977, 1981) during the period since World War II. Because the places where anthropologists typically conduct ethnographic fieldwork are parts of the so-called third and fourth worlds (Graburn 1981), they see the contemporary world as a product of the recent past, which involved internal or overseas colonization. Other social science disciplines also consider this when exploring the historical formation of imaginaries (heritage, nostalgia, postwar, "dark," etc.), and we can claim that concepts such as Rosaldo's (1989) "imperialist nostalgia" have been widely influential. Anthropologists claim their advantage stems from (1) their holistic approach, studying not only groups of people or communities but also the surrounding sociological contexts and, more recently, the temporalities of the situation; and (2) their long-term, "in-depth" field research, stressing participant observation and intimate knowledge. Though the study of tourism, an unusually mobile subject, sometimes forces anthropologists into "quick and dirty" fieldwork, resembling media reporters and market advisors (Graburn 2002), most anthropology of tourism is still in depth (Leite and Graburn 2009; Scott and Selwyn 2010).

Origins

Destination marketers have no monopoly over manufacturing the exotic or the extraordinary. The origins of tourism imaginaries are complex and difficult to pinpoint. They are always situated within wider sociocultural frameworks (Hutnyk 1996) and emerge not from the realm of concrete everyday experience but in the circulation of more collectively held images. Tourism imaginaries can be traced back to more general sources, including: parental and family milieu; early worldviews; early prototypes of self and alterity established through family interactions, stories, and attitudes, even including the animal world; early understandings of geography or "ownership" of inside and outside; and language, overt religion, and prayers. Close to these would be early schooling, including textbooks, readers, teachers, maps, and classes—the kind of information that often shapes our worldviews for life (Mota Santos, this volume). For much of the Western world, we could stress the early fundamental sociocultural context of upbringing (Graburn 2007).[5]

We should separate the above background sources from the normally cited proximate channels, especially the modern media. These channels include the visual and textual content of documentaries and fiction movies; art, museum exhibitions, and fairs; trade cards, video games, and animation; photographs, slides, video, and postcards; travelogues, blogs, and other websites; guidebooks and tourism brochures; literature, coffee-table books, and magazines; news coverage and advertising; official documents; and quasi-scientific media such as *National Geographic* (Lutz and Collins 1993). All of these play upon already internalized worldviews, directing them to specific destinations. There is a worldwide advertising industry creating these mediated messages, which anthropologists are beginning to reveal (e.g., de Waal Malefyt and Moeran 2003).

Another and immediate personal source of imaginaries originates from ongoing experience: the tourists' experiences include feedback and reverse gazes from destination communities, and from tour guides and other mediators (Salazar 2010a). This is part of what Bruner (2005) calls the ongoing "narrative" that is constantly churned over and updated *not just* in the light of ongoing tourist experiences and word of mouth from others, but also in terms of the ongoing *non*tourist life afterward (Graburn 2002; Harrison 2003)—people constantly reformulate (or reaffirm) their imagined worldviews. Tourism imaginaries of peoples and places cannot be considered simply as commoditized or commercial representations with an interpretative or symbolic content. They often propagate historically inherited stereotypes that are based on the myths and fantasies that form part of an imaginary or, as Leite calls it, an "imaginative reconstruction" (2005: 290).

Discourses of the past—Orientalism, colonialism, and imperialism—seem to be fertile ground for nostalgic and romantic tourism dreams. The imagery used in tourism to developing countries is often about an ambivalent nostalgia for the past—ambivalent because returning to the past is not what people actually desire (Bissell 2005). Appadurai (1996: 76–78) calls such nostalgia, without lived experience or collective historical memory, "armchair nostalgia" or "imagined nostalgia." The ambivalence is also captured in Rosaldo's notion of "imperialist nostalgia," described as "a particular kind of nostalgia, often found under imperialism, where people mourn the passing of what they themselves have transformed" (1989: 108). In any of its versions, "imperialist nostalgia uses a pose of 'innocent yearning' both to capture people's imaginations and to conceal its complicity with often brutal domination" (Rosaldo 1989: 108).

Critical scholarship reveals how broader cultural and ideological structures create and mediate tourism representations (Ateljevic et al. 2007; Hall and Tucker 2004; Morgan and Pritchard 1998; Mowforth and Munt 2008; Selwyn 1996; Urry and Larsen 2011). Images of difference have been (re)constructed over centuries of cross-cultural contact. In the case of Western tourism to developing countries, the circulating representations cater to certain images within Western consciousness about how the Other is imagined to be. Such imaginaries heavily rely upon the fictional worlds of literature, film, and the fine arts to give "authenticity" to peoples and places (Hennig 2002; Robinson and Andersen 2002; Urbain 1994). At the same time, tourism imaginaries do not exist in a vacuum, but have to contend with other circulating images and ideas. Global media streams overwhelm people with thousands of impressions of the world, in real time. In the case of developing countries, the competing imagery is often negative, and the media can be very selective in what they show or do not show their audiences.

Not surprisingly, the currently dominant tourism discourses draw upon and extend mythologized (colonial) visions of Otherness from popular culture, (travel) literature, and academic writings in disciplines such as anthropology, archaeology, and history (Clifford 1997; Pratt 2008; Said 1994; Salazar 2013; Torgovnick 1990). The discourses surrounding ecotourism, for example, are closely related to the much wider global ecological imaginary of late twentieth-century environmentalism, while nostalgia tourism often taps into commoditized (neo)colonial imaginaries. Henderson and Weisgrau, for instance, note how guidebooks about India remarkably mirror the accounts of nineteenth-century British colonial tourists, with a recycling of the mythic foci grounded in these earlier accounts, which evoke an Orientalist imaginary of India, "replete with moral judgments about the superiority of Western 'civilization', mixed with the desires evident in fantasies about romance, decadence, sensuality, cruelty, sex and the unfathomable" (2007: xvii).[6]

Sexual imaginaries apply to cultures and subcultures or, more correctly, to particular peoples and ways of life (Bishop and Robinson 1999; Frohlick 2010). Cowboys and the American West, like the Maasai warriors of East Africa (Salazar 2009), are "masculine" to most Western minds (whether the minds are attached to traveling bodies or not). Tibetans are excessively masculine to both male and female (Han) Chinese tourists, and they know it and take advantage of it (Zhang 2009). Conversely, as Schein (2000) and others have averred, most Chinese minority *minzu* ("nationality") are feminized in relation to the dominant Han Chinese, and they emphasize this kind of attractiveness in the ethnic tourism that is a pervasive part of China's contemporary development and "rural poverty alleviation." Sexual imaginaries are a common feature of cultural tourism where tourists are exploring and "penetrating" more marginal areas and peoples in a kind of conquest, a symbolic and sometimes a real historical parallel to colonial invasions and territorial conquests.

Focusing once more on the materials mostly evident in the chapters to follow, we find many features in common between Western (European and North American) tourists' imaginaries of non-Western people and destinations (Graburn and Gravari-Barbas 2011). Many instances exhibit what some would claim as "universal modern" (but most likely just "Western") "archetypes." These may be positive or negative, but most likely invoke familiar ambivalences: love/hate, fear/attraction, or noble/savage. For instance, there are implied or explicit "evolutionary" Stone Age "primitives," with "nasty, brutish and short" lives; warlike cannibals (Hobbes) versus the complementary view of the Other as natural, pure, and unspoiled (Rousseau). There have been many variations over historical time, with major tropes hinging on "tradition" and "modernity" (and perhaps postmodernity). Evolving ways of interpreting and living this evolutionary worldview are reflected, for instance, in some features of ethnic tourism and ecotourism. A more limited version of this worldview would look to the most recent past, using tropes of "colonialism" and "empire."

One temporal aspect of the modern imaginary is what Lanfant and Graburn (1992) have labeled the "smell of death," the fascination with the rare, the endangered, the about-to-disappear; in general, the (over)valuation of the old. Another temporal aspect is the tourist's need for escape from the here and now, to a more authentic life "elsewhere," in other places, other peoples' lives, other forms of nature, and literally in *other times,* as exemplified by archeology, history, or science fiction (cf. Salazar and Zhang 2013). Yet for tourists to succumb to allotemporal imaginaries requires suspension of disbelief, the ignoring of countersignals, and a disregard of the almost universal commodification. This is heightened by the common illusion that the absence of humans equals purity. Therefore, imaginaries of wilderness and nature as unspoiled and unpolluted are important in contemporary tourism (Tonnaer, this volume), succumbing to the illusion of time travel, often expressed as fantasy and dreams. Another powerful, closely related illusion is the equivalence of space with time. The distance traveled is often seen as a measure or a promise of time travel through history and cultural and natural difference. This is a replay of the evolutionary model, where things/people farther away are deemed to represent a more distant (and purer or more primitive) past, a more distant history, and an earlier time (Ferraris, this volume). Such time travel is aided by modern technologies such as media, science fiction, and variations of "daydreaming," such as New Age channeling.

One further aspect of the temporality of imaginaries is their stability or instability over time. Many imaginaries, especially those clinging to historically important places, are slower to change. Many historical cities have strong images that display them as museums of themselves, such as Kyoto and Nara in Japan or Oxford, Bruges, and Florence in Europe. Similarly, whole countries, such as England and Italy, work to maintain their image and "olde" traditional destinations, and go to great expense to ensure the maintenance of architectural fabric as well as the expected traditionally clothed persons such as Beefeaters, gladiators, and Swiss Guards. On the other hand, those places that were "discovered" in recent history and that have grown in popularity have to work at keeping their original "exclusive" and novel image, even as they suffer from their success and attract growing numbers of less affluent mass tourists (Di Giovine, this volume). This is one of the most thoroughly studied aspects of the control and manipulation of imaginaries.

Circulation

Images, discourses, and ideas have certain points of origin—in tourism many of them are marked by distinctly Western genealogies—but are now incessantly moving in global "rounds," not strictly circular, reaching new horizons and periodically feeding back to their places of departure. As with myths, the older the imaginaries, the longer they have been circulating, the harder it becomes to trace where they originated (Selwyn 1996). Imaginaries circulate unevenly, not freely; their spread is shaped by processes that delimit and restrict movement. In its articulation between the ideological and the material, the circulation of imaginaries requires some sort of material and institutional infrastructure of movement. In order to understand how this circulation works, we not only need to study what is circulating but also the sociocultural structures and mechanisms that make that circulation possible or impossible.

Empowered by imagined vistas of mass-mediated master narratives, tourism imaginaries have become global (Crouch et al. 2005). They are now sent, circulated, transferred, received, accumulated, converted, and stored around the world. Through this continuous circulation, tourism fantasies help in (re)creating peoples and places. Global tourism disembeds images and ideas of peoples and places from their original context, making them available through their transformation, legitimization, institutionalization, and distribution. Tourism images and ideas easily travel, together with tourists, from tourism-generating regions (which are also destinations) to tourism destination regions (which also generate fantasies) and back. However, tourism imaginaries do not float around spontaneously and independently; rather, they "travel" in space and time through well-established conduits, leaving certain elements behind and picking up new ones along the way, and continuously returning to their points of origin.

Tourism imaginaries are easily reembedded in new contexts by a process that constantly alters both the imaginaries and the contexts, building on local referents to establish their meaning and value (Salazar 2010a). It is no coincidence that "travel" is linguistically related to the French word *travail*, which means labor. Tourism involves networked orderings of people, natures, materials, mobilities, and cultures. In some destinations, tourism imaginaries are so firmly established and all-encompassing that they are difficult to escape. In other places, the images and ideas are much more diffuse and open to changes (Bruner 2005; M. Picard 1996). Indeed, reproduction processes are rarely without negotiation and resignification. The circulation of tourism discourses and imaginaries is, in many respects, a translocally negotiated process involving variously situated actors and their glocal engagements with tourism to (re)produce "stereotypic images, discredited histories, and romantic fantasies" (Bruner 2005: 76). Rather than mere projections, these transactions are negotiated in various ways and both restrict the lives of people and create new subject positions.

What material equipment "contains," carries, or serves as a mnemonic for tourism imaginaries? When it concerns a "self-imaginary" (typically where cultural difference is great), people often emphasize overt features such as their "race," that is, phenotypic characteristics, language, clothing, craft technologies, naming and sociocultural system, ownership of property and nature, hospitality, ritual, or athletic prowess. Particularly important are food and cuisine, especially when it is seen to be locally derived and manually processed, or not processed at all. Sacred places—waters (especially waterfalls), mountains, caves, sacred paraphernalia, graves, and grave goods play an important role, too. Then there are objects, often stressing the allotemporal and traditional links or "remnants": historical objects, old "treasures," conspicuous "survivals," often displayed in those hallmarks of local guidance for tourists, museums or cultural centers (Graburn 1998). The production of these, especially the material carriers and the stories that travel with them, are fomented by the "contact" zone (Bruner 2005; Clifford 1997).

This is particularly true of tourist arts and other souvenirs, which are powerful carriers of the iconic aspects of imaginaries. These range from replicas of key traditional symbolic arts to kitsch souvenirs, but also include many innovative products of the contact context, which carry simple but powerful key messages between cultures (Graburn 1976). Tourists may buy (in the pecuniary and the metaphoric sense) the souvenirs of the Others whom they visit. Indeed, buying mementos that hopefully capture and confirm the essence of the imaginary that they brought with them is much of the fun of the tourism experience. Lee (1999) has shown how different classes of tourists may seek closer relations with not only the exotic seller, but also the maker as part of the authenticity-confirming experience, carrying away with them the material objects that witness their prowess as ethnic tourists.

Thus, the tourist is taking a small part of the imaginary while affirming the host's self-imaginary (cf. Little, this volume). Souvenirs can be both the signs and symbols of imaginaries, which could be banal stereotypes or could be highly modified and personalized by their experiences, in many forms. In many instances, the souvenirs proffered satisfy a simple match with a particular imaginary, but they may not be made by the people visited. Indeed, they may be produced far away by methods that have little in common with the local culture (Zhong 2010). Tourists are complicit in creating their own "proofs" or evidences of tourism imaginaries. Prime are photographs, which can reproduce the imaginary expected and searched for or can represent a unique experience and thus be the bearer of newly formed imaginaries to be passed on by "word of mouth." Similarly, there are paintings, figurative images, guidebooks, menus, and party favors. Some of these carriers have to bear witness to more difficult aspects of the imaginary, such as climate and distance or exoticism. Clothes and cuisine are important material carriers of these aspects and easily incorporated into "word of mouth" transmissions, as well as being amenable to commoditized production.

Museums and theme parks are the more institutionalized bearers of imaginaries (Salazar 2010b). Like guidebooks, they often are prime guides for tourists' consolidation and exploration of imagined destinations (Mota Santos, this volume). Museums particularly function as guarantors of "objective" authenticity. Tourism destinations are often reconstructed or even erected as "museums of themselves," bearing and conforming to a tourist imaginary and a dialectical process that has often been labeled postmodern, but, as any student of architecture can tell you, has been common since the early Roman and Chinese eras. In sum, analyzing the global circulation of images and ideas of tourism—a constant interaction between documents, devices, and people—and seeking to determine the local dynamics of this exchange is a complicated matter. Imaginaries often become the symbolic objects of a significant contest over economic supremacy, territorial ownership, and identity. This does not mean that such imaginaries enter into public circulation with their meanings already defined according to some preexisting cultural matrix; nor are they innocent of history. As new forms of circulation come to shape our world to an unprecedented degree, understanding the historical specificities of these global processes is a central challenge for scholars. This becomes clear in the various chapters of this volume.

Tourism Imaginaries (in Plural)

Because of their historical concern with ethnographically and geographically marginalized peoples and, more recently, through critical anthropology's concern for socially and economically marginalized peoples, anthropologists have an unusually thorough understanding of "host" imaginaries, whereas most other social scientists only know or care about tourist imaginaries. Indeed, a feature of many chapters in this collection is the multiple focuses on tourist, tourism service provider, and host imaginaries, sometimes explicating the dialectic between them (e.g., Theodossopoulos, this volume; Swain, this volume). The foregrounding of the host's imaginary is closely related to what has been called the "counter-gaze" (Evans-Pritchard 1989; Hendry 2000). While most social science disciplines do of course acknowledge the power and influence of major nations'/peoples' self-imaginaries (as hosts) and their influence on the tourist imaginary, anthropologists stress the same with minority/formerly marginalized peoples and thereby give them "agency" in their interaction with the global world (see figure 0.1).

Bunten (this volume), for example, has focused her research on the world of indigenous and marginal peoples under the pressures of modern

Figure 0.1. Host "gazing" at guests in an ethnic village in southwest China (Copyright: N. Salazar).

tourism. She suggests that when indigenous peoples can control the images that they wish to meld into visitors' imaginaries, the images are favorable to the "marginalized peoples," often countering the negative images that have long inhabited dominant worldviews. They attempt to make visible the previously invisible; the images are always localized but contextualized, placing their modern selves in the world context. Moreover, they may be as fascinated with tourists/tourism as the visitors are with them. They try to stress that the imaginaries are based on a unique cultural core: bringing in mythology, history, their past, and their relation to the land/nature as "key symbols" (Ortner 1973). That is the ideal, valorizing their culture on their own terms. However, when the power imbalance is steep and the local peoples have only recently been thrust onto the world stage as "tourees," they may try to live up to the role thrust upon them (perhaps unconsciously), whether they believe in it or not. They may be acting out (consciously) this newly acquired part on the global stage, while protecting their inner beliefs and private lives, struggling against selling out, that is, becoming that figment of someone else's imagination (Stanley 1998).

While anthropologists traditionally analyzed tourism in terms of "hosts" and "guests" (Smith 1977, 1989; Smith and Brent 2001), recent research has reflected the more complex and fluid situation in most contemporary commercial tourism venues. There are nearly always a somewhat privileged set of mediators acting as fulcrum, filtering information and actions of tourists vis-à-vis locals (Salazar 2010a). In most tourism destinations of any scale, the "locals" and the "visitors" are by no means simple or solidary groups, but are themselves conglomerates of stakeholders. Outsiders include not only tourists, but also investors, travel industry staff, sellers and provisioners, technical and business experts (often expats), the press and the media, and often migrant workers. Locals include the owners and the propertyless, the workers and the uninvolved residents, proprietors, entertainers, suppliers, and possibly agriculturalists and anglers. In developing countries, there may be added complexities of national and international politics, nongovernmental organizations (NGOs), imperial "nostalgists," and the remnants of local traditional rulers and religious officials. Not all of these are concerned with creating or manipulating imaginaries, though many of them might find themselves constituent parts of someone's imaginings. Moreover, every community and status group has its own ideas about themselves that they wish to convince others, and about the others with whom they necessarily interact. There will always be a dialectic between these sets of ideas, just as there may be a dialectic between any one group's set of imaginaries and those of other groups with whom they have important relations. So, although there are never just two groups, "hosts" and "guests," there are always dualities both within groups and between any one group and its "Others."

There is clearly more at play in tourism than a mere replication of global tourism imaginaries. While on the discursive level tourism service providers are (re)producing globally dominant images and ideas, on the metadiscursive level they seem to be conveying a surprisingly dissonant message (Salazar 2005, 2006). There are many instances where shifts of role alignment occur and the common asymmetry between immobile locals and mobile tourists is blurred or temporarily interrupted. Two different logics are at work simultaneously: a logic of differentiation that creates differences and divisions, and a logic of equivalence that subverts existing differences and divisions. In some instances, tourism workers find creative ways to distance themselves from local people and align themselves on the side of the tourists. They prefer to position themselves as different from the represented locals and more similar to their foreign clients in a bid to enhance their own cosmopolitan status and to gain symbolic capital, using their privileged contact with foreigners to nourish their utopias of escape from the harsh local life.

WHAT TO IMAGINE NEXT?

The in-depth study of tourism imaginaries—tracing their historical and semiotic makings, while keeping the very material effects of the processes in view—reveals that they are potent propellers of sociocultural and environmental change, and essential elements in the process of identity formation, the making of place, and the perpetual invention of culture (K. M. Adams 2004). This is especially true of cultural tourism or tourism with cultural elements (Amirou 2000). We need to retain a clear idea about the chief interest groups behind these processes and avoid the mistake of seeing imaginaries as just a range of possibilities. Tourism imaginaries come to occupy a central position in a complex set of connections among very diverse societies, very dissimilar locales, and very different kinds of relations of production and consumption. They resonate most clearly in destinations, the physical and mental landscapes where the imaginaries of local residents, tourism intermediaries, and tourists meet and, occasionally, clash. As they are grounded in relations of power, they can never be politically neutral.

Whatever the form of tourism indulged in, people always travel with a set of expectations derived from various sources (Skinner and Theodossopoulos 2011). Much of this prior information removes uncertainty and reduces risk on the one hand, yet on the other hand can also be seen as a form of control that channels tourist experiences into predetermined forms.

Tourism spaces, set apart from the mundane world for the tourists, are in part spaces of the imaginary, of fantasy, and of dreaming. Places across the globe have different images attached to them. A series of social practices, ideologies, and behaviors derived from tourism imaginaries and their discourses subtly influence how people engage with the "Other" (cf. Tucker 2009). This is true for Western imaginaries of culture(s) in developing countries (Salazar 2010a), but also for non-Western imaginaries (e.g., Wynn 2007), for nature-related fantasies and their ecological consequences (e.g., Stepan 2001), or for imaginaries about the Western world by both Westerners and others (Carrier 1995).

The failure of both those studying tourism and those working in tourism to understand how imaginaries are embedded within local, national, regional, and global institutions of power restricts their ability to determine the underlying forces that restrict some tourism practices and not others, some imaginings and not others, and that make possible new hegemonies in new fields of power. Tourism imaginaries renegotiate political and social realities. The fierce local (and national) power struggle over globally circulating tourism imaginaries seeking to redefine peoples and places reaffirms that the social construction of place is still partly a process of local meaning making, territorial specificity, juridical control, and economic development, however complexly articulated localities become in transnational economic, political, and cultural movements. Even if many imaginaries have distinctive genealogies, we have to be careful not to exaggerate their coherence and consistency and we need to acknowledge the agency and autonomy of those represented, because the imaginative flow has certainly not been a one-way street (Salazar 2010a, 2011).

To be more inclusive and to overcome ethnocentric tourism imaginaries, we need to move far beyond a language of ethnic minorities and colonized indigenous peoples (Winter et al. 2008). Non-Western players have long been actively collaborating in the often unruly circulation of tourism imaginaries. In order to arrive at a more nuanced account of tourism, attention needs to be focused on the relationships between the various elements and relations of tourism circuits, and the contradictions, anomalies, and paradoxes that these entail (Nyíri 2006). In particular, attention should be paid to the ways in which values, meanings, and forms of knowledge can be altered, changed, and renegotiated at all points, from prior expectations to the point of purchase and beyond, and the ways in which different forms of knowledge are (re)constructed or, as often is the case in tourism, do not change at all.

Tourism imaginaries often shrewdly exaggerate the power of difference while neglecting and obfuscating the power of commonality. Especially in developing countries, imaginaries shape frameworks for cultural interaction and influence against a broader background of cultural dissimilarity and the imaginative possibilities this creates (e.g., to build up cosmopolitan capital). While tourism is often characterized by exoticized holiday package products, moving beyond an imaginary, which is blind to whom the Other really is, is still a possibility that tourism offers for intercultural personal growth. To be a tourist, but also a tourism service provider, is to be mobile and transient and to become involved, even if only superficially, in the worlds and lives of others. While tourism often stands for the commoditization of a one-dimensional culture, the exoticization and eroticization of contact with the Other, along with cosmopolitanisms constructed on the foundation of colonialism and Orientalism, it can also foster interpersonal relationships that involve genuine intercultural exchanges. These opportunities are tourism's "imaginative horizons," the blurry boundaries that separate the here and now from what lies beyond, in time and space (Crapanzano 2004). Such horizons profoundly influence both how all parties involved experience the tourism encounter and how they interpret this experience. Connections are made and unmade that reach beyond the specificity of time and place.

If we accept the possibility of tourism creating positive relations in a world hitherto unconnected, it becomes a key challenge to recognize and identify currently dominant tourism imaginaries, but also to actively create and operationalize new images and discourses that contest and replace tenacious imaginaries. This is a serious ethical imperative in which tourism scholars and educators obviously have a crucial role to play.

AN IMAGINATIVE ROAD MAP

This edited volume is divided into two complementary sections of five chapters each: "Imaginaries of Peoples" and "Imaginaries of Places." Rupert Stasch opens the first section by making a case in his chapter for methodological symmetry in the analysis of tourism encounters and their related imaginaries. He does this by examining the mutual imaginary constructions of Korowai of Papua and of the adventurous tourists visiting them. Tourism in Papua reveals many contradictions, and tourists and locals alike have exoticizing stereotypes about each other. Stasch focuses particularly on two key tropes of tourism interaction, namely, the nudity of Korowai and the payments made by the tourists. He shows convincingly how juxtaposing the imaginaries Korowai and tourists each bring to their encounters is a helpful way of getting access to important internal features of those imaginaries.

Studying another marginal indigenous group, the Emberá of Panama, Dimitrios Theodossopoulos examines the control of exoticization, knowing that this could involve either idealization (positive) or negative stereotyping, or sometimes both in a common state of ambivalence. He stresses how, at any given moment, parallel layers of exoticization participate and inspire any given tourism imaginary. Unlike the idealizing tourists, nonindigenous Panamanians, in their great majority, reproduce in their imagination of Emberá a different orientation toward exoticization: a patronizing and stereotyping perspective that he terms "unintentional primitivization." Theodossopoulos also discusses the role of the anthropologist as mediator of information for both local indigenous Emberá and, at other times, for curious tourists.

Alexis Celeste Bunten is concerned with recent efforts of indigenous peoples in Australia to take control of and operate the circuits and representations of ethnic tourism. In her chapter, she analyzes how the Aboriginal imaginary functions as a motivating force to visit Tjapukai Aboriginal Cultural Park. Bunten shows how supply and demand are overridden by hosts who use the opportunity to dismantle unfavorable aspects of their image and to shape more positive and less marginal narratives in rebuilding their culture, both for the tourist gaze and for their long-term cultural strength. This situation creates a double bind of the imaginary, in which tourists are conscious that Aboriginals play to an imagined authenticity that can never be reached (because it does not exist outside of the imagination), yet the indigenous people present heritage that is part of their lived experience within and outside the tourism context.

Margaret Byrne Swain engages with indigenous mythic tourism destinations as "imaginariums," the dialectic circulation of personal imaginings and institutional imaginaries. She does this by discussing the case of indigenous Sani Yi of southwest China, who have successfully positioned themselves as a literate, historical minority civilization with their own intellectuals. They have used the (exaggerated) "primitivist" imaginary proffered by neighboring Axi Yi peoples in a dialectic of identity strengthening. Swain addresses how indigeneity and cosmopolitanism become coimagined identities for Sani and Axi, from a shared era of French colonialism to Chinese ethnic tourism development. Her chapter helps us to explore universal and culturally specific collective and individual relations.

João Afonso Baptista addresses the implications that moral imaginaries have on the constitution of meanings in rural populations by zooming in on one powerful imaginative construction that has emerged in tourism as part of its moralization: the "community." He investigates the "reality" of the imagined in community tourism as found in Mozambique. Drawing on Charles Taylor's work to introduce a moral order and on Castoriadis to analyze the signifying of the imaginary, Baptista shows how "community" is a morally positive feature of a modern "Northern" imaginary (largely in response to the disappointment with modernity). He illustrates ethnographically how a collective social perspective given as an imaginary order legitimizes certain interventions by tourists and how it dialectically produces local self-representations.

"Imaginaries of Places," the second part of this volume, analyzes how places become part of a "truly global iconography, taking up a huge mental space in the public imagination," as Löfgren (1999: 215) has argued about famous beaches (see figure 0.2). Michael A. Di Giovine examines the complex situation surrounding the pilgrimages to a small Italian village in honor of the memory of the twentieth-century Catholic saint Padre Pio. In their competition for recognition of religious tourism, the people of the saint's birthplace, Pietrelcina, compete with those of his shrine at San Giovanni Rotondo with a productive dialectic of symbolic armaments. Di Giovine describes this as an "imaginaire dialectic," an ongoing process whereby imaginaries based on tangible events and images are formed in the mind, materially manifested, and subsequently responded to, negotiated, and contested through the creation of tangible and intangible re-presentations.

Federica Ferraris studies Cambodia's ancient and recent history as objects of touristic imaginary, the ways in which the two combine in the narratives tourism produces, and the imaginaries such accounts generate on Italian audiences. Based on oral accounts of tourists, promotional texts of

Figure 0.2. Cleaning up Kuta Beach, Bali: assuring the experienced reality matches the associated imaginaries (Copyright: N. Salazar).

Italian tour operators, and colonial travel literature, she argues that Cambodia, a destination that is very "distant" for contemporary Italian tourists, is taken to express distance in (past) time, resulting in an allotemporal imaginary of the meeting of incommensurate eras. Ferraris also describes how tour operators manipulate the exoticism experienced by tourists.

If imaginaries are central to tourism, this is even truer in the particular case of theme parks. Paula Mota Santos examines a colonial imaginary in a postcolonial time at Portugal dos Pequenitos (Portugal of the Little Ones). This miniature theme park of Portugal and its former empire was constructed during the fascist period (1940s). It is still a popular destination, in part because the miniature regional houses appeal to children, and the reproductions of the famous architectural landmarks of Portugal appeal to adults. The quality of the park as a landscape that organizes a spatial-temporal reality in a clearly bounded imaginary branched out from the late nineteenth- and early twentieth-century world's fairs to meet today's postmodern trope of place theming. This theme park (like all others) is a true work of the imagination: of those who designed it in the first half of the twentieth century, and of those who visit it today.

Kenneth Little describes in a very evocative way how sensations become narrativized in Belize. He tracks the meanings of ephemera, not for their intended and often banal expressions, but for their associations with people, circumstances, and events. Little scrutinizes the informal or unofficial creation of fleeting imaginaries—assemblages of configurations related to tropicalizations and images of paradise—that capture the attention of tourism resort inhabitants in personal and expected ways. He analyzes how seduction and shock are the generative affective forces that grow against the dream worlds of tourism imaginaries of a Caribbean paradise and its nightmares.

Last, Anke Tonnaer scrutinizes how national and regional identities and identifications are linked to emerging and often competing imaginaries. She introduces us to a recent movement in the Netherlands to let parts of the land go "wild" again, bringing back a premodern or a preinhabited "wilderness" stocked with relatives of extinct fauna such as the ancestor of domestic horses. With areas affectively named, such as "the Dutch Serengeti," ecopolitical compatriots are creating spaces of recreation where tourists are both needed as witnesses and shunned as spoilers. Tonnaer argues that it is the vitality of tourism imaginaries, more than the strength of nature itself, that determines the success of such projects.

In the afterword to this volume, Naomi Leite interrogates the theoretical concept of "imaginaries" itself. She characterizes the study of imaginaries as being essentially concerned with "shared mental life," a long-standing area of anthropological research, and examines theoretical and methodological implications of approaching "the imaginary" ethnographically. Leite makes thought-provoking analytical connections between the ten chapters and suggests some interesting trajectories for future research, both in terms of ethnographic and theoretical engagements. As stated in the afterword, the chapters that make up this edited volume add a nuanced perspective to the theme of how people and places are imagined in tourism. The cultural creativity and dialogical interactions of the various sets of imaginaries shows multiple agencies and contestations for power and control. Despite the different approaches to tourism imaginaries—as dialectic (Di Giovine), as assemblage (Little), or as imaginarium (Swain)—all authors stress the fact that tourism imaginaries are socially shared and are widely circulated, which is precisely what makes them so powerful and worthy of critical anthropological analysis.

NOTES

1. "Fantasy" is the original Greek word for imagination (developed, among others, in the work of Aristotle). In the context of tourism, the term is often used nowadays to denote more playful imaginaries related to things that are improbable or impossible (cf. Reijnders 2011).
2. This structuring function of imaginaries resembles somewhat the reasoning of Kant (2007), who saw the imagination (*Einbildungskraft*) as a synthesizing faculty by which the chaos of sensation is ordered and that reproduces representations by association. According to this line of thought, the human imagination serves as the bridge over the gap between mere sensation and intelligible thought.
3. This idea is related to the philosophical ideas of the French existentialist Sartre (2004), who argued that the imagination is intimately connected with personal freedom, for to imagine is to escape from the world.
4. Graburn (1972), for example, was employed for the academic year 1963–64 as a researcher studying intercultural relations and mutual imaginaries of the Inuit and Naskapi/Cree in northern Canada for the Cooperative Cross-Cultural Study of Ethnocentrism. The study was supported by a five-year grant from the Carnegie Foundation as "peace research" toward the understanding of why societies in contact generated mutual imaginaries about and behavior toward each other.
5. Salazar's image of Africa, for instance, was heavily influenced by growing up in Belgium, a country with a colonial past in central Africa that was never fully digested. As a child, he avidly read Hervé's classic but controversial comic strip album *The Adventures of Tintin in the Congo* (1931) and he watched innumerable documentaries and movies about the "dark continent" (Salazar 2010a: 33–34). Graburn remembers his first images of France coming from (1) newspapers

about World War II read from the age of four onward, and (2) the little blue French language textbook and its stories of traveling in France, encountered at the age of eight in French lessons at school in the UK.

6. Of course, we acknowledge that there were many different imaginaries being played out during the colonial era, too.

REFERENCES

Adams, Jacqueline. 2004. "The Imagination and Social Life." *Qualitative Sociology* 27, no. 3: 277–97.

Adams, Kathleen M. 2004. "The Genesis of Touristic Imagery: Politics and Poetics in the Creation of a Remote Indonesian Island Destination." *Tourist Studies* 4, no. 2: 115–35.

Amirou, Rachid. 1995. *Imaginaire touristique et sociabilités du voyage.* Paris: Presses Universitaires de France.

———. 2000. *Imaginaire du tourisme culturel.* Paris: Presses Universitaires de France.

Anderson, Benedict R. 1991. *Imagined Communities: Reflections on the Origin and Spread of Nationalism.* 2nd ed. New York: Verso.

Appadurai, Arjun. 1996. *Modernity at Large: Cultural Dimensions of Globalization.* Minneapolis: University of Minnesota Press.

Ateljevic, Irena, Annette Pritchard, and Nigel Morgan, eds. 2007. *The Critical Turn in Tourism Studies: Innovative Research Methodologies.* Amsterdam: Elsevier.

Bacchilega, Cristina. 2007. *Legendary Hawai'i and the Politics of Place: Tradition, Translation, and Tourism.* Philadelphia: University of Pennsylvania Press.

Barth, Fredrik. 1969. *Ethnic Groups and Boundaries: The Social Organization of Culture Difference.* Boston: Little, Brown.

Barthes, Roland. 1972. *Mythologies.* Trans. A. Lavers. New York: Hill and Wang.

Bishop, Ryan, and Lillian S. Robinson. 1999. "Genealogies of Exotic Desire: The Thai Night Market in the Western Imagination." In *Genders and Sexualities in Modern Thailand,* ed. Peter A. Jackson and Nerida M. Cook. Chiang Mai, Thailand: Silkworm.

Bissell, William C. 2005. "Engaging Colonial Nostalgia." *Cultural Anthropology* 20, no. 2: 215–48.

Brann, Eva T. H. 1991. *The World of the Imagination: Sum and Substance.* Lanham, MD: Rowman & Littlefield.

Bruner, Edward M. 1989. "Of Cannibals, Tourists, and Ethnographers." *Cultural Anthropology* 4, no. 4: 438–45.

———. 2005. *Culture on Tour: Ethnographies of Travel.* Chicago: University of Chicago Press.

Bunten, Alexis C. 2008. "Sharing Culture or Selling Out? Developing the Commodified Persona in the Heritage Industry." *American Ethnologist* 35, no. 3: 380–95.

Carrier, James G., ed. 1995. *Occidentalism: Images of the West.* Oxford: Clarendon Press.

Castoriadis, Cornelius. 1987. *The Imaginary Institution of Society.* Trans. Kathleen Blamey. Cambridge, MA: MIT Press.

Clifford, James. 1997. *Routes: Travel and Translation in the Late Twentieth Century.* Cambridge, MA: Harvard University Press.

Crapanzano, Vincent. 2004. *Imaginative Horizons: An Essay in Literary-Philosophical Anthropology.* Chicago: University of Chicago Press.

Crouch, David, Rhona Jackson, and Felix Thompson, eds. 2005. *The Media and the Tourist Imagination: Converging Cultures.* London: Routledge.

Dann, Graham M. S. 1976. "The Holiday Was Simply Fantastic." *Tourism Review* 31, no. 3: 19–23.

de Waal Malefyt, Timothy, and Brian Moeran, eds. 2003. *Advertising Cultures.* Oxford: Berg.

Di Giovine, Michael A. 2008. *The Heritage-scape: UNESCO, World Heritage, and Tourism.* Lanham, MD: Lexington Books.

Durand, Gilbert. 1999. *The Anthropological Structures of the Imaginary.* Trans. Margaret Sankey and Judith Hatten. Brisbane: Boombana Publications.

Echtner, Charlotte M., and Pushkala Prasad. 2003. "The Context of Third World Tourism Marketing." *Annals of Tourism Research* 30, no. 3: 660–82.

Edensor, Tim. 1998. *Tourists at the Taj: Performance and Meaning at a Symbolic Site.* London: Routledge.

Evans-Pritchard, Deirdre. 1989. "How 'They' See 'Us': Native American Images of Tourists." *Annals of Tourism Research* 16, no. 1: 89–105.

Fabian, Johannes. 2002. *Time and the Other: How Anthropology Makes Its Object.* 2nd ed. New York: Columbia University Press.

Frohlick, Susan. 2010. "The Sex of Tourism." In *Thinking through Tourism,* ed. Julie Scott and Tom Selwyn. Oxford: Berg.

Gaonkar, Dilip P. 2002. "Toward New Imaginaries: An Introduction." *Public Culture* 14, no. 1: 1–19.

Gold, John Robert, and Margaret M. Gold. 1995. *Imagining Scotland: Tradition, Representation, and Promotion in Scottish Tourism since 1750.* Aldershot, UK: Scolar Press.

Graburn, Nelson H. H. 1972. *Eskimos of Northern Canada.* New Haven, CT: Human Relations Area Files.

———, ed. 1976. *Ethnic and Tourist Arts: Cultural Expressions from the Fourth World.* Berkeley: University of California Press.

———. 1981. "1, 2, 3, 4 … Anthropology and the Fourth World." *Culture* 1, no. 1: 66–70.

———. 1998. "A Quest for Identity." *Museum International* 59, no. 4: 13–18.

———. 2002. "The Ethnographic Tourist." In *The Tourist as a Metaphor of the Social World,* ed. Graham M. S. Dann. Wallingford, UK: CABI.

———. 2003. *Tourism and Tradition: Culture as Resource or Commodity, with Respect to the Caucasus.* Moscow: International Institute of Peoples of the Caucasus (IIPC), Department of Caucasian Studies at the Institute of Ethnology and Anthropology.

———. 2007. "Tourism through the Looking Glass." In *The Study of Tourism: Anthropological and Sociological Beginnings,* ed. Dennison Nash. Amsterdam: Elsevier.

——. 2013. "Beyond Selling Out: Art, Tourism and Indigenous Self-Representation." In *Anthropologists Up Close and Personal: Works and Lives That Are Shaping the Discipline,* ed. Cris Shore and Susanna Trnka. Oxford: Berghahn Books.

Graburn, Nelson H. H., and Maria Gravari-Barbas. 2011. "Introduction: Imagined Landscapes of Tourism." *Journal of Tourism and Cultural Change* 9, no. 3: 159–66.

Gregory, Derek. 1994. *Geographical Imaginations.* Oxford: Basil Blackwell.

Guldin, Gregory E. 1989. "The Anthropological Study Tour in China: A Call for Cultural Guides." *Human Organization* 48, no. 2: 126–34.

Hall, C. Michael, and Hazel Tucker, eds. 2004. *Tourism and Postcolonialism: Contested Discourses, Identities and Representations.* London: Routledge.

Harrison, Julia. 2003. *Being a Tourist: Finding Meaning in Pleasure Travel.* Vancouver: University of British Columbia Press.

Henderson, Carol E., and Maxine K. Weisgrau, eds. 2007. *Raj Rhapsodies: Tourism, Heritage and the Seduction of History.* Aldershot, UK: Ashgate.

Hendry, Joy. 2000. *The Orient Strikes Back: A Global View of Cultural Display.* Oxford: Berg.

Hennig, Christoph. 2002. "Tourism: Enacting Modern Myths." In *The Tourist as a Metaphor of the Social World,* trans. Alison Brown, ed. Graham M. S. Dann. Wallingford, UK: CABI.

Hollinshead, Keith. 1998. "Tourism and the Restless People: A Dialectical Inspection of Bhabha's Halfway Populations." *Tourism, Culture & Communication* 1, no. 1: 49–78.

Hughes, George. 1992. "Tourism and the Geographical Imagination." *Leisure Studies* 11, no. 1: 31–42.

Hutnyk, John. 1996. *The Rumour of Calcutta: Tourism, Charity, and the Poverty of Representation.* London: Zed Books.

Kant, Immanuel. 2007. *Critique of Judgement.* Trans. James Creed Meredith. Oxford: Oxford University Press.

Kaspin, Deborah. 1997. "On Ethnographic Authority and the Tourist Trade: Anthropology in the House of Mirrors." *Anthropological Quarterly* 70, no. 2: 53–57.

Kearney, Richard. 1998. *Poetics of Imagining: Modern to Post-modern.* 2nd ed. New York: Fordham University Press.

Kunz, Hans. 1946. *Die anthropologische Bedeutung der Phantasie.* Basel: Verlag für Recht und Gesellschaft.

Lacan, Jacques. 1977. "The Mirror Stage as Formative of the Function of the I." In *Écrits: A Selection,* trans. Alan Sheridan, ed. Jacques Lacan. New York: W. W. Norton.

Lanfant, Marie-Françoise, and Nelson H. H. Graburn 1992. "International Tourism Reconsidered: The Principle of the Alternative." In *Tourism Alternatives: Potentials and Problems in the Development of Tourism,* ed. Valene L. Smith and William R. Eadington. Philadelphia: University of Pennsylvania Press.

Lee, Molly C. 1999. "Tourism and Taste Cultures: Collecting Native Art in Alaska at the Turn of the Twentieth Century." In *Unpacking Culture: Art and Commodity in*

Colonial and Postcolonial Worlds, ed. Ruth B. Phillips and Christopher B. Steiner. Berkeley: University of California Press.

Leite, Naomi. 2005. "Journeys to an Ancestral Past: On Diasporic Tourism, Embodied Memory, and Identity." *Antropológicas* 9: 273–302.

Leite, Naomi, and Nelson H. H. Graburn. 2009. "Anthropological Interventions in Tourism Studies." In *The Sage Handbook of Tourism Studies,* ed. Tazim Jamal and Mike Robinson. London: Sage.

Little, Walter E. 2004. *Mayas in the Marketplace: Tourism, Globalization, and Cultural Identity.* Austin: University of Texas Press.

Löfgren, Orvar. 1999. *On Holiday: A History of Vacationing.* Berkeley: University of California Press.

Lutz, Catherine, and Jane Collins. 1993. *Reading National Geographic.* Chicago: University of Chicago Press.

Marcus, George E., and Michael M. J. Fischer. 1986. *Anthropology as Cultural Critique: An Experimental Moment in the Human Sciences.* Chicago: University of Chicago Press.

Morgan, Nigel, and Annette Pritchard. 1998. *Tourism Promotion and Power: Creating Images, Creating Identities.* Chichester, UK: John Wiley.

Mowforth, Martin, and Ian Munt. 2008. *Tourism and Sustainability: Development, Globalisation and New Tourism in the Third World.* 3rd ed. London: Routledge.

Nash, Dennison. 1977. "Tourism as a Form of Imperialism." In *Hosts and Guests: The Anthropology of Tourism,* ed. Valene L. Smith. Philadelphia: University of Pennsylvania Press.

———. 1981. "Tourism as an Anthropological Subject." *Current Anthropology* 22, no. 5: 461–82.

Nyíri, Pál. 2006. *Scenic Spots: Chinese Tourism, the State and Cultural Authority.* Seattle: University of Washington Press.

Ortner, Sherry B. 1973. "On Key Symbols." *American Anthropologist* 75, no. 5: 1338–46.

Picard, David. 2011. *Tourism, Magic and Modernity: Cultivating the Human Garden.* Oxford: Berghahn Books.

Picard, Michel. 1996. *Bali: Cultural Tourism and Touristic Culture.* Singapore: Archipelago Press.

Pratt, Mary Louise. 2008. *Imperial Eyes: Travel Writing and Transculturation.* 2nd ed. London: Routledge.

Reijnders, Stijn. 2011. "Stalking the Count: Dracula, Fandom and Tourism." *Annals of Tourism Research* 38, no. 1: 231–48.

Ricoeur, Paul. 1994. "Imagination in Discourse and in Action." In *Rethinking Imagination: Culture and Creativity,* ed. Gillian Robinson and John F. Rundell. London: Routledge.

Robinson, Mike, and Hans Christian Andersen, eds. 2002. *Literature and Tourism.* London: Continuum.

Rosaldo, Renato. 1989. "Imperialist Nostalgia." *Representations* 26 (Spring): 107–22.

Roth, Ilona. 2007. *Imaginative Minds.* Oxford: Oxford University Press.

Said, Edward W. 1994. *Orientalism.* Rev. ed. New York: Vintage Books.

Salazar, Noel B. 2005. "Tourism and Glocalization: 'Local' Tour Guiding." *Annals of Tourism Research* 32, no. 3: 628–46.

———. 2006. "Touristifying Tanzania: Global Discourse, Local Guides." *Annals of Tourism Research* 33, no. 3: 833–52.

———. 2009. "Imaged or Imagined? Cultural Representations and the 'Tourismification' of Peoples and Places." *Cahiers d'Études Africaines* 49, no. 193–94: 49–71.

———. 2010a. *Envisioning Eden: Mobilizing Imaginaries in Tourism and Beyond.* Oxford: Berghahn Books.

———. 2010b. "Imagineering Tailor-Made Pasts for Nation-Building and Tourism: A Comparative Perspective." In *Staging the Past: Themed Environments in Transcultural Perspectives,* ed. Judith Schlehe, Michiko Uike-Bormann, Carolyn Oesterle, and Wolfgang Hochbruck. Bielefeld, Germany: Transcript.

———. 2011. "The Power of the Imagination in Transnational Mobilities." *Identities: Global Studies in Culture and Power* 18, no. 6: 576–98.

———. 2012. "Tourism Imaginaries: A Conceptual Approach." *Annals of Tourism Research* 39, no. 2: 863–82.

———. 2013. "Imagineering Otherness: Anthropological Legacies in Contemporary Tourism." *Anthropological Quarterly* 86, no. 3: 669-696.

Salazar, Noel B., and Yang Zhang. 2013. "Seasonal Lifestyle Tourism: The Case of Chinese Elites." *Annals of Tourism Research* 43, no. 4: 81–99.

Sartre, Jean-Paul. 2004. *The Imaginary: A Phenomenological Psychology of the Imagination.* Trans. Jonathan Webber. London: Routledge.

Schein, Louisa. 2000. *Minority Rules: The Miao and the Feminine in China's Cultural Politics.* Durham, NC: Duke University Press.

Scott, Julie, and Tom Selwyn, eds. 2010. *Thinking through Tourism.* Oxford: Berg.

Selwyn, Tom, ed. 1996. *The Tourist Image: Myths and Myth Making in Tourism.* Chichester, UK: John Wiley.

Sheller, Mimi. 2004. "Demobilizing and Remobilizing Caribbean Paradise." In *Tourism Mobilities: Places to Play, Places in Play,* ed. Mimi Sheller and John Urry. London: Routledge.

Skinner, Jonathan, and Dimitrios Theodossopoulos, eds. 2011. *Great Expectations: Imagination and Anticipation in Tourism.* Oxford: Berghahn Books.

Smith, Valene L., ed. 1977. *Hosts and Guests: The Anthropology of Tourism.* Philadelphia: University of Pennsylvania Press.

———, ed. 1989. *Hosts and Guests: The Anthropology of Tourism.* 2nd ed. Philadelphia: University of Pennsylvania Press.

Smith, Valene L., and Mary Ann Brent, eds. 2001. *Hosts and Guests Revisited: Tourism Issues of the 21st Century.* New York: Cognizant Communication Corporation.

Sneath, David, Martin Holbraad, and Morten Axel Pedersen. 2009. "Technologies of the Imagination: An Introduction." *Ethnos* 74, no. 1: 5–30.

Stanley, Nick. 1998. *Being Ourselves for You: The Global Display of Cultures.* London: Middlesex University Press.

Stepan, Nancy L. 2001. *Picturing Tropical Nature.* Ithaca, NY: Cornell University Press.

Stephen, Ann, ed. 1999. *Pirating the Pacific: Images of Travel, Trade & Tourism.* Aldershot, UK: Ashgate.

Strauss, Claudia. 2006. "The Imaginary." *Anthropological Theory* 6, no. 3: 322–44.

Taylor, Charles. 2004. *Modern Social Imaginaries.* Durham, NC: Duke University Press.

Thomas, Nicholas. 1994. *Colonialism's Culture: Anthropology, Travel, and Government.* Princeton, NJ: Princeton University Press.

Torgovnick, Marianna. 1990. *Gone Primitive: Savage Intellects, Modern Lives.* Chicago: University of Chicago Press.

Tucker, Hazel. 2009. "Recognizing Emotion and Its Postcolonial Potentialities: Discomfort and Shame in a Tourism Encounter in Turkey." *Tourism Geographies* 11, no. 4: 444–61.

Tylor, Edward B. 1889. *Primitive Culture: Researches into the Development of Mythology, Philosophy, Religion, Language, Art, and Custom.* 3rd ed. New York: Holt.

Urbain, Jean-Didier. 1994. *L'idiot du voyage: Histoires de touristes.* Paris: Éditions Payot & Rivages.

Urry, John, and Jonas Larsen. 2011. *The Tourist Gaze 3.0.* 3rd ed. London: Sage.

Vogler, Candace. 2002. "Social Imaginary, Ethics, and Methodological Individualism." *Public Culture* 14, no. 3: 625–27.

Wagner, Roy. 1975. *The Invention of Culture.* Englewood Cliffs, NJ: Prentice-Hall.

Winter, Tim, Peggy Teo, and T. C. Chang, eds. 2008. *Asia on Tour: Exploring the Rise of Asian Tourism.* London: Routledge.

Wynn, Lisa L. 2007. *Pyramids and Nightclubs: A Travel Ethnography of Arab and Western Imaginations of Egypt.* Austin: University of Texas Press.

Zhang, Jinfu. 2009. "Touristic Encounter, Identity Recognition and Presentation." *London Journal of Tourism, Sport, and the Creative Industries* 2, no. 1: 12–20.

Zhong, Xiaolian. 2010. "Research on the Localization and Delocalization Phenomenon of Tourist Souvenirs with the Tourist Souvenirs Market in Old Town of Lijiang of Yunnan Province as an Example." In *Tourism and Glocalization: Perspectives on East Asian Societies,* ed. Min Han and Nelson H. H. Graburn. Osaka: National Museum of Ethnology.

Part I

Imaginaries of Peoples

Chapter 1

Toward Symmetric Treatment of Imaginaries

Nudity and Payment in Tourism to Papua's "Treehouse People"

Rupert Stasch

This chapter seeks to advance the study of the imaginaries that structure cultural tourism by arguing for symmetric attention to perspectives of tourists and visited people. Such symmetry brings out more sharply what tourism imaginaries are, and what they do. I argue for such an approach through the example of encounters between international tourists and Korowai of Papua, Indonesia. My specific focus is exoticizing stereotypes that Korowai and tourists hold about each other, and these stereotypes' expression in concrete actions.

There are several levels to symmetry's value. One is that by juxtaposing different populations' stereotypy, each side's ideas stand out more sharply *as* imaginative. Putting different participants' models side by side highlights how "out of touch" each group is with the other's actual subjectivity, and thus how much the exoticizing stereotypy exists as a collective representation with a life of its own among the stereotypers. At the same time, this juxtaposition underscores similarities between different sides' processes of exoticization. We will see that Korowai and tourists stereotype each other in similar ways, without knowing it. This too throws into relief how much each side's stereotypy is an imaginative projection grounded in the lives of the stereotypers themselves and conditions of the tourism encounter.

Besides making imaginaries stand out more sharply, symmetry also helps us better discern the actual organization of tourism interactions as structures of "working misunderstanding" (Dorward 1974). When people relate closely across cultural disparities, all participants' imaginaries shape the articulations that emerge. I document here tourist and Korowai imaginaries' force in conditioning their perceptions and actions, but I also explore how articulations between Korowai and tourists are influenced by their imaginaries' openness and heterogeneity. Patterns of coordination across gulfs of mutual incomprehension depend not only on imaginaries' projective constraining of experience and practice, but also on their ambiguous character of pointing to possibilities other than themselves.

The empirical value of studying all participants' perspectives might seem obvious, but commitment to such an approach is still emerging in tourism studies and in the study of intersocietal articulations generally. There is a metatheoretical level to symmetry's value, having to do with the covert and lopsided power of the imaginaries of tourists on the intellectual horizons of tourism *scholars*. Analysis of tourism can easily be swayed by dominant ideological precepts of tourists' home societies, such as the idea of a fundamental difference of being between tourists and the people they visit, or the idea that the social position of tourist is false or immoral. I take up this theme in my conclusion, where I discuss the importance of the recent transition toward symmetry in the anthropology of tourism, within concern with symmetry in the cultural sciences generally.

AN OVERVIEW OF KOROWAI TOURISM

About four thousand Korowai live spread across five hundred square miles of forest in the southern lowlands of Papua, where they make their livelihoods by tending sago stands and banana gardens, as well as by fishing and hunting (figure 1.1). All their activities are shaped by high valuing of kinship and social bonds on the one hand, and high valuing of autonomy and equality on the other (Stasch 2009). This contradictory mix of values is reflected in people's practices of living far apart to avoid subjection to each other's wills, while also traveling constantly in pursuit of social connections. The overall landscape is a patchwork of forest territories each about one square mile in expanse, owned by different patriclans. In the past, people were only comfortable living on their own land or that of close relatives. Today this practice of living far apart coexists with residence in centralized villages. Village creation began in 1980 with the opening of the airstrip settlement of Yaniruma by Dutch missionaries. The missionaries left in 1991, but Korowai have continued to form new villages on their own initiative (shown by dots in figure 1.1). Roughly one-third of Korowai live in villages, one-third live on forest land, and one-third continuously alternate back and forth between both types of space (Stasch 2013). Until recently, the Indonesian government was an even more distant presence than church organizations. Korowai themselves have actively fashioned their modes of engagement with the wider state, market, and religious institutions they now know themselves to live amidst (Stasch 2001, 2014).

What Korowai are famous for internationally is their "treehouse" architecture. For over twenty years, international tourists and media professionals have been drawn to the area by these treehouses and by a further range of ways Korowai are thought to exemplify a condition of primitiveness and purity (figure 1.2). Tourist visits to the Korowai area began around 1990, first with brief visits by longboat to the far southwest corner of the Korowai lands, and later by chartered Cessna flights to Yaniruma. Overall, about

Figure 1.1. Korowai lands in Papua. Tourists arrive by longboat or airplane at the four villages with their names shown (Copyright: R. Stasch).

Figure 1.2. Members of a German tour group photographing the house of Saxip Bumxai (Copyright: R. Stasch).

five thousand tourists have visited Korowai or their closely related Kombai neighbors across recent decades. This is small even by comparison to the modest scale of arrivals in Papua's other main destinations, such as the Baliem Valley, the Asmat coast, and the Raja Ampat Islands. At the peak around 1997, several hundred tourists visited each year. But the more typical pattern has been for many months to pass with no visitors, followed perhaps by a burst of several groups in a few weeks. Growth in visitors has been inhibited by Papua's limited tourism infrastructure more generally, by political and military conflict surrounding Papuan desires to be an independent country, by wider ethnoreligious violence in Indonesia in the late 1990s, by the cessation of direct flights from Los Angeles to Papua in 1998, by the World Trade Center attack and Bali bombings in the early 2000s, and by the 2008 global economic downturn. Arrivals have also been constrained by the extremely high cost of plane or boat charters now needed to reach gateway villages on the edges of the Korowai lands.

Many visitors are highly educated professionals, and some are quite affluent. They include citizens of almost every European country and most settler colonial ones. In the 1990s, German and US nationals accounted for half of travelers, reflecting primitivism's special strength in Germany and the large size of the US traveling population. US tourists dropped away in the 2000s, while citizens of ex-Soviet bloc countries are now prominent. The median size of groups is four persons, and the maximum is about twelve. The destination's high costs, combined with its reputation for true primitivity, have meant that large portions of visitors are filmmakers and other media professionals (Stasch 2011a, 2011b).

Once they arrive at villages in the southwest, tourists set out on foot with local porters to visit Korowai living in treehouses on their forested clan lands. These treks last between one and ten days, and include events of Korowai performing subsistence activities for the groups. Some groups witness culminating stages of a sago grub feast, staying in housing built for them in advance at the feast site. Tourists are usually accompanied by a paid Indonesian or Papuan guide, who communicates with them in English. Most guides live near Jayapura on Papua's north coast, which tourists transit through on their flights from Bali or Jakarta. In the costliest packages, the guide works for an international tour leader who also accompanies the group.

Alongside communicating in English with clients, guides speak Indonesian with some Korowai (Stasch 2007). In particular, guides work closely with specific Korowai men who are established tourism specialists. These mediators translate in turn between Indonesian and Korowai, to convey visitors' desires to other Korowai. The overall situation is thus one of Korowai talking densely with each other in their vernacular, tourists likewise talking densely with each other in their home language, and a bottleneck of multistep translation between these groups via a small number of intermediaries.

This linguistic situation is one reason why tourist and Korowai ideas about each other circulate much more densely within each population than between them, even when the two groups are in each other's presence. Moreover, long before and after their direct interactions, Korowai and tourists alike devote much attention to the *idea* of the other. A core paradox of their relation is that both groups care intensely about their meetings, but each is mostly oblivious of the others' understandings. Their representations of the

other have a life of their own, grounded less in actual characteristics of the
stereotyped people than in sociocultural and psychological conditions of the
stereotypers themselves, or conditions of their meetings.

This is one reason the concept of tourism imaginaries is relevant to
the encounters. Scholars have used the noun "imaginary" to mean different things (bearing a variety of ambiguous relations to alternatives such as
"culture" or "semiotic order"). Yet many uses have in common that they fuse
two streams of thought about human consciousness: first, social scientists'
sensitivity to collective process and the world-constituting effects of ideas
(e.g., Castoriadis [1975] 1987; Taylor 2004); and second, philosophers' and
psychoanalytic theorists' sensitivity to the complex creativity and multiplicity of individual subjective makeup (e.g., philosophical ideas about "imagination" as interior faculty surveyed in Kearney [1988, 1991]). Such a fusion
is well suited to thinking about Korowai and tourists' highly creative and
projective *images* about each other.

TOURIST IMAGINARIES ABOUT KOROWAI

I already noted that tourists' travel is motivated by a notion that Korowai
instantiate a condition of primitive humanity. In other words, their visits to
Korowai flow from the vast cultural formation of contemporary global primitivism. Primitivism is any body of ideas in which one set of people imagines
another as archaic, not simply in time of actual living but in ontological
time: their very *being* is tied to an earlier epoch. This idea is expressed, for
example, in one US economist's diary entry recounting a feast on the Kom-
bai-Korowai borderlands, posted on his consulting firm's website:

> The dance continues. A child cries. It is today. It is 15,000 years ago. If there
> was ever any doubt that we were witnessing traditions whose roots disappear
> into long ago mists of time—they are gone. We are in the Stone Age—as the
> Stone Age here has been for millennium [*sic*] in this place. These people are so
> fully adapted into this place and this environment that they would only have
> changed as the jungle itself has evolved.[1]

In primitivist tourism of this kind, metropolitan travelers visit people
understood to be original and basic, to experience their complexly admired,
disparaged, and exoticized cultural attributes. The travelers describe their
cosmos as consisting of a Manichaean polarity of two types of humanity,
the *civilized* and the *primitive* (not always labeled by these specific terms).
This model's core contrast of contemporaneity versus archaicness is also
intertwined with an understanding that the civilized pole is economically

and technologically more powerful than the primitive, and a threat to its existence. Yet primitive humanity is superior to the civilized in morality, ecology, and aesthetics. It is a source of redemption or pleasure for inhabitants of civilization, while also being linked to fearful and inferiority-marked practices like cannibalism.[2] Primitivist ideas are familiar to tourism scholars from the documentary *Cannibal Tours* (O'Rourke 1987) and from early studies by Cohen (1989) and Bruner and Kirshenblatt-Gimblett (1994), as well as from blockbuster films like *Avatar, Dances with Wolves,* and many other cultural artifacts. There is now a worldwide boom in this type of tourism, referred to in different national and academic spheres under such designations as "indigenous cultural tourism," "Aboriginal tourism," "first nations tourism," "tribal tourism," and tourism of "minority nationalities."

That tourist imagery about Korowai has a life of its own is illustrated by certain words tourists apply to Korowai that do not fit their actual lives. Tourists commonly call specific old-looking Korowai men the "chief" of a group, even though Korowai do not recognize any such leadership roles or otherwise link adult age differences with authority. Tourists also routinely affirm that Korowai are "hunter-gatherers," even though most of their food comes from gardens right below their houses and from carefully managed sago groves. Often tourists call a Korowai feast compound or a garden clearing with two houses a "village," even though there were historically no Korowai words for "village" and no actual permanent settlements. These and other features of tourist discourse reflect a generic idea of primitive cultural others that preexists its application to Korowai.

Dozens of television shows and a hundred or more magazine and newspaper stories have played an important role in making Korowai iconic representatives of the idea of "Stone Age" existence in global primitivist imaginaries today. For example, in June 2009, five million French prime-time television viewers watched an episode of *Rendez-vous en terre inconnue* in which the pop singer Zazie was shown living in a Korowai household. A segment on Korowai treehouse building was featured as the culmination of the "Jungle" episode of the widely seen 2011 BBC and Discovery television series *Human Planet*. Articles about Korowai and Kombai have been published in such magazines as *National Geographic, Reader's Digest, Outside, Smithsonian,* and *The New Yorker*. Photographs of Korowai are prominent in Sebastião Salgado's recent *Genesis* exhibition and associated book (Salgado 2013), and numerous other travel books have been published detailing visits to them.

The market demand for these media products exemplifies the general pattern that international metropolitan audiences intensely *value* Korowai, and intensely value the idea of interaction with them across divides of radical difference. For tourists, a visit to Korowai has an aura of profound significance, as an enacted picture of the primitivist cosmos of two foundationally different kinds of humans (compare Adler 1989). MacCannell (1976) used the Goffman-derived contrast of "frontstage" and "backstage" to describe the general organization of tourism as a quest for authentic realities felt to lie behind regular-life appearances. Extending this metaphor, we could say that tourists understand Korowai trips as access to the backstage of humanity at large.

KOROWAI IMAGINARIES ABOUT TOURISTS: SIMILARITIES IN EACH SIDE'S STEREOTYPY

In the wake of studies by Said (1978), Todorov (1984), and others, it has become a common exercise for scholars to show that European or settler colonial exoticizing stereotypy about ethnic others is a representational system with logics of its own. My sketch of tourist primitivism above followed this pattern. Much rarer is detailed work on non-Westerners' stereotypy about Westerners. From studies that do exist (e.g., Basso 1979; Bashkow 2006; Vilaça 2010), it is unsurprising that Korowai have elaborate ideas about foreigners. Sketching these ideas now, my concerns will be to establish that this stereotypy also has a life of its own among the stereotypers, and to note striking parallels between each side's stereotypes.

For most Korowai, tourists have been a bigger presence than all other categories of radical strangers whom they have become newly concerned with across the last thirty-five years. Yet due to Korowai spatial dispersion, as well as the infrequency of tourist visits and the erraticness of where they go on the land, there are many Korowai who have never interacted with tourists or have met only one or two groups. However, talk *about* tourists circulates widely across the Korowai population, much as imagery about Korowai circulates widely in tourist-sending countries and is established in tourists' minds before they meet Korowai.

Linked to this wide circulation, Korowai strongly conceive tourists to exist as a *type*. This is well illustrated by the fact that to them "tourist" is an ethnic group (cf. Van den Berghe 1994: 16). Korowai call tourists by the word *tulis,* which they borrowed from Indonesian *turis.* But tourists are still *tulis* when they go home, and other people in those home countries are also *tulis. Tulis* is often for Korowai functionally equivalent to "white people" or "foreigners," but conceived as a single population with uniform ethnic characteristics. Tourists' typicality is at the level of ontology, or their very being, rather than at the level of a temporary activity. This Korowai emphasis on tourists as being a type is similar to tourists' feeling that to meet an individual Korowai person is to meet a walking embodiment of the transhistorical condition of "Stone Age" life.

Another parallel between tourist and Korowai imaginaries is construal of the generic other as dangerous. Besides calling the visitors *tulis,* Korowai also routinely call them *laleo,* which normally refers to a type of demonic monster humans become after death (Stasch 2009: 215–23). Korowai put daily effort into staying separate from these beings, who seek reunification with the living even though this would cause the living to die. Besides fearing the return of individual dead persons, Korowai also fear apocalyptic entry of the whole population of demonic dead into the world of the living. Applying the word "demon" (*laleo*) to all the new outsiders who have come to their lands in recent decades, with white tourists as the prototypic referent, most Korowai initially understood the new outsiders to be actual demonic dead, and have considered the foreigners' presence to be deeply threatening to their safety.

Different areas of the Korowai landscape have gone through locally controversial transitions from first being hostile to tourists to later greatly desiring their visits. As specific Korowai traverse this arc of feelings, their use of "demon" (*laleo*) becomes increasingly idiomatic. The word starts to mean just "human foreigner," distinct from its alternate sense of "demonic dead." Yet even this idiomatic reference to tourists as "demons" expresses a stance of residual deprecation and wariness. Fear of tourists' transgressive, violent character is also expressed in adults' portrayals of tourists as murderous boogeymen when talking to children, and in the idea that tourist photography involves dangerous separation of people's shades from their bodies. Imagery of tourists' dangerousness is similar to tourists' preoccupation with Korowai cannibalism, tribal violence, and weaponry, and with the dangerousness of their natural environment.

Alongside their shared categorization of the other as a dangerous monster, tourist and Korowai stereotypes also run parallel in figuring the other as a temporal limit. Calling tourists "demons," Korowai take up death and loss as their best precedent for the otherness of these new foreigners. This associates the foreigners with humans' end, while tourists see Korowai as humanity's beginning. The two sides also specifically map time into geography. For tourists, the Stone Age is a *place* they can visit (along lines discussed by Salazar and Graburn, this volume). So, too, Korowai today strongly link both tourists and the actual demonic dead to the newly rumored spatial form of the city. Korowai now routinely say that people go to cities when they die (Stasch n.d.). Their imaginative interest in experiencing cities after death has been partly fostered by meetings with tourists, who are known to live in cities as their prototypic settlement form.

Another parallel is each side's focus on material culture. The most prominent Korowai idea about tourists is that they have unlimited wealth, expressed by the assertion that tourists' food and money is not produced by labor but is instead "just there" (*yəpa ibo,* or *ibontop xondüp;* cf. Crick 1994: 133; Causey 2003: 92–95, 245–46n47; Theodossopoulos, this volume). This is partly based on Korowai seeing tourists eat only food made for them by expedition cooks. But it is also Korowai people's way of grasping the global commodity economy in general, in which the objects people eat or use are bought from others rather than made by the consumers. Korowai contrast tourists' practice of sitting in houses eating food that is "just there" with their own situations of descending from houses and struggling on the land to produce what they eat, the main context also when they are vulnerable to attack by witches and thus subject to death. The possibility of getting into the transactional stream with tourist wealth is what leads individual Korowai to shift from fearing tourists to desiring their visits.

Tourists similarly take Korowai people's material repertoire as the crux of their special condition. International visitors pay close attention to Korowai tools, weapons, household articles, genital coverings, and facial ornaments. It is based on specific Korowai persons' lack of imported manufactures that tourists judge how pure the Korowai they meet are in their isolation from the global order of monetized consumer culture and their embodiment of the desired primitive ideal.

In this way, each side figures the other as living without alienation from their conditions of material livelihood. Tourists marvel at Korowai people's production of all they need from the forest. Calling them "hunter-gatherers" reflects this investment in the idea that they live in seamless harmony with their environment: tourists in effect admire Korowai for having their food "just there" in surrounding nature, much as Korowai admire tourists for living in a paradise of effortless harmony with the commodity system. It is common for Korowai and tourists alike to express desire to "become" or "be like" the other, focused on material life. Korowai and tourist imaginaries thus converge in linking the other to not just fearful monstrosity but also utopian sacredness (a wider pattern of ambivalence also noted by Salazar and Graburn, this volume).

The two bodies of stereotypy circulate without Korowai or tourists knowing about the other's imaginings. The parallels between them make it even more obvious how much the stereotypes are projections of the stereotypers themselves. Tourists live in a world in which monetized social relating dominates most areas of activity, is conceptually and evaluatively polarized relative to other modes of social connection (Carrier 1991), and is morally suspicious. They project this anxiety onto Korowai in the inverted form of an ideal of direct provisioning from nature. The Korowai fantasy of tourists' unlimited access to money and food is a projection of their own characteristically New Guinean emphasis on exchange objects as prime media through which people know their social relations, and an inverted projection of their sense of their own lives as defined by ambivalent mortality-imbued labor on a natural landscape that provides for them but is also refractory to their desires and needs. Adjusted in wording, MacCannell's (2011: 11) view that "the ultimate other of the tourist subject is the *unconscious*" can be applied not only to tourists who visit Korowai, but also to Korowai in their own engagement with the visitors.

IMAGINARIES TALKING PAST EACH OTHER: INTERACTIONS AROUND NUDITY AND PAYMENT

There are many further important details to Korowai and tourists' abstract stereotypy about each other, but I have said enough to be able to turn to what happens in concrete interaction. Here the benefits of a symmetric approach fall more heavily in the direction of contrast: we see the two sides talking past one another. We also see further levels at which imaginaries structure all participants' orientations to tourism encounters. For example, the encounters are deeply shaped by the participants' contrasting ideological evaluations of which media of social relating matter most. The media I discuss here are nudity and payment.

Lack of imported clothing is the biggest issue tourists attend to in judging whether Korowai are exemplars of primitive humanity. Tour groups generally meet many Korowai in clothes before meeting any in traditional dress. When they do first come into the presence of a Korowai person in traditional dress, there is an obvious intensification of their attention: the tourists orient to the person visually, conversationally, and photographically with new liveliness. It is also common for tourists and guides to tell Korowai they are looking for people without clothes. When my friend Wayap once worked for a pair of tourists who made it to the Korowai area without the help of a guide (based on their ability to speak some Indonesian themselves), after a few days the tourists began disagreeing with Wayap's choices of direction to travel, because everyone they were seeing was wearing clothes. One of the tourists told him in Indonesian, "These are not Korowai!" (*ini bukan korowai*), to which he countered, "It's Korowai people in all directions. We all speak one language and are the same."

The reasons for this focus on nudity are numerous, and mostly tacit. An overview, though, was given by a Danish reality TV actor in response to my question to him about why the film crew directing his show did not wanted any clothed Korowai on camera:

> I think they look at the contrast between us white guys standing in our European clothes. It's much greater if it's only those Korowai standing there without clothes. If all the sudden [there is] a guy who looks like the Korowai standing in clothes like us, it takes out—it makes the distance smaller. Because there's the middle point, saying "okay maybe they're not that uncivilized as well, maybe they just took off the clothes to make good pictures." So definitely it's just a bigger leap from us standing there being all pale and fat to seeing those skinny muscular guys standing naked.

Commercial representations respond to special pressures of the media sphere that set them apart from regular tourism, but this actor's statement expresses a principle probably important to all tourists' experience: Korowai nudity is pivotal to experiencing the encounter in terms of a Manichaean gulf between civilized metropolitan self and primitive other.

Within this broad principle, a few more specific suggestions about the logic of nudity are worth mentioning, drawn from patterns of tourist discourse as well as from other scholarship. One is that nudity's status as the foremost sign of primitive purity is motivated again by an idea of *immediacy*. Wrapping their bodies with just rattan waistbands, leaf or nut penis coverings, fiber skirts, and other ornaments they have made from nature, Korowai only minimally separate themselves from their surroundings. There is also a broader parallel between the idea of primitive people as the foundational underside of humanity in general, and the concrete human body bare of coverings (figure 1.3). Primitivist tourism is an inquiry into the category "human," and tourists take the body as that category's most primordial sign. Modification of body surfaces is understood as a prime site where people express stances toward their humanness, including qualities of unalienated innocence, purity, and natural aesthetic and social virtue. The nude primitive body is a figure of a self completely unified with visibility to others.

Tourists' orientations are also likely informed by the Christian idea of prelapsarian nudity without shame, when Adam and Eve were clothed in the grace of God (Agamben 2011), and by an alternative Greco-Roman valorization of the human nude as an image of perfection (Barcan 2004). Their orientations also reflect a long practical history of Europeans understanding nudity as the repressed underside of a civilizing process in their own constitution and the leading sign of the ambivalent naturalness of people of the New World, the Pacific, or Africa (Barcan 2004: 154–65). During their own lives, tourists form the expectation that Korowai will be nude from the "look" that *National Geographic, Discovery Channel,* and similar media outlets promulgate as the concrete form of the primitive idea. The focus on nudity also reflects intense emphasis on vision in tourist convictions about knowledge and being generally. By this understanding, to see is to know, and the sight of an unclothed Korowai body is knowledge of a pure human state. There is probably an affinity between the idea of the primitive as a condition of purity outside the estrangements of tourists' regular lives, and a culturally and historically peculiar idea of *seeing* as itself a channel of deep knowing that is nonetheless also pure in not impinging on the external object in its essence. Finally, the focus on nudity is also informed by subtexts of erotic desire and the knowing of gender difference through the screen of primordial humanity.

Much as tourists concretize their primitivist imaginary by spotlighting Korowai nudity, Korowai concretize their imaginary by spotlighting material goods tourists possess and might give. Tourists do not understand payment as central to their relations with Korowai. Rather, they see it as a regrettable, morally fraught compromise, in keeping with their idea that what is special about Korowai is their externality to the global market economy (cf. MacCarthy forthcoming). The gulf between tourist and Korowai imaginaries in this area can be appreciated by the fact that Korowai commonly say the

Figure 1.3. A film crew enacting a desire to "be like them," after completing their film shoot (Copyright: R. Stasch).

whole reason tourists come to their land is to give them valuables. In one common turn of reasoning, Korowai say that tourists know that Korowai are "people without articles" (which is actually true of tourists' outlook, since by "articles" here Korowai mean imported consumer goods), and so the tourists are moved by "pity, longing, love" to come give them the things they lack (which is not true). Korowai also underline the positive value of their own cultural repertoire as a reason why tourists ought to be materially generous. They often link this to an idea that tourists are paid back home for the photos and stories they convey to their superiors (an idea held about all tourists, not just film teams). One man quoted to me these general thoughts that Korowai have about tourists:

> You foreigners [*laleo-alin*] are coming to our Korowai place and looking again and again. Tall houses, bows and arrows, string bags, big garden clearings, pandanus hair decorations, penis wrappers, waistbands, grubby bodies, all of this big work: when you tourists are happily coming, you go on photographing our articles, bodies, and land, and then over there with your people you keep getting lots of money. Give us money, give us axes and machetes. You don't come here because our place is bad; you come here because it's good.

Across diverse contexts of talk, Korowai describe payment as an integral and obvious part of the overall system of tourism transactions. They construe themselves and tourists as participants in a single system of exchange-based social relating, reciprocally answerable to each other in their material actions.

Intense concern with objects and payments has long been central to relations between Korowai themselves. In many contexts, Korowai understand giving or paying of objects to be the measure of whether people have a true relation (e.g., Stasch 2009: 232–50). The specific idea that tourists bring objects out of "love" (*finop*) in response to Korowai material deprivation also follows a well-established pattern of experience. Often when I have asked Korowai if some person felt "love" for another, they immediately talked about the food or other objects the one person gives the other. A particularly common and valued social act is to give objects to someone out of feelings of "pity" or "love" for them, provoked by the knowledge of the other person's lack of that object (Stasch 2009: 164).

Following these principles, Korowai are frequently intense in their requests to be paid well by tourists. If a clan stages a feast or builds a special, tall treehouse for tourists, when the tour group is preparing to leave it is common for the clan to increase the demanded main payment by hundreds of dollars above what was previously negotiated. Such changes are prompted by the hosts' contemplation of how much they have actually done for the tourists, how wealthy the tourists are, and how many relatives the money will need to be shared with. In these and many smaller transactional situations, Korowai may succeed in imposing into the encounter their own imaginative ideas about tourist wealth and about relating through objects. When tourists are aware of such processes rather than being sheltered from them by guides, they are sometimes deeply saddened. The Korowai focus on money and articles, although grounded in Korowai social principles, plays into tourists' sensitivity to payment and materialism as corrupt modes of relating, which they infer have been brought into Korowai lives by tourism itself.

While Korowai and tourist imaginaries sometimes swing into conflict in this way, the main pattern is for the imaginaries to talk amicably past each other. Each side takes as central what the other considers peripheral. Korowai narrate the payment element of tourism interactions as being seamlessly on the same plane as the ways they act toward tourists and their cameras, whereas tourists narrate the material transactions as being of a different order from who Korowai are and the true heart of the encounter. Juxtaposing tourist and Korowai imaginaries is a basic step by which it is possible to appreciate this overall structure of working misunderstanding. The juxtaposition also enables more specific insights into how a working misunderstanding actually "works," by highlighting that imaginaries consist of selective valuing of specific media of action. Tourists ideologize sight and visual appearance as holding special truth, while Korowai locate truth in giving and possession of tangible objects.

IMAGINARIES AS UNSETTLED AND HETEROGENEOUS

I have so far dwelled on relatively central ideas Korowai and tourists elaborate about each other. The concept of "imaginaries" helpfully evokes these ideas' collective character, and their shaping force on perceptions and actions of those who hold them. However, another side of the notion of "imaginaries" is that it also describes areas of psychic and cultural process that are open, ambiguous, incomplete, or contradictory, relative to more stabilized areas of symbolic order. This is emphasized, for example, in Lacan's contrast between the imaginary and the symbolic ([1966] 2006), Sartre's linking of imagination to freedom ([1940] 2004), or Crapanzano's notion of "imaginative horizons" (2004). Such openness and ambiguity is also prominent in stereotypy about exotic others. I will explore this issue further now, still focusing on nudity and payment. Besides their areas of bright attention, Korowai and tourist imaginaries also have areas of activity they accommodate but are *inattentive* to. Even in their core world-shaping content, these imaginaries may signal something more than themselves.[3] This heterogeneity is also important to how imaginaries structure interactions across difference.

In addition to nudity and payment each having special prominence in the respective outlooks of tourists and Korowai, these two channels of relating come into direct practical connection. For one thing, Korowai understand tourists to be *paying for* nudity. Sometimes they get this idea directly from guides or tourists, who tell them that payment depends on Korowai appearing in traditional dress. But the idea that tourists want to see Korowai without clothes is itself a feature of Korowai stereotypy about tourists that circulates independently of the presence of specific foreigners. Under such pressures, Korowai bodily appearance is a frequent focus of processes of staging. During almost every tour group's trek, at certain points clothed Korowai remove their imported garments in advance of the tourists' arrival, much as in the famous Gary Larson cartoon in which two islanders rush to hide their TV and VCR while anthropologists approach in the background (see also Theodossopoulos 2012).

Another practical connection between nudity and payment is that the most common thing Korowai do with cash earned in tourism is buy clothes, typically by entrusting the money to a relative traveling to a commercial center elsewhere. Tourists see Korowai clothedness as a loss of their valued and beautiful true character. They often remark about Korowai persons wearing heavily soiled and tattered shirts, shorts, or skirts: "They look like beggars." This response, with its intense moral and emotional charge, may reflect discomfort with a particular collapse of difference that clothing on Korowai bodies brings about in tourists' eyes: it puts them into a single system of material possession and economic inequality with the tourists, the system in which there are people who are wealthy and others who are destitute. Yet the actual rise in popularity of clothing among Korowai over the last twenty years has been greatly structured by the same Korowai egalitarian ethos that is expressed in the idea that tourists visit out of compassion for Korowai people's lack of wealth. One aspect of Korowai egalitarianism is aversion to standing out as a focus of attention, and sensitivity that other people might be silently judging one's negative attributes. This has given immense appeal to the new possibility of hiding one's body under clothing. Additionally, once clothing began to be adopted, this created a strong egalitarian desire to do what others were doing. One woman answered my question about why most Korowai have now taken to wearing imported clothes with the statement, "It's because of seeing our relatives regularly wearing shirts and shorts. We think, 'Let's do so too!' and we're putting them on." Or as another woman explained more elaborately: "People like clothes, because their relatives look at them having beautiful shorts and shirts, and are attracted. It is like desire for food or sleep. They look at clothes and are desirous. Someone else puts on clothes and another person sees and wishes to wear them too." Besides this affirmative element of positively desiring what others have, there is also a negative side to the egalitarian dynamic, in the form of widespread fear that a person without clothes will be "mocked" (*xulmo-*), again continuing earlier patterns of high interpersonal sensitivity to the judgments of others. Finally, a further main reason for clothing's rise is that it became a medium of expressing care among kin. The specific articles of clothing that most Korowai wear have been given to them by relatives, as a poignant act of love. There are thus many ways in which this change in Korowai cultural practice, which tourists would understand to have been caused by forces from tourists' own society, is actually a complex coproduction, driven by Korowai social sensibilities as well as the new conditions.[4]

The ethnography of Korowai experience of clothes underscores that tourists' ideas about nudity and clothedness are an imaginative formation of those tourists, not a universal. Furthermore, the pattern of Korowai undressing for tourists in order to get more clothes again exemplifies a process of imaginaries "talking past" each other. The two sides converge attentively on certain practical points of contact, while remaining mutually inconsistent in their wider understandings.

Yet these points of articulation also involve each side's imaginaries internally adapting to what is other than themselves. To Korowai, taking off clothes to appear in traditional dress does not make sense as something they would do for each other. But in relating to outsiders who value Korowai nudity, dressing down *does* make sense, in more than the ways allowed by models of deceptive staging of appearances held by those of us dominated by imaginaries of spectatorship and preoccupation with interior "sincerity"—imaginaries that make expressive performance ultimately an issue of the relation between self and self rather than self and other. Instead, dressing down for tourists is also a response to the otherness of others: an act of recognizing what they value, and enthusiastically making it available as a way to enter into transactions with them. Tourists' own frameworks would tend to describe the staging of nudity as a form of deception. Korowai by contrast more routinely use the verb *mbemo-*, "deceive, mislead," to describe what would happen if they did *not* don traditional dress for the visitors: the tourists would feel "misled" about the experiences they would have on their trip. This again locates the truth of relations in external performance toward another's desires. Korowai also say matter-of-factly that the reason tourists want to see "penis wrappers," "rattan waistbands," and "fiber skirts" in the first place is because they do not have those articles in their home country and thus "have not seen people without clothes" before.[5] The same imaginaries that pose tourists as living in a utopia of material plenty and as being a source of payments give Korowai a way of understanding tourists as oriented to something material too, that Korowai can provide as a relation-building gesture even if it is peripheral to what Korowai themselves value.

So, too, is tourists' imaginary pluralistic or conflicted. While their travel is oriented by the dream of an encounter with the backstage of humanity, signified by absence of clothing or commoditization, even this dominant aspect of tourists' imaginary is a fragile tissue. It coexists with payment-based relating as a tried-and-true underside of the travelers' imaginary, readily available to support the other dream. Despite their larger stance of desire for a nonmonetized world, most tourists do comfortably inhabit the activity of paying Korowai for goods or services at certain moments, ranging from the purchase of artifacts or food, to giving wages to porters, to compensating performers for exhibitionary activities. The different imaginaries' internal complexity are pivotal to how Korowai and tourist orientations articulate with each other in actual practice, despite each side's obliviousness of the other's dominant understandings.

A related important area of multiplicity in imaginaries lies in processes of learning and subjective transformation. Curiosity toward exotic others is, after all, a project of opening toward something supposedly outside one's received horizons. Perhaps some horizons are actually altered via such openings, in addition to other horizons becoming only more naturalized. While my account has been necessarily schematic, I will leave the setting of Korowai tourism with two examples of more complex play of imaginaries specifically in relation to nudity. First, on Korowai people's parts, in addition to their stances of transactional enthusiasm for providing tourists what they seek, they also occasionally express pride in the look of traditional dress, sparked by tourism encounters. For example, when tourists themselves sometimes take off their clothes in emulation of Korowai dress, Korowai commonly remark that if wealthy, literate, urban foreigners are happy to dress in the manner of past Korowai, so too Korowai themselves should not be embarrassed to do so. Persons watching the photo session in figure 1.3, for example, said that it made them think, "Why should we forest people be scared of taking off clothes?" Korowai also praise the beauty of tourists' bodies in these contexts, which is partly a tacit praising of traditional Korowai dress styles and bodily aesthetics. The Korowai man Yakop being photographed in figure 1.3 complimented the appearance of the Swiss photographer facing him, remarking that he looked like Yakop's own deceased father's brother. This comparison would never have occurred to me from my own memory of the deceased man's appearance, but it made sense if the focus was articles of dress and their gestalt relation to a general male human form.

The renewed pride in old dress styles stimulated by some tourists' actions may not be very consequential within today's wider shift to clothedness as the dominant norm. There are power asymmetries in the conditions under which Korowai and tourists respectively undress during their encounters, limiting the extent to which tourists putting on Korowai coverings and ornaments can unsettle broader hierarchies. But it is interesting that tourism prompts a discussion of other possibilities within the new Korowai imaginative order that otherwise takes clothedness as the standard.

My other example of more complex play of imaginaries comes from an interview with a northern European tour leader who has visited the Korowai area more times in connection with tourism than any other foreigner. Here are his thoughts prompted by a question I asked about tourists' responses to seeing Korowai in imported clothing:

> I think that they respect them as much even with old clothes and so on. For the being together and the experience, [clothedness] doesn't matter very much. But the tourists want to show relatives and friends back home where they have been, and those people have not been there, not been in contact with the locals, and they look at the clothes. That's the first thing they will see. "Oh, these poor people." That's their reaction. And I think that the tourists don't want to bring that impression with them home. I think that's maybe more [the reason for sensitivity to clothedness] than their own personal feeling. Because when you are there, you get to know the people, you go beyond the clothes, and get into the mind of the people and their personality and so on. And so you more or less forget the clothes. But showing somebody at home, you don't show the personality.... The clothing, that's just a surface. But if you are only one week with the Korowai, then it's only the surface you get to. Maybe that's why it's more sensitive to tourists than to an anthropologist who is staying there a whole year. ... And if you have been there a week, you think less of it [clothedness]. And a year, you don't think of it at all. It's important to understand the difference. Don't think that tourists are stupid or something. It's just the length of stay that makes the difference.

This description departs from the account of tourists' orientations I have earlier given in at least two major ways. First, my interlocutor describes his clients as going through a *weakening* of their initial imaginative concern with visuality and nudity as part of the encounter itself. They develop in its place an imaginary focused on a wider communicative field of copresence with individual persons, who begin to stand out in their complex particularity. Second, the tour leader's description points to a more varied ecology of imaginaries' existence than the simple dichotomy of visitors and visited (which Salazar and Graburn also advocate going beyond, this volume). Nudity emerges as a focus of articulation not only between the disparate imaginaries of tourists and Korowai, but also between the disparate imaginaries of tourists and their home country friends. The gap between what can be conveyed visually to those friends via photographs and a wider lived experience of direct encounters becomes itself an element in tourists' imaginative process.

These are just two examples of the play of "internal" heterogeneity in the imaginaries of tourists and Korowai, of a sort that a fuller study would need to examine more thoroughly. By briefly sketching these examples here, though, I hope to have laid some further groundwork for thinking of imaginaries as *systematically* dual. They are at once forceful constraints on thought, and a field of emergence of new ideas, or new hierarchies of which ideas matter most.

CONCLUSION: SYMMETRY'S VALUE

The symmetry advocated here is not new in anthropology and allied fields. Such a principle is arguably foundational to modern fieldwork-based ethnography, as it was institutionalized a century ago. One early explicit statement of the principle was the suggestion of Wagner ([1975] 1981: 31, 34) that New Guinean "cargo cults" amount to a "reverse anthropology" or "an interpretive counterpart of anthropology itself," different from anthropology's own culture concept, but symmetrically comparable to it as a formation of thought about human difference. Much further work influenced by Wagner has elaborated this idea (e.g., Kelly 2011; see also Hanlon's [1999: 71–75] independent notion of a "counter-ethnography," and the idea of a "counter-gaze" cited by Salazar and Graburn, this volume). The specific term "symmetry" is now associated with Latour (e.g., 1993), whose program for treating nonhuman entities as agents on a par with human actors is intertwined with rejecting any a priori assumption of a foundational difference between the West and the Rest. Chakrabarty's (2000) project to "provincialize" Europeans out of their tacit position as the singular subjects of history is another influential variation on this broad theme.

Opening this chapter, I suggested that there is a metatheoretical value to a symmetric approach to tourism, intertwined with its empirical value. By this, I have in mind that study of tourism has been dominated by imaginaries of tourists alone (a point also raised by Little, this volume). This is arguably true not only at the level of data but also of interpretive assumptions. One family of arguments that has recurred with special frequency in tourism studies holds that while tourists' goal is to experience something outside their system, actual tourism unfolds as the imposition of that system into places they engage with. For example, Enzensberger ([1958] 1996) charts tourism as having arisen historically as a project of escape from industrialized social relations, but then as itself proceeding by industrial logics. In the account of Frow (1991), tourism is characterized by an "internal condition of paradox," consisting of nostalgic longing for a lost world that is the projection of the tourists' own cultural condition. Many scholars document how tourists arrive at tourism sites with a strong "destination image" or "place image" (Shields 1991) originating out of the cultural and media processes of the tourism industry and the tourists' home societies (e.g., Thompson 2006; Stasch 2011a, 2011b). MacCannell (1976) sees tourism as enactment of a cultural logic of a quest for authenticity prompted by the experience of social differentiation under capitalist modernity, generating arrangements of the "staging" of experiences of revealed authenticity in tourism destinations. Greenwood (1989), Comaroff and Comaroff (2009), and others analyze tourism as leading to commodification of formerly noncommoditized areas of cultural life, and to the invention and fixing of local tradition in forms that did not exist independently of tourism itself. Probably the most frequent turn of interpretation scholars present about cultural tourism is that destinations and the people there are remade in the image of what tourists are seeking.

Such arguments are based on careful study of actual tourism processes, but they are also strikingly reminiscent of tourists' own ideas. Tourists routinely state that tourism leads to increased monetization of social relations and desire for mass consumer goods among visited people, and they routinely express anxiety that events might be artificially staged for their benefit. Expressions like "the tourist bubble," widely used by tourists and tourism professionals, contain the germ of a critical theory of tourism as projection of tourists' sociocultural system into visited spaces. The germ of such a theory is even more evident in the vast cultural phenomenon of contempt for the tourist figure, which arose historically in close tandem with the actual emergence of tourism, and which is widely internalized in tourists' own subjectivities of shame, disavowal, or critical reflexivity toward the category "tourist" as such (Urbain 1991; MacCannell 1976: 9–10). Researchers' practice of showing that tourism expands the very social logics tourists seek to escape is not original to academics, but is internally generated by tourism. This prominent "debunking" logic of tourism scholarship also resembles the quest for access to an authentic backstage commonly organizing tourism itself. Scholarly pleasure in the revealed truth that a cultural object is staged for tourism resembles tourists' pleasure in experiencing a true ritual performance, different from the staged kind that other tourists have seen (cf. Hoesterey 2012).

Against this background, the attention to host imaginaries that Salazar and Graburn (this volume) see as characteristic of anthropological work on tourism has special importance. It is not enough to *assert* that visited people's perspectives matter; there is the further problem of commitment to sustained fieldwork on the topic. It is largely anthropologists and anthropology-emulating scholars who have begun producing a body of work in which visited people's ideas are given truly as much documentary and theoretical weight as tourists' framings. A good indication of the contemporary arrival of such an approach is the attention to visited people's experiences shown by many contributors to this volume in their chapters here and their wider work, and the increasing availability of full-length ethnographies premised on such symmetry (e.g., Causey 2003; Tucker 2003; Adams 2006; Gillespie 2006). Yet scholarship based on extended fieldwork with visited people still accounts for only a small proportion of general academic output on tourism.

I have sought in this brief account to illustrate ways a symmetric approach helps bring out more vividly the organizing features of tourists' and visited people's imaginaries, and the organizing features of their overall encounter. Symmetry is also important for making sure scholars' own understandings of tourism are not covertly constrained by the critical anxiety about tourism structurally central to tourists' own positions, or by the equally central tourist ideology of radical difference in kind between visited people who *are* ethnic or cultural, and another set of people, tourists themselves, who are not. This last assumption, that Westerners are universal subjects rather than culturally and historically particular ones, is the conceit that has been exposed with such clarity in programmatic statements of authors like Wagner, Latour, and Chakrabarty. Symmetric ethnography of actual tourism encounters continues to be an area of important empirical follow-through on that theoretical promise.

NOTES

1. See http://www.johnhusing.com/Adventure_Kombai_Feast.htm (accessed 26 June 2013).
2. Tourists' sense of the superiority of primitive humanity on some dimensions is why many who visit Korowai use the term "primitive" only with hesitation or avoid it, because it connotes inferiority to "civilization." In European primitivism generally, celebration of the primitive has long coexisted with deprecation of it. But across the last hundred years or more, there has been a slight loosening of imperialist and social evolutionist models of archaic people's inferiority,

and a rise in popularity of romantic representations posing archaic humans as better than the stereotypers themselves. Tourism to Korowai is part of that trend.

3. Tonnaer (this volume, citing Bærenholdt et al. 2004) introduces the metaphor of tourist places as "sand castles," meaning they are fragile imaginative formations. Leite (this volume) raises the issue of the underdetermination of tourist experiences by collective imaginaries. These are additional forms of the openness I am referring to.

4. See Wiener (2005) for a similar situation in which Western tourists idealized the undress of visited people as a figure of primitive paradise superior to modernity, while those visited people began valuing clothedness as a figure of desired modernity. Korowai also link clothedness to modernity and a desired larger new socioeconomic condition.

5. Tellingly, under the influence of tourism interactions, the Indonesian word *asli,* "indigenous, authentic, original, real," has been borrowed by Korowai speakers to mean simply "naked." While for tourists and guides, the theoretical *idea* of primitive humans is one of a completely metaphysical condition of being, in actual communicative practice and in Korowai understanding of tourists' goals, *asli* takes on a highly physical focus.

REFERENCES

Adams, Kathleen. 2006. *Art as Politics: Re-crafting Identities, Tourism, and Power in Tana Toraja, Indonesia.* Honolulu: University of Hawai'i Press.

Adler, Judith. 1989. "Travel as Performed Art." *American Journal of Sociology* 94, no. 6: 1366–91.

Agamben, Giorgio. 2011. "Nudity." In *Nudities.* Palo Alto, CA: Stanford University Press.

Bærenholdt, Jørgen Ole, Michael Haldrup, Jonas Larsen, and John Urry. 2004. *Performing Tourist Places.* Aldershot, UK: Ashgate.

Barcan, Ruth. 2004. *Nudity: A Cultural Anatomy.* Oxford: Berg.

Bashkow, Ira. 2006. *The Meaning of Whitemen: Race and Modernity in the Orokaiva Cultural World.* Chicago: University of Chicago Press.

Basso, Keith. 1979. *Portraits of "the Whiteman": Linguistic Play and Cultural Symbols among the Western Apache.* Cambridge: Cambridge University Press.

Bruner, Edward, and Barbara Kirshenblatt-Gimblett. 1994. "Maasai on the Lawn: Tourist Realism in East Africa." *Cultural Anthropology* 9, no. 4: 435–70.

Carrier, James G. 1991. "Gifts in a World of Commodities: The Ideology of the Pure Gift in American Society." *Social Analysis* 29: 19–37.

Castoriadis, Cornelius. (1975) 1987. *The Imaginary Institution of Society.* Cambridge, MA: Harvard University Press.

Causey, Andrew. 2003. *Hard Bargaining in Sumatra: Western Travelers and Toba Bataks in the Marketplace of Souvenirs.* Honolulu: University of Hawai'i Press.

Chakrabarty, Dipesh. 2000. *Provincializing Europe: Postcolonial Thought and Historical Difference*. Princeton, NJ: Princeton University Press.

Cohen, Erik. 1989. "'Primitive and Remote': Hill Tribe Trekking in Thailand." *Annals of Tourism Research* 16, no. 1: 30–61.

Comaroff, John, and Jean Comaroff. 2009. *Ethnicity, Inc.* Chicago: University of Chicago Press.

Crapanzano, Vincent. 2004. *Imaginative Horizons: An Essay in Literary-philosophical Anthropology*. Chicago: University of Chicago Press.

Crick, Malcolm. 1994. *Resplendent Sites, Discordant Voices: Sri Lankans and International Tourism*. Chur, Switzerland: Harwood Academic Publishers.

Dorward, David C. 1974. "Ethnography and Administration: A Study of Anglo-Tiv 'Working Misunderstanding.'" *Journal of African History* 15, no. 3: 457–77.

Enzensberger, Hans Magnus. (1958) 1996. "A Theory of Tourism." *New German Critique* 68: 117–35.

Frow, John. 1991. "Tourism and the Semiotics of Nostalgia." *October* 57: 123–51.

Gillespie, Alex. 2006. *Becoming Other: From Social Interaction to Self-Reflection*. Greenwich, CT: Information Age Publishing.

Greenwood, Davydd. 1989. "Culture by the Pound: An Anthropological Perspective on Tourism as Cultural Commoditization." In *Hosts and Guests: The Anthropology of Tourism*, 2nd ed., ed. Valene Smith. Philadelphia: University of Pennsylvania Press.

Hanlon, David. 1999. "Magellan's Conquerors? American Anthropology's History in Micronesia." In *American Anthropology in Micronesia: An Assessment*, ed. Robert C. Kiste and Mac Marshall. Honolulu: University of Hawai'i Press.

Hoesterey, James B. 2012. "The Adventures of Mark and Olly: The Pleasures and Horrors of Anthropology on TV." In *Human No More: Digital Subjectivities, Un-Human Subjects and the End of Anthropology*, ed. Neil Whitehead and Michael Wesch. Boulder: University of Colorado Press.

Kearney, Richard. 1988. *The Wake of Imagination: Toward a Postmodern Culture*. London: Routledge.

———. 1991. *Poetics of Imagining: From Husserl to Lyotard*. London: HarperCollins Academic.

Kelly, José Antonio. 2011. *State Healthcare and Yanomami Transformations: A Symmetrical Ethnography*. Tucson: University of Arizona Press.

Lacan, Jacques. 1977. *Écrits: A Collection*. New York: W.W. Norton.

Latour, Bruno. 1993. *We Have Never Been Modern*. Cambridge, MA: Harvard University Press.

MacCannell, Dean. 1976. *The Tourist: A New Theory of the Leisure Class*. New York: Schocken Books.

———. 2011. *The Ethics of Sightseeing*. Berkeley: University of California Press.

MacCarthy, Michelle. Forthcoming. "'Like Playing A Game Where You Don't Know The Rules': Investing Meaning in Intercultural Cash Transactions." Ethnos.

O'Rourke, Dennis. 1987. *Cannibal Tours*. Los Angeles: O'Rourke & Associates; Direct Cinema Ltd.

Said, Edward. 1978. *Orientalism.* New York: Vintage Books.

Salgado, Sebastião. 2013. *Genesis.* Cologne: Taschen.

Sartre, Jean-Paul. (1940) 2004. *The Imaginary: A Phenomenological Psychology of the Imagination.* Paris: Gallimard.

Shields, Rob. 1991. *Places on the Margin: Alternative Geographies of Modernity.* London: Routledge.

Stasch, Rupert. 2001. "Giving Up Homicide: Korowai Experience of Witches and Police (West Papua)." *Oceania* 72, no. 1: 33–55.

———. 2007. "Demon Language: The Otherness of Indonesian in a Papuan Community." In *Consequences of Contact: Language Ideologies and Sociocultural Transformations in Pacific Societies,* ed. Miki Makihara and Bambi B. Schieffelin. Oxford: Oxford University Press.

———. 2009. *Society of Others: Kinship and Mourning in a West Papuan Place.* Berkeley: University of California Press.

———. 2011a. "The Camera and the House: The Semiotics of New Guinea 'Treehouses' in Global Visual Culture." *Comparative Studies in Society and History* 53, no. 1: 75–112.

———. 2011b. "Textual Iconicity and the Primitivist Cosmos: Chronotopes of Desire in Travel Writing about Korowai of West Papua." *Journal of Linguistic Anthropology* 21, no. 1: 1–21.

———. 2013. "The Poetics of Village Space When Villages Are New: Settlement Form as History-Making in West Papua." *American Ethnologist* 40, no. 3: 555–70.

———. 2014. "Korowai Engagement with Ideologies of Unequal Human Worth in Encounters with Tourists, State Officials, and Education." In *From "Stone-Age" to "Real-Time": Exploring Papuan Mobilities, Temporalities, and Religiosities,* ed. Martin Slama. Canberra: ANU E Press.

———. n.d. "Singapore, Big Village of the Dead: Cities as Figures of Desire, Domination, and Rupture among Korowai of West Papua." Unpublished manuscript.

Taylor, Charles. 2004. *Modern Social Imaginaries.* Durham, NC: Duke University Press.

Theodossopoulos, Dimitrios. 2012. "Indigenous Attire, Exoticization, and Social Change: Dressing and Undressing among the Emberá of Panama." *Journal of the Royal Anthropological Institute* 18, no. 3: 591–612.

Thompson, Krista A. 2006. *An Eye for the Tropics: Tourism, Photography, and Framing the Caribbean Picturesque.* Durham, NC: Duke University Press.

Todorov, Tzvetan. 1984. *The Conquest of America: The Question of the Other.* New York: Harper and Row.

Tucker, Hazel. 2003. *Living with Tourism: Negotiating Identities in a Turkish Village.* London: Routledge.

Urbain, Jean-Didier. 1991. *L'Idiot du voyage: Histoires de touristes.* Paris: Plon.

Van den Berghe, Pierre L. 1994. *The Quest for the Other: Ethnic Tourism in San Cristóbal, Mexico.* Seattle: University of Washington Press.

Vilaça, Aparecida. 2010. *Strange Enemies: Indigenous Agency and Scenes of Encounters in Amazonia.* Durham, NC: Duke University Press.

Wagner, Roy. (1975) 1981. *The Invention of Culture.* Chicago: University of Chicago Press.

Wiener, Margaret. 2005. "Breasts, (Un)dress, and Modernist Desires in the Balinese-Tourist Encounter." In *Dirt, Undress, and Difference: Critical Perspectives on the Body's Surface,* ed. Adeline Masquelier. Bloomington: Indiana University Press.

Chapter 2

Scorn or Idealization?

Tourism Imaginaries, Exoticization, and Ambivalence in Emberá Indigenous Tourism

Dimitrios Theodossopoulos

Scorn and idealization represent two dominant orientations in the exoticization of indigenous communities that host tourists. These two orientations also appear as dominant tropes in the tourism imaginary (Salazar 2010), shaping the negotiation of expectations during the tourism encounter (Skinner and Theodossopoulos 2011). In this chapter, I argue that these two types of exoticization often coexist in parallel in the tourist imagination, producing contradictions that set in motion the imagination of local hosts. The host communities gradually develop their own versions of exoticization, as they categorize and stereotype the tourists. Thus, at any given moment, parallel layers of exotization participate and inspire any given tourism imaginary. This realization can help us escape from a limiting vision of indigenous hosts as passive recipients of tourism imagination; it can also help us appreciate the agency of hosts in renegotiating their self-identity during the tourism encounter (see also Bunten 2008).

In this chapter, I explore these propositions in the context of Emberá indigenous tourism. I use as a case study the development of tourism in Parara Puru, an Emberá community in the Chagres National Park in Panama, where I have conducted anthropological fieldwork in the last seven years.[1] Tourism has provided the Emberá with opportunities to investigate the expectations of their guests and, in an effort to satisfy those expectations, respond to contradictory types of exoticization. These range from idealization, an attitude that reflects nostalgia for the idealized "vanishing savage" and lost worlds unaffected by (Western) civilizing processes (Clifford 1986; Rosaldo 1989; see also Conklin and Graham 1995; Ramos 1998; Gow 2007), to scorn, irony, and negative stereotyping, an attitude to which I refer as an "unintentional primitivization."

"Unintentional primitivization" encapsulates a more general ambivalence in the imagination of many tourists: an expectation that indigenous people may benefit from certain aspects of Western civilization—such as education for children and hospital care—while at the same time remain unaffected by other "corrupting" Western influences. In this respect, tourist expectations frequently oscillate between exoticism and primitivism, two visions of Otherness rooted in a "European world hegemony" established in the age of exploration (Friedman 1994: 4). In our age of increased global flows, such pervasive and ethnocentric imaginaries persist and shape the tourism encounter—and popular expectations of cultural sameness and difference—posing dilemmas for indigenous hosts, who attempt to negotiate their representation in contradictory-cum-exoticized terms (which may be simultaneously denigrating or idealizing).

Rather than remaining passive recipients of these two contrasting, and often parallel, modes of exoticization, the Emberá observe, categorize, and exoticize the tourists, too. They develop their own geographical awareness and imaginaries of cultural difference. Exoticization, I argue, can be a reciprocal process, targeting both the West and the Rest. It involves parallel processes that may reinforce each other, or may not overlap at all, but still contribute to the local and global negotiation of cultural difference. Thus, the negotiation of tourism expectations in the tourism encounter, and the study of exotic images reproduced by hosts and guests, can open the doorway to the systematic study of the tourism imaginary (see also Leite, this volume). Anthropology, with its attention to contextual specificity and meaning, can make a substantial contribution in this respect by comparing local and global imaginaries of the exotic, and how these are "challenged, contested, and transformed" (Salazar and Graburn, this volume).

In the context of Emberá indigenous tourism, the attention of the tourist audience—guided by exoticized expectations—has encouraged the Emberá who work in tourism to engage with their indigenous identity and its representation in a more systematic manner. This renewed interest of the Emberá in the details of their culture represents a new, emerging representational self-awareness; it encourages the accumulation of new knowledge about one's own cultural distinctiveness and, more importantly, a more confident articulation of this knowledge during communication with outsiders. Bunten (2008: 381) has referred to this type of self-representation as self-commodification, the construction of a marketable identity to employ in the tourism encounter, but one that does not seem alienating to the indigenous host. The anthropology of tourism has further established how the tourist encounter provides opportunities to rediscover, reflect upon, and reconstitute indigenous traditions (Abram et al. 1997; see also Graburn 1976; Smith 1989; Swain 1989; Selwyn 1996; Boissevain 1996; Stronza 2001; Coleman and Crang 2002; Bruner 2005; Leite and Graburn 2009; Salazar 2010).

The anthropology of tourism has aided academic analysis to escape from a static or dichotomous view of authenticity in the tourism encounter (Bruner 2005; Theodossopoulos 2013a, 2013b) and to appreciate expectation and imagination in tourism as transformative processes that shape local social realities, often in profound ways (Skinner and Theodossopoulos 2011). In the discussion that follows, I draw upon these lessons from the anthropology of tourism to explore the imagination of the exotic and the contradictions it entails and generates, first in the expectations of the tourists who visit the Emberá, and then in the reception of these expectations by the Emberá. As Bruce Kapferer has recently argued, "any and every context, situation or practice is potentially exotic to any other"; the challenge for the academic analyst is to "take advantage of an exotic recognition, without becoming either trapped in the exotic or devolving into exoticism" (Kapferer 2011).

Figure 2.1. Emberá men waiting for the arrival of the tourists (Copyright: D. Theodossopoulos).

THE TWO FACES OF EXOTICIZATION

We can easily identify two opposing tendencies in the exoticized tourism imaginary. The first involves a conceptualization of the exotic subject in terms of primitiveness and lack of civilization, while the second idealizes—in a Rousseauian fashion—the exotic subject as a noble savage, living in harmony with nature. With respect to the exoticization of Amerindian communities, these two tendencies have been identified before (see, e.g., Berkhofer 1978; Ramos 1998; Ulloa 2005), but in this chapter I would like to stress their interrelationship and the mixed messages they generate when applied to concrete local contexts. Thus, I will attempt here to approach indigenous tourism from a more integrated perspective that considers both "primitivization" and "idealization" in the exoticization of exotic Others.

The tendency toward scorn and denigration encourages the modernization of indigenous communities through the experience of tourism. Premodern communities are approached with prejudice—representing a "primitive" or "less civilized" state of human history—but tourism is perceived as a force able to elevate those less-than-perfect communities and bring them closer to the rest of the world. Thus, through tourism, premodern communities—which are imagined to exist in spaces far from civilization—gradually become partakers of the global community and, in this process, the nontourist exotic Other is imagined to become more similar to the tourist self.

In contrast, the idealizing tendency of the exotic imaginary is in most respects antitourist in its orientation. The basic presupposition here is that indigenous communities should ideally remain "uncontaminated" by the influences of modernity, representative of a primordial past or a static authenticity that denies the indigenous actors the possibility of change (see Theodossopoulos 2013a, 2013b). From this point of view, tourism, and the presence of tourists in the exoticized communities, poses a problem: it alters the idealized constitution of the supposedly noble premodern communities and corrupts those who (are imagined to) have been untouched by the corrupting influence of Western or urban society. I would like to stress here that the idealizing attributes of this second type of stereotyping could hide from our view that this is also a type of exoticization.

So we have seen so far that tourist exoticization oscillates between (1) a desire to make the "less civilized" Other more like the tourist self and (2) a yearning to preserve an uncontaminated version of indigeneity—an expectation of unshakable cultural integrity and purity (Ramos 1998: 70). The first orientation encourages the introduction of Western civilization's benefits into the indigenous experience, such as new forms of technology, education in schools, and medical care in hospitals, while the second remains passive—discouraging direct intervention or the economic "development" of the poor—and trapped within its idealizing vision of indigenous innocence.

Unsuspectingly, with regard to attitudes toward development and social change in indigenous society, some versions of the negative stereotyping frame of reference can be more "progressive" than their idealizing counterparts: they encourage contact and exchange of information (between tourists and hosts) or welcome the use of modern technologies by the hosts. Nevertheless, this "progressiveness"—representative of a less static attitude toward social change—is often complemented by an expectation of assimilation, which can be imperialistic, nationalist, or evolutionist in its orientation. In contrast, the idealizing frame of reference appears, at first sight, less progressive, as it reproduces an expectation of authenticity as isolation—a deeply static view of society (Theodossopoulos 2013b). Although static, we have to admit that this perspective encourages a greater respect for cultural difference.

More importantly, and as I will show in the following sections, the two contrasting modes of exoticization often work in parallel in the imagination of tourists, and manifest themselves in parallel ways in the lives of indigenous hosts. They also raise contrasting dilemmas for indigenous communities involved with tourism. Is it appropriate for indigenous actors to go

Figure 2.2. Emberá children learning how to type on the anthropologist's computer (Copyright: D. Theodossopoulos).

to university; use cellular phones and watch television; rely on shamanic medicinal ceremonies or go to the hospital; adopt (more clearly identifiable) indigenous practices when the tourists visit the community, but engage with nonindigenous practices when the tourists depart? I will now explore these dilemmas in the imaginaries and expectations that inform the Emberá-tourist encounter.

EMBERÁ CULTURAL TOURISM

Parara Puru looks at first sight like an isolated community forgotten by time and untouched by modernity. It is surrounded by dense forest and approachable only by dugout canoe. Thus, from the tourist point of view the community emerges "naturally" out of the green vegetation of the Chagres National Park. The appearance of the community—its thatched-roofed houses and the relaxed disposition of its inhabitants, who are dressed in indigenous attire—resonate with Rousseauian representations of life away from the tribulations of Western civilization. In the Western imaginary, the expectation of discovering authentic indigenous communities "far away" from the corrupting influences of modernity has been associated—under the influence of Rousseau—with expectations of sincerity, primordial authenticity, paradisiacal innocence, and purity (Bendix 1997; Lindholm 2008). "Tribal" or "native" cultures, such as the indigenous peoples of the contemporary world, have been and are still perceived as representing those qualities (see Salazar 2010).

In the twentieth century, popular ecology relied upon the appeal of the earlier romantic visions, further idealizing indigenous communities as being closer to nature or encapsulating the essence of ecological wisdom (Morris 1981; Ellen 1986; Conklin and Graham 1995; Milton 1996: 109–14; West and Carrier 2004; Carrier and Macleod 2005). The mass media has further reproduced the image of "ecological natives" as "integral components of an imperiled and exotic natural order, rather than a group of fellow humans in a complex network of social and natural relationships" (Ulloa 2005: 197). When tourists approach indigenous communities, they often do so with already-developed preconceptions of that type.

To the satisfaction of the tourists, the community of Parara Puru complies, in appearance and character, with the idealized expectations of its visitors. What is not directly visible at first sight is that indigenous tourism was introduced in Parara Puru as an alternative economic strategy, a new adaptation in response to unanticipated circumstances, such as the establishment of the Chagres National Park, which prohibited the Emberá from practicing their subsistence activities (e.g., cultivation and hunting). Indigenous tourism was also initiated at the very end of a period of significant social change, which included new patterns of residence and education in Spanish, but also new opportunities for political representation.

The grandparents of the residents of Parara Puru arrived at Chagres in the 1950s from Darién and established themselves, in dispersed settlement, on the River Chagres and the River San Juan de Pequeni (cf. Caballero and Araúz 1962). The establishment of the national park in 1985 was the beginning of a difficult period for the second generation of Chagres-born Emberá, several of whom had to move closer to nonindigenous communities and perform wage labor for outsiders. To survive under the restrictions imposed by the national park, the Emberá explored the option of cultural tourism. With the help of some NGOs and tourist agencies, they organized cultural presentations for tourists, which included dance, music, a simple meal, and an explanatory speech by one of the leaders of the community. A steady flow of tourists from hotels in Panama City and cruise ships transiting the Panama Canal allowed the Emberá to specialize in delivering presentations for tourists on a frequent, almost daily basis. In time, they learned how to share the profits generated from tourism, keep their accounts, meet the necessary safety regulations, and make links with tourism agencies interested in organizing tourist excursions. The agencies provided the infrastructure for advertising and transporting the tourists to River Chagres, where the Emberá receive the tourists and transferred them to their communities in motorized canoes.

The success of indigenous tourism in Chagres encouraged the Emberá to form concentrated settlements, villages that specialize in the development of tourism and are prepared to carry out cultural presentations for outsiders on a frequent, almost daily basis. The flexible manner with which the communities were composed and organized, and the overall decision to establish concentrated settlements, is part of a much more widespread process. Since the late 1950s, the Emberá of Panama started establishing spatially concentrated communities, which have government-funded schools and political leaders (Herlihy 1986, 2003; Kane 1994; Velásquez Runk 2009; Colin 2010). Although Parara Puru, the community I examine in this chapter, was founded only thirteen years ago, its foundation was part of a wider process of Emberá resettlement that took place in Panama.

Resettlement in concentrated communities has encouraged the organization of Emberá political leadership, with the introduction of elected community leaders and regional leaders. Such changes have enhanced, in some respects, the authority of men, and the political peripheralization of women (Kane 1994). Yet, with the introduction of tourism, many women started deriving alternative income from tourist arts, such as the construction of basketry, even in communities that do not directly entertain tourists (Colin 2010).[2] In Parara Puru, the profits from tourism—derived from a per capita entrance fee, which is negotiated with the tourist agents—are divided according to the degree of participation in the presentations for the tourists,[3] while money earned from the sale of artifacts goes directly to the vendors. The community maintains a united front toward its negotiations with tourist agents, and its leaders regulate the prices of artifacts to discourage competition and the lowering of prices.

The Emberá of Parara Puru hold regular community meetings in which they discuss the logistics of their engagement with tourism, reorganizing the division of labor, or making preparations for hosting large groups of visitors. In these meetings, they also share their experience with particular aspects of the tourist encounter, and assess how to improve certain parts of their presentation. In recent years, an increasing number of individual community members—younger and older men and women—have stepped forward and volunteered to take a more active role in the speech delivered to the tourists, a practice that allows them to receive and answer the questions of the tourists (with the help of nonindigenous tourist guides, who act as translators). My ethnographic presentation in this chapter draws from their continuously growing experience of the tourist encounter.[4]

Overall, the introduction of tourism has brought new challenges for the Emberá, one of which is the wider revalorization of Emberá cultural practices. From the point of view of the Emberá, the positive attention of the outside world is a new experience. The adult residents of Parara Puru were raised with the expectation—originating from the nonindigenous Panamanian society—that they should learn Spanish, dress in modern clothes, and adopt Western civilizational practices. In the context of previous discrimination and stereotyping in Panama, Emberá culture was caricatured as "primitive" or "uncivilized." With the introduction of tourism, however, the Emberá are receiving the message that their culture is now respected by tourists or travelers who come from countries more powerful and wealthier than Panama. This realization is now encouraging the Emberá to articulate a stronger identification with their culture, and project their indigenous identity to outsiders more confidently. Instead of hiding away from the non-Emberá world, an adaptation strategy that served them well in the past (Williams 2005), they are now reaching out to the international community, and gradually taking advantage of the new representational opportunities offered by an increasingly globalized world (Theodossopoulos 2009).

This emerging awareness of the respect, but also the expectations, of the wider world has inspired a renewed interest among the Emberá in the history and representation of their own culture. Now that a wider non-Emberá audience is increasingly paying attention to the Emberá, the Emberá desire to become more informed and more articulate tourist guides, able to describe a wider variety of cultural particularities that might interest a larger variety of tourists, including those who are more knowledgeable and inquisitive. It is in this respect that the manner of presentation to tourists, but also the explanation of the presentation, become acts of ever-increasing consequence.

TOURIST EXPECTATIONS AND THEIR RECEPTION IN PARARA PURU

The tourists who visit Parara Puru arrive with varied and unique combinations of expectations, based on preexisting popular stereotypes about life in the rainforest and diverse sets of knowledge about the position and relationship of indigenous communities relative to the wider world. As I have explained in the previous sections, tourist expectations about the Emberá range from an idealized nostalgia for the idealized "vanishing savage" and lost worlds unaffected by (Western) civilizing processes (Clifford 1986; Rosaldo 1989) to patronizing and discriminatory stereotyping that caricatures indigenous difference as primitiveness and lack of cultural sophistication. Yet, as I would like to stress in this section, in most cases, individual tourists combine in their commentary about Parara Puru elements from both the idealizing and the patronizing orientations of exoticization. Even when some tourists are willing to accept—to deferring degrees—that their indigenous hosts are subjects of the contemporary global and interconnected world, they struggle to escape from the two main tropes of exoticization mentioned above.

Although Parara Puru occasionally receives small groups of domestic (nonindigenous Panamanian) tourists, the great majority of tourists come from international destinations, mostly from North America, but also Europe and, to a smaller degree, Japan and other Latin American countries. Some of these tourists come from holiday resorts, while others are passengers on cruise ships that are transiting through the Panama Canal. They respond to tourist advertisements (promoted in their hotels or cruise ships) that offer a variety of excursions, one type of which is to "an Emberá village" or "an indigenous community" in the Chagres National Park, an excursion that has been, as the tourist agents explain, very popular in recent years.[5]

For the duration of the trip, the tourists are accompanied by nonindigenous tourist guides,[6] who shape to a certain degree the "precontact" expectations of their customers about the Emberá. The guides collect the tourists in buses or minibuses and have an opportunity to explain, during the bus trip, the practical aspects of the tour, and provide some information about the Emberá. The detail and quality of this information varies tremendously, according to the knowledge, experience, and enthusiasm of the tourist guide, some of whom have visited Emberá communities many times before and maintain friendships with Emberá individuals, while other guides improvise (due to lack of experience or preparation), mixing fact with fiction and contributing to the idealizing and/or stereotyping of the Emberá indiscriminately.

After arriving at Chagres, the tourists have their first glimpse of Emberá men, dressed in loincloths and with their bodies painted in traditional Emberá style. The Emberá help the tourists get aboard their motorized canoes—the Emberá are renowned for their skill in constructing and navigating canoes—which they use to transport the tourists to their communities. Particular tourism agencies have arrangements with particular Emberá communities, and each community knows when to expect and welcome each individual tourist group. They do so dressed in traditional attire and with traditional live music, which signify, from the Emberá point of view, an indication of respect toward the visitors.[7]

The tourists enter the community and have time to browse Emberá artifacts, such as baskets and wood carvings, which are usually arranged on tables in communal houses, where the cultural presentations take place. Normally, each Emberá family maintains a separate table of artifacts. The profits from the sale of artifacts comprise an important part of the family's annual income. So the tourists are encouraged to buy, and many of them do, aware or unaware that the local prices are much lower than the price of similar items in the airport or in urban tourist markets. Most Emberá communities entertain the tourists in a similar manner, which includes, as I mentioned above, a "traditional meal" of fried fish and plantains, a speech by one of the local leaders, and a dance presentation. Some tourists walk in the community, explore, take photos of the thatched roofs of Emberá houses, or in some communities receive an ethnobotanical tour by an Emberá expert in the medicinal properties of plants.

Sometimes, while walking in the community, tourists discover details of the daily life of the Emberá, such as items of clothing, electronic devices, or plastic toys that do not fit into their preconceptions about indigenous people in the rain forest. These discoveries contribute to their puzzlement about the exact position of the Emberá at the interface of tradition and modernity, and usually inspire the tourists to express pessimistic statements about culture loss and the eventual disappearance of all indigenous people. The idealizing nostalgia of these comments is often associated with ambivalence about the corruptive influence of technology and modernity on indigenous life. Some tourists adopt an extreme romantic idealism toward this issue, and mourn, in Rousseauian fashion, the lost innocence of "primitive" man, anticipating that Emberá culture will disappear due to exposure to the relentlessly homogenizing forces of our global era.

Some other tourists recognize that the Emberá, like other indigenous people, live in a modern world and are confronted with change, but approach change as an undesirable inevitability. Their recognition that the Emberá "have to" send their children to school or use modern medicine clashes with their disappointment at the discovery that some Emberá houses have televisions or at the view of modern T-shirts hanging on a laundry line along with traditional Emberá *paruma* skirts. Ambivalent views of this type—permeated by an idealizing spirit, mixed with realistic observations—are voiced by the overwhelming majority of international tourists. Yet, there are always a few tourists who side unequivocally with modernity, and caricature the Emberá with pointed comments that focus on their observable nudity and their assumed lack of knowledge of the civilized world. Domestic tourists are the most likely visitors, albeit not the only ones, to caricature indigeneity in these respects.

Complex, ambivalent, and (more or less) opinionated commentary that reflects the general orientations outlined above is often expressed by some tourist with a loud voice while the tourists are walking in the community or in the communal house in the presence of other tourists and the Emberá (who do not understand languages besides Spanish and Emberá). On many occasions during my fieldwork—which represents a continuous commitment, and for this reason I am using in this description the present tense[8]—I meet tourists wandering in the community or, even more frequently, the tourists discover me in my Emberá house. Some are curious about my identity, and after explaining that I am an anthropologist, they ask questions about the Emberá, most of which reflect the tourist's ambivalence about modernity and the future of indigenous people. Many tourists explain that have been pleasantly surprised by the "traditional" character of the community, and remark that, unlike other similar cultural tours they have taken, this particular tourist experience is very rewarding. Yet, and as I have explored in detail in my written work (see, e.g., Theodossopoulos 2013a), a small number of tourists try to discover elements of inauthenticity in the backstage of the tourist encounter (see also Stasch, this volume). This suspicion of inauthenticity can become more meaningful in the general context of idealistic nostalgia described above. As one tourist explained to me: "The community looks way too good to be true!"

The Emberá learn about the comments and expectations of the tourists from the tourist guides, who act as translators and have a stake in maintaining and improving the high level of tourist satisfaction. Complaints, communicated through the guides to the leaders of the Emberá, are disseminated to all members of the community during community meetings. The Emberá, however, have an additional opportunity to measure the expectations of their guests during the question time that follows the speech delivered to the tourists by one of the community leaders. The speech itself contains a brief summary of the history of the community and a description of its organization, the methods of artifact making and their value, and the components of the male and female traditional attire. At the end of this speech, the tourists address the Emberá speaker directly, and their questions (as well as the speaker's answers) are translated by the guides.

Some of the most representative questions the tourists ask address the following topics: (1) if the Emberá do, in real life, live in Parara Puru, a question that reflects the tourists' previous experience with cultural presentations by other ethnic groups that take place in locations outside the indigenous community, such as sites of historic significance (cf. Bunten 2011) or settings especially prepared for tourist performances (cf. Kirtsoglou and Theodossopoulos 2004); (2) if the Emberá wear their traditional attire all the time or only during the cultural presentations; (3) if they rely for medical treatment on their shamans or if they go to the hospital; and (4) if they have a school in the community. Questions of this type reflect a widespread weariness toward the commoditized nature of prearranged cultural presentations, and a general ambivalence about the position of indigenous groups in the interface of tradition and modernity. Thus, some tourists would recommend that Emberá children living in the rain forest should not be deprived of educational opportunities or medical care, but they would expect that adult Emberá rely on the therapeutic advice of their shamans.

The Emberá answer questions of this type in a diplomatic manner: they explain that (1) they do live in their own community permanently; (2) when the tourists depart, the inhabitants of the community take off their necklaces and bracelets to carry out their daily chores in a more comfortable manner (although they diplomatically avoid emphasizing the fact that they wear T-shirts both within and outside the community, while men also wear shorts); (3) some Emberá still rely on traditional medicine, but to solve more serious medical problems they take conventional medicines and go to the hospital; and (4) they have a primary school in the community and they cherish the education of their children. With respect to the last question, the Emberá receive the message that the tourists' admiration of premodern cultural lifestyles gives way in the face of their modern values about education.

Other types of exploratory questions asked by the tourists are, for the most part, less controversial, but can help us shed some light on the tourist imagination and curiosity. For example, tourists frequently ask: "Are you monogamous?" (Usual reply: "Yes"); "Where do you find partners to marry?" (Usual reply: "In neighboring Emberá communities, or in Darién, where many Emberá live"); "At what age do young people marry?" (Usual reply: "Girls at sixteen, boys a bit older, unless they want to continue their education"); "How do young people have fun?" (Usual reply: "Sometimes in social gatherings in neighboring Emberá and non-Emberá communities, sometimes locally"). When some of the same questions are asked by non-indigenous Panamanians, such as Panamanian students on an educational trip, the Emberá of Parara Puru might provide additional details to their answers, making more apparent to their interlocutors that they too live in the same nation and are not too different from them after all.

The feedback the Emberá receive from the tourist guides, and their direct experience of the questions that tourists ask during the "question time" encourage the Emberá to slightly underplay or accentuate their cultural difference in their attempts to guide their visitors to varied, well-known, or sometimes unexplored dimensions of their culture. When they are among

Figure 2.3. Emberá child looking at the arriving tourists from a high vantage point at the entrance of the community (Copyright: D. Theodossopoulos).

nonindigenous Panamanians, for example, they do not want to be the "un-civilized" Indians with the loincloths, yet they welcome the admiration of the international tourists who respect their cultural distinctiveness, including their practice of wearing the loincloths. But, more often than not, the two types of exoticization work in parallel. Some tourists, for example, are happy to know that Emberá kids are learning about computers at school, but they feel ambivalent about the use of Microsoft Excel to organize the community accounts and distribute the profits from tourism. They are happy with the idea that indigenous children should have an education about modern technology, but fail to contain their disappointment at the sight of Emberá children holding cellular phones in their hands. This has led my respondents in Parara Puru to hide their technology in the darker corners of their houses, consciously reproducing MacCannell's (1976) classic distinction between the front and backstage.

THE EMBERÁ OBSERVING AND IMAGINING THE TOURISTS

It is important to stress at this point that it is not only the tourists who observe the Emberá in the tourism encounter; the Emberá share similar opportunities to observe their guests, too. They are curious about the nationality of their guests and their respective countries. Often, while waiting for the arrival of particular tourist groups, or sometimes after their departure, the Emberá of Parara Puru would approach me with questions about countries such as England, France, or Italy (from which they receive regular visitors). They are interested in general information, such as demography, climate and language, and types of food available, or in matters that are more culturally meaningful to Emberá, such as if there are (in those countries) any rivers, how these rivers are, and what type of fish they sustain.

Through daily contact with diverse nationalities of tourists, the Emberá have come to recognize the ethnic categories of tourists that visit their community more frequently and some of their respective characteristics. Tourists from different nationalities behave differently, my respondents explain. Some, for example, the North Americans, are likely to buy many artifacts; others, such as the French, fewer; and some, the Germans are a case in point, purchase almost none. German tourists, I was told (and this was verified by my own observations), enjoy walking in the back regions of the community, sometimes with their guides, but very often unsupervised, and have a tendency to break away from their group or "get lost." The Italian men, a couple of teenage Emberá girls explained, enjoy posing for photos with Emberá women, even though the women themselves sometimes find this attention uncomfortable.

The comments made by the Emberá about different ethnic groups of tourists represent a significant breakaway from the old Emberá practice of avoiding contact with the outside world, a strategy that protected the integrity of the Emberá culture in the past but resulted in limited knowledge of the wider world. Nowadays, frequent interaction with tourists has facilitated the growth of a global awareness among those Emberá who receive and entertain tourists (Theodossopoulos 2010a, 2011). This increasing awareness of the wider world further instigates Emberá curiosity and inspires their geographical imagination:[9] the names of foreign countries are no longer abstract and irrelevant terms—trivial information in a geography school class taught by a nonindigenous teacher—but comprise recognizable categories representing real people, who have visited the Emberá and bought artifacts from them (or have interacted with them in a verbal or nonverbal manner).

As the Emberá organize their information and experiences with these new categories of outsiders, they develop their own stereotypes and exoticize their hosts and their behavior. Through this process, the Emberá develop their own imagination of the exotic Other and their own expectations of foreigners: the Germans who do not buy indigenous artifacts, the North Americans who buy too much, the Italians who pose for photographs with the local girls. One of the most salient local stereotypes is that of the rich and gullible *gringo*—the generic North American, wealthy, white individual (see Theodossopoulos 2010b)—who has money to spend and needs the guidance and the protection of the local knowledgeable actor, who can assume the role of the tourist guide and provide information, company, or entertainment, which has to be paid for.

Seen from this point of view, the Western tourist emerges as a resource to be exploited, a produce to be harvested for the benefit of the local community (see Theodossopoulos 2010a). In this process of stereotyping, the individual agency of the singular tourist is eliminated, in an attempt to redefine and encode the role of the local host. Stereotyping here can be understood as a way of thinking and redefining the category of the self (Theodossopoulos 2003; Brown and Theodossopoulos 2004). It is also important to note, and this point is related to my general argument in this chapter, that exoticization in the tourist imaginary is a reciprocal process, the result of the imaginative categorization of both indigenous and nonindigenous actors.

CONCLUSION: MANY PARALLEL
IMAGINARIES AND EXPECTATIONS

Undoubtedly, the tourism exchange has had an effect on Emberá culture, but one that has been so far—and as the overwhelming majority of my Emberá respondents maintain—constructive rather than destructive. Tourism imaginaries, "reembedded in new contexts" and built "on local referents"—such as the exotic appearance of the Emberá—"help in (re)creating peoples and places" (Salazar 2010: 15). The Emberá in the communities that receive tourists have seized the opportunity for improving their financial situation, but also for making their culture more widely known. From their perspective, the idealizing attention of the international audience positively contrasts with the previous stereotyping that they experienced in the past, especially in the context of relating with nonindigenous society in their own nation. Images of Emberá are now part of official national tourism campaigns, while photographs and short videos of their performances are posted on the Internet by the tourists themselves. This, by Emberá standards, unprecedented visibility entails a small but positive transformation of status, nationally and internationally (Theodossopoulos 2010a, 2011).

It can be argued that the warm reception of Emberá culture by the international tourist audience is the by-product of an essentializing gaze, which is based on previous Western preconceptions about the exotic. These revolve around static images of "an unspoiled and irrecoverable past" (Herzfeld 1997: 109), an unreflexive expectation to meet civilizations untouched by modernity, expressed through "the lament for things lost" (Howe 2009: 249). Rosaldo (1989) refers to this sentiment, or sentimental pessimism (Sahlins 2000), as "imperialist nostalgia": the children of modernity mourn what was lost by the dominating impact of their own societies. So they search among indigenous people, such as the Emberá, to discover and satisfy their Western aesthetic of premodern authenticity (Conklin 1997; Ramos 1998; Gow 2007; Santos Granero 2009).

Unlike the idealizing tourists, the great majority of nonindigenous Panamanians reproduce in their imagination of the Emberá a different orientation toward exoticization: a patronizing and stereotyping perspective to which I refer as "unintentional primitivization." Nonindigenous Panamanians communicate through this trope of exoticization the expectation that the Emberá will change and become more like themselves. Their scorn and irony for the "less civilized" Indians—with its simultaneous expectation that the Emberá will assimilate to mainstream society—encourages the modernization of the Emberá, and sharply contrasts with the idealizing perspective of the tourists, which encourages adherence to tradition, but discourages change.

The discrepancies between foreign and domestic tourists described above represent general orientations, but are not, strictly speaking, prescriptive. There are many foreign, but also domestic, tourists who combine in their expectations of the Emberá the idealizing and stereotyping perspective. They see the Emberá as "primitive" or "less civilized" people, but they are happy to think that they will remain so, guardians of an original authentic state of human existence. Other tourists state that the Emberá "should" become "more civilized"—and benefit from education and Western medicine—but they are sad to see the Emberá using mobile phones, wearing Western clothes, or hearing that they now disregard the medical advice of the shamans (see Theodossopoulos 2011). Thus, scorn and idealization coexist in the comments of the same groups of tourists, or even the very same individual tourists, adding complexity to the tourist encounter, but also reproducing contradictions that the Emberá have to tackle.

The Emberá, on their part, do not remain static or passive recipients of the imaginings of outsiders; they imagine their Others too. They observe, categorize, and stereotype the nonindigenous Panamanians and the tourists, developing their own imaginary, and expanding their geographical awareness. It is for this reason that I have adopted in this chapter an approach that does not treat indigenous people as passive victims of processes originating in the West. The Western imaginary of indigeneity, with its double standards, poses difficult puzzles to ethnic groups that welcome the attention of outsiders such as tourists (Conklin and Graham 1995; Conklin 1997; Ramos 1998; Salazar 2010). But indigenous hosts, for their part, also confront the challenges of tourist imagination. The Emberá, for example, continually polish their skill in deciphering and anticipating contradictory tourist expectations and explicitly communicate their desire to take advantage of the tourist economy. They now wish to reach out to the world and enhance the representation and visibility of their culture (Theodossopoulos 2009; Strathern and Stewart 2009); to derive some benefit from the globalizing economy; and to renegotiate—as other Panamanian ethnic groups have done (cf. Salvador 1976, 1997; Swain 1989; Howe 1998, 2009; Tice 1995; Young and Bort 1999; Guerrón-Montero 2006a, 2006b; Pereiro Pérez et al. 2010; Martínez Mauri 2011)—their relationship with the wider national and international community.

Thus, I argue, it would be simplistic to adopt an approach to the study of the tourism imaginary that focuses too narrowly on the power inequalities between hosts and guests, and traces the tourism imaginary as emanating, unidirectionally, from the imagination of the Western audience. Such a perspective would inevitably underestimate the ability of peripheral hosts to shape social life through the work of imagination (Appadurai 1996, 2001). The imagination of Western tourists does not merely affect the lives of indigenous hosts, but also provides inspiration for new local transformations. Indigenous actors, such as the Emberá, imagine and stereotype the tourists in their own terms—all the different varieties of outsiders.

These reflections can help us appreciate that imagination in the tourism encounter is a parallel, even reciprocal process that produces parallel imaginaries, which partly communicate with each other and partly not. Tourism imaginaries circulate unevenly, argue Salazar and Graburn in their introduction to this volume, but the imaginative flow is not "a one-way street" (see also Salazar 2010). Some routes of imaginary flow have a longer history and circulate images and expectations derived from a vast repository of idealizing or stereotyping perceptions of Others—literature, film, and a history of colonial inequality. Many other routes of imaginary flow have been carved more recently, and some are the product of the tourist encounter itself: tourists collect their own personal images (and lived experiences) of indigenous hosts (which may contradict or verify previous idealizing or stereotyping imagery), while, at the very same time, indigenous hosts observe and collect information about the tourists (which may contradict or verify previous images of the exploitative or exploitable colonial Other). The result of such parallel and reciprocal processes of "Othering" is a multilayered imaginary, to which both tourists and hosts contribute with their expectations, misinformation, personal experience, and "emancipatory" imagination (Appadurai 2001: 6). The resulting contradictions do not constrain the appeal of the tourism encounter, but, on the contrary, fuel original recombinations of tourism imaginaries.

NOTES

1. In total, I have spent seventeen months in the field, spread over periods of two and four months each year since 2005. My main field site, Parara Puru, was one of the first Emberá communities to develop indigenous tourism. It is located in the Chagres National Park, close to the flow of tourists who are visiting Panama City or cross the Panama Canal in cruise ships. During the course of my fieldwork, I have also made several comparative field trips to the Darién province, visiting Emberá communities that have developed, to a smaller extent, cultural tourism, or communities that aspire to develop tourism but have been unsuccessful so far (see Theodossopoulos 2007, 2010a).
2. A process that parallels the experience of the Kuna (Swain 1989), the neighbors of the Emberá.
3. The labor invested in cooking, dancing, playing musical instruments, transporting the tourists in dugout canoes, or delivering a speech.
4. Although I systematically compare Emberá and tourist views in this chapter, my intention is not to homogenize either group. In fact, the Emberá views of the tourists are not homogenous. In other publications, I have discussed in more detail diverging opinions within the Emberá world regarding particular

cultural practices, such as the perceived authenticity of Emberá dance (Theo-dossopoulos 2012a) or Emberá attire (Theodossopoulos 2012b, 2013a).

5. There are at least six Emberá communities in the general Panama Canal area that specialize in indigenous tourism; four of these are located within the Cha-gres National Park.

6. The tourist guides are employees or owners of Panamanian tourism agencies, most of whom are Panamanian and fluent in English, French, German, or Ital-ian, while a few are native speakers of these languages who now live perma-nently in Panama.

7. The dress code, music, and jolly spirit of the Emberá welcome to tourists is reminiscent of Emberá *chicha*—beer celebrations in the past, during which visi-tors from neighboring communities or settlements along different rivers were invited.

8. I visit Parara Puru every year and I remain in contact with some of its residents throughout the year by telephone and Internet communication. The use of eth-nographic present here does not indicate a static vision of the Emberá society, but, on the contrary, my awareness of the dynamic engagement of the Emberá with tourism, and the continuous flow of tourists in the community (at the time of writing).

9. Until the time of writing, none of the residents of Parara Puru had traveled abroad, although a few other Emberá, from other communities, have. On those rare occasions when a third party—such as a nonindigenous friend, an NGO, a Christian mission, or an institution—is willing to pay the cost of travel, the Emberá usually welcome the idea with excitement. This desire to travel reflects the older semimigratory lifestyle of the Emberá, which, in the past, necessitated a continuous expansion to new rivers, unclaimed rain forest lands, and hunt-ing territories (see, among many, Torres de Araúz 1966; Herlihy 1986; Isacsson 1993; Kane 1994; Williams 2005).

REFERENCES

Abram, Simone, Jacqueline Waldren, and Donald Macleod, eds. 1997. *Tourists and Tourism: Identifying with People and Places.* Oxford: Berg.

Appadurai, Arjun. 1996. *Modernity at Large: Cultural Dimensions of Globalization.* Min-neapolis: University of Minnesota Press.

———. 2001. "Grassroots Globalization and the Research Imagination." In *Globaliza-tion,* ed. Arjun Appadurai. Durham, NC: Duke University Press.

Bendix, Regina. 1997. *In Search of Authenticity: The Formation of Folklore Studies.* Madi-son: University of Wisconsin Press.

Berkhofer, Robert F. 1978. *The White Man's Indian: Images of the American Indian from Columbus to the Present.* New York: Vintage Books.

Boissevain, Jeremy, ed. 1996. *Coping with Tourists: European Reactions to Mass Tourism.* Oxford: Berghahn Books.

Brown, Keith, and Dimitrios Theodossopoulos. 2004. "Others' Others: talking about stereotypes and constructions of Otherness in Southeast Europe." *History & Anthropology* 15, no. 1: 3–14.

Bruner, Edward M. 2005. *Culture on Tour: Ethnographies of Travel.* Chicago: University of Chicago Press.

Bunten, Alexis. 2008. "Sharing Culture or Shelling Out? Developing the Commodified Persona in the Heritage Industry." *American Ethnologist* 35, no. 3: 380–95.

———. 2011. "The Paradox of Gaze and Resistance in Native American Cultural Tourism: An Alaskan Case Study." In *Great Expectations: Imagination and Anticipation in the Anthropology of Tourism,* ed. Jonathan Skinner and Dimitrios Theodossopoulos. Oxford: Berghahn Books.

Caballero, Vicente, and Bolivar Araúz. 1962. "Inmigración de indios Chocoes en Río Pequeni y algunos aspectos de su cultura." *Hombre y Cultura* 1, no. 1: 44–61.

Carrier, James, and Donald Macleod. 2005. "Bursting the Bubble: The Socio-Cultural Context of Ecotourism." *Journal of the Royal Anthropological Institute,* n.s., 11: 315–34.

Clifford, James. 1986. "On Ethnographic Allegory." In *Writing Culture: The Poetics and Politics of Ethnography,* ed. James Clifford and George E. Marcus. Berkeley: University of California Press.

Coleman, Simon, and Mike Crang, eds. 2002. *Tourism: Between Place and Performance.* Oxford: Berghahn Books.

Colin, France L. 2010. "'*Nosotros no solamente podemos vivir de cultura*': Identity, Nature, and Power in the Comarca Emberá of Eastern Panama." PhD diss., Carleton University.

Conklin, Beth A. 1997. "Body Paint, Feathers, and VCRs: Aesthetics and Authenticity in Amazonian Activism." *American Ethnologist* 24, no. 4: 711–37.

Conklin, Beth A., and Laura R. Graham. 1995. "The Shifting Middle Ground: Amazonian Indians and Eco-Politics." *American Anthropologist* 97, no. 4: 695–710.

Ellen, Roy. 1986. "What Black Elk Left Unsaid: On the Illusory Images of Green Primitivism." *Anthropology Today* 2, no. 6: 8–12.

Friedman, Jonathan. 1994. *Cultural Identity and Global Process.* London: Sage.

Gow, Peter. 2007. "Clothing as Acculturation in Peruvian Amazonia." In *Body Arts and Modernity,* ed. Elizabeth Ewart and Michael O'Hanlon. Wantage, UK: Sean Kingston Publishing.

Graburn, Nelson H., ed. 1976. *Ethnic and Tourist Arts: Cultural Expression from the Fourth World.* Berkeley: University of California Press.

Guerrón-Montero, Carla. 2006a. "Can't Beat Me Own Drum in Me Own Native Land: Calypso Music and Tourism in the Panamanian Atlantic Coast." *Anthropological Quarterly* 79, no. 4: 633–63.

———. 2006b. "Tourism and Afro-Antillean identity in Panama." *Journal of Tourism and Cultural Change* 4, no. 2: 65–84.

Herlihy, Peter H. 1986. "A Cultural Geography of the Emberá and Wounaan (Choco) Indians of Darien, Panama, with Emphasis on Recent Village Formation and Economic Diversification." PhD diss., Louisiana State University.

———. 2003. "Participatory Research: Mapping of Indigenous Lands in Darien, Panama." *Human Organization* 62: 315–31.

Herzfeld, Michael. 1997. *Cultural Intimacy: Social Poetics in the Nation-State.* London: Routledge.

Howe, James. 1998. *A People Who Would Not Kneel: Panama, the United States and the San Blas Kuna.* Washington DC: Smithsonian Institution Press.

———. 2009. *Chiefs, Scribes, and Ethnographers: Kuna Culture from Inside and Out.* Austin: University of Texas Press.

Isacsson, Sven-Erik. 1993. *Transformations of Eternity: On Man and Cosmos in Emberá Thought.* Gothenburg: University of Gothenburg.

Kane, Stephanie C. 1994. *The Phantom Gringo Boat: Shamanic Discourse and Development in Panama.* Washington DC: Smithsonian Institution.

Kapferer, Bruce. 2011. "How Anthropologists Think: Figurations of the Exotic." Huxley Memorial Lecture. *Journal of the Royal Anthropological Institute.*

Kirtsoglou, Elisabeth, and Dimitrios Theodossopoulos. 2004. "'They are taking our culture away': Tourism and Culture Commodification in the Black Carib Community of Roatan." *Critique of Anthropology* 24, no. 2: 135–57.

Leite, Naomi, and Nelson Graburn. 2009. "Anthropological Interventions in Tourism Studies." In *The Sage Handbook of Tourism Studies,* ed. Mike Robinson and Tazim Jamal. London: Sage.

Lindholm, Charles. 2008. *Culture and Authenticity.* Oxford: Blackwell.

MacCannell, Dean. 1976. *The Tourist: A New Theory of the Leisure Class.* New York: Schocken Books.

Martínez Mauri, Mónica. 2011. *La autonomía indígena en Panamá: la experiencia del pueblo kuna (siglos XVI-XXI).* Quito: Ediciones Abya-Yala.

Milton, Kay. 1996. *Environmentalism and Cultural Theory: Exploring the Role of Anthropology in Environmental Discourse.* London: Routledge.

Morris, Brian. 1981. "Changing Views of Nature." *The Ecologist* 11: 130–37.

Pereiro Pérez, Xerardo, Cebaldo de León, Mònica Martínez Mauri, Jorge Ventocilla, and Yadixa del Valle. 2010. *Estudio Estratégico del Turismo en Kuna Yala* (Primera Versión del Informe de investigación 2008–2010). Panama: SENACYT.

Ramos, Alcida R. 1998. *Indigenism: Ethnic Politics in Brazil.* Madison: University of Wisconsin Press.

Rosaldo, Renato. 1989. *Culture and Truth: The Remaking of Social Analysis.* London: Routledge.

Sahlins, Marshall. 2000. "'Sentimental Pessimism' and Ethnographic Experience; or, Why Culture IS NOT a Disappearing 'Object.'" In *Biographies of Scientific Objects,* ed. Lorraine Daston. Chicago: The University of Chicago Press.

Salazar, Noel B. 2010. *Envisioning Eden: Mobilizing Imaginaries in Tourism and Beyond.* Oxford: Berghahn Books.

Salvador, Mari Lyn. 1976. "The Clothing Arts of the Cuna of San Blas, Panama." In *Ethnic and Tourist Arts: Cultural Expression from the Fourth World,* ed. Nelson H. Graburn. Berkeley: University of California Press.

———., ed. 1997. *The art of being Kuna: Layers of meaning among the Kuna of Panama.* Los Angeles: UCLA Fowler Museum of Cultural History.

Santos-Granero, Fernando. 2009. "Hybrid Bodyscapes: A Visual History of Yanesha Patterns of Cultural Change." *Current Anthropology* 50, no. 4: 477–512.

Selwyn, Tom, ed. 1996. *The Tourist Image: Myths and Myth-Making in Tourism.* Chichester, UK: Wiley and Sons.

Skinner, Jonathan, and Dimitrios Theodossopoulos. 2011. "Introduction: The Play of Expectation in Tourism." In *Great Expectations: Imagination and Anticipation in the Anthropology of Tourism,* ed. Jonathan Skinner and Dimitrios Theodossopoulos. Oxford: Berghahn Books.

Smith, Valene L., ed. 1989. *Hosts and Guests: The Anthropology of Tourism.* 2nd ed. Philadelphia: University of Pennsylvania Press.

Strathern, Andrew, and Pamela J. Stewart. 2009. "Shifting Centers, Tense Peripheries: Indigenous Cosmopolitanisms." In *United in Discontent: Local Responses to Cosmopolitanism and Globalization,* ed. Dimitrios Theodossopoulos and Elisabeth Kirtsoglou. Oxford: Berghahn Books.

Stronza, Amanda. 2001. "Anthropology and Tourism: Forging New Ground for Ecotourism and Other Alternatives." *Annual Review of Anthropology* 30: 261–83.

Swain, Margaret B. 1989. "Gender Roles in Indigenous Tourism: Kuna Mola, Kuna Yala and Cultural Survival." In *Hosts and Guests: The Anthropology of Tourism,* 2nd ed., ed. Valene L. Smith. Philadelphia: University of Pennsylvania Press.

Theodossopoulos, Dimitrios. 2003. "Degrading Others and Honouring Ourselves: Ethnic Stereotypes as Categories and as Explanations." *Journal of Mediterranean Studies* 13, no. 2: 177–88.

———. 2007. "Encounters with Authentic Emberá Culture in Panama." *Journeys* 8, no. 1: 43–65.

———. 2009. "Introduction: United in Discontent." In *United in Discontent: Local Responses to Cosmopolitanism and Globalization,* ed. Dimitrios Theodossopoulos and Elisabeth Kirtsoglou. Oxford: Berghahn Books.

———. 2010a. "Tourism and Indigenous Culture as Resources: Lessons from the Emberá Cultural Tourism in Panama." In *Tourism, Power and Culture: Anthropological Insights,* ed. James G. Carrier and Donald V. L Macleod. Bristol, UK: Channel View.

———. 2010b. "With or Without Gringos: When Panamanians Talk about the United States and Its Citizens." *Social Analysis* 54, no. 1: 52–70.

———. 2011. "Emberá Indigenous Tourism and the World of Expectations." In *Great Expectations: Imagination and Anticipation in Tourism,* ed. Jonathan Skinner and Dimitrios Theodossopoulos. Oxford: Berghahn Books.

———. 2012a. "Dance, Visibility, and Representational Self-Awareness in an Emberá Community in Panama." In *Dancing Cultures: Globalization, Tourism and Identity in the Anthropology of Dance,* ed. Jonathan Skinner and Hélène Neveu Kringelbach. Oxford: Berghahn Books.

———. 2012b. "Indigenous Attire, Exoticisation and Social Change: Dressing and Undressing among the Emberá of Panama." *Journal of the Royal Anthropological Institute* 18, no. 3: 591–612.

——. 2013a. "Emberá Indigenous Tourism and the Trap of Authenticity: Beyond Inauthenticity and Invention." *Anthropological Quarterly* 86, no. 2: 397–426.

——. 2013b. "Laying Claim to Authenticity: Five Anthropological Dilemmas." *Anthropological Quarterly* 86, no. 2: 337–60.

Tice, Karin E. 1995. *Kuna Crafts, Gender, and the Global Economy.* Austin: University of Texas Press.

Torres de Araúz, Reina. 1966. *La cultura Chocó: Estudio ethnológico e historico.* Panama: Centro de Investigaciones Antropológicas, University of Panama.

Ulloa, Astrid. 2005. *The Ecological Native: Indigenous Peoples' Movements and Eco-governmentality in Colombia.* London: Routledge.

Velásquez Runk, Julie. 2009. "Social and River Networks for the Trees: Wounaan's Riverine Rhizomic Cosmos and Arboreal Conservation." *American Anthropologist* 111, no. 4: 456–67.

West, Paige, and James Carrier. 2004. "Ecotourism and Authenticity: Getting Away from It All?" *Current Anthropology* 45, no. 4: 483–98.

Williams, Caroline A. 2005. *Between Resistance and Adaptation: Indigenous Peoples and the Colonisation of the Choco 1510–1753.* Liverpool: Liverpool University Press.

Young, Philip D., and John Bort. 1999. "Ngóbe Adaptive Responses to Globalization in Panama." In *Globalization and the Rural Poor in Latin America,* ed. William M. Loker. Boulder, CO: Lynne Rienner.

Chapter 3

Deriding Demand

Indigenous Imaginaries in Tourism

Alexis Celeste Bunten

As Australia's largest and most successful cultural tourist attraction and the Australian domestic tourism industry's largest employer of Aboriginal people, Aboriginal-owned Tjapukai Aboriginal Cultural Park is the premier destination to experience Tjapukai culture.[1] As such, visitors look to this attraction to fulfill their expectations for "Aboriginal people" with whom they are already somewhat familiar through the imaginaries of the Indigenous Other. One visitor described the Tjapukai experience:

> While I was in Australia, I was looking for an appreciation of Aboriginal culture … What I wanted was someone to explain to me how Indigenous people lived, what they thought was important, and maybe explain to me what the "Dream-time" was. The only place I found this was at the Tjapukai Cultural Park. The people there gave a hands-on introduction to their culture. Learn how to throw a boomarang, a spear, make bush medicine, and lots more. It was fun, informative, and entertaining. (14 June 2011)[2]

Through a series of mediated presentations and activities, Tjapukai Aboriginal Cultural Park workers demonstrate iconic aspects of their culture that speak to imaginaries for the Indigenous Other as "close to nature," "magical," and "living relics." The day tour begins in the "magic space," a museum-like room that juxtaposes "authentic stone-age artefacts"[3] along-side contemporary Aboriginal art and experience. Visitors are invited to contextualize material culture through a looped screening of a documentary about Aboriginal history. While the "magic space" showcases Aboriginal cultural continuity, it evokes a "paradigmatic fossilization," in which Aboriginal hosts are "confined to the fixed status of an object frozen once and for all in time by the gaze of the Western percipients" (Said 1985: 92).

After visitors move through the "magic space," they are escorted to an outdoor amphitheater to watch Aboriginal guides present their culture through a narrated performance that freezes hosts into a Paleolithic past (Nesper 2003) through a fire-making demonstration and mimetic dance that highlights their connections to the animal world. Aboriginal guides then break up the audience into groups and escort them to experience more cultural demonstrations that frame the Aboriginal hosts as living hunter-gatherers whose specialized skills and knowledge help them to maintain a close relationship to the natural world. Finally, visitors return to the "Creation Theater," a sensory, multimedia experience that brings Tjapukai origin stories alive as live-action performers enact dreamtime visions by interacting with life-size holograms. Visitors must exit the park through the gift shop stocked with Aboriginal art, crafts, and other souvenirs to remind them of their trip.

The Tjapukai Aboriginal Cultural Park is simultaneously unique and banal. While the cultural traditions and intellectual property of the Tjapukai people could not faithfully be presented anywhere else or by any other people, this venue follows standard procedures for presenting culture. Typically, this takes the form of staging the world as a museum in which indigenous cultures are experienced in a uniform, sanitized, synchronic design, regardless of location and history.[4] By touring the sites of this global "museum," tourists can ultimately affirm and reinforce what they think they already know about the world presented in a predictable format (Bruner 2005). Bunten (2010: 294) describes this phenomenon as a "cultural tourism formula" that has presented indigenous peoples with a basic model to begin the process of taking control of their representation through tourism, albeit one designed to appeal to tourists' desires within the dominant systems of representation and consumption that underpin all cultural tourism.

This formula includes: (1) the greeting, (2) the friendly guide, (3) demonstrated use of the heritage language, (4) traditional architecture, (5) a performance, (6) a gift shop or souvenirs for sale, (7) demonstrations of traditional native crafts, and sometimes (8) a Westernized native feast. An assemblage of visitor reviews illustrates the formula in effect at Tjapukai:

You start with the "Magic Space," which is a strategically lit open space with beautiful artifacts, paintings telling stories and a fantastic painting with the Rainbow Serpent ... Then you basically move from one show to another ... You also have chance to talk to someone about Aboriginal weapons & medicines. Apparently green ant is great for hangover!!! (8 October 2011)

Dreamtime Theatre presentation was a fascinating look into the roots of Aboriginal beliefs. I really liked the live demonstrations of song, dance, and didgeridoo playing! The gift shop has a wonderful assortment of fabric panels, boomerangs, didgeridoos, and artwork for sale. My only wish is that I had more time. (26 October 2010)

With a final warning: "Let's be clear that it is not a 'National Geographic' type experience nor are you paying for one" (13 April 2010).

This chapter unpacks the relationship between the tourist gaze and hosts' manipulation of it, raising new questions about the nature and flexibility of the imagination. I have written it as a thought piece, designed to generate more questions than it answers through an examination of the ways the indigenous imaginary motivates visitors and hosts to engage with each other. In it, I argue that indigenous hosts are sophisticated culture brokers who are not just familiar with the indigenous imaginary, but can subvert it to support local goals.

The ideas introduced in this chapter are culled from my impressions visiting Tjapukai Aboriginal Cultural Park (on 25 June 2011) and those of visitors and workers gathered through correspondence, as well as primary sources available through the TripAdvisor website, the Tjapukai website, and promotional pieces, as well as secondary analysis culled from academic articles and graduate theses. Prior to visiting Tjapukai, I conducted over a decade of research on the topic of indigenous tourism, including two years of fieldwork working as an indigenous guide myself.[5]

As the first Aboriginal attraction of its kind in Australia, Tjapukai was founded in 1987 by a nonindigenous, North American couple with expertise in cultural theater and displaced Tjapukai people living in and around Cairns, Australia, the hub of tropical, Great Barrier Reef tourism. From humble beginnings as a touring Aboriginal dance group, the nucleus for today's Tjapukai experience took shape through a 1996 merger with Aboriginal groups and regional tourism operators who developed it into a cultural park attraction.[6] In 2004, the Aboriginal and Torres Strait Islander Commercial Development Corporation (renamed Indigenous Business Australia, IBA) acquired 19.93 percent equity in the park, and later increased its ownership to 100 percent to keep the park operating through the economic downturn in tourism. In accord with IBA's commitment to "increase the wellbeing of

Indigenous Australians by supporting greater economic participation and self-reliance,"[7] Tjapukai cultural presentations are vetted through elder consultants to ensure cultural integrity and protection of Tjapukai intellectual property. Like other indigenous-owned cultural tourism venues, Tjapukai has been actively involved in promoting Aboriginal culture from within, providing millions of dollars in jobs and revenue for the local Aboriginal community.[8] Despite critiques that the park is "too touristy," the cultural tourism formula clearly works for Tjapukai, garnering the park numerous tourism awards.

The recent expansion of indigenous-owned and operated tourism has been made possible through industry-wide trends, policies designed to boost economies through tourism, and reclamation of indigenous resources through legal settlements with colonizer states. The corporation that now owns Tjapukai was established directly following the 1989 Aboriginal and Torres Strait Islander Commission Act that established statutory corporations to manage reclamations. The act proclaims, *"The [Australian] Government expects that the Corporation will enhance the opportunities for Aboriginal and Torres Strait Islander people to begin to break free from the web of dependency and achieve a significant degree of economic independence."*[9] Indigenous Business Australia (IBA) describes itself as an integral partner within the government's Indigenous Economic Development Strategy, which seeks to close the gap between indigenous Australians and other Australians' standard of living.

The indigenous tourism sector does not merely reflect a current trend that capitalizes on difference as simply an opportunity for local development. Rather, indigenous tourism should be understood as part of a larger project among subaltern communities to redefine dominant notions of the Other in a postcapitalist global economy. Indigenous culture promoted at touristic destinations are products of Western ontologies that tend to isolate hosts' worldviews and traditions into fixed geographic and temporal spaces that comprise the landscape of tourist imagination. With more possibilities to make connections with potential customers, indigenous communities are taking advantage of these discourses in developing tourism sites.

Bunten and Graburn (2009: 3) describe indigenous tourism as "any service or product that is a) owned and operated at least in part by an Indigenous group and b) results from a means of exchange with outside guests." While indigenous control is the defining factor of this industry, it is limited by market demand. For this kind of tourism to generate business, visitors must agree that the hosts are indeed "indigenous" according to their own sets of criteria articulated through the language of imaginaries (and these may differ from those currently debated on the world stage).[10] This chapter is not an attempt to categorize exhaustively imaginaries of the indigenous

Other; rather, it examines their trajectories—where they came from, points of intervention, and where they are headed. Imaginaries possess dichotomous qualities; they are tacit and implicit, traveling backward and forward at the same time (see Salazar and Graburn, this volume). Some reflect stereotypes and fantasies about the "-ized" (Orientalized, colonized, globalized, etc.), while others are more site- and even person-specific. International imaginaries tend to be more generalized, such as the concept that indigenous peoples are "natural," whereas domestic imaginaries reflect particular colonizer settler histories, and more personal imaginings address a range of ideas that reflect upon the identity of those possessing the gaze.

Several scholars have pointed out that interactions between tourists and indigenous hosts result in perpetuating stereotypes of the Other (Evans-Pritchard 1989; Lujan 1993; Babcock 1994; Nicks 1999; Whittaker 1999) that appease visitors' desires and aspirations. While one take on this asserts that yielding to the tourist gaze reduces hosts to inauthentic caricatures of their "real" selves (Rossel 1988), I have argued elsewhere that indigenous hosts respond to the gaze through a carefully crafted commoditized persona that manipulates these stereotypes to subvert asymmetrical power relations (Bunten 2008). In fact, indigenous hosts view tourism as part of a larger strategy to shape their participation in the global economy in a way that honors culturally based values (see Tucker 2003; Wiketera and Bremner 2009; Bunten 2010; Endicott et al., forthcoming). They actively manipulate tourist imaginaries of the Other to shape industry trends and articulations of alterity at multiple levels. In doing so, hosts take advantage of the cyclical and reciprocal shape of the imaginary. The rest of this chapter tracks the imaginary as it circulates through a feedback loop between visitor to host and back to visitor again (cf. Salazar 2010).

TOURIST IMAGINARIES OF THE INDIGENOUS OTHER

People who visit indigenous tourism sites in one place tend to experience indigenous attractions in other countries, suggesting that similar motivations underlie touristic desires to visit indigenous peoples in general (Pearce and Moscardo 1999; McIntosh et al. 2000). An August 2011 visitor to Tjapukai explained, "Having experienced some rather disappointing 'culture park' type attractions in different countries, I was a little apprehensive about visiting Tjapukai, but was very pleasantly surprised." Another had an opposite reaction, "I love the Culture Center on Oahu and expected Tjapukai to be similar. I was very much disappointed" (29 August 2010). When visitors seek an impossible imaginary through the tourism context, they express cynical disappointment. Though Tjapukai makes no pretense that it is anything more than a place to encounter Aboriginal culture filtered through the tourism context, comparing reviews reveals contradictions in visitor satisfaction.

> The Park offered an excellent, multi-faceted portrayal of the Aboriginal experience—a play, a film, music/dance performance, didgeroodoo performance, food presentation, spear-throwing, boomerang-throwing, and exhibits ... Aborigine staff members interacted with us in very small groups [and] most of the activities and answered wide-ranging questions regarding Aboriginal life (both past and present) ... We very much appreciated the opportunity to learn about this ancient culture. (11 January 2010)

> Took my family to the Tjapukai by Night experience ... Fire Ceremony done extremely well and very entertaining ... Spirit visit done inside the building was professionally managed and awe inspiring ... I have a whole new view of the culture of these fascinating people. (19 March 2004)[11]

While some clearly appreciate an exposure to Aboriginal culture within the comfortable boundaries of the cultural tourism formula, others express disappointment.

> I know we are "tourists" and that most things are geared for us, but this one was a little too touristy for our liking. Although it gave us good insight into the Aboriginal culture, the dancing, spear throwing, it left us in a bit of a daze. (5 September 2010)

These comments reveal tourist expectations for Aboriginal hosts to reflect an ancient, spiritual, low-technological, and performative culture easily consumed through exhibition, activities, and one-on-one interaction. These expectations are imaginaries in the sense that they are uniformly shared across the spectrum of visitors and reproduced within the popular consciousness through hegemonic devises including mass media, the educational system, museums, and other sites where heritage is interpreted at a different scale of patrimony (see Salazar and Graburn, this volume). Several scholars have remarked upon the shaping of the tourist desire for the Other as an imaginary that cannot be met. Rossel (1988: 5) finds "exaggerations, misleading statements, and lies" that provided a certain way of understanding reality, and that offered the "tourist view." Likewise, Craik (1997) argues that tourist expectations originate in the tourist's origin culture rather than in the cultural offerings of the destination (see also Silver 1993; King 1997; Nuttal 1997).

Following this logic, the tourist imaginary is always subject to the visitor's expectation of reality, an egocentric pursuit characterized by self-delusion through simulacra (Ritzer and Liska 1997: 107). In order for the imaginary to be fulfilled, visitors must suspend their knowledge that the encounter is staged expressly for them. This creates a double-bind of the imaginary, in which visitors are conscious that hosts play to an imagined authenticity that can never be reached (because it doesn't exist outside of the imagination), yet hosts present heritage that is part of their lived experience within and outside the tourism context.[12] For example, Djabugay employees at Tjapukai demonstrate the didgeridoo, perhaps the greatest icon of Australian Aboriginals, yet performers acknowledge that their people neither made, nor played, the instrument in the past. The double bind of the imaginary demands to know what is authentic in this instance. That the Djabugay hosts' reality as tourism workers includes playing the didgeridoo, or that they didn't play it prior to the instrument's iconization as "Aboriginal" through the work of anthropologists and the Western music and tourism industries that served colonial desires to consume the Other?

One Tjapukai visitor wrote:

> I never really understand why people overly bash an attraction for being too touristy—Tjapukai park IS touristy—it doesn't pretend not to be, but it still delivers a pretty fun day ... No, it's not as authentic as if you tagged along on a National Geographic expedition searching for lost Aboriginees, but it tries to introduce people to a culture using fun activities, shows and exhibits ... by no means is it a complete or exhaustive education of Aboriginal history, but it's not watered down either. (12 October 2009)

This feedback clearly demonstrates that visitors understand that they are being presented with cultural bric-a-brac that indexes another type of cultural authenticity lived outside of the park. Despite their awareness of the constructed nature of the cultural tourism site made expressly for them, visitors use the language of authenticity as a benchmark from which to rate whether the quality of their experiences match their expectations. While it is fraught with contention within academic debates, "authenticity talk" is useful inasmuch as hosts, guests, and tourism mediators frequently refer to it to describe the tourism experience.

Handler and Linnekin (1984) argue that authenticity is highly sought after in contexts, such as tourism, in which people's lives are packaged into discrete stories as a reaction to the alienation felt in everyday modern life. By consuming the Other within a highly proscriptive tourism format, visitors are attempting to "feel authentic" themselves. However, tourists' notions of what is "authentic" are highly mediated by their own subjective experience. Building from Leach's (1961) theory of time as marked by cycles of sacredness and profanity and Turner's (1969) notions of liminality, Graburn ([1977] 1989) argues that tourists make meaning of their lives by experiencing a world outside of their own, through tourism as a pseudoreligious pilgrimage. The trope of "imperialist nostalgia" (Rosaldo 1989), or a longing for what one has destroyed in the past, is most often used to advertise the indigenous tourism experience as outside the humdrum of visitors' everyday lives.

Aboriginal people are heavily marketed (both by outsiders and in self-promotion) as "the world's oldest living culture" in ways that serve dominant power dynamics. Palmer (2004: 111) states that "non-Aboriginal Australians have increasingly drawn on emblematic images of Aborigines, the 'first people,' to provide their nation with a sense of national antiquity and distinctiveness." One Tjapukai reviewer observed, "I found the show a great insight into Australia's history and culture and something that I have not particularly had an interest in the past. I hope the Tjapukai tribe continue their great work and continue to show both national and international tourists a great insight into our [Australian national] history" (5 November 2008). Akin to the United States' doctrine of "manifest destiny," the Australian government actively promoted a romanticized notion of Australian Aboriginal peoples as stuck in the "dreamtime" to justify the theft of Aboriginal resources in founding modern nationhood. Coined by early twentieth-century salvage anthropologists who translated indigenous ontologies into colonial narratives of progress,[13] the Western imaginary of the "dreamtime" links "authentic" Aboriginal people to "empty" land, both under the management of settler colonial agents. Though many of the inhumane policies tied to the promotion of these imaginaries are long over, the tourism industry propagates these ideas through the transmogrification of complex indigenous beliefs into simplified images, sound bites, and ideas that can be easily consumed in highly mediated spaces, performances, and souvenirs.

Tourism tends to favor imaginaries of the Other invented during colonial periods of conquest, because they are a part of a shared consciousness that visitors actively seek out through their tourism experiences (Salazar 2013). In their efforts to meet the tourist gaze, indigenous hosts run the risk of smothering local interpretation with these kinds of narratives of conquest that once legitimized indigenous exploitation, and currently maintain an asymmetrical relationship between themselves and guests.[14] It is from within this framework, shaped by dominant discourses and ideologies, that indigenous tourism operates.

MEETING THE TOURIST IMAGINARY

Indigenous cultural tourism sites generally follow predictable formats that have proved to work in similar contexts. Ryan and Huyton explain that "one

reason why Aboriginal communities have looked to culturally based products is because they have little business experience and tend to repeat a
known successful product" (2002: 42). As the first purpose-built Aboriginal
tourism park in Australia, Tjapukai has co-opted the "model culture" format exemplified by the Mormon-owned Polynesian Cultural Center in Hawaii (Stanton 1989).[15] This format presents a sanitized version of culture that
is often compared to a precolonial past, in which performers follow what appears to be culturally proscribed gender roles, don "precontact" clothes, and
perform "traditional" songs and dances in the heritage language. All of these
performative and representational elements are adapted to the constraints of
the tourism environment. For example, songs and dances are shortened and
accompanied by an authorial translation in the dominant language.

One visitor to Tjapukai was disappointed by the superficiality of the
"model culture" on display: "We were looking forward to learning more
about the Aborigines at a dinner show. The show began with a poor re-
enactment of the tribe's history. The fire ceremony seemed authentic, but
once dinner began, authenticity was not seen very often. The song they
ended on sounded like a Disney animated movie soundtrack rather than a
lesson in history" (4 August 2004). On the other hand, the "model culture"
experience works for the mass tourist used to highly mediated experiences.
A reviewer commented, "Our family, which includes a 4 and 6 year old visited Tjapukai today and we enjoyed ourselves ... On arrival we were given a
map and info on the program and show times and in what order to do them"
(30 June 2011). Another corroborated, "We spent just over half the day there
and saw 5 shows/activities in that time. Overall, we found it very educational
and entertaining" (10 September 2011).

While it does not allow for a deeply personalized encounter with indigenous hosts, cultural parks such as Tjapukai successfully fulfill tourist
desires for the Indigenous Other in a controlled space, where visitors know
what to expect. As Barbara Kirshenblatt-Gimblett observes, "Sameness is
a problem the [tourism] industry faces. Standardization is part and parcel
of the economies of scale that high-volume tourism requires ... the industry requires a reliable product that meets universal standards, despite the
dispersal of that product across many widely separated locations" (1998:
152). The parallels in contemporary touristic representation grew out of
similar histories of colonizing objectification, epitomized in continuums of
"cultural evolution" from savagery to civilization reproduced in expository
texts, world's fairs, advertising, museum exhibitions, and theme park attractions, perhaps culminating in the "It's a Small World" ride at Disneyland
(Bunten 2010). Within this broad context, ethnographic displays of any sort
function as "trophies of conquest—command performances of manifest des-

tiny—and as carefully bounded representations that allowed this difference to be sampled at a safe distance" (Johnson and Underiner 2001: 45). Following this logic, effecting distance through self-commoditization legitimizes structures of domination (Mieu 2011).

Under these kinds of pressures to frame touristic notions of indigenous authenticity within the subjugator's imaginary and traditions of display (Kirshenblatt-Gimblett 1991; Fusco 1994; Stanley 1998), indigenous hosts have a limited ability to project culturally and politically nuanced presentations of themselves to their audiences. Tjapukai's general manager acknowledges where Tjapukai representation fits within the wider scope of the industry, stating, "Cultural tourism is an important part of the Australian tourism landscape. It has been around for countless generations. At Tjapukai, cultural tourism means expressing our living culture every day to guests from all over the world. It's a responsibility we take seriously—Edu-taining guests are what Tjapukai is all about."[16] In addition to "edu-taining," which implies brevity, the "fake" villages in places like this imply that the host culture is not to be taken seriously. The constructed nature of the site combines with the fact that visitors are paying something most indigenous peoples deem inalienable—cultural contact forces everyone, host and guest alike, to suspend their disbelief. Those who cannot "play along" with the irony of the context find themselves disappointed. One such visitor to Tjapukai explained:

> This is one of those experiences that years later, I still laugh about and consider it one of the hokiest and strangest live action shows I have ever seen. It was like one of those really, really bad dioramas you saw when you were a kid, touring the really bad museum with your classmates. Now just imagine the dioramas coming to life. This is the Tjapukai Show ... I still can't hear a didgeridoo without having flashbacks and then bust out laughing. (2 August 2007)

Another visitor left the same performance with an earnest desire for the "magical Aborigine" of her imagination:

> Then we went off to see a live performance of traditional Aborigines and songs and didgeridoo playing. This was enjoyable but for me lacked some atmosphere, I feel the fake rocks that make up the stage and other landscaping errors took away from the overall feel. A lot of money has been spent on other things and I think this could be made a whole lot better, a real rock amphitheater with aboriginal paintings surrounded by lush rainforest would make you feel like you were experiencing something magical. (30 June 2011)

While a cursory visit might leave the impression that Tjapukai and places like it are in the business of reproducing Western fantasies of the

Other, a closer look reveals there is a lot more going on. Like other mass entertainment genres, cultural parks can be approached on many different levels. Indigenous-owned tourism, in particular, tends to reproduce popular forms of cultural display, while simultaneously deconstructing it. Harkin (2003: 582) describes this phenomenon as "ironic" entertainment similar to the conventions of the popular television program *Seinfeld,* which "provided a running critique of sitcom conventions while at the same time employing those conventions effectively." He adds, "increasingly, Indian tourism will be defined by this touristic practice. Tourists seeking casinos and kitschy public versions of traditional culture will greatly outnumber and outspend those seeking authenticity" (Harkin 2003: 582).

Visitors recognize the irony inherent in practices of "staging authenticity," to varying degrees of satisfaction. One disappointed Tjapukai customer complained: "The performers seemed to be having a laugh among themselves. [It] felt like a private joke onstage we weren't privy to." Another offered a less cynical response to the "double bind of authenticity" taking place at Tjapukai: "As the taxi pulled up to the Tjapukai cultural park, I was expecting something either really hokey or very serious. What I found was something in between" (11 December 2002).

DERIDING DEMAND: INDIGENOUS IMAGINARIES AT WORK

Emblematic of the indigenous-owned and operated cultural tourism industry in general, Tjapukai Aboriginal Cultural Park does not slavishly reproduce Western ontologies of difference. No pretense is made that the simulated experiences of indigenous cultural tourism are "real," yet they construct liminal spaces where indigenous hosts invite guests to experience local culture through a mutually respectful exchange. Martha Brim (Djabugay), who has been with Tjapukai since 1996, confirmed, "Working at Tjapukai gives me the opportunity to work with my family and friends, meet people from different countries and not only share my culture with them but also learn a little about theirs." Similarly, Garina Brady (Djabugay), employed with Tjapukai since 2005 explained, "The most exciting things about Tjapukai is that I get to meet people from different countries and not only share my culture with them but also learn a little about them."[17]

Indigenous employees express a preference to work for these kinds of tour companies, where their personal experiences add value to the products they deliver. They come to work with a different sense of investment in their labor than what might be expected of workers in places that merely play to imaginaries of domination; their cultural identities are intimately tied to the workplace, a crucial site where workers' bodies, identities, ancestors, beliefs, and landscapes make up the tourist attraction. In this setting, one that is both indigenous and Western at the same time, employees seem to genuinely enjoy sharing aspects of their cultures, past and present, with their customers. They see their work as a way to celebrate their cultures and educate the mainstream public. Likewise, visitors can tell that workers are not burdened by the yoke of Western representation. One Tjapukai visitor remarked, "The Aboriginal hosts were the friendliest tour guides I have ever met. They made us feel a part of their culture in the friendliest way possible. They were smiling even when they thought we weren't watching" (23 November 2011). Another corroborated, "The staff were all excellent and clearly proud to share their background" (28 August 2011).

Through the cross-cultural tourism encounter, indigenous hosts navigate complex, entangled tourist imaginaries, including their own expectations for what they hope to get out of the workplace experience (see Bunten 2012).[18] Although they feel pressure to respond to the imaginaries implicit in the tourist gaze, indigenous tourism professionals often adhere to their own cultural norms of representation, protocols regarding the sharing of traditional knowledge and concepts of the self. For Tjapukai hosts, this entails protecting aspects of their culture that are secret and elder approval of those that are on display. Tjapukai proudly proclaims that the shows and activities offered have been approved by the traditional Aboriginal elders as a marketing tactic to verify the authenticity of its product.[19] Backstage, these checks and balances ensure Aboriginal control over products that follow local cultural protocols, rather than "selling out" culture to the whims of the tourist gaze. By respecting their own cultural norms while meeting certain aspects of the tourist gaze, indigenous tourism professionals maintain a sense of pride in sharing their culture, in addition to any monetary compensation.[20]

Parallel to indig museums

Hosts' own imaginaries about visitors are informed by their cultural attitudes toward guests and how to treat them, as well as historical relations between themselves and outsiders. For indigenous tourism workers, this often entails rectifying negative feelings about serving and entertaining members of the dominant society before engaging in any kind of tourism work. This process requires managing the very ideologies that excused ethnocide, and are constantly recycled within dominant tropes of difference. Resistance is an integral aspect of this process, a self-protective mechanism that balances out acts of self-exoticization. It is almost always hidden behind a mask of compliance (Scott 1990), utilized as a way to live through, but not necessarily resolve, problematic power relations (see Hall and Jefferson 1989). Assuming many different forms, it is usually undetected by those to whom it is directed (Salazar 2010). Resistance expressed in the cultural tourism setting is covert, varying in gradations of agency and intensity, "continually negotiated in the discourse and practice of everyday life" (Valaskakis 1993: 283). At its most basic and unconscious level, tour guides practice resistance simply by portraying themselves through a trope of cultural persistence in the face of dominant society. At the most consciously directed level, workers actively challenge stereotypes through both rehearsed and spontaneous commentary (Bunten 2008).

Tjapukai hosts convey their own imaginaries behind a "mask of compliance" that may appear "touristy" to some visitors and highly "authentic" to others. If they pay careful attention, visitors can gain a clear sense of how their hosts see themselves in time and their place in the world in relation to the colonizer settler nation. As at indigenous tourism venues elsewhere (see Bunten 2008), Tjapukai workers are engaged in varied levels of covert acts of resistance, which range from looping a documentary about the effects of colonization, to explaining that didgeridoos are not part of the regional repertoire, to a live presentation that explains how the incredible diversity of Aboriginal peoples defies stereotyping.

While the cornerstone of the Tjapukai experience is cross-cultural understanding, workers do not deny the intergenerational trauma of theft (of children, land, culture, ancestors, etc.) and colonization that has left Aboriginal peoples from across Australia with disparities in health, education, income, and employment. At the end of every performance, Tjapukai dancers play a song, titled "Proud to be Aborigine," that tells the story of colonization, cultural change, and reconciliation (Ellis 2007: 23). The lyrics state:

> Twenty thousand years we lived in peace a land a man was free to wander
> The white man came and pulled it down under
> The white man found a land he thought no one owned
> Spears can't fight guns and dynamite
> The white man came and pulled it down under ... The black and white should unite
> Be as brothers in the land down under
> Proud to be Aborigine
> We'll never die
> Tjapukai
> Always be our identity
> Proud to be
> Aborigine

While reconciliatory, this song covertly communicates the same sentiments on relations with the settler colonial nation as one Aboriginal commentator stated in a documentary titled *Dreaming As One*: "We are the custodian of Australia no matter which tribe you come from. We inherited the land. Not through the Western law but through our law and custom we own the land regardless. And our heart will always be here with the land. The government doesn't see it that way, that we are the true owners."[21]

The same documentary analyzed white imaginaries for the Indigenous Other: "Part of that search [for self-discovery] sometimes comes to indigenous peoples and [whites] wanting to know and expecting and starting to know something deeper than perhaps they understand they can go. So it becomes little bit of tension there." An Aboriginal woman interviewed for the documentary explains, "We'll teach anyone. Even other people who are interested in our culture to help keep it alive." While these statements might seem to contradict each other, they reveal the complex issues surrounding cultural perpetuation, traditional knowledge, and representation in the settler colonial context.

Critics of cultural commoditization used to discuss cultural producers as if they experience their own cultures in the bounded and discrete ways that they are sometimes presented on tour, or as if hosts cannot engage in metadiscursive action (MacCannell 1973; Greenwood 1989; Hewison 1987). In fact, most indigenous peoples do not experience their world as integrated culture, and may perform aspects of their identities that reflect both tourist and local imaginaries. In line with this perspective, Fienup-Riordan (2000: 167) sees heritage as "conscious culture" responding to demands and pressures that originate both within and outside native communities, "mediating new powers and attachments; relations with the land, among local groups, with the state and with transnational forces" (quoted in Clifford 2004: 6). While some think that commoditizing culture reinforces stereotypes that reproduce asymmetrical power relations with the unpleasant side effect of bastardizing "real" culture, others see cultural tourism sites as cultural border zones (Bruner 2005), or contact zones (Pratt 1992; Clifford 1997) where people from disparate backgrounds come face to face with each other to re-define their ongoing relations on both personal and ideological levels (Ellis 2007: 28; Bunten 2008).

[handwritten margin note: Heritage as conscious Culture]

DISCUSSION

The mandatory performance of the Other in the tourism context is a critical activity that reflects a double bind implicit within the representation of identity. Tourism workers' performances are in dialogue with tourist imaginaries, but they also reflect their own imaginaries about heritage, colonization, work, and the visitors themselves (cf. Salazar 2010). Like many of their indigenous counterparts around the world, Aboriginal development within the ethnocidal context of settler colonial economic and social structures poses unique challenges and opportunities for indigenous entrepreneurs. Indigenous tourism workers face opposition from factions within their own communities, who see the cultural representation within a capitalistic context as an extension of colonial domination.

According to this viewpoint, playing to the tourist imaginary becomes an implicit form of acceptance of narratives of conquest. As long as workers dress up in leather and play the didgeridoo, they reproduce stereotypes that uphold unequal power structures. Another faction within the Aboriginal community sees playing to the tourist imaginary as an important way to open up meaningful dialogue between hosts and guests, ultimately erasing imaginaries inherited from a previous era. Meanwhile, those non-Aboriginals who operate from a continuum of racist and dehumanizing tropes about Aboriginals assume that Aboriginals cannot possibly pull off a successful tourism business, beyond serving as exotic entertainment.

As the first Aboriginal tourism presentation of its kind in Australia, Tjapukai faced multiple sources of opposition to the staging of Aboriginal culture. According to a case study written for Indigenous Tourism Australia:[22]

> When Tjapukai began their Aboriginal theatre, they weren't even sure if the audience would be there. They had to win over a local community (both black and white), and a tourism industry unsure where to place a product like this, they also had to win the hearts and minds of an audience who had never before been exposed to anything like this. Where Tjapukai encountered prejudice, they answered it with humor and talent. When they found barriers, they charmed them out of existence with their passion and vision of what they wanted so much to achieve. Not only has Tjapukai succeeded to become Australia's premier Indigenous cultural attraction, it has paved the way for Indigenous tourism to develop in this country. Doing it first also meant they needed to do it so well they became the benchmark that those who followed. Most important was the content and style of the show; it illuminated Aboriginality for the first time. Tjapukai took what everyone believed was a novel idea and transformed it into a new industry. They have sustained the self-determination and economic independence of the Tjapukai community and created a multi-million dollar attraction that benefits an entire region.

Indigenous tourism operators recognize that tourism can provide a means to heal intergenerational wounds through cross-cultural dialogue in a mediated setting that applauds cultural difference while improving the basic conditions for individual workers and the local community. One Tjapukai worker explained:

My experience with tourism has changed my life. I now own 20 acres of land, my own house, and four-wheel drive. My standard of living and that of my family has been lifted dramatically ... Not only me, but my brothers and sisters who have stayed with Tjapukai have also lifted their standard of living. The economic and social benefits have flowed on to the entire community in increased respect for my people and greater integration between the white and black community. (quoted in Ryan and Huyton 2002: 60)

Comparing examples of indigenous tourism from around the world, Bunten (2010) argues that profitability, while important, is not the overriding factor driving tourism business operations. Rather, indigenous tourism is nearly always aligned with cultural perpetuation, ecological preservation, and promoting international peace as part of an overall community development vision. Former director for the Center for Aboriginal Economic Policy Jon Altman writes,

Aboriginal interests often consider development options in a context that includes social and cultural as well as economic components. Within this perspective, development is not limited to issues like material expansion, increased cash income, and high formal employment, but also involves social and cultural issues, the potential for increased political power, and the possibility of widened future options. (1989: 460)

Similarly, Notzke observes,

For the [Canadian] Inuvialuit in embracing tourism, the challenge is twofold: to protect the integrity of their land-based economy and way of life from trespass and interference of the tourism industry; and to engage in tourism activities in a way which enables the industry to fit into, nurture, and benefit community mixed economies to an optimum degree. (1998: 67)

Stocker (2009) discusses the Chorotega of northwestern Costa Rica and their efforts to develop cultural and ecotourism through the construction of a community house: "Oftentimes, scholars look at endeavors as either motivated by potential monetary gain or by community consciousness. This is a clear case in which the two goals are not so easily disarticulated from one another." Thus, while profitability is very important to these tourism businesses, it is not necessarily measured in dollars.

There is a difference between the tourism that accommodates a perceived tourist gaze at the expense of cultural integrity and tourism that is carefully crafted to appeal to tourists while upholding local values. Tourists can sense the internal colonization in the former. They comment to the effect that what they are seeing is "fake" or "quaint." On the contrary, those who experience the latter seem to reflect on the humanity they share with their hosts, sometimes with tears, or by embracing their new friends on their way out. Ultimately, visitors want to make a connection with their hosts.

This chapter has presented visitors' reviews at both ends of this continuum, analyzing the complex nature of the tourism experience through the concept of the imaginary. For indigenous communities, tourism is one of the primary settings in which their people are valued for their unique cultures and heritages in relation to the outside world. Through thoughtful planning, tourism can be a means for indigenous communities to take control of power expressed through imaginaries by providing an instrument to determine what to share and not share with visitors. At this early stage of critical research on the topic of indigenous tourism, many other questions remain to be explored, such as the role of state policy in limiting the scope and reach of indigenous tourism sites and whether or not these destinations can serve as a catalyst to support social movements. Is tourism really the context from which to construct new discourses of alterity? I think it is.

NOTES

1. "Tjapukai" culture may be a misnomer for some. According to the park's website (http://www.tjapukai.com.au/tjapukai-the-culture/, accessed November 28, 2011), Tjapukai refers to the Aboriginal peoples of the rain forest in Queensland, northeast Australia, though many have been forcibly removed due to colonization. While the website mentions that the "culture" refers to that of the Djabugay people, the park's official term for the culture is "Tjapukai"; therefore, this is the term I will use to refer to the Aboriginal culture portrayed at this venue.
2. All of the visitor reviews discussed in this chapter were culled from the TripAdvisor website. I have presented them in their original form, including spelling and grammatical errors, to reflect the voices of the reviewers. While I acknowledge that the things people write on websites may not be true, and may even be generated by the hosts themselves, I assume they are accurate representations of users' experiences at Tjapukai.
3. The quote "stone-age artefacts" was taken from the park's website, http://www.tjapukai.com.au/tjapukai-by-day/ (accessed November 28, 2011).
4. Others (Handler and Saxon 1988; Kirshenblatt-Gimblett 1998) have commented upon this "museumizing" of indigenous groups through the paradigm of tourism, noting that heritage politics are, according to Appadurai (1990: 304), "remarkably uniform throughout the world."

5. For more on my prior research and expertise on the topic of indigenous tourism, see Bunten (2005, 2008, 2010, 2011a, 2012).

6. Prior to this merger, the Djabugay people had very little control over the operations at the park, resulting in community needs and desires going unfulfilled (Schuler 1999). Therefore, despite the fact that it displayed Tjapukai culture to visitors, Tjapukai was not an Aboriginal business until owned by Aboriginal interests.

7. This quote was pulled from IBA's website at http://www.iba.gov.au/about-us/our-commitment/ (accessed 3 December 2011).

8. A quote from Tjapukai's "education fact sheet 4, tourism and marketing" (http://www.tjapukai.com.au/documents/FactSheet4.pdf/, accessed 15 January 2012) states that "since we began, we have returned over more $25 million dollars [AUD] in wages, profits, royalties and art sales to the Aboriginal community. We support many local schools, businesses, and organizations with donations and offer free off site performances. We value our local visitors and offer them specials throughout the year."

9. This quote was pulled from the IBA website at http://www.iba.gov.au/about-us/our-history/ (accessed 24 January 2012).

10. In a United Nations study, Martinez Cobo (1986: 5) defines indigeneity in terms of "those which, having a historical continuity with pre-invasion and pre-colonial societies that developed on their territories, consider themselves distinct from other sectors of the societies now prevailing in those territories, or parts of them. They form at present non-dominant sectors of society and are determined to preserve, develop, and transmit to future generations their ancestral territories, and their ethnic identity, as the basis of their continued existence as peoples, in accordance with their own cultural patterns, social institutions, and legal systems."

11. While all other reviews were culled from TripAdvisor, this review was taken from the website IgoUgo at http://www.igougo.com/review-r1344734-Great_Value_Great_Food_Great_Entertainment.html (accessed 24 January 2012).

12. A double bind of the imaginary results in a paradox in which visitors measure their experiences against expectations for authenticity that are lost once commoditized through tourism (Harkin 1995). Once it is indexed, however, the signifier ceases to be authentic.

13. For more discussion, see Barnes and Foley (forthcoming).

14. Nash (1977) argues that touristic interactions between host and guest endorse Western imperialism by replaying colonial relationships of dominance and servility inherent in tourist imaginaries of the Other.

15. Bunten (2010) has written about other cultural tourism parks around the world, including the Saxman Village in Alaska and the Tamaki Maori Village in New Zealand, that also resemble the Polynesian Cultural Center. Ellis designed her master's thesis analysis around the similarities between Tjapukai Aboriginal Cultural Park and the PCC, explaining that "both sites serve similar functions: that is, to educate and entertain primarily Western (European and American)

tourist audiences with both broad and more localized notions of 'native culture' through interactive displays, activities and dance performances. Both sites are located near major tourism centers—Waikiki in Honolulu, Hawaii and Cairns, North Queensland, Australia respectively—and require indigenous involvement, whether as performers, collaborators, or board members" (2007: 3).

16. This quote was taken from the Tjapukai website at http://www.tjapukai.com .au/david-hudson/ (accessed 24 January 2012).

17. These quotes were taken from the Tjapukai website at http://www.tjapukai .com.au/tjapukai-the-culture/dancer-profiles/ (accessed 12 December 2011).

18. The concept of a "host gaze" that is at the same time both independent of and in response to the tourist gaze refutes this notion of passive capitulation to dominant economies and systems of cultural representation (Bunten 2012). Just as tourists size up and coerce their hosts with the power of the tourist gaze, hosts interact with visitors based on a set of systematized beliefs about their guests. Like the tourist gaze, which can change over the course of the touristic experience, the host gaze is not static. As the tourist gaze is informed by long-held imaginary motifs about the culture being consumed, the host gaze is generated well before the tourist encounter. The host gaze changes through interaction with guests, and over the course of a tourism season. Ultimately, it becomes a memory of visitors long gone, and expectations for those to come.

19. From TripAdvisor: "Thank you very much for visiting Tjapukai Aboriginal Cultural Park. We are very pleased you enjoyed your Tjapukai by Day experience. The shows and activities we offer at Tjapukai have been approved by the Traditional Aboriginal Elders, hence why your experience was authentic and educational. We appreciate your support and we hope you return in the future" (30 August 2011).

20. While many cultural norms are observed, indigenous patterns of speech are often suspended within the tourism context. Fordham (1994: 17–19) and Mc-Garvie (1985: 12–15) have listed Djabugay communicative norms, including proscriptions against eye contact, the use of silence, and indirect communication, that are cultural barriers to communicating with English-speaking members of the dominant culture. As is the case among many other indigenous groups, these barriers must be surmounted in order to operate a tourism business. However, other cultural norms, such as gratuitous concurrence (agreeing to something out of politeness while harboring reservations), storytelling, and humor, lend themselves well to the kind of cross-cultural encounter made possible through tourism.

21. I accessed the trailer for the documentary *Dreaming as One* on YouTube at http:// www.youtube.com/watch?v=lrslieKK0Nk (accessed 2 January 2012. I was unable to locate this documentary, but the credits state that it was produced in 2008 by Dan Hottie.

22. This quote was taken from the Indigenous Tourism Australia website at http:// www.indigenoustourism.australia.com/casestudies.asp?sub=0604 (accessed 22 December 2011).

REFERENCES

Altman, Jon. 1989. "Tourism Dilemmas For Aboriginal Australians." *Annals of Tourism Research* 16, no. 4: 456–76.

Appadurai, Arjun. 1990. "Disjuncture and Difference in the Global Economy." In *Global Culture,* ed. Mike Featherstone. London: Sage Publications.

Babcock, Barbara. 1994. "Pueblo Cultural Bodies." *Journal of American Folklore* 107, no. 423: 40–54.

Barnes, Jill, and Dennis Foley. Forthcoming. "Repossession of Our Spirits: Struggles over the Touristic Packaging of Australian 'Dreamtime' Landscapes by State-Mandated Agencies at the Expense of Local Aboriginal Custodial Knowledge." Unpublished manuscript.

Bruner, Edward. 2005. *Culture on Tour: Ethnographies of Travel.* Chicago: University of Chicago Press.

Bunten, Alexis C. 2005. "Commodities of Authenticity: When Natives Consume Their Own 'Tourist Art.'" In *Exploring World Art,* ed. Robert Welsch, Eric Venbrux, and Pamela Scheffield Rosi. Long Grove, IL: Waveland Press.

———. 2008. "Sharing Culture or Selling Out? Developing the Commodified Persona in the Heritage Industry." *American Ethnologist* 35, no. 3: 380–95.

———. 2010. "More Like Ourselves: Indigenous Capitalism Through Tourism." *American Indian Quarterly* 34, no. 3: 285–311.

———. 2011a. "Consumption and Resistance in Native American Touristic Performance." In *Great Expectations: Imagination Anticipation and Enchantment in Tourism,* ed. Jonathan Skinner and Dimitrios Theodossopoulos. New York: Berghahn Books.

———. 2012. "You Never Know Who Is Going to Be on Tour: Reflections on the Indigenous Host Gaze from an Alaskan Case Study." In *The Host Gaze in Global Tourism,* ed. Omar Moufakkir and Yvette Reisinger. Oxfordshire, UK: CABI.

Bunten, Alexis C., and Nelson Graburn. 2009. "Guest Editorial: Current Issues in Indigenous Tourism." *London Journal of Tourism, Sport and Creative Industries* 2, no. 1: 2–11.

Clifford, James. 1997. *Routes: Travel and Translation in the Late Twentieth Century.* Cambridge, MA: Harvard University Press.

———. 2004. "Looking Several Ways: Anthropology and Native Heritage in Alaska." *Current Anthropology* 45, no. 1: 5–30.

Craik, Jennifer. 1997. "The Culture of Tourism." In *Touring Cultures: Transformations of Travel and Theory,* ed. Chris Rojek and John Urry. New York: Routledge.

Ellis, Tiffany M. 2007. *Going Native: Tourism, Negotiable Authenticity, and Cultural Production in the Polynesian Cultural Center and Tjapukai Aboriginal Cultural Park.* Master's thesis, Institute for Social and Cultural Anthropology, University of Oxford.

Endicott, Kirk, Lye Tuck Po, and Nurul Fatanah Zahari. Forthcoming. "Batek Playing Batek for Tourists at Peninsular Malaysia's National Park." In *Cultural Tourism Movements: New Articulations of Indigenous Identity,* ed. Alexis C. Bunten, Nelson Graburn, and Jenny Chio. Unpublished manuscript.

Evans-Pritchard, Deirdre. 1989. "How 'They' See 'Us': Native American Images of Tourists." *Annals of Tourism Research* 16, no 1: 89–105.

Fienup-Riordan, Ann. 2000. *Hunting Tradition in a Changing World: Yup'ik Lives in Alaska Today.* New Brunswick, NJ: Rutgers University Press.

Fordham, H. 1994. "Cultural Difficulties in Defense of Aboriginal Clients: Guidelines to assist lawyers in dealing with Aboriginal Clients." *Proctor,* March, 17–19.

Fusco, Coco. 1994. "The Other History of Intercultural Performance." *The Drama Review* 38, no. 1: 143–67.

Graburn, Nelson. (1977) 1989. "Tourism: The Sacred Journey." In *Hosts and Guests: The Anthropology of Tourism,* 2nd ed., ed. Valene Smith. Philadelphia: University of Pennsylvania Press.

Greenwood, Davydd. 1989. "Culture by the Pound: An Anthropological Perspective on Tourism and Cultural Commodification." In *Hosts and Guests: The Anthropology of Tourism,* 2nd ed., ed. Valene Smith. Philadelphia: University of Pennsylvania Press.

Hall, Stuart, and Tony Jefferson, eds. 1989. *Resistance through Rituals: Youth Subcultures in Post-war Britain.* London: Unwin Hyman.

Handler, Richard, and Jocelyn Linnekin. 1984. "Tradition, Genuine or Spurious?" *Journal of American Folklore* 97, no. 2: 273–90.

Handler, Richard, and William Saxon. 1998. "Dyssimulation, Reflexivity, Narrative, and the Quest for Authenticity in Living History." *Cultural Anthropology,* no. 3: 242–60.

Harkin, Michael. 1995. "Modernist Anthropology and Tourism of the Authentic." Annals of Tourism Research 22, no. 3: 650–70.

———. 2003. "Staged Encounters: Postmodern Tourism and Aboriginal People." *Ethnohistory* 50, no. 3: 575–85.

Hewison, Robert. 1987. *The Heritage Industry: Britain in a Climate of Decline.* London: Methuen.

Johnson, Katie, and Tamara Underiner. 2001. "Command Performances: Staging Native Americans at Tillicum Village." In *Selling the Indian: Commercializing and Appropriating American Indian Cultures,* ed. Carter Jones Meyer and Diana Royer. Tucson: University of Arizona Press.

King, John. 1997. "Marketing Magic: Process and Identity in the Creation and Selling of Native Art and Material Culture." In *Present Is Past: Some Uses of Tradition in Native Societies,* ed. Marie Mauzé. Lanham, MD: University Press of America.

Kirshenblatt-Gimblett, Barbara. 1991. "Objects of Ethnography." In *Exhibiting Cultures: The Poetics and Politics of Museum Display,* ed. Ivan Karp and Steven D. Lavine. Washington DC: Smithsonian Institution Press.

———. 1998. *Destination Culture: Tourism, Museums, and Heritage.* Berkeley: University of California Press.

Leach, Edmund. 1961. *Rethinking Anthropology.* London: Athlone Press.

Lujan, Carol C. 1993. "A Sociological View of Tourism in an American Indian Community: Maintaining Cultural Integrity at Taos Pueblo." *American Indian Culture and Research Journal* 17, no. 3: 101–20.

MacCannell, Dean. 1973. "Staged Authenticity: On Arrangements of Social Space in Tourist Settings." *American Journal of Sociology* 79, no. 3: 589–603.

Martinez Cobo, José R. 1986. *Study of the Problem of Discrimination against Indigenous Populations.* New York: United Nations.

McGarvie, Neil. 1985. *Inservice/Induction Kit for Use with Teachers of Aboriginal and Is-lander Students in Queensland Schools.* Brisbane: Department of Education.

McIntosh, Alison J., Angela B. Smith, and Takiora Ingram. 2000. "Tourist Experi-ences of Maori Culture in Aotearoa, New Zealand." Research Paper Number 8, Foundation for Research, Science and Technology. Dunedin, New Zealand: Center for Tourism, University of Otago.

Mieu, George Paul. 2011. "On Difference, Desire and the Aesthetics of the Unex-pected: The *White Masai* in Kenyan Tourism." In *Great Expectations: Imagination and Anticipation in Tourism,* ed. Jonathan Skinner and Dimitrios Theodossopou-los. New York: Berghahn Books.

Nash, Dennison. 1977. "Tourism as a Form of Imperialism." In *Hosts and Guests: The Anthropology of Tourism,* ed. Valene Smith. Philadelphia: University of Pennsylva-nia Press.

Nesper, Larry. 2003. "Simulating Culture: Being Indian for Tourists in Lac Du Flambeau's Wa-Swa-Ga Indian Bowl." *Ethnohistory* 50, no. 3: 447–72.

Nicks, Trudy. 1999. "Indian Villages and Entertainments: Setting the Stage for Tourist Souvenir Sales." In *Unpacking Culture: Art and Commodity in Colonial and Postcolonial Worlds,* ed. Ruth B. Phillips and Christopher B. Steiner. Berkeley: University of California Press.

Notzke, Claudia. 1998. "Indigenous Tourism Development in the Arctic." *Annals of Tourism Research* 26, no. 1: 55–76.

Nuttal, Mark. 1997. "Packaging the Wild: Tourism Development in Alaska." In *Tour-ists and Tourism: Identifying with People and Places,* ed. Simone Abram, Jacqueline Waldren, and Donald MacLeod. Oxford: Berg.

Palmer, Lisa. 2004. "Bushwalking in Kakadu: A Study of Cultural Borderlands." *Social and Cultural Geography* 5, no. 1: 109–27.

Pearce, Philip L., and Gianna Moscardo. 1999. "Tourism Community Analysis: Ask-ing the Right Questions." *Contemporary Issues in Tourism Development,* ed. Douglas G. Pearce and Richard W. Butler. London: Routledge.

Pratt, Mary Louise. 1992. *Imperial Eyes: Travel Writing and Transculturation.* London: Routledge.

Ritzer, George, and Allan Liska. 1997. "'McDisneylandization' and 'Post-Tourism': Complementary Perspectives on Contemporary Tourism." In *Touring Cultures: Transformations of Travel and Theory,* ed. Chris Rojek and John Urry. London: Routledge.

Rosaldo, Renato. 1989. "Imperialist Nostalgia." *Representations* 26: 107–22.

Rossel, Pierre. 1988. "Potlatch and the Totem: the Attraction of America's North-west Coast." In *Tourism: Manufacturing the Exotic,* ed. Pierre Rossel. Copenhagen: International Work Group for Indigenous Affairs.

Ryan, Chris, and Jeremy Huyton. 2002. "Tourists and Aboriginal People." *Annals of Tourism Research* 29, no. 3: 631–37.

Said, Edward. 1985. *Orientalism.* Middlesex, UK: Penguin Books.

Salazar, Noel B. 2010. *Envisioning Eden: Mobilizing Imaginaries in Tourism and Beyond.* Oxford: Berghahn Books.

———. 2013. "Imagining Mobility at the 'End of the World.'" *History and Anthropology* 24, no. 2: 233–52.

Schuler, Sigrid. 1999. "Tourism Impacts on an Australian Indigenous Community, a Djabugay Case Study." MA thesis, University of Sunshine Coast.

Scott, James. 1990. *Domination and the Arts of Resistance: Hidden Transcripts.* New Haven, CT: Yale University Press.

Silver, Ira. 1993. "Marketing Authenticity in Third World Countries." *Annals of Tourism Research* 20, no. 2: 302–18.

Stanley, Nick. 1998. *Being Ourselves For You: The Global Display of Cultures.* London: Middlesex University Press.

Stanton, Max E. 1989. "The Polynesian Cultural Center: A Multi-Ethnic Model of Seven Pacific Cultures." In *Hosts and Guests: The Anthropology of Tourism,* 2nd ed., ed. Valene Smith. Philadelphia: University of Pennsylvania Press.

Stocker, Karen. 2009. "Authenticating Discourses and the Marketing of Indigenous Identities." *London Journal of Tourism, Sport and Creative Industries* 2, no. 1: 62–71.

Tucker, Hazel. 2003. *Living With Tourism: Negotiating Identities in a Turkish Village.* London: Routledge.

Turner, Victor. 1969. "Liminality and Communitas." In *The Ritual Process: Structure and Anti-Structure.* Chicago: Aldine Publishing.

Valaskakis, Gail. 1993. "Parallel Voices: Indians and Others." *Canadian Journal of Communication* no. 18: 283–298.

Whittaker, Elvi. 1999. "Indigenous Tourism: Reclaiming Knowledge, Culture and Intellectual Property in Australia." In *Tourism and Cultural Conflicts,* ed. Mike Robinson and Priscilla Boniface. Wallingford, UK: CABI.

Wiketera, Keri Ann, and Hamish Bremner. 2009. "Maori Cultural Tourism or Just Being Ourselves? Validating Cultural Inheritance." *London Journal of Tourism, Sport and Creative Industries* 2, no. 1: 53–61.

Chapter 4

Myth Management
in Tourism's Imaginariums
Tales from Southwest China and Beyond

Margaret Byrne Swain

"Imaginariums," a playful term used to name places or destinations that engage the imagination, like museums or toy stores, is applied here to tourism sites where personal imaginings and institutional imaginaries dialectically circulate (see Salazar and Graburn, this volume). My intention is to locate tourism imaginaries, building on Noel Salazar's understanding of imaginaries as "socially transmitted representational assemblages that interact with people's personal imaginings and are used as world-making and word-shaping devices" (2012: 864). Connections between local tales and global imaginings (Burawoy 2000) underlie cosmopolitan world-making potential for mythical tourism (Buchmann 2006) to express universal hero archetypes in diverse geocultural settings. Mythic destinations may appeal to a wide range of domestic and international tourists. This chapter engages circumstances around indigenous mythical tourism in the Zomian borderlands of southwest China, raising questions about the agency of culturally distinct small societies for self-determined imaginariums in response to state interventions.

The Sani Yi, an indigenous literate culture branded by their Ashima tale through film, illustration, writing, and commerce, dominate established tourism in Yunnan's Shilin (Stone Forest). In contrast, the neighboring Axi Yi have recently embraced transnational tourism with popular commoditization of their oral myth-based fire festival, described by tourists as "wild," frenzied," and "primitive" (Peng and Lu 2011). Both Yi groups also embrace historical nostalgia through "ethnic culture and ecological tourism village" development, a type of rural idyll (Phillimore 2002). I will address how indigeneity and cosmopolitanism become coimagined identities for Sani and Axi, drawn from shared eras spanning French colonialism to Chinese ethnic tourism development.

IMAGINARIUMS, MYTHICAL TOURISM, AND MYTH MANAGEMENT

Tourism imaginariums shape how and by whom a landscape becomes imagined, and what that imagining might entail. The how of tourism imaginariums has political, economic, and ideological foundations, much as Selwyn (1996) has cogently argued in his overview of tourism mythology. Politically, tourism flows between global axes of cores and peripheries, while global consumer culture and transnational labor migration shape tourism economies. Ideologically, tourism circulates ideas about authenticity, both in terms of tourist myths believed to re-create authentic feelings and knowledge, and the tourees' myths, stories, and understandings of authentic feelings and knowledge, mediated by the how, whom, and what of a particular local destination. Who populates a tourism imaginarium includes tourists, the tourees, and observers such as tourism researchers, intersecting at both externally directed and internally reactive levels (Selwyn 1996: 9). The "what" of a tourism imaginarium refracts location in time and space. Indigenous/ethnic tourism is often postcolonial, portraying particular tourist myths: of the tourees being frozen in time, living in a paradise, or enacting the uncivilized Other (Tucker and Akama 2009). Thinking beyond binaries, such as how the tourees enact and react to tourist myths, the tourees may also embody cosmopolitan desires.

Selwyn (2000: 403) concludes that myths are stories "at once 'liberating' in the sense that they are vehicles for imagining the possible, and 'desirable' in that they lead perception away from the pragmatic realities of history and political economy. In these senses tourism myths reveal one sort of truth in the process of concealing another." A cosmopolitan question encountered in tourism mythology asks what is universal, and what is culturally specific. The attraction of universal themes in dialectical relationship with diverse cultural understandings drives mythical tourism. Specific legends drawn from local stories, translocal literary works, and/or films, mythical imaginings about local populations by dominant groups (stereotypes, homogenizations), and marketing ploys to build a brand form the bases for mythical tourism. Destinations shaped by tourist expectations intersecting with the tourees' production of mythical experiences (Buchmann 2006) could be fulfilling a postcolonial fantasy and/or providing the familiarity of a universally recognizable hero story in a Jungian sense, with questions of gender set aside (Nicholson 2011). Myth management of specific tourism sites articulates imaginariums as places where circuits of global markets, national politics, and local identities connect. Identity groups engage their political and cultural capital with divergent institutional imaginaries in mythical tourism development. Connections between local tales and global imaginings underlie the cosmopolitan potential for mythical tourism to express universal archetypes in local, diverse geocultural landscapes.

INDIGENOUS COSMOPOLITANS

Debates about how indigeneity and cosmopolitanism, potentially opposite imaginaries, can be coproduced (Swain 2011b) have relevance to mythical tourism development. Rather than thinking in binaries such as local/global, rooted/mobile, barbarian/civilized, timeless/contemporary, and tradition/modernity, it is productive to think of these concepts as complementary, including the possibilities of indigenous cosmopolitans. Tensions between autochthonous claims to being the original people of a place and cosmopolitanism engagement with the world outside the home community or place may melt through hospitality and travel. In Appiah's (2006) perspective, cosmopolitanism can be distinguished from competing universalisms by engagement with plurality, in ethical celebration and regulation of difference through mediating rights.

Cosmopolitanisms

Interest in cosmopolitan theory revived in the 1990s as a way to analyze globalization. "Cosmopolitanisms" became a pluralized term in international literature, indicating the many ways of understanding this construct as identity, a consciousness or worldview, a global process, or a monolithic cultural companion to global capitalism. Three dialectical strands are evident in Western cosmopolitan theory: moral (universal values, ethics, multiculturalism), political (rights, citizenship, democracy), and cultural (mobilities, consumption, hybridities, networks) (Delanty 2006). These strands reflect distinct theoretical positions as well as areas of interest in various types of cosmopolitanism.

The early twenty-first century's global transformation of modernity has been mapped by some scholars as the "cosmopolitan condition" that connects human information webs, mobilities, and commodity flows. Cosmopolitanism can be celebrated for challenging various ethnocentric, sexist, racialized, national narratives, but critiqued for associated global rootless hybrid cultural forms, standardized mass commodities, images, and practices. A kind of cosmopolitan citizenship or identity based on mobility and connoisseurship and consumption of people, places, and cultures may develop into intellectual and aesthetic orientations toward cultural and geographic difference (Swain 2009).

New international scholarship on Chinese cosmopolitanism draws from understandings of *tianxiaguan* (all under heaven) and *shijie zhuyi* (worldism) (Swain 2013). A Confucian worldview, *tianxia,* promotes an inward-looking order, or a kind of soft power, that shapes official nationalism, state sovereignty, and territorial integrity. *Tianxia* is seen to have three main components: physical (the earth), philosophical (human heart), and political (global governance). Zhao (2009) argues that *tianxia* is a way of harmony for all humanity, much better than a Western idea of global citizenship based on *polis* or nation-state.

Shijie zhuyi, in contemporary Chinese, is an outward-looking concept, glossed as "cosmopolitan" in other languages, and indicates an ever-changing world. *Tianxia* does not account for all of the struggles, tensions, and inconsistencies within China's engagement with the modern world. Compared to the *tianxia* civilizing project, *shijie* does not presuppose a division of civilized and barbarian or the acculturation of Other subjects. It stresses a dynamic and relational understanding of the world. We can see *tianxia* and *shijie* as complementary opposites, promoting stability and openness to change, that form Chinese cosmopolitanisms (Barabantseva 2009). The complexity of China's relations with the world cannot be grasped through simply opposing the traditional Chinese worldview and state cultural authority to the Western-dominated organization of the world.

Indigenous and Indigeneity

Cosmopolitanism indicates an inclusive global citizen identity with diverse origins, while indigeneity refers to a specific global postcolonial identity of native or aboriginal peoples who claim some self-determination. Political solidarity for minority rights may motivate an indigenous group to function as an ethnic group with symbolic and strategic goals.[1] We can see that ethnic and indigenous identities both have claims to territory, cultural and language practices, and common ancestors, while claims of indigeneity focus also on dispossession and/or submission to colonizing forces. Globally, indigeneity and ethnicity are prime sources of multiculturalism, a concept that is celebrated and debated as a cosmopolitan ideal and as a perceived impediment to global equity and peace. An imagined identity community (Anderson 2006) based on flexible definitions of what it means to be indigenous intersects with rights-based social constructs and universal moral claims. Indigeneity is an evolving construct that has potential repercussions for global governance and equity-based democratic or socialist state regulations (Merlan 2009).

ETHNIC/INDIGENOUS TOURISM IN CHINA

Localized indigenous tourism has evolved globally to emphasize both ethnic and ecological resources, based on an indigenous group's cultural identity and territory and controlled somewhat from within by the group, buffering direct incorporation into transnational markets. The Chinese state denies that indigenous peoples exist within their borders, although there is a rising consciousness of indigeneity among specific groups (Swain 2011b). The official *tianxia* logic is that all nationalities in China suffered and struggled together against the aggression of foreign (European) colonizers. Any complications of this scenario with acknowledgement of the internal colonization of minority groups by the Han majority are unthinkable.[2] As China grapples with rapid globalization, it is evident that a monolithic Han Chinese majority is also expressing its diversity, celebrating regional cultural identities, landscapes, and linguistic distinctions, giving rise to nostalgic recreations for festivals and local tourism. Domestic ethnic tourism in China has grown exponentially. By the late 1980s, there were four major ethnic minority tourism sites in Yunnan: Shilin, Dali, Xishuangbanna, and Lijiang, which have been joined by Luguhu and Zhongdian (now Shangri-La) in major state promotion. These new sites in northwest Yunnan are part of The Nature Conservancy's Three Rivers watershed project. A clear indication of the region's cosmopolitan potential is the 2010 publication of the first Chinese-language version of Lonely Planet's Yunnan guide for independent travelers looking for the unusual.

Yunnan in Zomia

The perception of Yunnan[3] as an out-of-the-ordinary place, both remote and diverse, has been a theme throughout China's history. Recently it has been included in Zomia, an academic imaginarium first constructed by Willem van Schendel and then redefined by various scholars (Michaud 2010: 187) to categorize a past geographical region of remote highlands stretching from Afghanistan and Tibet through Yunnan to Vietnam. Colonial conditions, limited resource extraction, and the fleeing of peoples away from states up into the hills marked off this location. Zomia's contact zones now provide ideal locations for investigating ethnic tourism of "barbarians by design," in Scott's terms (2009: 8), local agency in response to state interventions, and global circuits of tourism imaginaries.

Zomia is an imaginary construct that helps us analyze how past power dynamics in a region have shaped diverse small-scale societies into varied economic development routes, even when the same strategy is used, in this case tourism. Toured indigenous/ethnic groups' myths or cultural stories mixed with consumer expectations become managed by the state and global commerce. In our current era of globalization within Zomia's borderlands, strategic uses of ethnic heritage for tourism can support coproduction of indigeneity and cosmopolitanism in neighboring communities with distinct cultural configurations (Swain 2011b).

Given that about one-third of Yunnan's population comprises twenty-five officially recognized minorities, divided into many additional subgroups, there is certainly potential for ethnic/scenic tourism development. This began in the late twentieth century with state and private tourism ventures selling ethnic minority/indigenous identities, often presenting homogeniz- ing images and marketable experiences while fostering the lure of authentic ethnic diversity. Some minority or indigenous people working in tourism may be empowered through the marketing of identity traits as commodities for sale, although results here, as worldwide, are uneven (Swain 2011a).

Sani and Axi Yi Myth Management in Indigenous Tourism

I will develop this argument by contrasting the Sani and Axi, two of twenty- eight state-recognized branches of the Yi minority nationality. Their ances- tors settled centuries ago in the limestone karst topography of southeast Yunnan within and around what is now the Shilin County tourism district and Mile County. Based on origin claims in a region colonized by Han Chi- nese and Europeans, one could call them indigenous peoples, an identity embraced by Sani intellectuals. Sani and Axi societies have dealt with at least three waves of globalizing change in their region over the past century, each with a translocal civilizing project. The first wave was French Catholi- cism, brought to them in the 1880s during an era of European imperialism. French missionaries, primarily ordained priests of Les Missions Étrangères de Paris (MEP), were active throughout Yunnan by the 1870s. Often interested in local languages and customs beyond their utilitarian potential, MEP missionaries' records provide valuable historical materials for current studies of and by indigenous peoples.

Father Paul Vial arrived in the region in 1888, with a highly ambitious plan to missionize and modernize indigenous society (Swain 2011c). He focused on Sani communities, in part because of interest in their written language, but included Axi in his panoptic gaze and church school-building efforts. Vial recorded his world through photography, no mean feat given technology and field conditions. In the MEP archives, I came across a small trove of Vial's postcards that he had produced in 1908 as a fund-raising effort for the missions. Using his photos spanning twenty years, these postcards introduced images of Sani and Axi people to French consumers in the enduring trope of travel, sending messages to and from home. Of all these cards, one truly intriguing imagining is a juxtaposition of two photographs, featuring Sani and Axi nursing mothers. From a Western point of view, much can be read into these images, including: indigenous Madonna; imperial soft porn of the Other; or contrasting natives—well-kept, potentially literate Sani versus poor, savage Axi.

Fellow MEP missionary Alfred Liétard settled among the Axi in late 1898. By 1900, he reported that things were going well in a letter to his superiors (in the MEP archives), detailing his schools for both girls and boys that built on Vial's earlier efforts. In 1904, Liétard published a review of missionary work with the Axi in the popular press journal *Les Missions Catholiques* (Liétard 1904: 93–96), where he noted an origin myth of the Axi: that they once had their own books, but because the characters were written on dried dough, the books crumbled with time and were lost. As Scott (2009: 220–23) observed, this narrative of lost literacy is one found among groups throughout Zomia, and may be tied to strategic retreats from state systems and other forms of dominance.

Catholic missions with the Axi and Sani persisted until the revolution, and have some followers still in both groups. Their survival during this next era was precarious, with most Christian converts going underground. In 1949, the beginning of the communist civilizing project brought a world vision and global social organization that created a new kind of communal citizen, with often disastrous local results. Post-Mao reforms led to a third wave of change when China opened to a new world of global capitalism in the 1980s that translated into tourism development within numerous indigenous ethnic minority homelands.

For the Sani, an imaginarium has grown with their scenic location in and around the Shilin national geopark, which includes: literate animistic rituals; an annual harvest-time fire torch festival; and ongoing celebrations of a highly reimagined female-centered ur-myth about Ashima, with attending music, dance, and film tourism, having a decidedly "civilized" native appeal. The presence of an indigenous writing system cannot be underestimated in the designation of an ethnic minority group as somewhat civilized in Chinese popular thought. In Yunnan, that would also include Naxi, Dai, and Tibetans. Conversely, the lack of indigenous writing makes a group less civilized and more barbarian, and quite possibly more exciting for tourist consumers. The Axi imaginarium builds on this "barbarian by design" (Scott 2009) motif, with no manicured national park in their homeland, but rather rough countryside outside of the Mile County town. Axi nonliterate animistic religion, a well-known dance performance, an uninhibited but organized annual festival to celebrate a male mythic hero's discovery of fire, and other festivities all now contribute to their tourism development.

Axi and Sani communities share landscape, resources, histories, Yi language similarities, and sometimes family. Their intangible cultural heritage translates fluidly between both groups. Sani and Axi women produce fine embroidery for their distinct traditional costumes and less involved work for tourists. Their music and dance are so intertwined that the Axi Tiao Yue (Axi Dance under the Moonlight) is frequently performed by Sani entertainers in the national park, and a large three-string drum guitar plays a major part accompanying both Sani and Axi dancing. "Ethnic cultural and ecological village" destinations are another form of tourism development shared by both groups, along with nostalgia for French colonialism through French-style wine production in Mile County near Axi villages, French colonial knowledge in Shilin tour books, and Catholic churches in Axi and Sani communities.

SANI TOURISM

In 1978, China had its "Opening to the Outside World" following decades of isolation. Soon, itinerant Sani women peddlers were migrating to Kunming to change money on the black market and sell their handicrafts to tourists. Shilin Park began to be refurbished, after its neglect during the Cultural Revolution. The Shilin (formerly Lunan)[4] Yi Nationality Autonomous County government identified tourism as a primary "pillar" within long-term regional development plans in 1987. Tourism marketing has focused on the impressive limestone landscape and a commoditized form of Sani ethnic identity. The region is branded as "Ashima's hometown," based on Sani lore about a golden girl who turned to stone.

During the 1990s, per capita income and employment in private sector and informal tourism grew rapidly (Shi 2000). Sani and Han have opened guesthouses, hotels, restaurants, and souvenir shops outside the park and are employed in various jobs within the park. Some two million tourists (1.9 million being domestic) visited Shilin during 1999. Since then, tourism growth has leveled somewhat, with 2.7 million tourists in 2009 (Swain 2011b). In 2004, the Shilin National Park became a UNESCO Geopark site and, in 2007, a World Heritage site.

Much of the background work on the marketing potential of cosmopolitan heritage drawn from French colonialism was accomplished in the early twenty-first century by a small group of Sani intellectuals: a French-educated Catholic teacher, a government historian, a professor at the Nationalities University in Beijing, and a local politician with a PhD in history and a sterling rural Communist Party pedigree. A focus on Sani indigenous culture and French colonial history targets both international tourists looking for nostalgia and domestic tourists looking for global sophistication. On a six-language Chinese travel website, the text about Shilin states that the park was "officially founded in 1931, but at the turn of the twentieth century, a French missionary named Paul Vial revealed its wonder to the West" (Cadieux 2007).

Ashima International Research Conference

Sani intellectuals also organized an international research conference held in August 2004 to commemorate the state's fiftieth anniversary of publishing the Sani narrative poem, "Ashima," and the fortieth anniversary of the release of the film *Ashima*. As the English invitation letter explained: "Today 'Ashima' has already gained its well-deserved worldly reputation and is recognized as a cultural heritage of humanity by all people," which I would frame as indigenous cosmopolitanism (Swain 2011a).

Fifty scholars were invited to present on Ashima-related cultural production or socioeconomic development issues (i.e., tourism). Both the poem and tourism commoditization of the region literally meld the heroic protagonist Ashima into the surrounding stone landscape (Swain 2005). In his welcoming toast, the Shilin County Chinese Communist Party vice-secretary expanded on these themes:

> Ashima is a mysterious legend. It is the symbol of beautiful Shilin ... [W]e sincerely hope that all guests can enjoy the beautiful natural landscape as well as the unique elegance of Ashima culture; ... strengthen communication and

cooperation between the world and Shilin, and we'll appreciate your advice on our county's development.

Conference materials included a holographic Chinese/English souvenir book celebrating both Ashima cultural production anniversaries. Presenters were not identified by ethnicity, but by informal assessment, the majority were Sani, with a few other ethnic minority scholars, a few Han Chinese, and a sprinkling of international guests—myself and another researcher from the United States and nine people affiliated with Korean and Japanese universities, many of whom were Chinese scholars. We attended presentations for several days, and then attended the annual Huobajie, the Sani fire torch harvest festival that has become a massive tourist draw to Shilin Park.

What is still an indigenous harvest celebration held in small communities is now also commoditized into a grand tourist and local event, with impromptu dancing contests and vendors selling festive foods and souvenirs crowded into the fairgrounds outside of a huge stadium holding a purported one hundred thousand people. It was a great finale for the conference, right down to the Korean pop stars' performance. One of the stars, the daughter of a presenting scholar, graciously received quite a bit of attention from the US delegates, who were readily labeled as the festivities' "*Yang* [foreign] Ashima and Ahei" (Ashima's companion). The organizers' cosmopolitan wish, to link this most indigenous but highly manipulated myth to the world, became embodied in our presence, with our spectacle, scholarship, and entertainment as part of the global canon of "Ashima culture."

In coordination with the conference, an impressive five-volume collection of new scholarship was published, *The Ashima Culture Series,* edited by Zhao Deguan, a rising Yunnan politician, scholar, and Sani native of Shilin (Bender 2004). To celebrate the poem's production and publication, honored guests included several members of the original *wenhua gongtuan* (culture work group), elderly Han women who had fascinating stories to tell. When they were teenagers full of revolutionary zeal, they lived with Sani people for months, transcribing translators' work from the Sani language into Chinese. Government culture workers ultimately combined materials from a number of sources into the ur-Ashima myth. Based on Sani *bimo* (religious leaders) poetic recitations for rites of passage, the life story of a "golden girl" became transformed into the revolutionary tale of Ashima, who fights for her rights and defies an evil property owner, aided by her beloved brother Ahei, only to drown and then become one with the local karst landscape.

After its first publication in Yunnan, the standardized poem then went on to be translated into a number of languages for international distribution, including Russian, English, and Japanese. The English edition that I bought in the late 1980s was first published in 1957. In the 1990s, parallel with the rise of tourism, Ashima-inspired literature began to appear in the popular Chinese press, especially anthologies and guidebooks. *The Shilin Tourism Cultural Series,* published in Beijing in the mid-1990s, includes an index in English and Japanese for books on the Sani by mainly Sani re-

Figure 4.1. Sani vendor dressing up tourists at the Ashima rock, Shilin Park (Copyright: M. Swain).

searchers, a poetry anthology, and a landscape-viewing guide, all liberally referencing Ashima.

A 2004 series features an edited volume of writings by foreigners (including me) concerning Ashima's hometown, and the life story of Yi minority film actress Yang Likun, who played the part of Ashima in the film. Sadly, her life was destroyed by persecution during the Cultural Revolution. Yang's husband, now a successful international entrepreneur, presented his biography of her, *My Sorrows Are like Ashima's,* at the conference. His wife's story is a strong reminder of China's recent turbulent past, while her image feeds the Ashima imaginarium. Photographs of Yang as Ashima, taken from the film, adorned many of the conference's publications and are used prominently in Ashima imaginings.

Regional Sani Tourism Development

The movie *Ashima* weaves together mythical, scenic, postcolonial, indigenous, and cosmopolitan tourism landscapes, ending with Ashima literally becoming a rock, identified as being in the national park. That rock is a hugely popular destination, where tourists regularly dress up in faux Sani clothes for souvenir photographs (figure 4.1). Multiple staged Sani performances present cultural song-and-dance tourist shows ranging from gaudy costumes, bright lights, fast music, and karaoke to presentations by mature performers wearing "real" Sani clothing and singing "real" Sani songs (some of which are from the movie).

The film has been reissued on DVD, including an English subtitled version, for international distribution. A recent Chinese film comparing Ashima and Ahei to Romeo and Juliet underscores an important change in the story from *bimo* chant to movie. Ahei is Ashima's lover, not her brother, in the 1964 movie. Segments of the original film are available on YouTube. In sum, the cosmopolitan potential of Ashima's story, and consequently Sani tourism imaginaries, promotes cultural diversity, with Sani characteristics, and universal values, in the mythic sign of the hero's journey and her sacrifice, for both tourists and tourees.

Besides mythical Ashima, another basis for Sani tourism development has derived from the tourists' myth of an imagined rural idyll. During the late 1990s, projects to promote "ethnic cultural and ecological village" tourism began in various Sani communities outside of the Shilin National Park. A Ford Foundation project utilized this approach with five pilot villages (Yin 2003), two of which were Sani: Yuehu (Moon Lake) in Shilin County (Xie 2010) and Xianrendong in Qubie County, to the southeast (Xu 2007). A top-down team of stakeholders comprised of the provincial government, NGOs, urban academics, regional government officials, and some locals guided each site's project. Although a stated goal was sustainability, the lack of "bottom-up" engagement in project design (Xie 2010) lead to variable results and predictable economic disparities. Yin (2003: 44–46) reported that Yuehu villagers said the project's organizing meeting was as large as those held for land reform in the 1950s were. This enthusiasm, however, was focused on a few aspects of Sani culture and limited individual involvement. The Yunnan Provincial Tourism Administration website (2011) promotes Yuehu as a Sani ethnic village that specializes in performance, the annual Sani *mizhi* (sacred forest) festival, and day trips, in a picturesque lakeside site evoking Ashima and Ahei.

Xianrendong also has a beautiful setting that draws tourists to a Sani area outside of Shilin County. Strong local leadership, a sophisticated planning process, and community investment created a firm base for tourism development. By 2006, local inns, called *nongjiale* (happy farmhouses), were well established in the village, providing services by villagers strategically marketing their rural livelihood for urban tourists searching for rustic charm (Xu 2007: 154).

The Shilin County government started its own second wave of development in 2005, with seven pilot villages and a budget of over one million US dollars. This effort focused on buy-ins from the local elite and villagers at the onset, creating a complex web of stakeholders driving each pilot project (Xie 2010). One project is in Danuohei, a Sani village regionally renowned for its stone-crafted houses, and, not too surprisingly, it is also the hometown of the politician Zhao Deguan, who was instrumental in the organization of the Ashima International Research Conference. The project design clearly includes the tourees, from local farmer to provincial elite; the tourists, both domestic and international; and the observers, both researchers and government agents. Efforts in Danuohei to document and revitalize intangible cultural heritage include embroidery arts, singing, dancing, hemp cultivation, and weaving; knowledge about making musical instruments, tools, and buildings; *bimo* sacred knowledge; and Yi writing.

Villagers have compiled "indigenous ethnographies" and videos of village life, created a local museum, participated in summer Sani culture camps for students,[5] and some families have opened tourist hostels. Tourism has become a lifeline for this village, its success due to resources, planning, and investment not available to every village. But even here not everyone agrees or shares equally. They have created a rural idyll imaginarium of happy, singing and dancing, mythological, artistic, animistic indigenous people. An Ethnic Odyssey 2 CNTV (2011) production on the Yi visited Danuohei, recording that "walking through a village you get a sense of the local way of life, simple and pleasant. No matter what village you are in, the sound of singing and dancing fills the air." What CCTV and visiting tourists do not hear are the French colonial Catholic church bells, just over the hill.

AXI TOURISM

A parallel tourism imaginarium has developed in some Axi villages, building on indigenous oral myths, annual festivals, other tangible and intangible heritage, and the rural idyll. By the early 2000s, Mile County infrastructure had developed and, with that, the possibilities for local Axi tourism began to flow along better highways, power lines, and communications. I will focus on the Axi villages of Hongwan, known for its annual fire festival, and Keyi, an ethnic culture and ecological tourism village known as the home of the Axi Dance under the Moonlight. Hongwan is a small rural village in the mountains outside of Mile County town, where, post–Cultural Revolution, the fire origins myth ceremony has been revitalized and believed to be the most authentic enactment (Yunnan Adventure 2009). Several thousand people from the countryside join in. In 2004, the regional Xiyi township government decided to fund the Hongwan event to encourage tourism (China Discover 2010). During the festival, local folk come to visit, tourists are charged an entrance fee, and tour groups are beginning to attend as well. By 2010, some forty thousand domestic and international tourists attended, and two thousand paid additional photographer fees (Yunnan Explorer 2010).

The festival celebrates the mythical origins of fire building brought by cultural hero Mudeng to Axi people, who were often cold and hungry until Mudeng rubbed wood together and built the first fire via friction. A reenacting of this story involves naked men painted with mineral designs, who represent their ancestors, guided by the local *bimo* through a series of rituals in the sacred forest. The next day begins with extinguishing the old fires in the village, celebrating with song and dance, ritual rekindling of the fire, and jumping over new bonfires. To quote one tourism website (Yunnan Adventure 2009), "the grotesque penis that some of the dancers show with pride points out also to the relationship of this festival with old fertility cults." This seems to be a rather fine example of "barbarians by design" (Scott 2010).

Peng and Lu's (2011) study of intangible heritage in the Axi fire festival notes that the current ritual leader has decided to borrow a bit of tangible heritage from his literate Yi neighbors, having special clothes made with the word *bimo* written in Yi script to mark his status. During the 2010 festival, government planners added a new element by holding Yi traditional wrestling matches while the ritual was going on. These competing events ended up curtailing time available for the fire ritual, as Axi participate sequentially, not simultaneously. Peng and Lu (2011) conclude that government interventions for entertainment can threaten Axi intangible heritage and tourist levels could drop off. While China enacted a national intangible heritage law in 2011, it remains to be seen how this relates to protection for heritage tourism development.

The Keyi Yi culture ecological village is somewhat easier to reach by main road than Hongwan. This village has been designated as the birthplace of the oral creation epic of Axi people, as well as the Axi Tiao Yue (IUAES 2009: 59). While Hongwan is inundated once a year, Keyi is open for business year-round. A 2006 CCTV travelogue program commented that Keyi is a must on your travel itinerary, welcoming visitors in "traditional style" with a dance if you call ahead. Keyi has been manicured with mural paintings on external walls, including one wall mural photograph featured on a tourist blog (Ethnic China 2009) that shows an enthusiastic Axi couple dancing literally on top of the globe. Clearly, they have a grasp of indigenous cosmopolitanism.

In 2008, the Axi Tiao Yue was added to the National Intangible Heritage List and the dance then became the focus of a highly orchestrated Mile County festival beginning in 2009, which attracted tens of thousands of villagers to the event as well as many tourists to the Keyi-Hongwan region (In Kunming 2010). European grape wine production, introduced to the countryside by French missionaries more than one hundred years ago, has been revived as a commodity and as another form of regional tourism. Images of beautiful young Axi girls in native dress are used to market the wine, especially to tourists.

CONCLUSIONS

Since 2001, I have periodically surveyed tourism representations of Yunnan ethnic/indigenous minorities on the Internet, noting little difference in those brief phrases of Internet-speak portraying their interpolated identities, partial impressions that provide interpretations, or representations unauthorized by the community in question (Swain 2011a). Internet information on Yunnan's ethnic tourism from government promotion, tour companies, or tourist blogs often presents a given ethnic minority as happily singing and dancing all day long, as crafty traders to be bargained with, or as folkloric heroes. These interpolated identities reflect hegemonic systems creating "ethnic minority" in contrast to ideas about what constitutes identities for toured indigenous minority peoples and their beholders. Cyber tourism discourses on cultural diversity emanate from multiple paradigms of authenticity, indigeneity, and cosmopolitanism. Internet imaginariums refract back into real-life efforts of minority ethnic groups to claim greater agency in tourism development. The subjects are reading their representations, as Formoso (2010) has argued for Zomian denizens, and sometimes they are in charge. Khampa Caravan, a touring company in the Shangri-La region, provides one such example. Their multilanguage website (Khampa Caravan 2011) details cosmopolitan backgrounds of the all-Tibetan owner-operators and extensive crew, as well as the many tour packages they provide, featuring indigenous cultures and diverse natural environments. We have seen in this chapter that some Sani also have high-powered cosmopolitan input in their tourism development, and the mural in Keyi of global Axi dancers has profound meaning.

Cosmopolitan Myth Management and Imaginariums in Indigenous Tourism

Sani and Axi tourism development is shaped by intersecting indigenous tales and tourists' myths about postcolonial idylls. In 2011, Internet tourist blogs on the region seemed much more interested in Axi "primitive" spectacle than "civilized" Sani poetic Ashima fare. However, most tour company sites featured a day trip to Shilin Park and a Sani village, rather than a somewhat longer trip from Kunming to visit Axi sites. While the scale of Axi tourism is significantly smaller than Sani, they are providing a distinctly desirable destination, with the allure of being more remote and barbarian in comparison to the Sani. Sani and Axi imaginariums are constituted from shared historical experiences in contiguous rural habitats, related language and material culture, and very distinct cultural repertoires of the imaginary. Their heroes vary by gender and journey. One became a sign of their culture within the physical landscape, the other invented critical cultural knowledge—how to start a fire. Furthermore, the telling of their story varies, from written records in one case and oral literature in the other.

Management of these mythical elements, as we have seen, takes distinct directions, reflecting the material and the messages being sent. In 2009, the Sani village of Danuohei and the Axi village of Keyi were primary field trip sites for the sixteenth International Union of Anthropological and Ethnological Sciences (IUAES) Congress, held in Kunming.[6] Brief and objectifying presentations of the sites in the IUAES handbook (2007), two laudatory Chinese press stories about these visits (Xinhua 2009a, 2009b), and anthropologists blogging about their reactions to the field trips as academic tourists (Antropologi 2009) provide a window into external myth management and reaction to it by consumers expressing both cosmopolitan ideals and political critique.

The IUAES descriptions focus on geographical location, the population of "almost pure ethnic people," and claims to fame. Danuohei is lauded for the protection of Yi culture, where old-time "tree worship" is completely preserved and 98 percent of the houses are built in the village's unique stone style (IUAES 2007: 58). Keyi is promoted as the birthplace of Axi intangible heritage, with an oral origins myth and signature dance (IUAES 2007: 59). Xinhua online news ran a photo-essay on Danuohei (2009b) and a written story about Keyi (2009a). The Danuohei story featured nine photographs detailing the village's geographical setting, stone houses, local people in ethnic dress, a tiger face–shaped gate marking a place of ritual,[7] and other cultural productions, but not a word about Ashima. The next day's article about Keyi was focused significantly on international anthropologists' purported appreciation for China's minority policies, while noting the Axi people's creation myth and dance, but not the barbarian celebration of the Axi creation of fire myth. Touted as the essence of Axi culture, the dance's indigenous cosmopolitan potential is marked by the observation that it has been performed in various countries outside of China, including the United States, Poland, and Korea.[8]

The anthropologists' blog (Antropologi 2009) starts with a riposte to Chinese authorities' propaganda generated about and from the IUAES Congress. Seven commentators weighed in with their responses on China's repressive ethnic/indigenous policy and anthropologists being entertained by "happy minorities and their songs and dances." Several field trip participants spoke about the tensions inherent in tourism myth management. In contrast to claims of Axi ethnic homogeneity in Keyi, one blogger noted that he saw *Hui* (Muslim) families, a Christian church, and evidence of Han families in the village. When some visitors were critical of the authenticity of Axi culture being presented, the official response was "what you see here is real." Likewise, a participant on the field trip to Danuohei commented that they experienced a "staged managed show by ethnic villagers," with no space for conversation with locals about their opinions. In these highly managed encounters for visiting anthropologists, the government, with some collusion of the villagers, chose to portray a rural indigenous idyll, rather than indigenous archetype hero myth tourism. This short-circuits the local idyll and hero myth imaginarium generally marketed by the tourism industry, government agencies, and local communities to domestic and international tourists, on the Internet, and on the ground.

Figure 4.2. Destroying the Sani village of Wukeshu in Shilin for tourism development (Copyright: W. Swain).

The agency of culturally distinct small societies to self-manage tourism imaginariums depends on locating circuits of local tales and global imaginings, as we saw in the Ashima International Research Conference; response to state power, manipulations, and protection, as seen in the Axi fire festival; and tourists' myths of the rural indigenous idyll and postcolonial Other, as explored in the ecocultural villages of Danuohei and Keyi. Times are not idyllic in some Sani communities. Wukeshu, the village by the national park's main gate, was bulldozed down in August 2011 to make way for new tourism construction (figure 4.2). A struggle over this went on for several years, but now the government has exercised eminent domain. Some villagers refused to move, and over fifty were jailed. Across a main highway from old Wukeshu is a new community of modernistic townhouses, available for the villagers to purchase when their old homes are destroyed. The houses are of shoddy construction and urban in feel, with no room for community gardens or even a small household patch. The community is being torn apart for tourism development in a hegemonic imaginarium with little room for self-management.

Tourism imaginariums adapt to global markets, national politics, regional governments, and local identities, combining cultural and political capital into multiple imaginaries. As illustrated by our examples from Yunnan, strategic uses of ethnic heritage for tourism can support coproduction of indigeneity and cosmopolitanism in some communities, though often with contested control of resources. For Chinese domestic tourists visiting indigenous sites, the imaginarium they help produce could reinforce ideas distinct from their hosts' about China's territorial claims, while "along with the locals they become immobile backdrops to Chinese modernity" (Nyíri 2010: 165), drawing particularly from *tianxia* thinking.

In this brief encounter with Sani and Axi in southwest China, I have promoted an idea of tourism imaginariums as a way to acknowledge the importance of place in how destinations shape circuits of imagining among all the stakeholders coproducing tourism imaginaries. I have also expanded on a predominantly Western genealogy of tourism discourse that will benefit from additional perspectives, looking specifically at cosmopolitan mobility and tourism in China. China's *tianxia* cosmopolitanism in tourism imaginaries promotes minority nationality unity in diversity (*minzu tuanjie*), the nation's place in the world, heritage, and ecological treasures, while upholding China's soft power and hierarchical order. *Shijie* cosmopolitanism in China's tourism imaginaries shapes ideas of modernity, global marketing and finance networks, corporate cultures, indigenous identities, global environmental concerns, and a drive for change. *Tianxia* and *shijie* have the potential of moderating aspects of Chinese society that each cosmopolitan system engages in distinct ways, while providing nuanced ideas of and for China in the world. In a similar vein, cosmopolitan conditions from Western perspectives may promote imaginaries of both commonality and difference (Leite, in this volume), shaping tourism imaginariums.

NOTES

1. My touchstone for what constitutes ethnicity is the straightforward "purported common descent and purported cultural commonality" (Harrell 1995: 4).
2. China's postponement of the International Congress of Anthropological and Ethnological Sciences scheduled in Kunming during the 2008 Olympics to a year later showed that even though indigeneity does not officially apply in China, the state is vigilant about incursions by more rambunctious "ethnic minorities," like Tibetans or Uighurs.
3. Literally "south of the clouds," meaning very far from central control.
4. In 1997, the county name was changed officially from "Lunan," a Chinese version of the Sani language name, to "Shilin," or Stone Forest, for tourism branding.
5. I taught a Ford Foundation–funded field methods workshop in 1993 for Chinese researchers in Danuohei. Even then, there was strong awareness of the tourism potential of the village.

6. Field trip preparations were influenced by provincial politics, and the distance of these communities from Kunming, making them ideal destinations for day trips.
7. See Xie (2010) for details on building this "traditional" gate for tourist consumption. Such a gate was not even imagined when I was in the village several times throughout the 1990s.
8. This mirrors the claims in the 1950s of international stature for the Ashima myth, published in various languages.

REFERENCES

Anderson, Benedict. 2006. *Imagined Communities.* New York: Verso.
Antropologi. 2009. "IUAES: Anthropologists 'Praise' Chinese Government's Relation to Minorities." http://www.antropologi.info/blog/anthropology/2009/iuaes-anthropologistspraise-chinese-government (accessed 4 June 2011).
Appiah, Kwame. 2006. "The Case for Contamination: No to Purity; No to Tribalism; No to Cultural Protectionism: Toward a New Cosmopolitanism." *New York Times Magazine,* 1 January: 31–38, 52.
Barabantseva, Elena. 2009. *Change vs. Order: Shijie Meets Tianxia in China's Interactions with the World.* Manchester: British Inter-University China Center, BICC Working Paper Series, No. 11.
Bender, Mark. 2004. "Review of Zhao Deguang, ed. (2003). *Ashima wenxian huibian* [A Collection of Ashima Literature]." *Asian Folklore Studies* 62, no. 1: 149–52.
Buchmann, Anne. 2006. "From Erewhon to Edoras: Tourism and Myths in New Zealand." *Tourism, Culture & Communication* 6, no. 3: 181–89.
Burawoy, Michael. 2000. "Introduction: Reaching for the Global." In *Global Ethnography: Forces, Connections and Imaginations in a Postmodern World,* ed. Michael Burawoy, Joseph Blum, Sheba George, Zsuzsa Gille, Teresa Gowan, Lynne Haney, Maren Klawiter, Steven Lopez, Seán Ó Riain, Miller Thayer. Berkeley: University of California Press.
Cadieux, Louise. 2007. "Shilin: Lost in the Stone Forest." *China Today,* http://www.chinatoday.com.cn/English/e2007/e200706/p28.htm (accessed 11 November 2007).
CCTV. 2006. "Honghe Trip II." http://english.cctv.com/program/travelogue/20060323/100594_4.shtml (accessed 4 June 2011).
China Discover. 2010. "Mile." http://www.chinadiscover.net/china-tour/yunnan-guide/Yunnan-honghe-mile.htm (accessed 4 June 2011).
CNTV. 2011. "Travelogue 2011-03-02 Ethnic Odyssey 2, Chuxiong: Yi Minority." http://english.cntv.cn/program/travelogue/20110302/103166.shtml (accessed 4 June 2011).
Delanty, Gerard. 2006. "The Cosmopolitan Imagination: Critical Cosmopolitanism and Social Theory." *The British Journal of Sociology* 57, no. 1: 25–47.
Ethnic China. 2009. "Keyi: A Museum Village of the Axi Yi." http://www.ethnic-china.com/Yi/yikeyi.htm (accessed 4 June 2011).

Formoso, Bernard. 2010. "Zomians or Zombies? What Future Exists for the Peoples of the Southeast Asian Massif?" *Journal of Global History* 5: 313–32.

Harrell, Stevan. 1995. "Introduction." In *Negotiating Ethnicities in China and Taiwan,* ed. Melissa Brown. China Research Monograph 46. Berkeley: University of California Institute of East Asian Studies.

In Kunming. 2010. "2nd Mile Axi Dancing Under the Moon Festival Kicks Off." http://en.kunming.cn/index/content/2010-08/10/content_2260611.htm (accessed 4 June 2011).

IUAES. 2007. "Agreements: IUAES Newsletter #69." http://www.glocol.osakau.ac.jp/iuaes/nl/069.html (accessed 30 May 2011).

———. 2009. "16th World Congress Handbook." Kunming: China Union of Anthropological and Ethnological Sciences.

Khampa Caravan. 2011. http://www.khampacaravan.com/ (accessed 4 June 2011).

Liétard, Alfred. 1904. "Les Ashi." *Les Missions Catholiques* 36: 93–96.

Merlan, Francesca. 2009. "Indigeneity: Global and Local." *Current Anthropology* 50, no. 3: 303–33.

Michaud, Jean. 2010. "Editorial: Zomia and Beyond." *Journal of Global History* 5: 187–214.

Nicholson, Sarah. 2011. "The Problem of Woman as Hero in the Work of Joseph Campbell." *Feminist Theology* 19, no. 2: 182–93.

Nyíri, Pál. 2010. *Mobility and Cultural Authority in Contemporary China.* Seattle: University of Washington Press.

Peng, Zhaorong, and Fang Lu. 2011. "Consuming Heritage: How Ethnic Groups Face the Heritage Tourism—A Case Study on the Fire-Worship Ritual of Yi Ethnic Group Used Upon the Mass Tourism." In *Exploring Ethnicity and the State through Tourism in East Asia,* ed. John Ertl. Report 13. Kanazawa: Kanazawa University Japan-China Intangible Cultural Heritage Project.

Phillimore, Jenny. 2002. "Women, Rural Tourism Employment, and Fun(?)." In *Gender/Tourism/Fun(?),* ed. Margaret Swain and Janet Momsen. Elmsford, NY: Cognizant Communication Corporation.

Salazar, Noel B. 2012. "Tourism Imaginaries: A Conceptual Approach." *Annals of Tourism Research* 39, no. 2: 863–82.

Scott, James C. 2009. *The Art of Not Being Governed: An Anarchist History of Upland Southeast Asia.* New Haven, CT: Yale University Press.

Selwyn, Tom. 1996. *The Tourist Image.* London: Wiley.

———. 2000. "Myth." In *The Encyclopedia of Tourism,* ed. Jafar Jafari. London: Routledge.

Shi, Junchao. 2000. "Ashima: Yongheng de meili yu xiaoying—Shilin xian da luyou xiandai de wenhua gainian" [Ashima: Effects of eternal charm—modern notions in Shilin County tourism]. In *Shilin Yizu* [Shilin Yi people], ed. He Yaohua and Ang Zhiling. Kunming: Yunnan Jiaoyu Chubanshe.

Swain, Margaret. 2005. "Desiring Ashima: Sexing Landscape in China's Stone Forest." In *Seductions of Place: Geographical Perspectives on Globalization and Touristed Landscapes,* ed. Caroline Cartier and Alan Lew. London: Routledge.

———. 2009. "The Cosmopolitan Hope of Tourism." *Tourism Geographies* 11, no. 4: 505–25.

———. 2011a. "Commoditizing Ethnicity for Tourism Development in Yunnan." In *Moving Mountains: Ethnicity and Livelihood in Highland China, Vietnam, and Laos,* ed. Jean Michaud and Tim Forsyth. Vancouver: University of British Colombia Press.

———. 2011b. "Ethnic Tourism and Indigenous Cosmopolitans." In *Exploring Ethnicity and the State through Tourism in East Asia,* ed. John Ertl. Report 13. Kanazawa: Kanazawa University Japan-China Intangible Cultural Heritage Project.

———. 2011c. "Franco-Catholic Modernizer Paul Vial: His Legacy Amongst the Sani Yi." In *Explorers and Scientists in China's Borderlands, 1880–1950,* ed. Denise Glover, Stevan Harrell, Charles McKhann, Margaret Swain. Seattle: University of Washington Press.

———. 2013. "Chinese Cosmopolitanism (Tianxia he Shijie Zhuyi) in China's Heritage Tourism." In *Cultural Heritage Politics in China,* ed. Tami Blumenfield and Helaine Silverman. New York: Springer.

Tucker, Hazel, and John Akama. 2009. "Tourism as Postcolonialism." In *The Sage Handbook of Tourism Studies,* ed. Tazim Jamal and Mike Robinson. Thousand Oaks, CA: Sage.

Xie, Chunbo. 2010. "Ecomuseum or Ethnic Cultural and Ecological Village? The Case of Safeguarding ICH in Monkey Lake Sani Village, Yunnan, China." http://www.sac.or.th/databases/fieldschool/?page_id=891 (accessed 28 May 2011).

Xinhua. 2009a. "Overseas Anthropologists: Adventure in Chinese Ethnic Village 'Eye Opening.'" http://news.xinhuanet.com/english/2009-07/30/content_1179 8026.htm (accessed 4 June 2011).

———. 2009b. "Yi Ethnic Group in S. China's Yunnan Province." http://news.xinhua net.com/english/2009-07/29/content_11792507_6.htm (accessed 13 December) 2011).

Xu, Judy. 2007. "Community Participation in Ethnic Minority Cultural Heritage Management in China: A Case Study of Xianrendong Ethnic Cultural and Ecological Village." *Papers from the Institute of Archaeology* 18: 148–60. http://pia-journal.co.uk/article/view/pia.307/416 (accessed 21 June 2011).

Yin, Shaoting. 2003. "A Work Report on the Project for Construction of Ethnic Cultural and Ecological Villages in China." *Chinese Sociology and Anthropology* 35, no. 3: 37–50.

Yunnan Adventure. 2009. "Axi Fire Worship Festival of Yi ethnic group in Mile County." http://www.yunnanadventure.com/YunnanGuide/Axi-Fire-Worship-Festival-of-Yi%20ethnic-group-in-Mile-County.html (accessed 4 June 2011).

Yunnan Explorer. 2010. "Yunnan Festivals: Axi Fire Worship." http://www.yunnen-explorer.com/festivals/hongwan/ (accessed 4 June 2011).

Yunnan Provincial Tourism Administration. 2011. "Xianrendong, a Fairytale of Pu-zhehei." http://en.ynta.gov.cn/Item/576.aspx (accessed 4 June 2011).

Zhao, Tingyang. 2009. "A Political World Philosophy in Terms of All-under-heaven (Tian-xia)." *Diogenes* 221, no. 1: 5–18.

Chapter 5

Tourism Moral Imaginaries and the Making of Community

João Afonso Baptista

"Our place," the British manager of an internationally distinguished eco-lodge located at the shore of Lake Niassa in Mozambique said, "is 100 percent sustainable and ethical, and part of the revenues goes directly to the communities around here." He had offered me an informal tour into the environmental technologies of the hand-built lodge. A few hours of conversation later, he commented on tourists' criticisms and how he tried to find solutions. After tourists complained about the indiscretion of the waterless toilets, for example, he engineered a system that directed a stream of water through the bowl but changed nothing about the mechanics of the waste removal system. Following the demonstration of the toilet flushing system, the manager whispered to me, "Tourism is all about illusions" (12 April 2008).

The plethora of new terms of virtuosity that academics and those in tourism have applied to represent tourists and leisure activity (e.g., responsible, sustainable, eco, green, sensitive) is part of a contemporary broad movement that Jim Butcher (2003) called "the moralization of tourism." Ethical tourism encompasses, perhaps better than any other designation, the quest for this movement, serving as an umbrella term to enclose all morally superior forms of being on holiday. Despite its benign character, we should not lose sight of the forces behind this movement, which are at the center of this chapter: the advent of ethical tourism has as much to do with the "modern moral order" in the North Atlantic societies (Taylor 2002) as with capitalizing on it. Concretely, the contemporary expansion of ethical forms of tourism run alongside the broader growth in demand for ethical goods

and services of "illusion" driven by psychological needs—to resort to Jacques
Lacan's (1977) conceptualization of imaginary—in "Northern" societies.

From an anthropological perspective, ethical tourism should be interpreted within the modern politics of lifestyle and the processes of subject
formation in tourist-consumers' own societies. The incorporation of these in
worldwide tourism activity has generated a wave of ethical "new tourisms"
(Mowforth and Munt 2009). With this expansion, new illusions, fantasies,
and imaginaries are materialized in the tourism arena. This chapter focuses
on one powerful imaginative construction that has emerged in tourism
as part of its moralization: the community. What are the forces operating
behind individuals' actions that inform spending holidays in, or donating
tourism revenues to, communities in Africa as manifestations of ethics in
modernity?

"Community-based," an ethical fashion in tourism, "undoubtedly, remains the option of choice for most nongovernmental organizations (NGOs)
and governmental agencies that include tourism in their developmental
portfolio" (Weaver 2010: 206). Although this may seem obvious, it is worth
emphasizing that the starting point for any community-based project is de-
marcating a specific group of people as "the community" (Sangameswaran
2008: 388). The question that therefore arises is: what makes a community
in, or for, tourism? Not surprisingly, the discussion around this *making* necessarily leads to an analysis extending beyond the field of leisure activity—if
one can surpass fields in an era where everything is increasingly mingled
(Bauman 2000)—namely, the hidden nature of the ethical consumer society.
Perhaps the central question should be simply: why is the concept of community used in the ethical way that it is?

By considering the growing popularization of community-based tourism, this work focuses on the implications that tourism moral imaginaries
have on the constitution of meanings in and of rural populations. I further
consider the centrality of local processes of appropriation and, in turn,
their role on the disposition of certain imaginaries, imaginaries that can
ultimately be capitalized on. As Benedict Anderson noted, "Communities
are to be distinguished ... by the style in which they are imagined" (2006: 6).
The imagined, however, is an essentially determined creation, and "reality"
and "rationality" are its products (Castoriadis 1975: 8). Along these lines, in
this chapter I critically analyze the global drivers behind the materialization
of the imaginary of community into *the group* according to which some rural
populations live. I attempt to demonstrate how the deterritorialized modali-
ties of power that induce the constitution of community as a moral subject
enable historically subjugated peoples to develop strategies of recognition
that meet the standards of *an* universalized ethic. These processes of local

legitimacy, it can be argued, come with an obvious cost: they camouflage a politics of ideological dominance mostly run by nongovernmental development regimes over those same peoples who vie for recognition.

COMMUNITY IN CANHANE

I conducted fieldwork in Mozambique for three months in 2006 and for almost the entirety of 2008. My goal was to study the implementation of the first community-based tourism project in the country, which took place in the southwestern village of Canhane. The project was not the outcome of an initiative of its residents. In 2001, the Maputo office of the Swiss NGO Helvetas was awarded funds from the United States Agency for International Development (USAID). The funds were distributed from the USAID branch located in Nelspruit, South Africa, and intended to support the construction and further maintenance of a lodge that would provide both a cultural experience for tourists and benefits to the local population. After several consultations in the district of Massingir, the village of Canhane was selected for the project. A lodge was built there and opened to tourists in May 2004.

The first time I spoke with the headman of Canhane in private was in February 2008. As soon as he started talking, one word emerged predominantly in his discourse: "community." Although he spoke Shangane, the local language of Canhane, he always said this word in Portuguese (*comunidade*). At one point, he said: "[T]he *comunidade* is benefiting from tourism, and because of tourism revenues the *comunidade* now has a new classroom, which helps the education of the children of the *comunidade*" (18 February 2008). In one single sentence, he used the term "community" three times, all in the context of the benefits of tourism. Interestingly, however, "community" is a foreign concept to Canhane, with no direct translation in Shangane—the closest concept is *munti,* which can roughly be translated as population. This means that the concept derives from a normative order that comes from elsewhere but that, despite its extrinsic origins, serves to represent the local society from within. Hence, there is a broader dimension to the use of the term "community" in Canhane. This rhetoric allows emblematizing the residents in accordance to an extrinsic, but self-identitarian, imaginary condition that values them.

As discussed below, the community of Canhane is an imaginary that can be explored, among other ways, by the analysis of the narratives supporting it. Yet, it is important to recognize the practical possibilities of imaginaries: they can be materialized. The performances matching the imaginary of community are what led Canhane to be an object of moral realization, organization, and consumption in tourism. In this chapter, I am interested specifically in what underlies the usage and appropriation of the imaginary of community for self-representation, particularly in the context of ongoing community-based ventures in the "South." What might the appropriation of the idea of community by the residents of Canhane reveal about the nature of the moral order in which they participate?

STORY WITH A PURPOSE

What I am going to report here was told to me by the elders of the village of Canhane: those residents who proclaimed themselves experts in local history. Hence, this is a story by the Canhaners about themselves. These narratives about the past define their sense and aspiration of "who we are today" and, in turn, determine relations in the present.

Before present-day Canhane was named, the area was known as Ngovene, meaning founded by the Ngovene family lineage. However, at some point, Ngovene was taken by a different ruling lineage—the Zithas. "All started," a resident explained to me, "when this place was under Valoi Ngovene's chieftaincy" (18 February 2008). Accordingly, on one occasion, a man called Marunzele Zitha arrived at the banks of the Elephants River, considered to be under Ngovene's rule. He was tired because he had been paddling on a wooden trunk and only using one oar. Therefore, he opted to stay for the next days, and while there, he fell in love with a woman whom he later married. The chief, Valoi Ngovene, offered him a parcel of land—approximately the same area of actual Canhane. Marunzele Zitha accepted the offer and established his life on that land with his wife.

At that time, the population of Ngovene had to pay an annual tax to the local chief. The payment was made through pits of canhu fruit. When the time came to pay, Marunzele Zitha and his family decided to mix almonds (the inner part of the pits of canhu) with dried human and animal feces, offering the mixture to the Ngovene chief. It was Marunzele Zitha's way of protesting the customary practice. His attitude was understood as a public manifestation of disrespect for tradition and local social order. He and his family were then named *vá canhane,* which means a group of people that is stubborn and breaks the rules. Valoi Ngovene was very angry and complained to Marunzele Zitha about his obstinate behavior. Soon after, Marunzele Zitha became sick and died. After his death, there was no rain in Ngovene. The population became extremely worried, and finally, a year later, the council of the residents consulted the local witch doctor, who informed them of the cause of the drought: Marunzele Zitha was angry with them. According to the witch doctor, the solution was to organize a cere-mony in which the *vá canhane*—Marunzele's descendants—had to participate. During the ceremony, it started to rain heavily. Afterward, the local chief and the elders of Ngovene decided to make peace with the *vá canhane* people and gave them another opportunity to be included in the local social life.

However, on another occasion, when the time to pay the tax again ar-rived, the oldest son of Marunzele Zitha, called Covane Zitha, decided to replace the mandatory pits with an elephant horn. Again, the population considered this a disobedient act in which the authority of the Ngovene chief was publicly challenged. This time, the council of the elders decided to kill Covane Zitha. But Valoi Ngovene, who as the local chief had the final say, did not accept this and opted to let Covane live according to his own rules. "This was when the community was born," said a resident after I had asked him about the origins of Canhane's territorial borders (26 January 2008). From the moment Valoi Ngovene gave independence to Covane's territory, Covane Zitha became known as *Canhane* (stubborn) and his lands as *the lands of Canhane,* which inevitably led to the later common use of the single word "Canhane" to refer to the area.

Fundamentally, the (hi)story of Canhane is a discourse of exclusivity. The stubborn personal attitude that is associated with the origin of the vil-lage represents the quest for uniqueness by its residents. Canhane is indeed the only village in the region that was not founded by the Ngovene lineage: "Canhane is Zitha," the headman's cousin once told me, "Zitha and Can-hane mean the same" (7 February 2008). However, more in line with what I want to focus on in this chapter, such a story of exclusiveness also serves to institutionalize in the present the locale and its residents as a moral and distinctive society: a community.

According to the residents' accounts, the subject formation of commu-nity was informed by the constitution of historical boundaries, by which Canhaners differentiate themselves from others—not just physically, but by extension also through their symbolic past. This view of community aligns with Anthony Cohen's suggestion that all communities are based on the symbolic construction of "map references with which the individual is so-cially oriented" (1985: 57). Following this interpretation, communities can be hypothetically conceptualized as institutional arrangements of demarca-tion, which nevertheless are driven by "radical imaginary"—to use Cornelius Castoriadis's (1986: 143) idea that acknowledging history is impossible with-out creative imagination.

In January 2008, I met with the director of the Mozambican NGO that took over the management of the community-based tourism project in Canhane after the Swiss Helvetas closed its offices in Maputo. He told me:

"When we first arrived there, they were much disorganized and not aware of their potential, and we had to hire a person to research their historical background. But now they changed completely, they are much empowered and already acting as a community" (18 January 2008). Explicitly, being a community empowers, and the "history of Canhane," as it is announced in the informative folders provided in the Covane Community Lodge to tourists, is important for that. Nonetheless, the empowerment of a certain group of people can only take place if, and only if, they engage in the broader system of values of those who manifest the intention to empower them. Concretely, the moral character of the tourism project in Canhane is what informs the "history of Canhane" and being a community as valuable assets, and thus as empowerment mechanisms. Therefore, the remembered history and the transmission structures of collective memory used for the constitution of the community of Canhane inform a certain "kind of truth": the "truth" of the past required by the circumstances of the present. This "truth" of Canhane is not neutral, and informs socioeconomic interests brought, as we will see, by nongovernmental regimes. The presentation of themselves and the fact that Canhaners' self-distinction is now, more than ever, an important matter, are part of the modern politics of legitimacy and recognition within these regimes (cf. Baptista 2012a). Underlined here is Canhaners' perception that their contemporary distinctiveness is valuable capital that legitimizes their participation in the broader tourism market and access to development opportunities.

In theoretical terms, the community that derives from this appears to be in line with the idea of "communities of memory" (Bellah et al. 1996; Booth 2006). In this context, the transmission of memories is used to foster collective identity, to support meaning, and to justify or challenge the present. The community of Canhane is based on a dominant (hi)story that, by reproducing a shared past, helps constitute the social background from which Canhaners produce their common sense of attachment to the land. As such, the community ultimately gets its internal coherence not only in a mythic past but also in the continuous reaffirmation of that same version of the past in the present. Tourism is a privileged field to attest to this strategic procedure. For example, one of the first official measures the residents took after being targeted for developing the tourism project was to decide the name of the lodge. They opted for "Covane," the name of their first community leader. That is, tourism served as a medium to express the relevance of a past in the present.

However, the link between their legendary past—Covane—and their quest for collective exclusivity in the present becomes more evident in their selection of the second word for the lodge: community. Canhaners wanted to transmit the idea that they were a socially coherent unit that emerged from Covane's rule over the territory. The lodge was therefore named "Covane Community Lodge." This naming process reflects their campaign for exclusiveness and indicates how imaginaries about the past can be objectified, maintained, and capitalized on through discourse and tourism practice.

The impact of collective memory in Canhane is also evident in the knowledge the residents have about the constitution of the village. The way this circulates internally is far more elaborated than the same kind of knowledge and its transmission in neighboring populations. Indeed, in the surrounding villages of Cubo and Tihovene, the residents seem to be much less aware of their local past. In the village of Cubo, for example, when I first asked the headman about their history, he quickly exclaimed: "I have no idea!" (17 October 2008). I had similar experiences in the village of Tihovene. Nevertheless, what might be at the core of such a distinction between these villages and Canhane is what both leaders told me to justify their lack of knowledge about the local history: "Nobody has asked me that before" (17 October 2008, for Cubo; 21 October 2008, for Tihovene).

As I already suggested, the contemporary interest in, and consciousness of, local history by the residents of Canhane derives from their introduction into a broader system that values them as an expression of community. In practice, and contrasting with the surrounding populations, the residents' engagement in their (hi)story is maintained, if not intensified, because they are continuously asked about it. More importantly, the relevance of their (hi)stories about themselves results from the importance they attribute to those who request the information, mostly tourists and "development experts" who visit the village. These people are perceived as a hope, an opportunity, and a way of integration in a broader system of possibilities that surpass the local, national, and even continental dimension.

The local (hi)story serves as an attribute for the constitution of the community of Canhane. But what gives the value of the local (hi)story in that process—or what Michel Foucault would have called "its conditions of emergence, insertion and function" (1972: 163)—is the background of those who ask about it. The social mores of the questioners are the framework that leads Canhaners to specific expectations that, finally, are to be met by their own condition—being a community. In general, what makes expectations a crucial force in tourism is the will for social and individual action, but also the ability to shape the sense of "who we are" in destination societies. Expectations are not just a set of ideas by anticipation; rather, they are what provide coherence to actions and consumption behavior (e.g., going to the Kruger National Park in South Africa to see the "big five"). The governing of expectations in the modern era means also the governing of consumption

practices. The expectations for the authentic, the underdeveloped, the exotic, the guilt-free, and the ethical are all typically driving forces in modern
tourism consumption.

The story the elders told me about their village is a product of *interaction,* of an external request that, nonetheless, for the residents serves to
strategize and make sense of their present collective lives. Following this
reasoning, the consequential institutionalization of Canhane as a community is a matter of the politics of legitimacy and recognition within a system
that involves Canhane's articulations with tourism and, as approached later,
development industries. The Mozambican village demonstrates how imaginaries are processes concretized by interaction (see Leite, this volume). But
more fundamentally, Canhane has to be understood within the nongovernmental galloping regimes that hover upon most of the "developing world"
and, by extension, the paradigms that these rely on. *The group* of Canhane is
a product(ion) of the modern moral order that induces capitalization on the
ideal of community in tourism.

SOCIAL MORAL ORDER

The context that allows individuals to make sense of any given act is limited,
for the simple reason that it does not encompass everything. Human mechanisms of perception are based on circumscribed images through which life
is understood. This is not to say, however, that all the background images of
each individual are static and necessarily in conformity with the established
social order. They may also invalidate it and instill disorderly practice, help-
ing the constitution of new meanings. As Zygmunt Bauman (2000) famously
suggested, we live under the constant blurring of solid frames of reference.
Yet, despite the contingent character of modernity, societies still have a basis
that provides their individuals with some sense of alliance. "Within this outlook," Charles Taylor argued, "what constitutes a society as such is the metaphysical order it embodies" (2002: 115). That is, the actions of individuals
in any society and the meanings they attribute to their and other actions
are allocated in a framework that binds them together. A crucial part of this
framework is what Taylor called the "moral order."

Taylor attributed the emergence of the modern moral order to Hugo
Grotius and John Locke, philosophers writing in the seventeenth century.
Since then, "this idea increasingly has come to dominate our political thinking and the way we imagine our society ... it tells us something about how
we ought to live together in society" (Taylor 2002: 92). The modern idea
of moral order became omnipresent in people's actions as "one in which

our purposes mesh, and each in furthering oneself helps the others" (Taylor 2002: 96). Taylor (2002: 93) noted that moral order has undergone an expansion in extension (more people live by it) and in intensity (the demands it makes are heavier and more ramified). Additionally, I would also suggest a third expansion: capitalizing on the very ideal of moral order. This expansion is mostly the outcome of late capitalism's forces and "neoliberal" ideologies, some of them driven by global development institutions that revolve around accessing financing for self-reproduction and (morally justified) external intervention.

Along these lines, the idea of moral obligation and rights that individuals and societies have in regard to one another have generated new fields of agency and market opportunities. The emergence of ethical modes of tourism, for example, can be integrated into such an expansion, in which a certain moral background is used to justify consumption, production, and business. But what makes Taylor's idea of a common moral background relevant for the arguments in this chapter is that it did not result from human invention: "it was designed by God," the author said (2002: 96). Taylor's analysis leads us to an obvious conclusion. Underlying the individuals' ways of making sense of the modern world is the ethics of human coexistence—the moral order—that in turn draws on the social imaginary as constructed by a greater being. In the same vein, Castoriadis argued that a "fundamental creation of the social imaginary, the gods or rules of behavior are neither visible nor even audible but *signifiable*" (1997: 183). Imaginaries are thus presented as crucial determinants in the way we "signify" our world, produce commonality (Leite, this volume), and constitute subjectivity. They support the articulations and distinctions of what matters and of what does not (Castoriadis 1975: 465), among other determinants, through prescribing what is to be moral. Therefore, imaginaries inform social moral order; they are normative; they constitute and are constituted by society; they provide the cognitive structure that allows humans to make sense of, lead to, and justify moral action; and, crucially, they are contemporary attributes for doing business. Castoriadis restated it in this way: "[T]o understand a society means, first and foremost, to penetrate or reappropriate the social imaginary significations which hold this society together" (1991: 85).

What I suggest, thus, is that we should keep Taylor's idea of imaginaries as informing the modern moral order in mind when analyzing community-based tourism. Why? Because community in this context is largely an institutionalized imaginary that constitutes and is constituted by the moral order in tourists' societies. As Salazar and Graburn observe in the introduction to this volume, "In the case of Western tourism to developing countries,

the circulating representations cater to certain images within Western consciousness about how the Other is imagined to be." Tourism imaginaries
do not exist in a vacuum. In practice, the institution of the imaginary of
community through tourism projects in the "South" embodies, materializes,
and animates the moral order in the very societies of those who quest for
community—the "North."

COMMUNITY AS LACK

There are certain words that carry so much emotional strength in tourism
that they only need to be read or heard to trigger the imagination of tourists. Take "safari" (the Swahili word for long journey), "wilderness" (which
derives from the Old English word "wildeor," meaning wild deer), or even
"African life" (to James Ferguson, this enters Western imagination as "simply a polite name for poverty" [2006: 21]). As is obvious by now, this chapter
is about yet another word. The focus is on the concept of community as an
ideal of a pure and pristine social bond; an imaginary impossible to realize
that, nonetheless, carries persuasive power and that becomes a *performance of
collective existence* for many people.

From national ministries (e.g., "Experience the Best of Dominica
through the Eyes of a Community")[1] to travel agencies (e.g., "reach and experience the heart of real South Africa in a small community")[2] and NGOs
(e.g., "Combine teaching and living in a Tanzanian community with adventure travel"),[3] references to community in tourism have become popular
(Salazar 2012). These attempts to capture the spirit of community are not
mere descriptions of an imaginary, but take part in the construction of the
idea of community itself; they create, reproduce, and validate tourists' expectations about an ideal. These in turn lead to creative agency and performative engagement by some of the populations in the destination areas in
order to meet such an ideal. Therefore, the discourse of community and its
circulation in tourism are not innocent. These are part of the marketing of
imaginaries that ultimately intends to profit from the strategic moral subject
of community. The question that remains is: what gives the imaginary of
community so much value and moral worth in tourism?

Before answering this question, it is important to acknowledge that, although "the idea of the loss and recovery of community may be seen as
together constituting the millennial tradition in Western thought" (Delanty
2010: 9), a clear definition of community remains a problem (Wolfe 2005:
10). Community relies on abstractions (Hart 1998: xxxiii); it represents the

aspiration of salvation (Kamenka 1982); it is symbolic (Cohen 1985); it indicates the "points of reference brought into play in particular situations and arenas" (Gusfield 1975: 41); it "is based on a subjective feeling of the parties" (Weber 1947: 136); it is the communion with the sacred (Augustine [1886] 2009); it addresses a utopian imagination of social relations in which "it is less and less clear whether the realities which the portraits of 'community' claim to represent are much in evidence, and if such realities can be found" (Bauman 2000: 169). As Gerard Delanty summarized it, "community has been an important basis of modern social relationships as an imaginary order" (2010: 36).

Despite its imaginary condition, what is certain is that the concept of community is situated, from the seventeenth century onward, in critiques of modernity. Classical sociologists saw the very idea of advancing modern society as being in opposition to the ideals underlying the moral order. The essential basis of this view was that human harmony, closeness, solidarity, and values of trust (what Ferdinand Tönnies (1988) attributed to the social unit of *Gemeinschaft*) were being replaced by competition, disharmony, and insecurity. Community became entrenched in the modern moral order as nostalgia about an imaginary past but also as a contemporary moral solution to problems caused by those same conditions brought about by modernity. In contrast to the impersonal modern era, community is "good because its members cooperate" (Tuan 2002: 307); it provides "a social organizational foundation for mobilization, as networks of kinship, friendship, shared crafts, or recreations offer lines of communication and allegiance" (Calhoun 1982: 897). As such, community means "hope and the wish of reviving … the closer, warmer, more harmonious type of bonds between people" (Hoggett 1997: 5).

To Bauman (2000), insecurity and precariousness play a crucial role in the modern recovery of community. For the author, the subjugation of modern life to motion, deterritorialization, and uncertainty leads to a diffuse anxiety about the present and the future. This, in turn, means precariousness and the propagation of conditions of insecurity. "We miss community," Bauman said, "because we miss security" (2001: 144). Accordingly, the vision of community complements this lack: it "is that of an island of homely and cozy tranquility in a sea of turbulence and inhospitality" (Bauman 2000: 182). However, such a source of peacefulness and coziness does not exist as a natural entity, except perhaps as a utopia (Delanty 2010: 91). In this sense, community was never lost, because it was never born. It offers only a comfortable illusion or promises a utopia (Delanty 2010: 91); a utopia, that is, primarily an imaginary, completing a lack.

THE MARKETING OF IMAGINARIES:
COMMUNITY IN TOURISM AND DEVELOPMENT

The social imaginary has a function: to satisfy social needs, aspirations, and fantasies. Hence, the birth of any imaginary can be linked to the context that gave, and gives, coherence to its formulation. The ongoing global popularity of the imaginary of community relies on the promise of the antithesis of social progress based on processes of individualization and competition in North Atlantic societies; that is, a safe haven, a dream destination, and groups to which people can belong or that they can trust forever. In tourism, the attractiveness of community is perhaps better understood through Nelson Graburn's idea of inversion. Graburn identified tourism as "one of those necessary breaks from ordinary life that characterizes all human societies" (1983: 11), a "ritual inversion" from everyday life. Facing the general pessimism over modern life, the contemporary attraction for communities lies in them as reproducing difference—inversion—for tourists.

In particular, the imaginary of communities in Africa has a moral significance. It encompasses a metaphorical moral world, an idyllic togetherness of "pure" structure of relationships, representing thus the inversion of individualized, competitive and precarious modern life that characterizes most tourists' home societies. In this sense, imagination proves to be an important element of modern subjectivity in constituting moral agency and making sense of ethical tourism consumption. The imaginaries that constitute the moral order in "Northern" tourists' societies bring new priorities, moral demands, and standards for action in the "South." In this sense, the tourists who consciously choose to go to community-based lodges have come to be referred to as inherent components of moral (and) development programs (Butcher 2003). This is manifested in terms of their ability to alleviate the underdevelopment innate to the imaginary of the communities they visit: the virtuous tourist has emerged (Baptista 2012b).

In practice, however, the use of the imaginary of community in tourism rests ultimately on the righteousness of consumption. Accordingly, as is implicit in tourism and development discourses, the product for sale in community-based tourism is not just any kind of product; it is a moral one, which means it has to match the imaginaries that constitute the modern moral order of the tourist-consumers. In assisting the commodification of the imaginary of community, the community-based tourism specialty is a response to the broader growth in demand for ethical goods and services mostly in, and for, Northern Atlantic societies. Community-based tourism is a product of this Northern context, and it is largely through this moral system of global regulation that communities in the "South," such as Canhane, are incorporated into the global tourism market and bound to specific rationalities of production and consumption.

Moreover, the underlying force that leads to such a capitalization on moral imaginaries is highly driven by nongovernmental regimes. The nongovernmental development industry capitalizes on the inherent images of purity, goodness, and poverty of communities in Africa, legitimizing a raison d'être for the development apparatus. As such, communities are discursively used in many development contexts. In Mozambique, from the offices of nongovernmental departments in cosmopolitan Maputo to the countryside, the term "community" has been productively appropriated for its developmental moral aptitude, namely, to ask for funds from international donors, with tourists being part of these (see Baptista 2011). In this sense, the use of discourses of community in development and, in turn, by the community members themselves helps constitute a space of inter/invention, in which the revenues generated (e.g., deriving from funds, donations, or tourism consumption) are morally justified through, and for, the imaginary of community. Consequently, those who constitute the imaginary—the community members—become locked into the regime of power and knowledge that the imaginary of community produces.

Frequently, advocates of community-based organizations (CBOs) highlight their character of empowerment. Yet they also emphasize that "CBOs need various forms of support to enable them to make a productive contribution to rural development" (Opare 2007: 256). In addition to other methods, and in the name of "community capacity building," such support is materialized through abundant consultations, courses, and workshops promoted at the local level. Following this logic, the community-based tourism enterprise in Canhane has justified numerous externally driven actions. Examples include codes of conduct for dealing with tourists (2004), a handicraft course (2005), a management training course (February 2008), English I (March–April 2008), a bartending course (July 2008), English II (October 2008), a course on conservation and sustainable planting methods (30 September to 4 October 2008), a course on "community ownership of land" (September 2008), a workshop on analysis and identification of profitable sections (6 October 2008) (see figure 5.1), and a waiter training course (1–5 December 2008).

Every action mentioned was funded by external organizations. The English I course in March and April of 2008, for example, was financed by "Spanish *mola* from the World Tourism Organization,"[4] as the director of the organizing Mozambican NGO said (1 April 2008). In practical terms, the tourism project has generated constant parallel funding for the participating NGOs, who invested it in "community capacity building." The predominance of such actions shows how the community-based tourism project has served as a way of introducing not only tourism and tourists, but also "development," its rationale, and its "experts" into a society that was constituted as a "community" exactly for that reason.

Chetan Kumar noted that "images of 'community' are central to issues of project implementation" (2005: 279), while Bauman observed that "all communities are *postulated;* projects rather than realities" (2000: 169). Inescapably, thus, the prevailing homogeneous moral rhetoric about community in the nongovernmental development industry should be perceived as a discursive strategy that assists in the moralization of interventions. However, what we should remember also here is that the images of community that Kumar mentioned and that legitimize project implementation are products of the moral imaginary order familiar to the "North." Therefore, using community, a core concept of that order, makes community-based projects more convincing, intrinsically good, implicitly assumed to have moral value, and potentially profitable. This is why the imagination plays a determinant role in constituting modern moral subjectivity, as ethics, justifying global intervention at the local level, and doing business.

In conclusion, the extensive system that reveals the imaginary of community as the moral subject of needs generates a field of inter/invention.

Figure 5.1. Workshop in Canhane (Copyright: J. Baptista).

A domain of reality that calls for help emerges, and ethical tourism and nongovernmental development industries self-identify as the appropriate mechanisms to intervene. The concept of community entails the moral imaginary through which "neoliberal" and nongovernmental institutions can best exercise their intentions. For that reason, the constitution of communities is an act of power, which corroborates Eva Brann's (1991) general idea of imagination as a world-shaping power. Quoting the director of the South Bakundu Forest Regeneration Project in Cameroon, Barrie Sharpe wrote: "If they don't have a 'community' we'll make them form one, and then we'll order them to participate" (1998, quoted in Kumar 2005: 280).

So far, I have attempted to show how the moral imaginary of community in tourism is imbedded in "neoliberal" and nongovernmental regimes. But what I still have not dealt with is how such an element of globalizing moral order is appropriated and reproduced by the local community's members. The following section addresses this issue.

THE VALUE OF COMMUNITY AND ITS MECHANISMS OF EXCLUSION

In October 2008, the Mozambican NGO working in Canhane organized another English course. The course was projected for fewer than fifteen attendees, which included a fisherman living in the neighboring village of Cubo who guided tourists through the Elephants River, showing them the local ways of fishing. On the second day of the course, a "development expert" from an international NGO based in Maputo and a representative from the Mozambique Ministry of Tourism attended the class. They had been invited by the Mozambican NGO to experience informally "community capacity building" and tourism impact in Canhane. During the class, the teacher, who was the receptionist at the lodge but also had the responsibility of "being the link between the community and the lodge" (25 January 2008), as he told me once, suggested the election of a class delegate. His proposal generated an aura of indecision in the room, so both the NGO and Ministry of Tourism representatives recommended the fisherman from the village of Cubo. However, the class proceeded without a definitive decision on the issue.

On the fourth day of the course, I met the fisherman at his home in Cubo. I asked him how the course was going. He said, "I don't know, and I don't care! I was kicked out of it the day after you and the other people from Maputo were there" (4 October 2008). Apparently, on the third day of the course, when the "development expert," the Ministry of Tourism representative, and myself were not present, the rest of the attendants accused him of not being a member of the community of Canhane and, therefore, unable to benefit from the English course. He told me, "They came with this stupid argument that I'm not from the community. But they forget that I'm the one who contributes more to them with my patience with the tourists … because, in the end, the majority of the money the tourists pay for my guiding tours goes to them, not to my family." Visibly irritated, he continued, "This is not the first time that such a thing happens … whenever foreigners interact with me in front of them, they act like, 'You are not from the community,' or 'We are the ones who need to be helped'!" The quarrel was later confirmed by the teacher of the English course.

Wayne Brockriede noted that a "rhetorical act occurs only within a situation, and the nature of that act is influenced profoundly by the nature of the encompassing situation" (1968: 12). This means that each rhetorical act fits into the characteristics of ongoing processes. Accordingly, the way the Canhaners speak about community must be understood within the broader situational context that gives it relevance and meaning. Being in the community is, in the ongoing community-based process, a value, an opportunity, and therefore needs to be exclusionary: "You are not from the community."

As with all symbolic creations, being the community must continually be revived and sustained by discourse. Canhaners' discourse of community is informed by a reflexive self-validating quality in accordance with an imaginary order from the "North," an universalized imaginary order that structures tourism consumption worldwide, allowing the expansion of production of moral goods and services to the core of rural populations in the "South"—in particular, something that the tourist's home culture has lost, such as the sense of purity, spirituality, closeness to nature, and the condition of community. The discourse of community has colonized the Canhaners' discourse about themselves, which in turn has become a discourse of opportunity that meets the normative standards for "neoliberal" market integration. By adopting such a discourse, the local residents engage in rhetoric as a process of adjusting people to ideas. More precisely, when speaking about community, the Canhaners create and authorize an entity that did not exist as such before the implementation of the tourism project by the nongovernmental institution. As such, the Canhaners constitute themselves as the proof of what is said, incarnating and validating a morally justified target for both tourism and development. This attests to the idea that the globalization of the imaginary order in the "South" may produce new forms of locality based on the production and performance of morals ("We are the ones who need to be helped"), but that are in line with broader "neoliberal" and nongovernmental ideals.

In Canhane, community is an enabling concept: adopting that trademark enables the residents to be a niche market and thus be part of the modern world. In this sense, numerous Canhaners strategically incorporate and exercise such an externally given position and participate in development ideology by projecting the act of being helped into the sphere of ethical tourism. Indeed, the community of Canhane is a product of the confluence of interests between development and tourism (Salazar 2004). Fundamentally, the Canhaners have adopted the rhetorical force (community) that best represents and expresses them in a market context in which development and tourism merge into each other: *developmentourism* (Baptista 2011). In sum, Canhaners, as a community, are being organized and constitute themselves not only as a market but also as specialized producers in, and of, developmentourism.

CONCLUSION

I am currently living in rural Angola, in a place that, by the same logic explained above, could be seen as a "community." It counts no more than 550 people and the housing area does not exceed 14 square kilometers—characteristics somehow similar to the Mozambican village of Canhane. However, to my knowledge, nobody refers to this constellation as a community. The residents present it as Cusseque or just "the neighborhood" (*o Bairro*). Angolans in general—the ones who know it—call it the Village of Cusseque (*Aldeia de Cusseque*). The governmental authorities are more formal and prefer to use its official name: Village of Cusseque in the Municipality of Chitembo (*Aldeia de Cusseque no Município de Chitembo*). Contrary to Mozambique and Canhane, such community-less naming is not only common but also institutional in southeast Angola. The most obvious explanation for this, perhaps, is that Cusseque was never targeted by nongovernmental development and tourism industries.

But why mention the Angolan village of Cusseque now? Cusseque is simply the place where I am currently conducting fieldwork. There is a risk in elaborating this in the final part of this chapter. To write a scientific text while conducting fieldwork has traditionally been considered a methodological mistake. "The field" in anthropology carries for the researcher the aura of mysticism, charm, discovery, and loneliness, but not of clairvoyance. My intention of revealing the fieldwork's context of my writings, however, is not to minimize the scientific relevance of my work. On the contrary, this chapter is as legitimate as if it were written in any other *space of rationality*.

By revealing the circumstances in which these pages were written, I intend to touch on the core of the chapter: the faculty of the imagination in the constitution of authoritative realities. "The field" in anthropology shares the same realm of "community" in the developmental and touristic Canhane, because both are a product of the imaginary that, in turn, assists in organizing knowledge and agency. This means that, although Marxist visions see modern society as being essentially a product of absolute rationality, imaginaries play a central role in structuring these same processes of rationalization, and anthropology is not an exception. This ethnographic work is thus by itself a contestation of an authoritative imaginary—"the field"—structuring the anthropological rational.

It is widely argued today that knowledge is a product of power. Like rationality, power is regulated by the mental structure that produces it: the imaginary. Following from this, through institutionalizing certain peoples as communities—conspicuously via discourse—nongovernmental and "neoliberal" regimes produce knowledge through which they subject them. In Canhane the tourism moral imaginary of community is a system of meaning. It constitutes the modern version of "who we are." However, such an imaginary also operates and becomes important within broader existing systems of meaning and power—in particular dictated by the ethical market. Therefore, inducing such an imaginary in Canhane means trapping or encasing Canhaners within a normative condition derived from the moral order of the "North," which they do not control.

Most importantly, I suggest that we should be more suspicious about community as an axiomatic term and treat it instead as an ideology of interests. The imaginary of community in tourism is a "Northern" response to the disappointment with progress. But community must be understood as being more than in tension with modern society. It is also an expression of modernity that has become central to some peoples' lives, such as the residents of Canhane. Nevertheless, and perhaps above all, the deeper impulse behind the moral imaginary of community is the willingness to imagine a better world.

NOTES

1. Ministry of Tourism and Legal Affairs of Dominica, http://www.community tourism.dm (accessed 16 September 2011).
2. Real Gap, http://www.realgap.com/Africa (accessed 18 September 2011).
3. Frontier, http://www.frontier.ac.uk/projects/78/Tanzania-Adventurer (accessed 18 September 2011).

4. In Mozambique, money is commonly referred to as *mola* ("spring" in English). Its connotation derives from the fact that money allows people to move.

REFERENCES

Anderson, Benedict. (1983) 2006. *Imagined Communities.* London: Verso.

Augustine. (1886) 2009. *The City of God.* Peabody, MA: Hendrickson Publishers.

Baptista, João. 2011. "The Tourists of *Developmentourism*: Representations 'From Below.'" *Current Issues in Tourism* 14, no. 7: 651–67.

———. 2012a. "Tourism of Poverty: The Value of Being Poor in the Non-governmental Order." In *Slum Tourism: Poverty, Power and Ethics,* ed. Fabian Frenzel, Ko Koens, and Malte Steinbrink. London: Routledge.

———. 2012b. "The Virtuous Tourist: Consumption, Development, and Nongovernmental Governance in a Mozambican Village." *American Anthropologist* 114, no. 4: 639–51.

Bauman, Zygmunt. 2000. *Liquid Modernity.* Cambridge: Polity Press.

———. 2001. *Community: Seeking Safety in an Insecure World.* Cambridge: Polity Press.

Bellah, Rellah, Richard Madsen, William Sullivan, Ann Swidler, and Steven Tipton. 1996. *Habits of the Heart: Individualism and Commitment in American Life.* Berkeley: University of California Press.

Booth, James. 2006. *Communities of Memory: On Witness, Identity, and Justice.* New York: Cornell University Press.

Brann, Eva. 1991. *The World of the Imagination: Sum and Substance.* Lanham, MD: Rowman & Littlefield.

Brockriede, Wayne. 1968. "Dimensions of the Concept of Rhetoric." *Quarterly Journal of Speech* 54: 1–12.

Butcher, Jim. 2003. *The Moralization of Tourism: Sun, Sand … and Saving the World?* London: Routledge.

Calhoun, Craig. 1982. *The Question of Class Struggle: Social Foundations of Popular Radicalism during the Industrial Revolution.* Chicago: University of Chicago Press.

Castoriadis, Cornelius. 1975. *L'institution et l'imaginaire.* Paris: Seuil.

———. 1986. *Instituição Imaginária da Sociedade.* Rio de Janeiro: Paz e Terra.

———. 1991. *Philosophy, Politics, Autonomy: Essays in Political Philosophy.* Oxford: Oxford University Press.

———. 1997. *World in Fragments: Writings on Politics, Society, Psychoanalysis and the Imagination.* Palo Alto, CA: Stanford University Press.

Cohen, Anthony. 1985. *The Symbolic Construction of Community.* London: Tavistock.

Delanty, Gerard. 2010. *Community.* London: Routledge.

Ferguson, James. 2006. *Global Shadows: Africa in the Neoliberal Order.* Durham, NC: Duke University Press.

Foucault, Michel. 1972. *The Archaeology of Knowledge.* London: Tavistock.

Graburn, Nelson. 1983. "The Anthropology of Tourism." *Annals of Tourism Research* 10, no. 1: 9–33.

Gusfield, Joseph. 1975. *Community: A Critical Response.* Oxford: Blackwell.

Hart, Roderick. 1998. "Introduction: Community by Negation: An Agenda for Rhetorical Inquiry." In *Rhetoric and Community: Studies in Unity and Fragmentation,* ed. Michael Hogan. Columbia: University of South Carolina.

Hoggett, Paul, ed. 1997. *Contested Communities: Experiences, Struggles, Policies.* Bristol: Policy Press.

Kamenka, Eugene, ed. 1982. *Community as a Social Ideal.* New York: St. Martin's Press.

Kumar, Chetan. 2005. "Revising 'Community' in Community-Based Natural Resource Management." *Community Development Journal* 40, no. 3: 275–85.

Lacan, Jacques. 1977. "The Mirror Stage as Formative of the Function of the I." Trans. A. Sheridan. In *Écrits: A Selection,* ed. Jacques Lacan. New York: W. W. Norton.

Mowforth, Martin and Ian Munt. (1998) 2009. *Tourism and Sustainability: Development, Globalisation and new Tourism in the Third World.* New York: Routledge.

Salazar, Noel B. 2004. "Developmental Tourists vs. Development Tourism: A Case Study." In *Tourist Behavior: A Psychological Perspective,* ed. Aparna Raj. New Delhi: Kanishka Publishers.

———. 2012. "Community-Based Cultural Tourism: Issues, Threats and Opportunities." *Journal of Sustainable Tourism* 20, no. 1: 9–22.

Sangameswaran, Priya. 2008. "Community Formation, 'Ideal' Villages and Watershed Development in Western India." *Journal of Development Studies* 44, no. 3: 384–408.

Opare, Service. 2007. "Strengthening Community-Based Organizations for the Challenges of Rural Development." *Community Development Journal* 42, no. 2: 251–264.

Taylor, Charles. 2002. "Modern Social Imaginaries." *Public Culture* 14, no. 1: 91–124.

Tuan, Yi-Fu. 2002. "Community, Society, and the Individual." *Geographical Review* 92, no. 3: 307–18.

Tönnies, Ferdinand (1957) 1988. *Community and Society.* New Brunswick: Transaction Books.

Weaver, David. 2010. "Community-Based Tourism as Strategic Dead-End." *Tourism Recreation Research* 35, no. 2: 206–208.

Weber, Max. 1947. *Social and Economic Organization.* New York: Free Press.

Wolfe, Alvin. 2005. "Network Perspectives on Communities." *Structure and Dynamics: eJournal of Anthropological and Related Sciences* 1, no. 4: 1–25.

Part II

Imaginaries of Places

Chapter 6

The Imaginaire Dialectic and the Refashioning of Pietrelcina

Michael A. Di Giovine

Since the inception of tourism studies in the 1970s, the notion of tourist imaginaries has factored into numerous research projects, management plans, and tourism models—though to varying degrees, directness, and methodological rigor. In general, these and other studies have helpfully revealed how tourism is both an individual and collective endeavor; how various groups imagine the same sites differently, and employ different strategies for defining the place in accordance with their varied ideologies; how such notions are diffused across geographic, linguistic, and cultural barriers; and ultimately how places are "made" not solely in the physical sense, but in the varied and disparate minds of those who profess membership in the equally diverse social worlds surrounding these sites. But while many notions of the "imaginary" center on the imaginative, the remembered, the narrative, or the otherwise *immaterial*, we must remember that they often crystallize as tangible re-presentations that physically circulate, and often materially shape and impact sites. As archaeologist Kathleen Morrison reminds us, "Places are created, imbued with meaning, argued over, changed, remembered and forgotten, but to see them simply in terms of ideas is to miss their critical phenomenological and material dimensions" (2004: 5; see also Morrison 2009). In this chapter,[1] I examine the material and immaterial changes in a small town—the result of newfound interest in the village by tourists and religious devotees of a contemporary Catholic saint born there—to posit the existence of an "imaginaire dialectic,"[2] an ongoing process whereby imaginaries based on tangible events and images are formed in the mind, materially manifested, and subsequently responded to, negotiated, and contested through the creation of tangible and intangible re-presentations.

TOURIST IMAGINARIES IN THE LITERATURE

Tourism is a voluntary, temporary, and perspectival interaction with place and especially the peoples contained within it (Di Giovine 2009: 57). As a form of sightseeing (or site-seeing), tourism is predicated on the visual, or, better, on perception (Di Giovine 2009: 155–56; cf. Urry 2002). The seductive draw of destinations is at once immaterial and material, imagined and "authentic" in every meaning of the word. Although the term "imaginary" became a popular buzzword in anthropology only toward the end of the 1990s (Strauss 2006: 233), when globalization theory challenged traditional notions of geopolitically situated communities (cf. Giddens 1990; Harvey 1991; Robertson 1992), the notion of place and community as largely imagined entities was embraced by social science at least as early as Benedict Anderson's seminal *Imagined Communities* (1983), although Marxists and 1970s structural anthropologists had certainly conceptualized the "imagined" earlier (often as an obscuring, superstructural force).

Yet it was Daniel Boorstin, in his book *The Image: A Guide to Pseudo-Events in America* ([1961] 1994), who, probably unwittingly, first associated this term with tourism, and in the process provided the impetus for a fruitful debate that gave birth to the serious social scientific study of tourism. In short, Boorstin argued that tourism revolves around inauthentic pseudoevents; and that contemporary tourists seek out these superficial, hollow re-presentations of romanticized ideas that exist largely in the mind. Writing in part as a response to Boorstin (Di Giovine 2009: 165), Dean MacCannell argued in his watershed work *The Tourist* that tourists were genuine yet often unwitting in their quest to encounter these romantic imaginaries; unable to fulfill these lofty desires, the travel industry itself perpetuates "staged authenticity" ([1976] 1999: 98). MacCannell further revealed the importance of tourist images and imagined concepts in his semiotic theory of how a tourist attraction is formed through a site-visitor-marker synergy, while Valene Smith ([1977] 1989) the next year addressed the importance of such imaginaries—particularly in the form of photographs and souvenirs—upon a traveler's return home.

One can likewise cite Dennis O'Rourke's ethnographic film *Cannibal Tours* (1988), Mary Louise Pratt's *Imperial Eyes* (1992), and Edward Bruner and Barbara Kirshenblatt Gimblett's seminal essay "Maasai on the Lawn" (1994) as major contributions to understanding how imaginaries are packaged and performed for tourists. Such emphasis has continued to the present day. Mike Robinson and David Picard's edited volume *The Framed World* (2009) stands as quite possibly the most thorough examination of the role of photography in creating and disseminating particular tourist imaginaries to date (see also Crang 1997). The role of the producers of these imaginaries have also been examined: in *The Heritage-scape: UNESCO, World Heritage, and Tourism* (2009), I examined how the narratives of "unity in diversity" are shaped, contested, and diffused—in text and image, in conservation practices, and in management plans—for tourists by UNESCO and its collaborating stakeholders through its World Heritage Convention.

Building on Hegel ([1834] 1956) and Said (1994), Peter Merrington (2001) examined Orientalist "colonial and imperial imaginary" and its indigenous reception in tourism development within postcolonial states in Africa, while both Yael Zerubavel (1995) and Nadia Abu El-Haj (2001) analyzed the ways in which contested archaeological sites in Israel are imbued with changing imaginaries of the ancient Levant for touristic consumption (domestic and foreign). Panivong Noriendr (1996), Penny Edwards (2007), and Tim Winter (2007) all examined how colonial imaginaries were converted into nationalist representations in postcolonial Cambodia's attempts to present itself, in part, to Western tourists. While these and similar works often portray tourism as an act of playing out colonial imaginaries, the aforementioned works of Pratt and Bruner and Kirshenblatt-Gimblett remind us that the tourist space is a liminal contact zone (Pratt 1992) that necessitates acts of mediation and translation; in an almost Goffmanian way (cf. Goffman 1967), tourist practices anticipate, negotiate, and re-present the Other's imaginaries. Indeed, Noel Salazar's monograph, *Envisioning Eden* (2010a), examined the all-important mediatory role of tour guides in developing countries for translating, negotiating, and explaining regional and national imaginaries to outsider visitors.

Justifiably, most of these studies build on mediation theory, and helpfully analyze with great ethnographic rigor a particular form of mediation—Salazar's aforementioned examination of tour guides in developing countries is an example par excellence, since guides straddle both realms of insiders and outsiders, and are capable of (and employed particularly for the purpose of) translating local concepts into imaginaries that are intelligible to outsiders (cf. Katriel 1997). Still other works deeply examine a particular point within the trajectory of this mediatory experience—an image's creation, dissemination, or reception.

Yet the reality of tourism is that there are many mediators at work simultaneously, and there are just as many tourist imaginaries as there are tourists. Indeed, elsewhere I have argued that tourism is not predicated solely on a host-guest dichotomy, but rather is created through a Bourdieuian "field" of production (Bourdieu 1993): a structured, totalizing set of relationships, often in conflict, that order a diversity of "epistemic cultures" (Knorr-Cetina 1999)—systems of groups with their own culturally specific knowledge, cosmologies, and ritualized practices that transcend geographic boundaries—who struggle to stake their claim to, define, and ultimately utilize the imaginaire of the site or destination (cf. Di Giovine 2009: 9, 21–22, 42–48; Di Giovine 2012a). This is thus a much more complex process, as all parties in the touristic experience simultaneously produce, receive, and reproduce these imaginaries—often with much contestation, negotiation, and "position-taking." It is therefore apropos to take a step back and examine the process from a macroscopic perspective, from the point of view of this total "field."

In this chapter, I examine how tourist imaginaries impact, both tangibly and intangibly, the southern Italian village of Pietrelcina. While small, the town welcomes some six hundred thousand religious tourists from around the world, thanks to global devotion to its favorite son, the twentieth-century Capuchin friar and stigmatic St. Padre Pio of Pietrelcina. In the span of a decade, Pietrelcina has completely refashioned itself in relation to other imaginaries of Pio, promulgated by various epistemic groups within the cult's field of production: the Capuchin friars at Pio's shrine in San Giovanni Rotondo, the Vatican, the international media, tour operators, service providers, devotees and secular tourists, locals, and a powerful, global network of prayer groups. In detailing the diverse and contested re-presentations of Pietrelcina and Padre Pio, it seems that such radical alterations in the very sociocultural and architectural bones of the town is not the product of simple mediation within a linear trajectory of production, dissemination, and consumption, but rather is articulated through what I term the "imaginaire dialectic," a complex process of presenting, imagining, re-presenting, and re-imagining site materiality within the field of touristic production at a site. While this dialectic is a lengthy and ongoing process that is obscured through time as imaginaries are modified and re-presented, thanks to the relatively recent occurrence of this phenomenon at Pietrelcina, this case study helpfully reveals many of the diverse refractions of tourist imaginaries, illustrating the imaginaire dialectic at work.

THE IMAGINAIRE DIALECTIC

The term "imaginary" has sparked several different, and often competing, definitions throughout its long history. For my usage, I draw on several aspects of this intellectual history, but it is best to clarify that I do not intend for "imaginary" to mean an abstract "ethos" or cultural schema composed of symbolic structures, in Castoriadis's terms ([1975] 1987), nor an individuals' psychosocial map, as Lacan defined it ([1949] 1977)—for the latter, I'm partial to Wallace's (1956, 2003) similar, and, I think, more evocatively termed concept of a "mazeway" that an individual feels he must negotiate. I also do not use the term "imaginary" as a code word for pure fantasy or illusion, as Marxists like Althusser ([1970] 1971) have done. Imaginaries are authentic—they are real in the sense that they serve to frame and provide meaning for a tourist site, sometimes even crystallizing in tangible images and written narratives.

Rather, by "imaginaries" I mean the constantly deepening, individually instantiated mix of remembered narratives and images that serve to inform an object or place's meaning. This follows Salazar's definition of an imaginary as the "representational assemblages that mediate the identification with Self and Other ... schemas of interpretation rather than explicit ideologies" (2010a: 6–7), which builds on Vogler's evocative characterization of imaginaries as "complex systems of presumption—patterns of forgetfulness and attentiveness—that enter subjective experience as the expectation that things will make sense generally" (2002: 625). Salazar's use of the term "representational assemblages" is important in this definition, for it references the fact that imaginaries are a finely woven fabric of re-presentations and mental images that will inevitably modify, deepen, and change over time.

This ongoing process of modification is the "imaginaire dialectic." By "dialectic," I am referencing the Hegelian process whereby pure being is contradicted or contested, then contradicted and contested again (Hegel [1807] 1977: 111–18)—much like an image in a hall of mirrors reflects its opposite, then reflects the opposite of that again, and so on. Indeed, Lacan (1977) had already intimated that an imaginary is the fruit of such a dialectical process when he likened it to a child's image in a mirror. Yet, I wish to better tease out the difference between an "imaginaire" as a thing (or notion), and the "imaginaire dialectic," which is the process by which the thing constantly forms and re-forms. As a "secular ritual" (Graburn 2001), tourism cultivates this process of animating and contesting imaginaries not only between people or groups, but within the very minds of individuals; they are formed while planning and preparing for a tour (the ritual's "separation" or preliminary phase), they are contested and negotiated as the tourist interacts with the place in situ (the liminal phase), and finally they are processed, reformulated, re-presented, and disseminated upon "re-aggregation" at home (Di Giovine 2009: 155–85). What I argue here is that this process is multiplied dialectically as diverse individuals from different epistemic groups interact with the site and each other; they react to, contest, and stake positions on each other's imaginaries, and finally re-present their own, new imaginaries about the place in text and image, oral narrative, and material preservation. Ultimately, meaning and materiality is re-formed through such a dialectical process, this "imaginaire dialectic."

THE IMAGINAIRE DIALECTIC AT WORK IN PIETRELCINA

This process of forming and re-forming imaginaries is just what occurred in Pietrelcina, Padre Pio's birthplace. A small, isolated town of three thousand inhabitants from six major extended families who traditionally made their living on self-sufficient farming, Pietrelcina is located in one of the poorest regions of Italy, and one that is the most resistant to change (Davis 1998). Its people are highly devotional; they honor their patroness, the Madonna della Libera, with two annual festivals in remembrance of when she liberated the town from a cholera outbreak in 1854.

Padre Pio was born into this highly religious, kinship-oriented environment on 25 May 1887, was ordained in 1910 after several illnesses, and celebrated his first Mass on the altar with Mary's holy effigy the following Sunday. Later that year, Pio experienced a vision of Jesus and Mary while sitting under an elm tree at his farm in the countryside of Piana Romana, immediately outside the town, where he herded sheep. This vision left red marks and extreme pain in his hands, side, and feet—an "invisible stigmata," as hagiographers now call it. They went away after a year, and in 1918, Pio was sent to a small Capuchin friary in the remote town of San Giovanni Rotondo, 135 kilometers away, never to return. It was in the choir loft of this friary that Pio, praying to God to be a sacrificial victim to end the slaughter of World War I and the Spanish flu that was decimating the region, received the physical stigmata in late 1918 that catapulted him and San Giovanni Rotondo into the international religious tourism track. Within a year, the town averaged five hundred pilgrims a day (Saldutto 1974:125; Luzzatto 2009: 42); this number grew exponentially as images and stories of Pio and his miraculous abilities to cure the sick spread throughout the international press. Devotees were frenzied: "locals and outsiders reached the point of penetrating the convent armed with scissors, to furtively steal what was perceived from afar as relics: the crowd ... cut pieces of his vestments, shirts, belts, even the chairs that Padre Pio sat on" (Allegri 1999: 185).[3] They were drawn by word of mouth, aided by the swift distribution of *santini,* wallet-sized prayer cards, emblazoned with an image of his bleeding hand on them.

National and international newspapers also played a major part in disseminating images and narratives of Pio and his thaumaturgic abilities from the very beginning of Pio's ministry. The first published miracle occurred on 30 May 1919–less than a year after Pio received his stigmata–when an Italian infantryman, Antonio Colonnello, whose leg was paralyzed after a grenade explosion in World War I, told reporters that his leg was healed "completely and instantaneously" after Pio's stigmatized hand touched it (*Il Giornale d'Italia* 1919). Stories of such encounters quickly circulated, particularly concerning Pio's disposition toward those who would come for the sacrament of reconciliation; it was believed he knew one's sins before they were confessed. He was frequently gruff with those who came out of curiosity rather than out of contrition. An Italian immigrant in America told me that a skeptic from the countryside around Benevento came to visit Pio, who said to him, "I know you don't believe in me; why did you come?" Pio then took the visitor's thumb between two fingers and pressed down so hard it left a black mark in the shape of Pio's silhouette; it would stay with the visitor the rest of his life, and he would proudly show it off as a badge of honor. Viscerally fusing narrative and visual images, such first-person testimonies were (and continue to be) extremely powerful in constructing and diffusing imaginaries of Pio, inside and outside of Italy (see, e.g., Keane 2008; Rega 2009), and in fostering pilgrimage to the sanctuary, where they would be called upon, compared, and negotiated against individual pilgrims' own experiences with Pio or his tomb–consequently coalescing into new imaginaries in a dialectical fashion.

This process also led to the development of San Giovanni Rotondo and its touristic infrastructure. With donations from devotees and pilgrims, Pio constructed an immense hospital, the Casa Sollievo della Sofferenza (the Home for the Relief of Suffering), to help deal with the influx of sick pilgrims in 1956; and just months before his death in 1968, a larger church dedicated to the Madonna della Grazia (Our Lady of Grace) was inaugurated. But while San Giovanni grew exponentially thanks to imaginaries of a thaumaturgic friar who could heal the sick, knew one's sins before they confessed them, and bore the marks of Christ's crucifixion, Pietrelcina was clearly left behind. Pilgrims in search of healing had no reason to visit Pio's obscure birthplace when they could commune directly with him; this conceptualization continues even after his death. Numerous tour sponsors in Ireland and Italy state that they have little desire to make the detour to Pietrelcina when the object of their devotion is Pio's tomb; of the six million annual pilgrims, only 10 percent stop in Pietrelcina.

From early on, the residents of San Giovanni Rotondo–the Sangiovannesi–were aware of the special "resource," so to speak, that their town was given. The Vatican attempted several times throughout Pio's ministry to suppress his cult, which it believed was the product of misguided popular piety; an early attempt to move Pio resulted in extreme protest and political maneuvering on the part of locals. One fanatic even charged up to Pio with a pistol and shouted, "Better dead among us than alive for others!" (Pio da Pietrelcina 2008: 398–99). San Giovanni Rotondo also "embargoed" Pio's relics after the friar's death; in the absence of any relics during the period of Pio's public exhibition (*ostensione*) in 2008–9, Pietrelcina made several futile requests to exhibit Pio's body temporarily in the town (cf. Di Giovine 2011a). Likewise, in 2013, the townspeople of San Giovanni Rotondo rose up when a Capuchin spokesman announced that the order was going to bequeath the reliquary containing Pio's heart to Pietrelcina; after civic authorities collected nearly one thousand signatures and threatened to appeal to Pope Francis, the Capuchin order relented. And threatened by the ascendant popularity (and impending canonization) of Mother Theresa and Pope John Paul II, the shrine has diffused images of the two soon-to-be saints venerating Pio's tomb, symbolically linking their growing cults with San Giovanni Rotondo–centric imaginaries.

When Pio was still alive, Pietrelcinesi were not only cognizant of their marginalization, but also felt entitled to the fruits of his internationally spreading cult. In several instances, Pietrelcinesi visiting Pio asked him why he allowed San Giovanni Rotondo to reap the material benefits of pilgrimage (including wealth, infrastructural development, and "traffic") while his hometown stagnated. Pio made reference to both the past and the future in his purported two-part answer. First, he reminded them that "Jesus was in Pietrelcina, and everything happened there." Second, he promised, "I have valorized San Giovanni in life, Pietrelcina I will valorize in death" (Da Prata and Da Ripabottoni 1994: 160, 163). Although these oft-recited quotes are believed to constitute a prophecy for Pietrelcina's regeneration after Pio's death in 1968, Pietrelcinesi did not immediately see Pio's promise fulfilled. Though the sites associated with Pio's birth and invisible stigmata were set aside as shrines, there is also little indication that locals attempted a concentrated effort to develop tourism in the region. Few material improvements were made to the town's infrastructure, the main streets were a patchwork of asphalt and stones, and abandoned homes were left to decay.

Yet Pietrelcinesi began to contest the predominant imaginaries that envisioned San Giovanni Rotondo as the axis mundi of the cult through narrative and image. In particular, they self-published a number of Pietrelcina-centric hagiographies that focused on the first thirty years of Pio's life, linking him with their town's history (cf. Montella 1987; Tretola 1988; Bonavita 1989). These narratives provided the earliest concretized imaginaries of Pio's connection with Pietrelcina for public consumption. They were less a marketing endeavor than the fruit of an acute need to "set the record straight" in the minds of Pietrelcinesi, who viewed Pio not as a patron saint—an "intimate, invisible friend"—like the worldwide network of devotees (including Sangiovannesi), but rather through a kinship idiom as a family member (Di Giovine 2012a, 2012b): Pietrelcinesi had already been naming their children "Pio," praying to him, decorating their homes with his images, and orally circulating stories about their personal experiences with him (as the Italian immigrant with the mark of Pio on his thumb did).

The imaginaries valorizing Pietrelcina as the foundation of Pio's ministry originally complemented the particular hagiographic understanding of Pio that was solidifying around San Giovanni Rotondo, thanks to a particularly effective marketing machine run by the Capuchin friars, who founded no less than five magazines, a publishing house, a radio station, and, in the present day, a satellite TV station and an Internet site—in all, an endeavor that nets over 120 million euro per year (*Italy Magazine* 2008). It also both reflected and set the stage for increased interest in Pietrelcina by Vatican experts and devotees following Pope John Paul II's formal opening of Pio's canonization process in 1982 (the *nihil obstat*). As the media reported on happenings within the process, interest grew. International visitors whose imaginaries were less connected to his shrine—and who were thus more receptive to alternative narratives—began to come in the 1980s, while Italian pilgrims and seasoned devotees—whose imaginaries of Pio were strongly tied to their remembrances of interactions with the friar or visits to his tomb—only arose a decade later. But by the mid-1990s, visitation to Pietrelcina reached a fever pitch. "At that time it was so packed you couldn't breathe," said one Irish guide who had been leading tours since the 1970s (Di Giovine 2010: 279).

In response to the increased interest in Padre Pio's bucolic origins, Pietrelcina's "very popular mayor" at the time, Pio Iadanza, engaged a group of architects from the University of Naples to suggest a restoration plan for the city. The team not only studied the layout of the town, but also conducted survey and interview research with locals and those catering to the nascent tourism industry in Pietrelcina. The idea was not merely to conserve the existing structures, but rather to reimagine the city to better coincide with both the imaginaries of locals and that of outsider devotees who came to the town looking to understand better Pio's bucolic and reverential upbringing, as portrayed in the hagiographies. What they suggested was a project of "urban transformation"—a synergy of conservation and reconstruction, "guaranteeing each other's existence" and "restoring life and utility" to the town (De Feo 1995: 9).

This radical plan was not without opposition; a certain faction of Pietrelcinesi, originally led by Domenico Masone, petitioned to block the work. He would later succeed Iadanza as mayor and would then change his tune, car-

rying out the former mayor's plan. In classic Italian style, Masone's critics
suggest that economics played a central part:

> He was the head of the opposition, Masone, it was he who went knocking on
> doors collecting signatures against the work in the piazza. But in the end, when
> you assume the leadership, and you're told, "Look, this money will come to you
> if you do this," you have to be courageous and utilize the funds rather than not
> carrying it out. (interview, 10 August 2010)

This informant's words are important not only for the juicy gossip, but also
for revealing the powerful potentiality of tourism to generate funding. Aided
by the touristic "discovery" of Pietrelcina, the Iadenza-Masone project began
a practice of linking the economic potential of tourism to successful grant
applications for infrastructural development, restoration, and the "recovery"
of traditional practices—despite the fact that tourists continued to visit for an
average of two hours and generated little revenue. And in the process, these
initiatives re-created, and revitalized, the urban space. Masone himself commented: "We don't have any ancient things, just old things.... In nine years,
we took an old town and made it completely new. A little with money from
the European Community, a little from the Campania region, the State, etc.,
we've made everything new" (interview, 31 July 2010).

This comment, however, suggests not merely economic motivations,
but a deeper concern with how Pietrelcina would be imagined by millions of
tourists and devotees around the world who consumed visual images of the
town. Indeed, in 1999, when tourism to Pietrelcina reached its frenzy—and
when De Feo's urban transformation project was still being debated—a television crew came to Pietrelcina to film a documentary entitled *Padre Pio:
Sanctus* (Damosso 1999) for the Italian national television station, Rai 1.
Dedicating a full sixteen minutes to Pio's early life and upbringing, this
hour-long documentary was groundbreaking because it was the first to use
footage from Pietrelcina itself. Marked by slow, languid pans across an intensely verdant countryside surrounding Pietrelcina, the documentary both
responded to, and certainly deepened, imaginaries of an idyllic Italian hill
town, not unlike those of the cobblestoned and wine-soaked Tuscany. It
also included footage of Pietrelcina's streets and edifices. While Padre Pio's
homes and churches had been restored after an earthquake in the 1970s and
another the following decade—thanks in part to Italian Americans and the
New York–based Padre Pio Foundation—the documentary's footage reveals
a hodgepodge of rickety buildings, gap-toothed stones peeking from patches
of crumbling asphalt, and a central piazza used as a parking lot for old cars.
In an interview, Masone seemed to have been tacitly referencing this sight,
which not only disturbed these idealized images of a traditional town, but

no doubt were embarrassing to portray to those whose impressions of Pietrelcina had not yet been formed:

> It's something so natural and obvious, that when you realize that your clothes are a little older, you buy new clothes to be more presentable.... You bathe, you shave, you prepare yourself for the party. [You do this] not only for the dignity of the place's inhabitants, but also to give a more dignified welcome—to show respect—to those who visit. So that our territory can have dignity, that our hospitality can be comfortable, honest, and acceptable particularly to those who come in a spirit of prayer. (interview, 31 July 2010)

Today, pilgrims who visit Pietrelcina are receptive to Pietrelcina's new look, which prompts them to recall stories of Pio and to exchange accounts of miracles and other supernatural phenomena that the saint has performed in their lives. The stones seem to act as mediators between the past inhabitant of Pietrelcina and the present pilgrim: "Just think, he sat right here outside the church waiting for it to open. My kids, I couldn't get them to go to church; I had to bribe them" (Irish pilgrim, 8 August 2009). These elements also seem to be effective in fulfilling their expectations of a "classic southern Italian village" that has been developed in the media. Numerous pilgrims echo the sentiments of an Italian who said: "It was just as I imagined, only maybe a little cleaner" (Italian pilgrim, 27 June 2009). Other comments reveal the importance of the imagination in co-creating the touristic experience (cf. Leite 2007): "With a little imagination, you can know how it was back then. The structures are all the same" (Italian pilgrim, 27 June 2009).

Although the management of these sites make no comparisons to San Giovanni Rotondo, many tourists have been overheard favorably comparing Pietrelcina's aesthetics to that of modern San Giovanni Rotondo. "I like Pietrelcina better than San Giovanni Rotondo," one Italian declared as he rested with two women of the same age; they agreed that it was "enchanting" (24 July 2009), as opposed to San Giovanni Rotondo, which, in its modern architecture, imposing size, and richly adorned aesthetics appeared incongruous with Pio's biographical narrative. Even pilgrims who correctly figured that Pietrelcina "was more rustic back then," nevertheless positively recognized the restoration's value: Pietrelcina "needs to be cleaned and organized. To maintain it, to let the future see how it was, for the people who will come—you have to maintain it like that" (Italian pilgrim, 27 June 2009).

But the completion of Pietrelcina's restoration effort in 2006 was met with greater iconographic contestation, as San Giovanni Rotondo had just inaugurated a new megachurch designed by internationally renowned architect Renzo Piano, and decorated by world-class sculptors such as Mimmo

Paladino and Arnaldo Pomodoro. The crowning achievement—other than the 8,300-person basilica and the beautifully landscaped piazza—envisioned as a "church without walls" that can accommodate 35,000 devotees—is Pio's new crypt, adorned with scintillating vermillion and golden mosaics by noted Slovenian mosaicist Marko Ivan Rupnik. By constructing this, the Capuchins in San Giovanni Rotondo fulfilled a long-standing desire to become "the next Assisi"—that is, a sustainable destination not only for future devotees of the saint, but also for future secular tourists who wish to see the most representative art and architecture of our era. At nearly 800 years after St. Francis's death, Assisi ranks as one of the top tourist attractions of Italy. In addition, "of the visitors who go to Assisi, 10 percent go for the saint. The rest go for Giotto," one site manager told me (interview, 31 July 2010).

This ambition has necessarily caused a reimagining of Padre Pio, in both narrative and image. On the one hand, many devotees from Ireland, Italy, and the United States are shocked by what they perceive as a modern, richly adorned, self-celebratory edifice that is incongruous with a traditional, humble, quietly suffering priest: "It's not that it's ugly or a monstrosity, it's just that it's very, very modern with respect to who Padre Pio was" (Italian pilgrim, 27 June 2009). "Renzo Piano is a world-class architect," said ninety-year-old Zì Umberto, Pio's family friend and former neighbor, who donated part of his land in Piana Romana for a modern sanctuary to "Blessed Padre Pio," inaugurated in 2000. "But I'm against it. It's a stadium, not a church" (interview, 9 October 2009). Many also point out that while Pio used the donations he was given by the faithful to charitably construct San Giovanni Rotondo's immense hospital, the Capuchins today melted down the thousands of gold bracelets, necklaces, and wedding bands given as ex-votos to create Pio's new crypt, and they believe that he would not be happy in his new "pharaonic" resting place (Colafemmina 2010b). Some have even gone as far as to argue, in extreme detail, that the church is really a Masonic temple (cf. Villa and Adessa 2006; Colafemmina 2010a). A contingent of Pio's family members even sued to stop his body from being put into the new crypt in 2010, to no avail. These contestations have forced the Capuchins to go on the offensive; they disseminated images, books, and television interviews, paintings of Pio, and quotations from Pio's writings that would suggest the saint's long-standing desire for just this very construction.

Such conflicting views of Pio have sometimes even forced pilgrims to stop and assess their culturally situated imaginaries of Pio and his relationship to the institution of the Catholic Church. For example, most Italians I have interviewed criticize what they consider a commodification of Pio's body, and the "business" of the Capuchins and the Vatican at San Giovanni Rotondo; this is in line with traditional anticlerical thought in the northern

Mediterranean since the Counter-Reformation (cf. Riegelhaupt 1984; Behar 1990). As Ellen Badone asserts, these cultures continue to privilege direct and reciprocal relations over more rational, economic, and legalistic ones instituted by the Council of Trent—and thus criticize attempts of the Vatican to co-opt the charisma of saints as a commercialization of the cult (1990: 13–15).

On the other hand, Irish Catholics—who exist as minorities in an Anglo-British milieu—are generally more receptive to forms that reveal the wealth and strength of the cult, and the Catholic Church in general. In one bus ride to the Rome airport after visiting both Pietrelcina and San Giovanni Rotondo, over forty pilgrims held an engaging debate on the merits and drawbacks of the new, modern basilica. One man integrated distinctively Irish imaginaries with that of San Giovanni Rotondo: "Somebody might disagree with the amount of money that was spent on Renzo Piano's basilica because there's so much poverty in the world—but in Ireland, in times past, there was poverty and famine. The only thing that stood out and remained past those generations are the churches. Hopefully it'll outlive [our generation, too]" (field notes, 24 September 2010).

On the other hand, the construction of Renzo Piano's new church, and Pio's subsequent translation (ritual movement of relics) to the crypt below it, has also created an avenue to iconographically solidify and consolidate imaginaries of San Giovanni Rotondo as the center of Pio's cult. This is achieved primarily through Rupnik's mosaic cycle leading down to the crypt, which juxtaposes scenes from the life of St. Francis—the first stigmatic and the "grandfather" of Pio's Capuchin order—with similar scenes from Padre Pio's life. They not only create new imaginaries linking Francis with Pio, but also Assisi with San Giovanni Rotondo. One particular scene is telling; it is a frieze of Pio convalescing in his parents' house in Pietrelcina. The rendering of the one-room home matches that of the actual house as it appears today: small, sparse, and with a solitary square window directly across from the entrance where a viewer could survey the scene (see figure 6.1). For pilgrims at Pietrelcina, it is a picturesque sight conforming to their romanticized expectations of Pio's rustic youth, with the window opening up to the verdant Pietrelcinese hillside. Yet Rupnik does not depict the hillside, but instead, anachronistically, the façade of Pio's friary in San Giovanni Rotondo—a symbolic conflation of the two towns that might suggest, contrary to what Pietrelcinesi feel, that everything really happened in San Giovanni Rotondo (see figure 6.2).

Pietrelcinesi have been progressively contesting such re-presentations by responding with their own images and narratives of the saint that underscore those aspects of Pio's life that he spent tangibly enmeshed in Pietrel-

Figure 6.1. Recreation of Pio's childhood home in Pietrelcina (Copyright: M. Di Giovine).

Figure 6.2. Scene from Marko Ivan Rupnik's fresco cycle depicting Pio convalescing at his family home in Pietrelcina (Copyright: M. Di Giovine).

cina's social networks, the supernatural events that are imagined to have occurred there, and Pio's devotion to their patroness, the Madonna della Libera. Around Pietrelcina, one can find numerous images of Pio as a young child, such as the stained-glass windows and the bronze doors in Pietrelcina's cathedral, which depict primarily scenes from Pio's youth—from his birth and baptism to early ecstatic visions and the aforementioned convalescence at his parents' home. And in the reconstructed central piazza a giant mural, complete with a map of the town, couples imagined images from Pio's childhood with famous images of Pio (one when he was young, and one when he was older in San Giovanni Rotondo), thus attempting, through mental association, to integrate new Pietrelcina-centric images of Pio into preexisting imaginaries. This mural not only provides information to visitors, but also localizes common imaginaries of Pio within the geography and topography of the town itself. The city also launched a branding campaign built around museologically inspired billboards that feature an image and relevant biographical details of a locality associated with the saint under the boldfaced heading, "Pietrelcina: City of Padre Pio."

And perhaps directly responding to imaginaries of Pio's bucolic shepherding childhood, a Via del Rosario (Way of the Rosary) was constructed in the woods connecting his home in Pietrelcina with his farmhouse in the countryside of Piana Romana. The pathway literally cuts through a dark forest, over a bubbling stream, up hills and around large stones, and, finally, past farmhouses, granaries, fields, and barns before emerging at his family's *massaria,* or farmhouse—and Zì Umberto's church, which was constructed there in 2000. Though the pathway appears natural, the fruit of generations of Pietrelcinesi farmers trekking from their city homes to their fields in the countryside, landscape designers were actually called in to create it. This illustrates how, once again, outsiders' imaginaries have impacted the physical foundations of the town itself. But while no doubt intended for outside tourists—Pietrelcina's biggest problem from the tourism standpoint is its small size and lack of activities that will keep visitors overnight—those who utilize the Via del Rosario the most are its locals; the town's church organizes a rosary pilgrimage once a month from April to September, and a special pilgrimage along the route to commemorate the anniversary of Pio's invisible stigmata draws most of the townspeople, old and young. One advertisement of these monthly pilgrimages reads:

> The Via del Rosario is a route that connects Pietrelcina with Piana Romana, which Padre Pio walked while reciting the Holy Rosary. Who knows how many graces he obtained for our souls through the many rosaries he recited along this

very path. It is up to us to rewalk [this path] to obtain from our heavenly *Mamma* all of the graces we need for ourselves, for all those we hold dear, for our Church and for the world.

As this quote reveals, Pietrelcina, too, employs similar tactics to conflate imaginaries concerning the Virgin Mary, Padre Pio, and Pio's devotional ministry in San Giovanni Rotondo with actual, physical locations in and around Pietrelcina. For locals, it further serves as a reimagining of their understandings of Pio and his life in their town, and a way of "putting themselves in his shoes," much like the spiritual exercises developed by St. Ignatius of Loyola are encouraged for Jesuit novices (cf. Fleming 1978). This embodied experience will create new, collective imaginaries—ones that bring devotees' focus to this small town, and to its narrative: "Jesus was in Pietrelcina, and everything happened there."

PIETRELCINA IN THE WORLD

These changes have also prompted a dialectical response from other institutions that had not been included in the refashioning of Pietrelcina. Reacting to the impetus by the town council and the church to re-create the town in accordance with tourists' imaginaries of the Pio narrative, Pietrelcina's Archeoclub has redefined itself and its mission from a lay archaeological organization to more of a historic preservation society. In interviews with several members, they see themselves as having become de facto a necessary watchdog for the town's "authenticity," advocating for the conservation of preexistent structures rather than their re-creation. Their initiatives in this regard are threefold. First, they are working to preserve the original skyline of the hill town by attempting to block the demolition of certain abandoned buildings, which have been left fallow after their owners emigrated to northern Italy and the Americas. Second, they try to recover material structures of the town that have been sold off or pillaged by pilgrims, such as the original wooden door of the cathedral, which was replaced several years ago with monumental bronze doors depicting Pio's early life. For the Archeoclub, this original door—existent at the time of Pio—has more archaeological value than the artistic one, and they have collected funds to purchase it back from the city of Foggia, outside San Giovanni Rotondo, which purchased it. And third, the Archeoclub continues to excavate the farmland outside of Pietrelcina to recover artifacts from the area's "non-Pio" history, particularly the Roman and Lombard periods (see Iasiello 2004). These are on display in the Archeoclub's new headquarters, which itself is a laudable example of historic preservation: outside, the façade remains the same, blending into the small piazza in front; but inside, the space is modern, well lit, and includes an innovative upstairs exhibition space.

There are also signs in Pietrelcina that more modifications to the urban footprint are in the works—modifications that imply a growing move by town officials themselves to refashion the town not solely as an integral component in the Padre Pio narrative, but also as a social, cultural, and political actor in broader regional and national society. A Spanish architect who examined the city's restoration plans with me pointed out that the town's previous reconstruction has opened new doors for the demolition of certain palazzos at the far end of the piazza, enabling the central square to be enlarged along its axis. Indeed, the present government has been active in promoting mass events in the piazza, which, should it prove successful, may necessitate a larger central space. Food-filled festivals (*sagre*) are held in the summertime, including the "sagra dei carciofi," which celebrates the Pietrelcinese artichoke (*carciofo*); long regarded as the village's "traditional" agricultural product (although it was only introduced in the nineteenth century), the artichoke is now believed by locals to have been one of Padre Pio's favorite foods (Di Giovine, forthcoming). The mayor and the tourism board have also been instrumental in bringing "culture" to Pietrelcina in the form of daily concerts in the piazza during the summer months; for the past few years, local student bands, international jazz musicians, Eastern European folk dancers, Neapolitan puppeteers, and even opera singers have performed in the town square—despite the fact that most inhabitants do not particularly profess an interest in these art forms.

This is not to say that officials in Pietrelcina have abandoned Padre Pio as the originator of their revitalizing imaginaries. The most prominent disseminator of imaginaries centered on Padre Pio and Pietrelcina is the annual concert, "Una Voce per Padre Pio," which is shown live throughout Italy on the national television station Rai 1. Although its name refers to the San Giovanni Rotondo magazine and media conglomerate, *Voce di Padre Pio,* this concert—which features top Italian pop stars who couple their singing performances with testimonies of their devotion to Padre Pio—is held against the backdrop of Pietrelcina's newly restored cathedral. In 2010, even the Italian prince Emanuele Filiberto of Savoy (whose family was allowed to return from post–World War II exile in Switzerland in 2002 and has become a television personality in his own right) was on hand to discuss his mother's devotion to the friar. Fourteen years after its inception in 1999, the show continues to win the most shares in viewership the night it airs live (see ASCA 2013).

As the years progress, explicit discourses linking Pio with Pietrelcina seem to be more prominent on this televised show. In 2013, for example, the show's longtime host, Massimo Giletti, asked famed Italian singer Toto Cutugno about his impressions "of this small village ... which had given birth to Padre Pio." Cutugno's reply replicated (or perpetuated) the imaginaries that Pietrelcinesi were promoting: "You feel a particular magic here. You feel well—with yourself—and you know that the one who's protecting you is Padre Pio" (field notes, 28 June 2013). Importantly, this concert reconceptualizes Pietrelcina's role in the world and conjures up new imaginaries, for it is also a telethon to support two Pio-affiliated organizations in Africa: the "Villaggio di Padre Pio" (Padre Pio Village), a home for abandoned, severely handicapped children in in Bombouaka, Togo, that was founded in 2010; and a hospital and youth center in the Ivory Coast named after St. Luigi Orione, a priest and contemporary collaborator of Pio's who was canonized in 2004. And since 2012, another edition of the concert has been held in Toronto, Canada, which boasts a large number of southern Italian Americans, including Pietrelcinesi. Called, appropriately, "Una Voce per Padre Pio nel Mondo" (A Voice for Padre Pio in the World), it caps an annual, weeklong celebration each September that purposefully conflates devotion to Pio and a celebration of Italian-American ethnicity. Such activities reveal once again how Pietrelcina, reacting to the narratives and images circulating around it, continues to reimagine itself and its relationship to other actors within the cult of St. Padre Pio.

CONCLUSION

This chapter illustrated the "imaginaire dialectic" by examining the changing narratives, images, and touristic practices surrounding the shrine of Padre Pio in San Giovanni Rotondo and the saint's hometown of Pietrelcina. Ultimately, Pietrelcina's reconstruction cannot be viewed simply as a commercial endeavor to attract more visitors, but neither is it solely a crystallization of locals' understandings about the place. Rather, it is one step in a broader, more historically situated process of producing, consuming, reacting to, and re-producing conflicting imaginaries of the town and its connection to Padre Pio espoused by a diversity of social actors within the cult's broader field of production. This is not a linear, evolutionary process—one marked by inevitable progression or development. Rather, as competing imaginaries refract off of each other, like images in a hall of mirrors, they will respond to one another, meld together, create new, competing imaginaries, and deepen, complexify, and modify each other. Nor is this simply a process within the minds of these actors, but, as revealed by the restoration of Pietrelcina, the construction of Renzo Piano's new basilica, the translation of Pio's body to the golden crypt, and the extension of Pietrelcina's missionary outreach in Africa and North America, there is a very real, physical aspect to the imaginaire dialectic.

Pietrelcina is small, but this case is not insignificant. Examining the imaginaire dialectic at work in Pietrelcina has broader implications for the social scientific study of tourism and pilgrimage by complexifying our understandings of the ways in which a destination's meaning is fashioned, contested, and refashioned. Just as the saint's significance cannot be readily boiled down to a particular chain of events or uncontested characteristics by a singular authority, neither can a destination's meaning, religious or not, be determined by one particular entity. Rather, like Pio himself, his shrines vary in meaning as imaginaries associated with them vary over time. Indeed, the model of an imaginaire dialectic complicates the simplistic, linear narrative of the development of a tourist site, first, by recognizing the agency of multiple, conflicting actors and groups of actors; second, by recognizing the impact of time itself; and third, by complicating the sense of space implicated in the ways in which a particular destination's imaginaries are formed.

First, viewing the significance of a site as being produced through a dialectical process, rather than a "hagiographic" one, can lead to the recognition of tourism as a "democratizing" activity, at least in the production of imaginaries. As Salazar and Graburn point out in this volume's introduction, imaginaries are produced not exclusively by governments or destination marketers—though certainly they may wield hegemonic or "top-down" power—but through an individual agent's total immersion in constantly circulating, historically and culturally contingent flows of ideas and images. These imaginaries may or may not be related to a particular site, but they are always utilized on an individual level to understand, make meaning of, re-present, contest, or confirm specific imaginaries concerning a particular place—which will then dialectically impact other producers of these imaginaries. Although most studies trace the changes in San Giovanni Rotondo's cityscape to development plans, this chapter argued that it is also a result of responses to conflicting imaginaries (most recently concerned with Pietrelcina).

Second, this model reveals that time itself plays a fundamental role in shaping the current imaginaries of a particular destination. These imaginaries are not stagnant in any way, but rather are constantly modifying, refracting, and changing throughout time. While certainly revealing a considerable sense of rivalry (see also Di Giovine 2012c), the case of Pietrelcina and San Giovanni Rotondo shows that meanings change with each passing day in response to new events. These meanings are based on the constant refashioning of imaginaries concerning the dual shrines that occurs precisely through prolonged processes of reception, negotiation, and re-presentation.

Third, this implies a broader, and more complex, understanding of the space involved in the production of tourist imaginaries. On the one hand, this dialectic does not take place in a hermetically sealed location; as Salazar and Graburn, Leite, and the other contributors to this volume assert, it cannot be contained or restricted by any geographic or sociopolitical boundaries. It is perhaps for this reason that tourism ministers, site managers, and tour operators are constantly acting and reacting to new developments in, new markets for, and new opinions of a particular site (Di Giovine 2009); their processes of marketing or "imagineering" (Salazar 2010b) seem neverending. Indeed, since the otherwise laudable studies of San Giovanni Rotondo have been single-sited, and have largely left other actors such as those in Pietrelcina out of their analyses (i.e., see McKevitt [1991] 2000; Confessore 2005; Mesaritou 2012), there runs a risk of reductionism that obfuscates the dialectical process of "positioning and position-taking" (Bourdieu 1993: 30) by site managers responding to initiatives and imaginaries by the cult's other stakeholders. A holistic analysis of tourist sites such as these might require multisited or "global" ethnographic methodologies (see also Di Giovine 2011b).

On the other hand, we must be careful not to assume necessarily broad universality of these imaginaries, either in their diffusion or their reception. Anthropology teaches us that these general ideas and images that help one to comprehend and re-present site-specific imaginaries—components of those "webs of significances" (Geertz 1973: 5) that constitute a culture—are socioculturally and historically contingent. Nor is tourism monolithic; social scientists have long pointed out that different cosmologies, cultures, and historical developments create different forms of tourism, types of tourists, tourist behaviors, and even gazes through which tourists perceive a particular site (see, e.g., Graburn 1983; Urry 2002; McCabe 2005; Di Giovine 2009). While the imaginaire dialectic is not necessarily constrained by geographic or social boundaries, in certain circumstances it may, paradoxically, be more localized—creating, at times, certain culturally contingent convergences in the way groups imagine a particular destination. And as Salazar and Graburn point out, these groups will negotiate the reception of such imaginaries in culturally contingent ways, too. Thus, it is possible to talk, as I do above, of groups espousing "distinctive" imaginaries of a particular destination—ones that circulate or flow through particular sociocultural, temporal, and/or geographical conduits.

The case of Pietrelcina certainly reveals this; based on different ideas and images of the role of saints and the Catholic Church in medieval history, Irish, Italian, and American pilgrims each make meaning of, contest, and refashion imaginaries of Pio in relation to his poverty in different ways. Many of these notions are themselves dialectically reinterpreted and re-presented within these cultural groups, and then color other groups' interpretations more forcefully when they "escape" or "leak" out of such conduits—through intercultural touristic interactions during pilgrimages, through conventional publishing, blogging, and posting to websites, or even through talking with members of one's extended, global network. Just as we can say that there are as many tourist imaginaries as there are tourists, it is also possible to assert that there are certain imaginaries that conform to particular cosmologies or cultural schemata more than others. It is ultimately for this reason that it is incumbent that tourism researchers understand and appreciate the complexity of the imaginaire dialectic, for it is through such complex processes of reception, negotiation, and re-presentation that the significance of sites as small as Pietrelcina or as large as San Giovanni Rotondo is determined.

NOTES

1. A highly abridged version of this chapter has appeared in Di Giovine (2012c). The author would like to thank the Associazione Italiana di Anglistica (AIA) and Carocci Editore for permission to utilize that article as a basis for the present chapter.
2. I use the French *imaginaire* instead of the English "imaginary" to avoid misrepresenting it as an adjective, which would erroneously convey the notion of an imagined (imaginary, false, or unreal) dialectic. Rather, I use "imaginary" or *imaginaire* as a noun; it is a dialectic of producing and reproducing imaginaries.
3. Unless otherwise noted, all translations from Italian publications and interviews are my own.

REFERENCES

Abu El-Haj, Nadia. 2001. *Facts on the Ground.* Chicago: University of Chicago Press.
Allegri, Renzo. 1999. *Padre Pio: Un Santo fra Noi.* Milano: Mondadori.
Althusser, Louis. (1970) 1971. "Ideology and Ideological State Apparatuses (Notes Towards an Investigation)." In *Lenin and Philosophy and Other Essays by Louis Althusser,* trans. Ben Brewster. New York: Monthly Review Press.
Anderson, Benedict. 1983. *Imagined Communities: Reflections on the Origin and Spread of Nationalism.* London: Verso.
ASCA (Agenzia Stampa Quotidiana Nazionale). 2013. "TV/Ascolti: Rai, 'Una voce

per Padre Pio' vince prima serata." 29 June. http://www.asca.it/news-Tv_ascolti_
_Rai____Una_voce_per_Padre_Pio___vince_prima_serata-1292550-ATT.html
(accessed 30 June 2013).

Badone, Ellen. 1990. "Introduction." In *Religious Orthodoxy and Popular Faith in European Society,* ed. Ellen Badone. Princeton, NJ: Princeton University Press.

Behar, Ruth. 1990. "The Struggle for the Church: Popular Anticlericalism and Religiosity in Post-Franco Spain." In *Religious Orthodoxy and Popular Faith in European
Society,* ed. Ellen Badone. Princeton, NJ: Princeton University Press.

Bonavita, Antonio. 1989. *Come Parlavano i Pietrelcinesi: Il Dialetto di Padre Pio.* Pietrelcina: Centro Studi e Richerche Storiche.

Boorstin, Daniel. (1961) 1994. *The Image: A Guide to Pseudo-Events in America.* New
York: Vintage Books.

Bourdieu, Pierre. 1993. *The Field of Cultural Production.* New York: Columbia University Press.

Bruner, Edward, and Barbara Kirshenblatt-Gimblett. 1994. "Maasai on the Lawn:
Tourist Realism in East Africa." *Cultural Anthropology* 9, no. 4: 435–70.

Castoriadis, Cornelius. (1975) 1987. *The Imaginary Institution of Society.* Trans. K.
Blamey. Cambridge, MA: MIT Press.

Colafemmina, Francesco. 2010a. *Il Mistero della Chiesa di San Pio: Coincidenze e strat-
egie esoteriche all'ombra del grande Santo di Pietrelcina.* Lamezia Terme: Edizioni
Settecolori.

———. 2010b. "La Traslazione di San Pio: Fra Ipocrisie e Miserie Umane." *Fides et
Forma* blog, 8 April. http://fidesetforma.blogspot.com/2010/04/la-traslazione-di-
san-pio-fra-ipocrisie.html (accessed 16 April 2011).

Confessore, Ornella. 2005. "Padre Pio e Il Santuario Di San Giovanni Rotondo."
Melanges De l'Ecole Francaise De Rome: Italie Et Mediterranie 7, no. 2: 713–26.

Crang, Mike. 1997. "Picturing Practices: Research through the Tourist Gaze." *Progress in Human Geography* 21, no. 3: 359–73.

Da Prata, Lina, and Alessandro Da Ripabottoni. 1994. *Beata Te, Pietrelcina.* Pietrelcina: Convento "Padre Pio"–Frati Minori Cappuccini.

Damosso, Paolo. 1999. *Padre Pio: Sanctus* (documentary film). Rome: Rai.

Davis, John. 1998. "Casting off the 'Southern Problem': Or the Particularities of the
South Reconsidered." In *Italy's Southern Question: Orientalism in One Country,* ed.
Jane Schneider. Oxford: Berg.

De Feo, Carla Maria, ed. 1995. *Pietrelcina: Memoria, Tradizione, Identità.* Naples: Florio
Edizioni Scientifiche.

Di Giovine, Michael A. 2009. *The Heritage-scape: UNESCO, World Heritage, and Tourism.*
Lanham, MD: Lexington Books.

———. 2010. "Rethinking Development: Religious Tourism as Material and Cultural
Revitalization in Pietrelcina, Italy." *Tourism: An International Interdisciplinary Journal* 58, no. 3: 271–88.

———. 2011a. "Re-Presenting Saint Padre Pio of Pietrelcina: Contemporary Ways of
Seeing a Contemporary Saint." In *Saints: Faith without Borders,* ed. Françoise
Meltzer and Jas Elsner. Chicago: University of Chicago Press.

———. 2011b. "Tourism Research as Global Ethnography." *Anthropologies* (April). www.anthropologiesproject.org/2011/04/tourism-research-as-global-ethnogra phy.html (accessed 5 November 2013).

———. 2012a. *Making Saints, Re-Making Lives: Pilgrimage and Revitalization in the Land of St. Padre Pio of Pietrelcina.* Unpublished dissertation, University of Chicago.

———. 2012b. "Passionate Movements: Emotional and Social Dynamics of Padre Pio Pilgrims." In *Emotion in Motion: Tourism, Affect, and Transformation,* ed. David Picard and Mike Robinson. Surrey, UK: Ashgate.

———. 2012c. "A Tale of Two Cities: Padre Pio and the Reimagining of Pietrelcina and San Giovanni Rotondo." *Textus: English Studies in Italy* 1: 157–69.

———. Forthcoming. "The Everyday as Extraordinary: Religion, Revitalization and the Elevation of *Cucina Casareccia* to Heritage Cuisine in Pietrelcina, Italy." In *Edible Identities: Exploring Food and Foodways as Cultural Heritage,* ed. Ronda Bru-lotte and Michael A. Di Giovine. Surrey, UK: Ashgate.

Edwards, Penny. 2007. *Cambodge: The Cultivation of a Nation, 1860–1945.* Honolulu: University of Hawai'i Press.

Fleming, David L. 1978. *The Spiritual Exercises of St. Ignatius: A Literal Translation and a Contemporary Reading.* St. Louis, MO: Institute of Jesuit Sources.

Geertz, Clifford. 1973. *The Interpretation of Cultures: Selected Essays.* New York: Basic Books.

Giddens, Anthony. 1990. *The Consequences of Modernity.* Palo Alto, CA: Stanford University Press.

Il Giornale d'Italia. 1919. "Il Miracolo di un Santo: Un Soldato Guarito Istantanea-mente a S. Giovanni Rotondo." 1 June.

Goffman, Irving. 1967. *Interaction Ritual: Essays on Face-to-Face Behavior.* New York: Pantheon Books.

Graburn, Nelson H. H. 1983. "To Pray, Pay and Play: The Cultural Structure of Japanese Domestic Tourism." *Cahiers du Tourisme, Centre des Hautes Etudes Touris-tiques,* ser. B, 25: 1–89.

———. 2001. "Secular Ritual: A General Theory of Tourism." In *Hosts and Guests Revis-ited: Tourism Issues of the 21st Century,* ed. Valene Smith and Maryann Brent. New York: Cognizant Communications.

Harvey, David. 1991. *The Condition of Post-Modernity.* Malden, MA: Blackwell Publishers.

Hegel, Georg W. F. (1807) 1977. *Phenomenology of the Spirit.* Trans. A. V. Miller. Oxford: Oxford University Press.

———. (1834) 1956. *The Philosophy of History.* Trans. J. Sibree. New York: Dover Publications.

Iasiello, Italo. 2004. *Dall'IRAP all'Archeoclub: Quarant'anni di Ricerche Archeologiche in Pietrelcina.* Pietrelcina: Archeoclub d'Italia–Sede di Pietrelcina.

Italy Magazine. 2008. "Padre Pio Tomb 'Desecrated.'" 22 May. http://www.italymag .co.uk/italy/religion/padre-pio-tomb-desecrated (accessed 1 June 2008).

Katriel, Tamar. 1997. *Performing the Past: A Study of Israeli Settlement Museums.* Mahwah, NJ: Lawrence Erlbaum Associates.

Keane, Colm. 2008. *Padre Pio: The Irish Connection.* Edinburgh: Mainstream Publishing.

Knorr-Cetina, Karin. 1999. *Epistemic Cultures: How the Sciences Make Knowledge.* Cambridge, MA: Harvard University Press.

Lacan, Jacques. (1949) 1977. "The Mirror Stage as Formative of the Function of the I." In *Écrits: A Selection,* trans. Alan Sheridan. New York: W. W. Norton.

Leite, Naomi. 2007. "Materializing Absence: Tourists, Surrogates, and the Making of Jewish Portugal." In *Things That Move: Material Worlds of Tourism and Travel,* ed. Mike Robinson. Leeds, UK: Centre for Tourism and Cultural Change.

Luzzatto, Sergio. 2009. *Padre Pio: Miracoli e Politica nell'Italia del Novecento.* Torino: Einaudi.

MacCannell, Dean. (1976) 1999. *The Tourist: A New Theory of the Leisure Class.* Berkeley: University of California Press.

McCabe, Scott. 2005. "Who Is a Tourist? A Critical Review." *Tourist Studies* 5, no. 1: 85–106.

McKevitt, Christopher. (1991) 2000. "San Giovanni Rotondo and the Shrine of Padre Pio." In *Contesting the Sacred: The Anthropology of Pilgrimage,* ed. John Eade and Michael J. Sallnow. Urbana: University of Illinois Press.

Merrington, Peter. 2001. "A Staggered Orientalism: The Cape to Cairo Imaginary." *Poetics Today* 2, no. 2: 323–64.

Mesaritou, Evgenia. 2012. "Say a Little Hallo to Padre Pio: Production and Consumption of Space in the Construction of the Sacred at the Shrine of Santa Maria Delle Grazie." In *Ordinary Lives and Grand Schemes: An Anthropology of Everyday Religion,* ed. Samuli Schielke and Liza Debevec. New York: Berghahn Books.

Montella, Carmine. 1987. *Padre Pio, Pietrelcina e Pietrelcinesi, dalla fine dell'800 alla metà del '900.* Pietrelcina: Centro Studi e Ricerche Storiche.

Morrison, Kathleen. 2004. "On Putting Time in Its Place: Landscape History in South India." Paper presented at the University of Pennsylvania Ethnohistory Workshop, April 2004.

———. 2009. *Daroji Valley: Landscape History, Place, and the Making of a Dryland Reservoir System, Vijayanagara.* New Delhi: Manohar.

Noriendr, Panivong. 1996. *Phantasmatic Indochina.* Durham, NC: Duke University Press.

O'Rourke, Dennis. 1988. *Cannibal Tours* (documentary film). Canberra: Ronin Films.

Pio da Pietrelcina. 2008. "Epistolario VI: Corrispondenza con Diverse Categorie di Persone." In *Pio (Padre),* ed. Melchiorre da Pobladura and Alessandro da Ripabottoni. San Giovanni Rotondo: Edizioni Padre Pio da Pietrelcina.

Pratt, Mary Louise. 1992. *Imperial Eyes: Travel Writing and Transculturation.* London: Routledge.

Rega, Frank. 2009. *Padre Pio and America.* Rockford, Ill.: TAN Books and Publishers.

Riegelhaupt, Joyce. 1984. "Popular Anti-Clericalism and Religiosity in Pre-1974 Portugal." In *Religion, Power and Protest in Local Communities: The Northern Shore of the Mediterranean,* ed. Eric R. Wolf. Berlin: Mouton.

Robertson, Roland. 1992. *Globalization: Social Theory and Global Culture*. London: Sage.

Robinson, Mike, and David Picard, eds. 2009. *The Framed World: Tourism, Tourists and Photography*. Surrey, UK: Ashgate.

Said, Edward. 1994. *Orientalism*. New York: Vintage Books.

Salazar, Noel B. 2010a. *Envisioning Eden: Mobilizing Imaginaries in Tourism and Beyond*. Oxford: Berghahn Books.

———. 2010b. "Imagineering Tailor-Made Pasts for Nation-Building and Tourism: A Comparative Perspective." In *Staging the Past: Themed Environments in Transcultural Perspectives*, ed. Judith Schlehe, Michiko Uike-Bormann, Carolyn Oesterle, and Wolfgang Hochbruck. Bielefeld, Germany: Transcript.

Saldutto, Gerardo. 1974. *Un Tormentato Settennio nella Vita di P. Pio da Pietrelcina (1918-25)*. Rome: Pontificia Università Gregoriana.

Smith, Valene, ed. (1977) 1989. *Hosts and Guests: The Anthropology of Tourism*. 2nd ed. Philadelphia: University of Pennsylvania Press.

Strauss, Claudia. 2006. "The Imaginary." *Anthropological Theory* 6, no. 3: 322–44.

Tretola, Sergio. 1988. *La Madonnella nostra: La Confraternita e il Culto della Madonna della Libera in Pietrelcina*. Pietrelcina: Centro Studi e Ricerche Storiche.

Urry, John. 2002. *The Tourist Gaze*. 2nd ed. London: Sage.

Villa, Luigi, and Franco Adessa. 2006. "Una 'Nuova Chiesa' Dedicata a San Padre Pio: Tempio Massonico?" Special issue, *Chiesa Viva* 33, no. 381 (March).

Vogler, Candace A. 2002. "Social Imaginary, Ethics, and Methodological Individualism." *Public Culture* 14, no. 3: 625–27.

Wallace, Anthony F. C. 1956. "Revitalization Movements." *American Anthropologist* 58, no. 2: 264–81.

———. 2003. *Revitalizations and Mazeways: Essays on Culture Change*. Lincoln: University of Nebraska Press.

Winter, Tim. 2007. *Post-Conflict Heritage, Post-Colonial Tourism: Tourism, Politics and Development at Angkor*. London: Routledge.

Zerubavel, Yael. 1995. *Recovered Roots*. Chicago: University of Chicago Press.

Chapter 7

Temporal Fragmentation
Cambodian Tales

Federica Ferraris

This chapter is conceived as an exploration of the notion of tourist imaginaries revolving around a specific host-guest relationship: the one between Italian tourists and Cambodia as a tourism destination. I argue that the imaginary emerging from tourist accounts of Italian tourists' trips and the one emerging from brochures of Italian tour operators is mainly formed around an idea of Cambodia as a past suspended by the present, following Johannes Fabian's (1983) notion of "allochronism" (i.e., the location of a spatially distant Other in a time of the past), which entangles a denial of coevalness (i.e., the destination lives in a time different from the one of the tourist). I will show that such images, far from being novel, have informed the imaginary of Cambodia since colonial times (Loti [1912] 1991), reaffirming that "tourism imaginaries do not float around spontaneously and independently; rather, they 'travel' in space and time through well-established conduits, leaving certain elements behind and picking up new ones along the way, and continuously returning to their points of origin" (Salazar and Graburn, this volume).

More specifically, the fields of inquiry are Cambodia's ancient and recent history as objects of tourism imaginaries, and the ways in which the two combine in the narratives tourism produces, and, subsequently, the imaginaries such accounts generate among Italian audiences. I use three different textual sources as material for my analysis. The main element are the oral accounts of tourists and travelers who have visited Cambodia over a span of almost ten years (1992–2001), who I interviewed (Ferraris 2004), followed by texts of Italian tour operator catalogs and websites (1999–2002, 2010–11). I also refer to colonial travel literature and to some interview excerpts of expatriate tour operators living and working in Phnom Penh. My aim is to demonstrate that being geographically "far" means often to be "out" of the present time.

The chapter is structured in five sections. First, I provide some theoretical and methodological considerations about the ethnographic present. The second section revolves around the complementary views of Harvey ([1990] 2004) and Giddens (1990, 1991) regarding space-time compression/distantiation and the implications for the study of tourism imaginaries. In the third part, I focus more specifically on time and times (that is, the times of travel), and address the relationship that exists between the ways travel accounts are structured and the use of the ethnographic present in anthropological literature. I then provide some reflections about how tourism discourses on Southeast Asia, and on Cambodia more specifically, can be thought provoking, in order to explore the temporal displacement that tourism imaginaries can engender. The fifth section presents some updates about the Italy-Cambodia touristic relationship and some concluding remarks.

THE ETHNOGRAPHIC PRESENT

Anthropological studies on tourism have often highlighted the need to examine contemporary travel as an extremely multifaceted phenomenon. Like scholars who have spoken of the coexistence of dissonant elements in globalization processes (Giddens 1991), those investigating tourism are more and more keen to underline the multiple elements tourism is made of, the superposition and the melting of different ways, sometimes even opposite, of being "tourists" and "doing tourism" (Alneng 2002; Harrison 2003; Salazar 2010; Simonicca 2007). If on the one hand there seems to be a reasonable agreement among academics in highlighting that it is impossible to describe the various manifestations of tourism univocally, many have made attempts to interpret such complexity with a variety of analytical tools that go beyond the usual anthropological methods. If "ethnography is a written description or, more generally, a representation of social organization, social activities, symbolism, interpretative and communication practices, etcetera, of a defined group of people" (Fabietti 2000: 35), it also should be "the result of a research process—also defined as ethnography—conducted partially through the objective and detached observation as well as through a participation from the inside, a self-identification with the studied individuals" (Fabietti 2000: 35).

Therefore, if writing and describing are central to the production of anthropological knowledge, it becomes of primary importance to construct an analysis of Cambodia's representations emerging from tourism encounters, and to have an in-depth look at those conceptual knots that contribute to the construction and interpretation of a more metaphorical than physical research context. The choice of devoting a specific reflection to the time and place of diverse tourism experiences of Cambodia is motivated by the conviction that, through an ethnographically "thick description" (Geertz 1973: 4), it is possible to highlight the multiplicity of aspects coexisting within a single travel experience. In particular, I believe that it can reveal the complexity of potential readings that, through tourism, can be derived from a specific context, becoming itself a pretext to reflect upon the relation between cultures created in tourism encounters. For this reason, the ethnographic analysis I have dealt with is influenced by the notion of multilocality suggested by Marcus, who analyses the "emergence of, if not a multi-sited research, then at least a multi-sited research imaginary in the pursuit of ethnography" (1998: 3).

Data must be considered the outcomes of an inquiry that has not explored a physical "field," that still exists and is tangible, an inquiry in which the representations have been proposed by the diverse social actors that move within the specific context of touristic Cambodia. Answering Geertz's invitation to consider the reciprocal impacts that diverse parties, the "touristified" and the "touristifier," have on one another (1997: 20), I will therefore present what the image of Cambodia that visitors have experienced is.[1] I am here thinking of images and representations as snapshots perpetuating a fixed picture of the visited context, with an impact on the production and reproduction of the imaginary (of the exotic, the Orient, and, more specifically, Cambodia).

However, such snapshots are intended as dialogic constructions between the concrete experiences of the visitors and what the local context promotes, highlighting the role tourism has in shaping the image of contemporary Cambodia. Political discourses of the Cambodian government on tourism development, as well as the real disentanglement that the latter seems to have in relation to the social actors of the local contexts where its development is promoted, indeed attest to how complex the dynamics of political and symbolic negotiation are within tourismifying contexts.

In fact, my interest in tourist accounts responds to a specific goal that I set as the main hypothesis of my research, namely, to investigate whether and to what extent the direct, albeit superficial, knowledge resulting from the spread of tourism in Cambodia would help to confirm or contest the double imaginary that I saw emerging from a visit to the market of Siem

Reap during preliminary fieldwork: a mix of ancient and contemporary history, archaeological romance, and genocidal terror, where T-shirts representing Angkor were hanging next to others with imprints of the maps of skulls that are preserved in the killing field of Choeung Ek, or replicas of guidebooks and travel novels of colonial and present times are found side by side with books about contemporary history and biographies of genocide survivors.

My conversations with tourists often begun with a question: "Why Cambodia?" A middle- to upper-class couple, retired professionals who had joined an organized group tour to Cambodia, Laos, and Bangkok in 2001, hinted at the genocide argument at the beginning of our conversation, indulging the concept several times, as in this quote:

> Cesare: For years … you are young, I don't know what you can remember, but we only heard of Vietnam! It was … I don't know how to say …
>
> Beatrice: … It was our daily bread …
>
> Cesare: For sure, … it was the very heart of military policy, international relations was Vietnam.
>
> Beatrice: And Cambodia, Laos, and Cambodia as a side dish. (Rome, 19 June 2002)

For others, the interest is less overtly declared, but sites of memory seem to fit overwhelmingly with contemporary tourist itineraries. Speaking of Tuol Sleng, Ilaria, a mature postgraduate student in her thirties who visited Cambodia and Vietnam on her own in 2002, says: "I really planned to go there … also to realize, to see what had happened" (Bologna, 21 March 2003).

To my question about what places she visited in Phnom Penh, Elena, a forty-year-old high school English teacher who visited Cambodia and Vietnam with a small party of six independent travelers, replied:

> Elena: We visited what we had to, we went to the museum, the prison …
>
> Federica: Ah, you mean the Genocide Museum …
>
> Elena: No, the other, we visited the other one [the National Museum]. It's pretty well managed, I would say. (Turin, 14 December 2002)

One of my research hypotheses, therefore, was to verify whether the image of Cambodia as a destination was mainly built around the idea of Angkor, the great archaeological complex that is accessed through a network of services (hotels and restaurants, airport, commercial premises) available in the neighboring town of Siem Reap. Such an imaginary of the country, as in the case of Mercille's research about Tibet (2005), has undoubtedly been shared collectively and reproduced socially, not only through travel and touristic materials and accounts, but also through other means, such as documentaries, movies, and video games (above all Lara Croft; Winter 2002).

As a result, Cambodia is often advertised as a destination primarily to audiences interested in archaeology, which reiterates, sometimes implicitly, sometimes overtly, that there is a gap between contemporary Cambodia—a poor country with a tragic recent history and a low potential in terms of socioeconomic development—and the mythical empire of Angkorian Cambodia, which rose between the ninth and fifteenth centuries BCE and which expanded its rule over most of Southeast Asia (Chandler 1998: 29). The magnificence of the shrines, as well as the charming fusion of architecture and tropical trees, are among the most frequent suggestions building up the touristic imaginary of Cambodia, both on the part of the tourist industry and on the part of the tourists and travelers, attesting to an overlap between the imaginary provided by tourism and the snapshots it builds on, and the imaginary reconstructed by tourists after their journeys: Cambodia is identified with Angkor, and Angkor is the image of the glorious Cambodian history.

In the case of Italian tourists, the fact that for many Cambodia is identified exclusively with the great archaeological park of Angkor Wat is probably due to the fact that sojourns in the country are usually extremely limited both in terms of time (a few days to maximum one week) and space (sites of interest, notably in the case of organized tours, are almost exclusively Angkor, the capital of the past, and Phnom Penh, the capital of the present). Therefore, emerging narratives and related imaginaries of this country are clearly influenced by spatial-temporal constraints, which are emphasized by the problems of mobility caused by the continued presence of land mines.[2]

In a country like Cambodia, undergoing a profound and rapid transformation process, such descriptions, even when compared from a diachronic point of view, allow us to take snapshots of the changing shape and reality. These dynamics are reflected both in the accounts of those who visited the country twice in different years, and in comparisons of various tales of travelers who visited the country in diverse moments.[3] Not only are there just as many tourist imaginaries as there are tourists (Di Giovine, this volume), but even in the same tourist's multiple experiences, the imaginary of the country changes, and sociocultural changes "ruin" the imaginary of an untouched and enchanted context (see also Theodossopoulos, this volume).

Yet, tourist accounts are not the sole typology of existing narratives of Cambodia as a tourism destination. In fact, when preparing for the trip, either alone or with an organized group, tourists access travel guides—both the *Lonely Planet* and the *Guide du Routard* are available in Italian—or promotional magazines and tour schedules provided by tour operators.[4] I have defined these "a priori descriptions," because they are materials used by tourists in preparation for their travel. Such depictions can also dwell on sources other than those provided by the tourism industry (see Salazar and Graburn, this volume; Salazar 2009). The travel narratives of the tourists back home are "a posteriori descriptions," informed by the subjective experience of the Cambodian context.

The reflections that follow are inspired by the analysis of the imaginaries emerging from both kinds of descriptions: they show, in my view, how different the "times" and "places" of touristic experiences of one destination may be. The plurality of elements arising from these stories shows how many diverse "Cambodias" may in fact coexist, despite a trend in the construction of its tourism imaginary tending to reduce it to its archaeological past and to its "primordial" dehistoricized contemporary condition.

TIME-SPACE COMPRESSION AND DISTANTIATION

"What is certain is that for all, being a tourist represents a time-out-of-time, a liminal period removed from the constraints of normal, everyday routine" (Boissevain 2002: x). The concepts of space and time and their possible interpretations are indeed extremely important to understand fully contemporary tourism imaginaries. Considering carefully theoretical analyses of time and space in the contemporary world can provide useful insights for the ethnographic study of the tourism experience. I rely particularly on an argument developed by Inda and Rosaldo (2002: 1–34). Referring to the notions of space and time, they take into account and compare two apparently opposite approaches: David Harvey's "time and space compression" ([1990] 2004: 284–307) and Anthony Giddens's "time and space distantiation" (1990, 1991). These notions seem to me particularly apt to the study of tourism and the construction of space and time in tourism imaginaries.

Let us consider first Harvey's space-time compression. The time needed to do things, the empirical distance between different places in space that shrink progressively, the automation of the transport network, and the presence and proliferation of social actors working for tourism services all convey the idea that potential tourists will be able to reduce the time needed to organize and manage their trip. Likewise, the existence and spread of increasingly faster transport has helped to significantly reduce distances. Indeed, it is now possible in a span of a few hours to find ourselves in places geographically and culturally distant from our ordinary life.

The suggestion of such speed sometimes even distorts our own travel memories, as in the case of Caterina, who went to Cambodia with her husband Ettore for three weeks, invited by a colleague involved in a research project there. When asked about the trajectory to reach the country, Caterina affirmed she did not have a stopover in Bangkok, but landed directly in Phnom Penh:

> Federica: You have traveled to Rome, so … you did Rome-Bangkok and from there you go …
>
> Caterina: No, no, Rome-Phnom Penh, we did …
>
> Federica: Yes, with a stopover in …
>
> Ettore: No, no, without a stopover …
>
> Federica: I mean, have you changed airplane, there was a direct flight …
>
> Caterina: Ettore, please, haven't we had a direct flight? Yes …
>
> Ettore: Phnom Penh-Rome.
>
> Caterina: Why not? We did not stop …
>
> Ettore: We didn't get off …
>
> Caterina: We didn't have to change aircraft, at all … I mean, we boarded in Rome and we arrived in Phnom Penh. (Rome, 26 March 2002)

In reality, a direct flight from Rome to Phnom Penh has never existed, nor did it operate at the time of their visit in 1998, as I verified afterward.

Even in promotional brochures, tour operators play with the idea of space-time compression: "Rallo Worldwide: Close to distant lands" (Rallo Worldwide-Boscolo Group 2002: 3); "When in Rome, do as Turisanda does" (Turisanda 2001: 2).[5]

> Service and assistance have always been at the core of our planning, along with the respect for the traveler, who by choosing Tours Service knew he could count … on the best and fastest air connections, directly operated by reliable carriers. Over the past 25 years, much has changed … and the time to reach the most important destinations in Southeast Asia, Australia, and the South Pacific has been significantly reduced by the introduction of nonstop flights. (Tours Service 2001: 3)

In these examples, tour operators invite their potential customers to choose distant destinations emphasizing their being nearby, eliminating the spatial distance that still remains the key ingredient of the offer but is no longer an obstacle: fast connections become the means to reach the Other promptly. Tourists, too, can express this idea of compression, like this travel blogger who wrote soon after his return: "I'm back. About 20 hours ago I was on the other side of the world, and now I'm here, waiting to collapse in my bed."[6]

However, in flyers and catalogs, as well as in oral accounts, there can also be suggestions that indicate a greater adherence to the model of Giddens, who defines globalization as "the interlacing of social events and social relations 'at a distance' with local contextualities" (1991: 21). In Giddens's model, compression seems to contribute to a broadening of experiences and social relationships; in the case of tourism we can see this interpretation represented by those brochures, guides, and accounts that place more emphasis on the gap between the ordinary experience of space and time in everyday life and those experienced while on tour. The following excerpt from a catalog seems to be informed by such a reading, which extends the distance between places of origin and destination to evoke in potential tourists a lust for the exotic:

> Imagine a picturesque landscape, the meeting of new people, and the silence of the great outdoors. Imagine yourself touching the symbols of more distant countries, leaving the passion to overflow so to live intense emotions. Imagine discovering lost civilizations and ancient cultures, to reach distant destinations, unique places that make you feel special. Imagine, and explore the charming world of Caleidoscopio. (Viaggi Del Ventaglio 2001: 3; see also Viaggi Del Ventaglio 2002, 2003)

Antonio, a forty-year-old veterinarian who visited Cambodia with an NGO-organized sustainable tourism tour, seems to embody this interpretation of space and time in his own words:

> I was reading Terzani's book *Un Indovino mi Disse,*[7] before the departure and throughout the trip, ... this helped me, in a sense. However, I could not imagine, even remotely, what I finally found.... I mean, what you think you'll see when you go to a place you've never seen, it's your own self-made template. Then, quite the opposite, you enter step-by-step ... starting from the length of the flight, you have to ... it's like if you are thrown into another [dimension], traveling all night ... it's always you, you reach Bangkok, and in Bangkok you find yourself in a situation ... beyond the mental chaos you suffer because of the jet lag, the climate which is so different, everything ... so for all these hours you're there, you're in a ... confused state of mind, you don't even realize where you are. (Rome, 11 January 2003)

The flight is "long," and is described as an experience suspended between two worlds. There is a sort of a priori representation of the destination, influenced by the reading of a book, an autobiographic travel novel written by an

Italian correspondent from Asia that has become a famous piece of contemporary Italian literature. However, we can read also the sense of distance, physical and metaphorical, between what has been imagined, even based on detailed information, and what instead becomes the concrete travel experience. There does not seem to be space, in this account, for Huggan's pointed reflections on contemporary air travel, which become "a marker of the everyday" (2009: 2). Here, travel is still "a badge of the exotic" (Huggan 2009: 2).

Space and time, compressed and distantiated together: this is how they appear in the words of tourism discourse, whether printed in catalogs, guides, and brochures or produced by tourists in their own oral and written accounts of the sites visited.

OF TOURISTS AND ANTHROPOLOGISTS: CONFLICTING OR CONVERGING?

Ethnography and Anthropology of Tourism vis-à-vis Ethnic and Cultural Tourism

So far, I have focused my attention on the imaginary of Cambodia produced within tourism. But what about the anthropological gaze? Is it innocent in such a production or does it play its own part? In a provocative essay, Malcolm Crick described the anthropologist and the tourist as two actors who, despite the attempts of the first to distinguish from the latter, could be considered as "distant relatives" (1995: 205). Indeed, they all "are travelers and collectors—both literally and metaphorically—in the space of the 'other'" (Crick 1995: 207). They all go "elsewhere" looking for abstract and concrete items to improve their own status. Whether this means an advancement in the academic career for the anthropologist (through the publication of fieldwork-based academic articles and books), or a collection of souvenirs and iconic witnesses that the tourist brings back to complete his/her account to those who remained at home, both collect and reappropriate symbolic and material objects that attest to the encounter with the Other and, with it, to the attainment of the prestige that such encounters engender.

Of course, there are also differences, and Crick himself underscores this: the seriousness of anthropology versus the frivolous character of leisure travels, the length of stay (long versus short), the kind of relationship the anthropologist creates with the locals compared to the superficial contact the tourist can have with them,[8] the greater preparedness concerning local traditions and society, and finally, a deeper search of "authenticity" compared to the tourist, who is believed to be satisfied by fictional artificial cultural performances.

Paraphrasing Geertz (1975), for the anthropologist the description must be thick, while for the tourist a thin one would be sufficient (see also Bruner 1989: 112; Crick 1995: 217). This is a rather harsh imaginary of tourists on the part of anthropologists, somewhat nuanced over the past decades by the increasing attention the discipline has given to the complex issues related to the globalization of tourism. Similar to the anthropologist, the tourist brings back to a domestic audience his or her own representation of the country visited. Undeniably, there are significant differences between these narratives. Still, it is worth reflecting on some common features that allow us to assimilate the writing of anthropological literature of the twentieth century to the ways in which travel narratives are shaped.

From the Ethnographic Present to Travel Narratives

Since postmodern reflections have entered the anthropological debate, the question of how to represent the contemporary presence ("coevalness," intended as living in the same time) of anthropologists and natives within fieldwork descriptions has become crucial. The significance of this issue is underscored by Marcus and Fischer (1999), who analyze anthropology's theoretical experiments that have dealt with the matter of time. Speaking of ethnographers of the twentieth century, they highlight how these have often been accused of a deep synchronic bias: "The setting of ethnographic accounts in a timeless present does not arise from a blindness to history and the fact of the continual social change, but rather is a tradeoff for the advantages that bracketing the flow of time and the influence of events offers in facilitating the structural analysis of systems of symbols and social relations" (Marcus and Fischer 1999: 95).

Fabietti shows how the "strict rules of description" used in ethnographic writing have been subject to changes "depending on the period and on the prevailing 'paradigm'" (1999: 120). The unique, unchanging element has been the use of the present tense, through which anthropologists tend to "present" the cultures they study. Apparently, we could ascribe this choice to the fact that the present tense reflects "the encounter, the coevalness, their 'being there' at the same time of the ethnographer and his/her interlocutors" (Fabietti 1999: 120). But the ethnographic present "contains many more elements 'culturally determined' than what we commonly think" (Fabietti 1999: 120), and, concretely, this has brought anthropological literature about "natives" to contribute to the reification of cultural elements and dynamics. The problematic nature of the description Fabietti refers to is such that a sum of ethnographic accounts, determined in terms of time by the permanence of the anthropologist in the field, is put in a timeless discipline of anthropology in the corpus, so that "in addition to producing undue generalizations probably has the effect to 'build' a people ... largely outside of history" (Fabietti 1999: 122).

Travel accounts by tourists are not narrated in the present tense and, unlike the ethnographic account, the story of the trip is narrated primarily through use of the past tense: "I went for the first time when I was [in Vietnam], then I went a second time with Sabina" (Luciano, Rome, 14 January 2003). In addition, there is usually an attempt to locate the time of the travel from a chronological point of view:

> Federica: Do not you remember the year, approximately ... ?
> Sabina: About nine years ago. (Rome, 3 December 2002)

> Due to various circumstances, in the end we managed to organize it in 2001. (Nino and Sara, Milan, 15 November 2002)

If the travel story is narrated in the past tense, the fact remains that, even after ten years, the tourist who was there at the time will describe it as it was: crystallized by his or her own experience and the historical moment of the visit. In doing so, years later when he or she describes Cambodia again, the tourist uses a narrative construction in the past tense, but provides the audience snapshots of Cambodia related to the period in which the trip was undertaken. In the perception of the tourist, "Cambodia" is and remains the one that was experienced at the time of the visit.

So, for example, even years later, Cambodia is the country where, "In many temples there were soldiers around us ... is not that they said, instead: 'Now we will accompany you,' but even if we were splitting, we always had a soldier next to us" (Sabina, Rome, 3 December 2002), and where, "The most beautiful hotel there was, believe me, was actually very modest. Rather, it was huge, and claimed to be luxurious. The bathroom, you could skate in it, as it was enormous ... but it was decadent" (Sabina, Rome, 3 December 2002). Such placing somewhere else in space and time that emerges from living the exotic sightseeing trip may not be entirely innocent. Today, tourists are trying to put the Other in a space that is "outside" of time and overtly express their intention with a lively sense, as Sabina does:

> Twenty years ago, India was not what it is today ... Take Kathmandu, for example, Kathmandu as I saw it myself, I refused to go in the last time I went. I do

not want to see the asphalted square. I want to see the market square with the dust … I don't want to ruin my memories. (Rome, 3 December 2002)

If, indeed, "tourism results from a basic binary division between the ordinary/every day and the extraordinary" (Urry 2002: 12), the more "modern" the locals become, "the less interest they have for [the] occidental tourist" (Bruner 1995: 224). Similar processes have been described across the globe (Salazar 2009: 59; Winter 2009). Hence, in order to make sense of their experience, tourists—and the industry that promotes exotic destinations—need to create, or at least amplify, the distance between the self and the local. Therefore, it is not enough to travel thousands of miles. Because we live in a world in which space and time have suffered a compression, "travel cannot be the experience of discovery and intercultural contact that it used to be" (Jean, Phnom Penh, 19 October 2001).

Travel narratives, then, function similarly to classic ethnographic texts in the reading of Fabian (1983): geographical and cultural Otherness is reinforced by a culture of denial between the contemporary context of departure (which is also that of return) and the place visited. In the case of descriptions of Cambodia I analyzed, such denial is expressed mainly by ignoring cultural dignity in contemporary Cambodia's cultural production, and by constantly recalling a historical and archaeological past that, with its artistic and architectural heritage, overwhelms an underdeveloped and impoverished present. More important for our discussion becomes the need to address the issue of the time within which Cambodia is inserted as a place of the "Elsewhere."

ALLOCHRONISM AND ORIENTALISM IN CONTEMPORARY CAMBODIA

A Cambodia Out of Time: Denial of Coevalness in Cambodia's Tourism Imaginary

In the way in which tourism is related to a context, the "Other" mainly refers to reflections proposed by Fabian (1983), who retraces the steps that have helped to place Otherness in a temporal, as well as spatial, "Elsewhere." The central concept that emerges is "allochronism," or the location of the Other in a different time (the past) than that of the narrator, author, or ethnographer. The central object of Fabian's argument is a critique of anthropological knowledge as generator of allochronism. Focused on the analysis of the constitution of anthropology as a science and the rereading of texts that have become its theoretical and methodological foundation,

Fabian's reflections about the topos of the journey identify some mechanisms that underlie the ways of interaction between the self and the Other within tourism.

In the case of tourism in Cambodia, there are two discourses about time that seem to coexist, and that, although at times contradictory, partially replicate allochronism (see Bunzl 2002). The practice of travel, Fabian argues, has risen in the history of Western thought and has contributed to the process of secularization and naturalization of time. With the advent of modernity, there is a "succession of attempts to secularize Judeo-Christian Time by generalizing and universalizing it" (Fabian 1983: 2). Travel became, at least potentially, "every man's source of 'philosophical,' secular knowledge" (Fabian 1983: 6), allowing the individual to become acquainted with Otherness by moving in space. This thirst for knowledge about the Other is aimed at better knowing oneself: the more exotic a place, the closer it is to our own past. But while contemporary anthropological thought has long revealed the workings of allochronism, such awareness does not emerge from the descriptions of exotic travel that I came across during my research. The risk of generalization is high, however, both in a priori narratives (guides, brochures, tourism itineraries) and in a posteriori ones (oral accounts, travel blogs). In Francorosso's brochures, for example, Cambodia is presented as follows: "A wandering writer left his travel notes at the beginning of the century, after visiting Cambodia. '... I did not think we could still feel an emotion so deep in front of the ruins of the past, a feeling of such an intense discovery'" (2001: 54; see also Francorosso 2003).[9]

The description above was written at the beginning of the twentieth century. But as Franceschi reminds us, already in the nineteenth century, during its colonial expansion in the region,

> France began ... to churn out reports of infantry officers and sailors, of frightened and curious soldiers, of pedantic professors, of fascinating and reluctant travelers, some of encyclopedic nature, some rather autobiographical, yet sentimental. ... Drawn either as handbooks to collect, or as objective scientific documents, their apparent intention to provide for objective knowledge ... hides in reality the ideology of the French rationalist and encyclopedic thought typical of the eighteenth century that ... has greatly contributed to the construction and crystallization of precise stereotypes. (2001: 55)

Such stereotypes demonstrate "how the contemporary imaginary of Southeast Asia, and more specifically the one of tourism, has been strongly nurtured and shaped by glossy, rarefied, romantic, eccentric or surreal images of these characters" (Franceschi 2001: 56). With the publication of *A Pilgrimage to Angkor*, Pierre Loti ([1912] 1991) narrates the achievement of his childhood dream of visiting Angkor: "That evening, then, … I was rummaging through some yellowed papers brought back from Indochina in the baggage of my dead brother … There was a picture besides which I stood shivering: gigantic bizarre towers entrapped by exotic branches all around, the temples of the mysterious Angkor!"[10]

Loti's writing is part of the prolific literary production that characterized the exploratory and colonial age, when descriptions often contained elements of cultural imperialism. According to Loti, early twentieth-century Cambodia represented a modest survival of the ancient Khmer culture. Narrating briefly the history of the people of Cambodia and the mysterious Khmer empire, from Funan to his age, Loti writes:

> It seems that the town of Angkor saw the peak of its glory during the Buddhist era, and the invading forest preserves its secret. Small contemporary Cambodia, upholder of complicated rituals whose meaning are lost, is a final remnant of this vast Khmer empire, which for more than five hundred years has ceased to exist under the silence of trees and mosses.[11]

Fabian refers in particular to James Boon's *The Anthropological Romance of Bali* (Boon 1977, quoted in Fabian 1983: 134–36), a text attesting to the existence of an iconic trend in symbolic anthropology:

> Boon's project is carried out with elegance and persuasiveness. His central concern might in fact be quite close to the one pursued in these essays: The ethnography of Bali must be understood in the context of "temporal perspectives" … which successively and cumulatively have contributed to constituting "Bali" as a topos, i.e. a striking and significant place of return and reference in Western anthropological discourse. From the time of its discovery as a "paradise" by the Dutch, to Mead and Bateson's delight at finding its people superbly photogenic, … down to the touristic packaging of the island in our days, … the Western image of timeless Bali was maintained with unwavering tenacity. (Fabian 1983: 134–35)

To return to Loti's Cambodia, his description of its inhabitants, and in particular of the region of Siem Reap, seems to capture the "iconic trend" and to display a certain propensity to allochronism: "We go across villages, quiet and beautiful as in the golden age, where people look at us passing through, smiling of shy benevolence. The race seems more and more mixed with Indian blood, because many girls have big black eyes, shaded like those of the dancers."[12] Here we are faced with an embodiment of Lowenthal's theory, where cultural, historical, and ethnic tourism are becoming increasingly popular and widespread as a vehicle for a sense of nostalgia for the premodern (Graburn 2001: 49; Lowenthal 1985).

But in today's travel proposals, it is not possible to place all the countries of Southeast Asia in a distant past. Hence, many promotional descriptions combine the idea of past and "future." In other words, travel always takes tourists into another time. For instance, a description of a tour to Vietnam, Cambodia, and Thailand, states: "A tour that delves into the fascinating atmosphere of Vietnam, through the sights of its city ... and then moves in search of the remains of the ancient Khmer empire in Cambodia ... concluding in Bangkok, with its city skyscrapers and magnificent temples, it's Travel back in time" (Francorosso 2001: 138). Similarly, in a brochure promoting the Orient:

> We have an ambitious goal: to offer travels that open your mind, "cure" your spirit, and represent a durable investment in time. Let our East become yours too; do "a leap into the past, a jump into the future"! This is the essence of an immense territory, inhabited by peoples so different and so alike at the same time, in constant development, without abandoning the bond with their traditions and their soul. The signs of a glorious past are visible at every corner and contribute to the creation of an extraordinary landscape: an exciting and unique "mélange," where mysticism and vitality, past and future, metropolis and jungle take turns. (Kuoni Group-Gastaldi Tours 2002: 5)

The Orientalist Gaze of Cambodia's Tourism Imaginary

Such promotional tourism discourse is paradigmatic of a certain mode of comparing the self (us) to the East (them), as is well explained in Said's *Orientalism* (1978). Narrowly defined as "a field of learned study" (Said 1978: 49), Said reminds us that "any account of Orientalism would have to consider not only the professional Orientalist and his work, but also the very notion of a field of study based on a geographical cultural, linguistic and ethnic unit called the Orient" (Said 1978: 50). It follows that

> Orientalism is a field with considerable geographical ambition. And since Orientalists have traditionally occupied themselves with things Oriental ..., we must learn to accept enormous, indiscriminate size plus a salient almost infinite capacity for subdivision as one of the chief characteristics of Orientalism—one that is evidenced in its confusing amalgam of imperial vagueness and precise detail. (Said 1978: 50)

In the case of contemporary Cambodia, this "stereotypical knowledge" is applied almost exclusively to the past of the Khmer empire. Contemporary history, represented in particular by the genocide that occurred during the

1970s, is reduced to an indirect reference in the majority of tour descriptions. It is a kind of historical caesura that would interrupt an atemporal and aesthetic description of the Khmer people, represented as an unchanging cultural entity until the late 1960s. The work of Sciortino (2003) confirms this. He describes a contrast, real or manufactured, between the present situation and "the vision of a 'gentle land inhabited by people who are always smiling' that is endemic in the accounts of travelers of the nineteenth century and in the memories of international consultants and journalists over the Sixties" (Sciortino 2003: 79).

The rupture caused by the regime of Democratic Kampuchea, which Sciortino has shown to be the most common explanation given by the "Cambodian residents—both expatriates and locals" (2003: 79), is another topos in the descriptions offered by brochures of Italian tour operators. For example, promoting a tour itinerary entirely devoted to Cambodia and Laos, an operator writes: "These are the new emerging markets of Southeast Asia. In Cambodia, finished with the horrors of civil war, shines the eternal light of Angkor, the ancient capital, which rises like a mirage in the middle of the jungle, the largest and most spectacular archaeological site in Asia" (Mistral Tour Internazionale-Quality Group 2000: 33). But in describing the very same tour two years later, the mention of the civil war "magically" disappears, making room for an elsewhere truly "Other," in space and in time: "From the quiet and idyllic landscapes of Vientiane and Luang Prabang to the wondrous architecture of the monuments of Angkor" (Mistral Tour Internazionale-Quality Group 2002: 34).[13]

This reticence is also strategically used by the Italian tour operator I interviewed in Phnom Penh. He affirmed, without hesitation: "With groups of 20 people, I usually reach the room with the pictures[14] and the ladies gesticulate to announce they'll wait for us outside" (Sergio, Phnom Penh, 23 October 2001). He also explained his disagreement with the idea of promoting the genocidal sites, referring to his own experience as tour guide and expatriate living in Cambodia:

> I don't push Tuol Sleng. I was there for the first time in 1990 and came out in shreds. Having been there at least thirty-forty times, I still come out shocked ... Of course, this is an important site to understand the history of the country, but now even Cambodians don't want to go there, why should we? (Sergio, Phnom Penh, 23 October 2001)

It almost seems that with the erasure of the past created by the Khmer Rouge, the only past remaining is the motionless and invariable era of the Khmer empire, brought to the light of the present by tourism—a present that cannot change. Emblematic are the words of a tour operator, promoting services in Cambodia, which promise that tourists will "discover a different Orient static in time" (Kuoni Group-Gastaldi Tours 2012).

CONCLUDING REMARKS: 2001–11

Over a span of ten years, since I first studied the construction of Cambodia as a touristic destination, it still seems a vivid idea that the traveler visiting this country will be confronted with an unchanging world. But a few changes have also occurred in the meantime. First, fewer Italian tour operators are promoting tours to Cambodia. Of the twenty-three operators active in Cambodia during my original research, nine are not traveling to the country anymore, eight are not offering any more packages to the country, and one was declared bankrupt. This decrease is compensated for by the diversification of existing products. Although the majority of tours are still focused exclusively on Angkor and Phnom Penh, new destinations have been added, so that other sites are appearing in tourism brochures: archaeological sites, seaside resorts, and the hills hosting ethnic minorities. Moreover, Cambodia seems to have become one of the favorite destinations of Italian independent travelers, as attested by the large number of travel blogs and travel accounts on some of the most important Italian websites.[15]

In this chapter, I have highlighted how the Italian tourism imaginary related to contemporary Cambodia is produced. I have presented examples of how tour operators and tourist accounts describe the experience of the journey in Cambodia, swinging between imaginaries of time-space compression and distantiation. I have described how tourist accounts produce a crystallization of the context visited as unchanging and unchangeable. I have then highlighted the similarities and differences between anthropology and tourism, and explored anthropological notions of coevalness (Fabian 1983) and Orientalism (Said 1978) to show how the denial of the first and the affirmation of the latter are significant in understanding the imaginary of contemporary Cambodia that tourism produces.

Indeed, if the Other lives in a present that does not change, then its time is past compared to ours, with all the repercussions that similar representations convey. A quote from a brochure is emblematic of this attitude:

These are cultures emerging thousands of years ago from China and India … They are sensational and advanced cultures that have created monumental works where man, eager of immensity, manifests in practice its spiritual dimension…. We have the chance to meet this extraordinary dimension, which is sometimes asleep in the Western man, who on the road toward economic productivity has not always clearly demonstrated an ability to determine the scale that differentiates humankind from other living creatures. These people now need us, our attention; they need our skills, the awareness offered by education, our scientific knowledge and technological evolution, and even more they need the capacity that the West has now acquired to understand the importance of enhancing the historic, traditional, social and environmental heritage having experienced the often irreversible damage resulting from the contempt of diversity, cultural homologation, inattention to the environment, finally from selfishness and presumption. Perhaps it is utopian to think of the means granted without asking anything in return, maybe it's an achievement to be done, perhaps this trip is another opportunity for reflection. (Siesta Tour Operator 2001: 172; see also Siesta Tour Operator 2010)[16]

The dual narrative voice through which Indo-Chinese cultures are presented to potential travelers is typical. First, the age-old tradition of the spirituality of these peoples and their degree of civilization, witnessed through demonstrations of architectural "monuments" that still prove their greatness. Second, the need to pay "attention" to these people, to whom the West has to offer its "capacity," having the courage to give without asking anything in return. So, on the one hand, there is the majesty of past, while, on the other hand, the present time emerges. While history is unquestionably central to the understanding of the current sociocultural situation, the period of colonial rule and the geopolitical conflicts of the Cold War have been silently removed. What seems to prevail is a tendency to "reflect" on "their" backwardness—their being in a time that is not ours.

NOTES

1. My interviewees' travels to Cambodia took place between 1987 and 2002. Tour operator interviews in Phnom Penh were collected in October 2001. Tour catalogs and brochure excerpts relate to 2000–3 and 2010–11. Bloggers quoted visited Cambodia in 2010, but websites analyzed host accounts dating from 2001 to 2011.
2. Lorenzo, a young backpacker who defined himself as "an engineer with a vocation in classical studies," visited Cambodia with a party of five to reach a friend that was volunteering in the country; when asked what he talked about when back in Italy, he said: "The things that, a bit cynically, made us laugh ... like the guides that tell: 'Don't get off the road, there are mines.' You think 'Mines?!?' and they really are out there! So, one thinks always they vaguely exaggerate, but there are" (Milan, 16 December 2002).

3. For instance, Luciano, a psychoanalyst with a deep passion for Oriental architecture, visited Angkor first in 1987 and again in 1992 as an independent traveler on a tour of two weeks in Cambodia and Laos together with Sabina. This is nine years before Elena, who was there in 2001 for the very first and last time. Caterina and Ettore presumably experienced a politically less worrying climate than Sabina did in 1992 or Sergio in 1995, but more thrilling compared to Antonio and Elisa, or Claudio and Lorenzo, who were there in 2001; not to mention the travel bloggers of Turisti per Caso in 2009–10 (see http://turistiper caso.it/a/magazine/diario/cambogia/ [accessed 2 March 2012]).

4. Avventure nel Mondo, a renowned company that combines tour organization with independent traveling, hands out to its customers a handbook containing information on history, culture, society, and potential attractions. Sergio, an urban policeman in his fifties who visited Cambodia with Avventure nel Mondo in 1995, told me: "There was a handbook, that we were given by Avventure, containing a collection of articles on this issue … and then, visiting Tuol Sleng & Co., there's a lot of history to read about" (Poggio Rusco, 20 March 2002).

5. English translation of "Paese che vai, Turisanda che trovi."

6. http://turistipercaso.it/cambogia/58683/lettere-dalla-kampuchea.html (accessed 22 January 2012).

7. Literally, "A diviner told me" (Terzani 1995).

8. Though Graburn (2002) has pointed out that anthropologists studying tourists and other mobile modern subjects may be limited to short "quick and dirty" field research at destinations, with much less well-rounded knowledge of the tourists than desired.

9. Despite keeping Cambodia and Indochina on its homepage as destinations, Francorosso is currently not offering any package to the country (see http://www.francorosso.it/vacanze/estremo_oriente/indocina/index.asp [accessed 2 March 2012]).

10. "Ce soir-là donc, … je feuilletais des papiers jaunis, revenus d'Indo-Chine dans les bagages de mon frère mort…. il y avait une image devant laquelle je m'arrêtai saisi de frisson: de grandes tours étranges que des ramures exotiques enlaçaient de toutes parts, les temples de la mystérieuse Angkor!" (Loti [1912] 1991: 1198).

11. "Il semble que, sous le bouddhisme, la ville d'Angkor connut l'apogée de sa gloire, et la forêt envahissante en garde le secret. Le petit Cambodge actuel, conservateur de rites compliqués au sens perdu, est un dernier débris de ce vaste empire des Khmers, qui depuis plus de cinq cent ans a fini de s'éteindre sous le silence des arbres et des mousses" (Loti [1912] 1991: 1198).

12. "Nous traversons des villages, tranquilles et jolis comme à l'âge de l'or, où les gens nous regardent passer avec des sourires de bienveillance timide. La race semble de plus en plus mélangée de sang indien, car beaucoup de jeunes filles ont des grands yeux noirs, ombrés comme ceux des bayadères" (Loti [1912] 1991: 1193).

13. The description is the same as the latest brochure I accessed online: http://www
.qualitygroup.it/sites/all/themes/quality/bookreader/index.php?catalogo=esto
#page/61/mode/1up (accessed 2 March 2012). This was the case for many of
the catalogs I compared between the period of my research (2000–3) and more
recent offerings (2010–12).

14. The reference here is to a panel with photographs of the victims of the Khmer
Rouge regime, recorded, imprisoned, tortured, and murdered in the S-21
prison, better known as Tuol Sleng, a former high school in the outskirts of
Phnom Penh, where between seventeen thousand and thirty thousand people
were jailed.

15. Cambodia is the second destination in Indochina and fourth in Asia to be visited by backpackers of vagabondo.net (http://www.vagabondo.net/viaggiare-in/
Asia [accessed 2 March 2012]); on Turisti per Caso, a website associated with
a popular TV series, the travel diaries concerning Cambodia are mainly related to trips made between 2007 and 2011 (http://turistipercaso.it/a/magazine/
diario/cambogia/ [accessed 2 March 2012]).

16. This quote was used in 2001 to introduce a tour combining Myanmar and Cambodia. Currently, the tour operator's website reserves the quote exclusively for
Myanmar. With what happened in the 1970s becoming a more and more distant
memory, aid and cooperation are not central anymore in depicting Cambodia.

REFERENCES

Alneng, Victor. 2002. "'What the Fuck Is a Vietnam?'" *Critique of Anthropology* 22, no.
4: 461–89.

Boissevain, Jeremy. 2002. "Preface." In *Tourism: Between Place and Performance,* ed.
Simon M. Coleman and Mike Crang. New York: Berghahn Books.

Boon, James A. 1977. *The Anthropological Romance of Bali, 1597–1972.* Cambridge:
Cambridge University Press.

Bruner, Edward M. 1989. "Tourism, Creativity and Authenticity." *Studies in Symbolic
Interaction* 10: 109–14.

———. 1995. "Ethnographer/Tourist in Indonesia." In *International Tourism: Identity and
Change,* ed. Marie-Françoise Lanfant, John B. Allcock, and Edward B. Bruner.
London: Sage.

Bunzl, Matti. 2002. "Foreword." In *Time and the Other: How Anthropology Makes Its Object,* 2nd ed., Johannes Fabian. New York: Columbia University Press.

Chandler, David. 1998. *A History of Cambodia.* Updated 2nd ed. Chiang Mai, Thailand: Silkworm Books.

Crick, Malcolm. 1995. "The Anthropologist as Tourist: An Identity in Question." In
International Tourism: Identity and Change, ed. Marie-Françoise Lanfant, John B.
Allcock, and Edward B. Bruner. London: Sage.

Fabian, Johannes. 1983. *Time and the Other: How Anthropology Makes Its Object.* New
York: Columbia University Press.

Fabietti, Ugo. 1999. *Antropologia Culturale: L'Esperienza e l'Interpretazione.* Roma: Laterza.

Fabietti, Ugo, Roberto Malighetti, and Vincenzo Matera. 2000. *Dal Tribale al Globale: Introduzione all'Antropologia.* Milan: Bruno Mondadori.

Ferraris, Federica. 2004. "Angkor, Angkar: La Cambogia Contesto e Pretesto per una Lettura Antropologica del Turismo." PhD diss., University of Milano–Bicocca.

Franceschi, Zelda A. 2001. "Sulla Via dei Mandarini, in Pellegrinaggio ad Angkor: La Città che Riempie la Metà del Cielo ..." *Afriche e Orienti,* nos. 3–4: 54–60.

Geertz, Clifford. 1973. *The Interpretation of Cultures: Selected Essays.* New York: Basic Books.

——. 1997. "Cultural Tourism: Tradition, Identity and Heritage Construction." In *Tourism and Heritage Management,* ed. Wiendu Nuryanti. Yogyakarta, Indonesia: Gadjah Mada University Press.

Giddens, Anthony. 1990. *The Consequences of Modernity.* Palo Alto, CA: Stanford University Press.

——. 1991. *Modernity and Self-Identity.* Cambridge: Polity Press.

Graburn, Nelson H. H. 2001. "Secular Ritual: A General Theory of Tourism." In *Hosts and Guests Revisited: Tourism Issues of the 21st Century,* ed. Valene Smith and Mary-Ann Brent. New York: Cognizant.

——. 2002. "The Ethnographic Tourist." In *The Tourist as a Metaphor of the Social World,* ed. Graham M. S. Dann. Wallingford, UK: CABI.

Harrison, Julia. 2003. *Being a Tourist.* Trent: University of British Columbia Press.

Harvey, David. (1990) 2004. *The Condition of Postmodernity.* Oxford: Blackwell.

Huggan, Graham. 2009. *Extreme Pursuits: Travel/Writing in the Age of Globalization.* Ann Arbor: University of Michigan Press.

Inda, Jonathan X., and Renato Rosaldo, eds. 2002. *The Anthropology of Globalization: A Reader.* Oxford: Blackwell.

Loti, Pierre. (1912) 1991. "Un Pèlerin d'Angkor." In *Voyages: 1872–1913.* Paris: Robert Laffont.

Lowenthal, David. 1985. *The Past Is a Foreign Country.* Cambridge: Cambridge University Press.

Marcus, George E. 1998. *Ethnography through Thick and Thin.* Princeton, NJ: Princeton University Press.

Marcus, George, and Michael J. Fischer. 1999. *Anthropology as Cultural Critique: An Experimental Moment in the Human Sciences.* Chicago: University of Chicago Press.

Mercille, Julien. 2005. "Media Effects on Image: The Case of Tibet." *Annals of Tourism Research* 32, no. 4: 1039–55.

Said, Edward W. 1978. *Orientalism.* New York: Penguin Books.

Salazar, Noel B. 2009. "Imaged or Imagined?" *Cahiers d'Etudes Africaines* 193–94, no. 1: 49–72.

——. 2010. *Envisioning Eden: Mobilizing Imaginaries in Tourism and Beyond.* Oxford: Berghahn Books.

Sciortino, Giuseppe. 2003. "Come Distruggere il Capitale Sociale: Lezioni dall'Esperienza Cambogiana." *Inchiesta* (January–March): 76–85.

Simonicca, Alessandro. 2007. "Turismo fra Discorso, Narrativa e Potere." *Ricerca Folklorica* 56: 7–29.
Terzani, Tiziano. 1995. *Un Indovino mi Disse.* Milan: Longanesi.
Urry, John. 2002. *The Tourist Gaze.* 2nd ed. London: Sage.
Winter, Tim. 2002. "Angkor Meets Tomb Raider: Setting the Scene." *International Journal of Heritage Studies* 8, no. 4: 323–36.
———. 2009. "Conclusion: Recasting Asian Tourism Towards an Asian Future." In *Asia on Tour: Exploring the Rise of Asian Tourism,* ed. Tim Winter, Peggy Teo, and T. C. Chang. New York: Routledge.

TOUR OPERATOR BROCHURES AND WEBSITES

Francorosso. 2001. "Estremo Oriente." Summer 2001.
———. 2003. "Estremo Oriente." Summer 2003.
———. 2012. "Estremo Oriente." http://www.francorosso.it/vacanze/estremo_oriente/indocina/index.asp (accessed 2 March 2012).
Hotelplan. 2011. "Catalogo Birmania-Indocina-Thailandia."
Kuoni Group-Gastaldi Tours. 2002. "Oriente." Winter 2002–3.
———. 2012. "Oriente." Winter 2011-2. http://www.kuoni.it/destinazioni/cambogia.php (accessed 2 March 2012).
Mistral Tour Internazionale-Quality Group. 2000. "Estremo Oriente Catalogo Ottobre 2000–Novembre 2001."
———. 2002. "Estremo Oriente Catalogo Ottobre 2002–Novembre 2003."
———. 2012. "Estremo Oriente Catalogo Novembre 2011–Ottobre 2012." http://www.qualitygroup.it/sites/all/themes/quality/bookreader/index.php?catalogo=esto#page/1/mode/1up (accessed 2 March 2012).
Rallo Worldwide-Boscolo Group. 2002. "Asia." May–October 2002.
Siesta Tour Operator. 2001. "Eurasia: Catalogo 2001–2002."
———. 2011. "Laos e Cambogia: Regni d'Acqua." http://www.toassociati.it/ (accessed 2 March 2012).
Tours Service. 2001. "Oriente & Oltre." October 2001–April 2002.
Turisanda. 2001. "Il Grande Oriente." April–October 2001.
Viaggi Dell'Elefante. 2011. "Oriente Oceania 1 Aprile 2010/31 marzo 2011."
Viaggi Del Ventaglio. 2001. "Caleidoscopio Oriente." April–October 2001.
———. 2002. "Caleidoscopio Oriente." May–October 2002.
———. 2003. "Caleidoscopio Oriente." May–October 2003.

WEBSITES AND TRAVEL BLOGS

http://turistipercaso.it/a/magazine/diario/cambogia/ (accessed 2 March 2012)
http://www.vagabondo.net/viaggiare-in/Asia (accessed 2 March 2012)
http://www.viaggiavventurenelmondo.it/nuovosito/viaggi/viaggiindocina.htm (accessed 2 March 2012)

Chapter 8

The Imagined Nation

The Mystery of the Endurance of the Colonial Imaginary in Postcolonial Times

Paula Mota Santos

Portugal was the first European nation to embark on the colonial project (1415) and the last to dismantle it (1975). The colonial project was not only long-lived but also widespread. At its height the Portuguese colonial empire encompassed territories in South America, East and West Africa, and Asia (the Indian subcontinent, Australasia, and the Far East). Colonial rule is thus an important element in Portugal's history.

Located in Coimbra, central Portugal, Portugal dos Pequenitos (Portugal of the Little Ones) is a theme park of circa 2.5 hectares in which the whole of Portugal as a colonial empire is represented through miniaturized examples of the vernacular architecture of each mainland province and each colonial possession. The park was officially opened in 1940 during the Estado Novo (New State) right-wing dictatorship of António Oliveira Salazar. In that year, the regime promoted nationwide celebrations of the eight hundredth anniversary of Portugal's emergence as a nation-state. The park is thus firmly set within the ideological principles of the regime that declared *O Império* (the Empire) as *uno e multiracial* (unified and multiracial). Because of this ideological imprint of the park, Portugal dos Pequenitos has been written about mostly in relation to its past and to its role in the regime's propaganda.[1] However, this chapter will not be focusing primarily on the park's past, but on its present.

In existence now for over seventy years, Portugal dos Pequenitos is reputedly the most visited tourist attraction in Coimbra today. Coimbra is the seat of the oldest Portuguese university (1290), and as such, it offers numerous heritage-based points of interest to its visitors. However, the number of visitors to Portugal dos Pequenitos is higher than to the university grounds.[2] According to the park's director, from May to June visitors are mostly primary school groups, while in the months of July, August, and September family groups are predominant. One might think that the primary school visits would account for Portugal dos Pequenitos' status as the most visited tourist attraction in Coimbra. However, the majority of the park's visitors are not children: in 2008, 52 percent of the visitors were between fourteen and sixty-five years old.[3] So the question arises as to how it is that a space built within the very clear and defined ideological principles of a fascist dictatorship and a colonial regime, principles presumed to belong to the past, constitutes itself in the present as such a strong tourist attraction? How does a colonial place still entice visitors in a postcolonial era?

This chapter will correlate issues of identity and of space, to then draw on lines of thought related both to exhibition spaces—the world's fairs of the late nineteenth and early twentieth centuries—and to themed spaces such as cities (e.g. Las Vegas) and amusement parks (e.g. Disneyland). The reflection on these types of places as "representational systems" (Hall 1997), that is, as material entities that represent something beyond themselves, and their link to the relationship between space and identity will constitute the framework to be applied in this analysis of the present-day reality of Portugal dos Pequenitos. Lacking as yet a consistent ethnography of visitors to the park,[4] and in the absence of useful visitor statistics, namely, range and ratio of nationalities, this chapter analyzes the imaginary of Portugal dos Pequenitos mostly from the standpoint of the Portuguese citizen, as most of the understanding of the effect of Portugal dos Pequenitos' imaginary results to date from study trips to the park and respective in-class discussions with architecture students (primarily Portuguese citizens) who attended my anthropology of space classes over the last five years.[5] I will argue that the diverse and often puzzling visitor-related realities encountered in the present in this colonial theme park make it clear that Portugal dos Pequenitos is a "rhizomatic" (Deleuze and Guattari 1987) space.

THE IMAGINARY: IDENTITY, SPACE, AND NARRATIVE

In this volume, the imaginary is defined as a socially transmitted representational assemblage (which in this chapter is seen as embodied in the understanding of social identity as narrative) that is used as a meaning-making and world-shaping device (an understanding objectified in this chapter by considering space as meaningfully and socially constructed and, in this case, clearly objectified in the theme park under analysis). Following this understanding implies viewing identity and space as intertwined (Santos 2003). Narrative as a meaningful construction of the self by a situated agency is both a producing and a produced element of this entanglement.

The phenomenological stance states that the self is primarily understood as living in the world. Heidegger's theory of the self (1997) has severe shortcomings, namely, the fact that it does not accord space to intersubjectivity (Lash 1996), and it can dangerously promote a coterminous relation between space and truthfulness of identity (Harvey 1996)—stances not underwritten by this text. What I bring here of Heidegger's theory is the definition of the self as a situated (*Da*) being (*Sein*) and his claim that existence is fundamentally a "being-there," that is, a temporally structured intelligibility of the place in which we find ourselves, in which we dwell. Thus, social identities are herein taken as always spatially located, albeit the nature of space is much more diverse than Heidegger's approach ever contemplated. However, independent of the nature of space, Lefebvre's *dictatum* that space is always a social product (1991: 26) remains a central understanding in the analysis presented here.

Like Heidegger, Ricoeur (1992) also consistently rejects any Cartesian claim for an absolute transparency of the self to itself that would render self-knowledge independent of any kind of knowledge of the world. For Ricoeur, as for Merleau-Ponty (1989), the knowledge of the world is an embodied knowledge because the self is essentially an embodied being, an entity that is both made possible and constituted by its material and cultural situation. Under the phenomenological stance, space as place (Heidegger's "dwelling") becomes a centrality, because not only is the knowledge of the self always a knowledge acquired through being-in-the-world, but the body itself is also the place from where we know the world. According to Heidegger (1997), social identity in the sense of selfhood is always an ongoing project, and *Dasein* is taken as a situated self that is basically a narrative (Thomas 1996: 43).

According to Ricoeur (1991), in order to express the complex historical present in which actions take place, one must have a kind of discourse that can articulate both the strands of actions and events and their human contexts. The kind of discourse that does this is *narrative*. Thus, for both Heidegger and Ricoeur the concept of *narrative* evokes a continuous process of creation of meaning through action: the self is meaningfully constructed through situated agency, that is, through being in the world and intervening in the world. Heidegger (1997) translates this general stance through the concept of "dwelling" and of "care," while Ricoeur (1991) does it through the understanding of "action as text" and as "performance."

In narrative, the meaning of the set of actions being told is constructed through not only the selection of events to be told (the partiality of perspective), but also by the order in which they are told (the structure). The imaginary of the tourist world is a narrative in the sense just outlined, which occurs as a particularly acute instance in themed spaces, and especially so in theme parks. The imaginaries and narratives of themed parks create meaning through the act of ordering, constituting the significant world being enunciated and visited, and thus performed. And because it is not space alone that establishes a themed space (Lukas 2007), the experience of visiting a themed place has as much to do with this believability of the theme as does architecture (see Santos 2014). Identity (Portugal, the nation-state), space (the grounds of the park itself), and narrative (the way the identity on display is transmitted to the visitors as they walk through the grounds of the park) are the central elements in Portugal dos Pequenitos that weave together the imaginary of the park, both as initially designed over seventy years ago and as experienced by today's visitors.

Through the confluence of identity, space, and narrative, Portugal dos Pequenitos assumes the quality of a "chronotope," a setting or a scene organizing time and space into a representable form (Clifford 1997: 25). This quality of a scene organizes a spatial-temporal reality into a single and clearly bounded form, producing a meaning-laden "experientiation"[6] of a place, a lived imaginary, the genealogy of which can be seen as having branched out from the landscapes of the late nineteenth- and early twentieth-century world's fairs to meet today's postmodern trope of place theming. Turn-of-the-century international exhibitions, themed spaces, and the embodied experientiation of miniature worlds are thus the main strands that weave themselves into Portugal dos Pequenitos as a representational space.

WORLDS IN EXHIBITION:
COLONIAL FAIRS AND THEMED PLACES

Imaginaries are intangible realities and the only way to study them is by focusing on the conduits through which they become objectified (Salazar and Graburn, this volume). The turn-of-the-century world's fairs and present-day themed spaces are two such conduits. Although colonial exhibitions had been held since 1866, it was not until 1883 that the first colonial exhibition took place in Europe. In that year, the Dutch held Europe's first international exhibition devoted primarily to colonialism. This exhibition marks the beginning of a period in which we see the imperial powers routinely organizing colonial expositions to build support for imperial policies (Rydell

1993: 61). These events usually included pavilions dedicated to the colonies, with reconstructions of the local architecture, objects, and ways of life of the overseas territories. These reconstructions were, on occasion, complemented by native inhabitants of the colonial possessions, who were brought to the fairs and displayed as part of the spectacle of the imperial world.

Themed spaces objectify ideas in urban spaces (Eyssartel and Rochette 1992): the avenues, streets, and squares of the colonial and international fairs of the turn of the century represented the world through a "paracity." They assumed the quality of a metaphor for a civilized, hierarchically structured, and thus meaning-laden world. Not only was the broader, that is, non-Western, and, at the time, colonial world represented there, but it was also "tamed," made "civilized," by being made part of an idealized and meaningful order, similar to that of an urban layout, with its center and peripheries. In these exhibitions, the colonial Other was made to assume a place in a spatial structure which the European visitor to the grounds could easily feel familiar with, and thus could easily negotiate spatially. Strolling through the carefully designed grounds of a make-believe paracity that objectified the world, the European visitors experienced the wonderment of colonial difference without ever feeling spatial disorientation.

Themed spaces are not only an industry of the imagined, but also a "condensation-place," a space where different sets of signification intersect with themselves (Eyssartel and Rochette 1992; Lukas 2008). Thus, although the reality on display in the international fairs is always the wider world, exhibitions always accentuated a particular theme. In the case of the colonial exhibitions, "colonial" was the theme of the display. The Strip in Las Vegas and Disneyland are two leisure places that epitomize themed leisure spaces. Regarding Las Vegas, I want to point to both the use of copy and scale (the Venetian's full-size replica of the Doge's Palace and the Paris's half-scale replica of the Eiffel Tower are two examples). From the original Disneyland park opened in 1955, I want to underline its urban layout and the centrality of a certain idea: an imaginary of the nation through the coupling of theme and space. Looking beyond the immediate commercial side of Disneyland, it is possible to see how, when taken as a whole, the park's themed spaces, laid out along its streets and squares, are places that objectify "a USA," the one imagined by Walt Disney himself. The themed nuclei of the park at the time of its opening–Main Street USA, Adventureland, Frontierland, and Tomorrowland[7]–when taken together speak of an idea of the spirit of America as a nation. For Disneyland's imagineers, the park's Main Street USA was what the real Main Street should be like. "What we create … is 'Disney realism,' sort of utopian in nature, where we carefully program out all the negative, unwanted elements and program in the positive elements" (Zukin 1991: 222).

Portugal dos Pequenitos is a world on display. Not the whole world as portrayed in the world's fairs or international exhibitions, but the whole of the Portuguese world at the time of the park's construction: the colonial empire, *uno e multiracial*.[8] Nowadays, the park presents itself as displaying the whole of the Portuguese-speaking world, a community of diverse cultures that, as a result of its historical past (the colonial era), shares a common language. In Portugal dos Pequenitos, we can find the devices mentioned in relation to the Las Vegas Strip—the use of the copy (replicas of real buildings) and the alterations of scale (use of the miniature)—and Disney's Anaheim park—the urban layout (the hierarchical relations resulting from organization along the streets and squares of the park) and the objectification of an imaginary of the nation (the diversity in unity). The genealogy of these latter elements, as found in Portugal dos Pequenitos, is most frequently referred to in relation to colonial rule and the national identity celebrations that took place in 1940. However, to these we must add the centrality of the child in the park's chosen rhetoric of space, that is, the use of the miniature as a technique of the (collective) self. Overarching all of the elements so far mentioned is Portugal dos Pequenitos' ludic nature as a place of leisure. This is translated both into its present-day self-presentation as a theme park, and its success as the most visited tourist attraction in Coimbra, reflecting the park's insertion both in the postmodern trope of place theming and in the realm of the posttourist.[9]

PORTUGAL DOS PEQUENITOS

The Past

The park was built through the actions of a Coimbra man of substance, Fernando Bissaya-Barreto—a doctor and university professor, a local philanthropist preoccupied with the living conditions (health) and the upbringing (education) of the small children of working-class mothers, and, on occasion, a man of the regime. Cassiano Branco, one of the leading names in Portuguese architecture, was commissioned to design the park. The grounds are divided into five themed areas that were built in different stages from 1938 up to the early 1960s when the park was finally completed (figure 8.1).[10]

Portugal dos Pequenitos emerged as the playground of a day care center for working-class children. Its construction follows Bissaya-Barreto's previous and ongoing philanthropic work for the benefit of early and later childhood. The Jardim e Casa da Criança Raínha Santa Isabel (The Saint Queen Isabel Garden and Children's Home) follows the model of a previ-

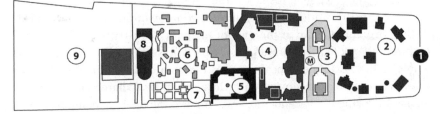

Figure 8.1. Portugal dos Pequenitos (Source: Fundação Bissaya Barreto/Portugal dos Pequenitos; Copyright: L. Salt & P. Santos).
(1) Entrance
(2) Overseas Portugal (Portuguese-Speaking Countries*)
(3) Insular Portugal (Azores and Madeira)
(4) Monumental Portugal
(5) Coimbra Ensemble
(6) Mainland Portugal (Regional Houses*)
(7) Formal Gardens
(8) Children's House
(9) Playground Area
* Present-day designation of the area

ous children's home in Coimbra, the so-called Ninho dos Pequenitos (Little Ones' Nest). Although the opening date for Portugal dos Pequenitos is often referred to as 1940, there are local newspaper reports from 1939 of visits to the gardens of the Casa da Criança Rainha Santa Isabel (Montês 1939). This shows that the place, at the time only constituted by the day care center (figure 8.1, point 8) and the Mainland Portugal section (figure 8.1, point 6), was open and running well before the grand opening of the Estado Novo–related national identity celebrations in June 1940. With regard to this type of playground built for the day care center, it should be noted that Bissaya-Barreto was a follower of the "pedagogical discourse of the New School" (Sousa 1999: 177). Contrary to a book- and classroom-based form of learning, the New School advocated instead "learning through doing." Portugal dos Pequenitos was thus created as a ludic-pedagogical device for the education of working-class children.[11]

The fact that by 1939, that is, well before the official opening of the national identity celebrations of 1940, Portugal dos Pequenitos was already open and running as a child day care center shows that the construction of the park was primarily a result of a concern for the welfare and education of small children from deprived families. To this social welfare context one must then add the national identity propaganda of the regime. However, it must be noted that the end of the Estado Novo regime, with the democratic revolution of April 1974, brought about the beginning of a "fall from grace" for Bissaya-Barreto and for Portugal dos Pequenitos, which lost its attraction to visitors. The Brazilian pavilion was burgled during the postrevolutionary times of 1974: its semiprecious gems collection was stolen and the pavilion was left with very few of the objects it had on display (Matos 2010: 11).[12] This pavilion only reopened in 2003, and is now home to a multimedia display on the maritime voyage that led to the sighting of Brazil by Portuguese navigators.

In spite of the frequent emphasis on the ideological connection with the Estado Novo, namely, by academic literature, the park's connection to the right-wing dictatorship and its national identity politics seems to have been lost on today's visitors. Looking at the information available for present-day visitors, such as the park's official website and its "History" section, we find reference to Portugal dos Pequenitos' construction as "a pedagogical park dedicated to young children,"[13] but on the home page of the website (the one users access first) the grounds are referred to as the "oldest theme park in Portugal."[14] It is to this present-day quality of theme park that I will turn next.

The Present

To the broad issues related to both Anderson's (1983) nations as "imagined communities," and to the experientiation of the park imagineers' work on its quality as a chronotope, one has to inevitably add the individual and collective imaginaries that the visitors, as differentiated nation-state citizens, carry with them as they walk through the park. Particularly relevant are the differences between visitors who are citizens of countries that have a historical and, quite often, colonial link to Portugal, and those from countries that do not. What follows arises mostly from my understanding as an academic and also as a Portuguese citizen who has visited the place both as a child and as an adult (the latter as an academic), as well as those expressed by my under- and postgraduate students who have visited Portugal dos Pequenitos as part of course assessments on the relationship between space and social identity (2008–12). The Portuguese citizen quality is used here in the sense of having been socialized within the Portuguese school system, with all that it entails in terms of learning the history of the nation and of the world from a specific standpoint: as a subject of the Portuguese nation-state.

The first section to be built was Mainland Portugal/Regional Houses (figure 8.1, point 8). The original entrance (still there, but hardly noticed by today's visitors) was located on its eastern side, between points 5 and 7 on the map, and led directly to the Mainland Portugal/Regional Houses ensemble (figure 8.2 top). Since the 1960s, visitors not only enter the park through a more conspicuous structure (figure 8.2 bottom), but they are also immediately immersed in the "exotic" world of the Overseas Territories/Portuguese-Speaking Countries section of the park. With the building of the new entrance, Mainland Portugal/Regional Houses changed from being the first to being the last section to be reached by the park's visitors.[15]

Present-day Portugal dos Pequenitos is no longer presented as the colonial empire. The reality presented, although materially the same, is now of the community of Portuguese-speaking countries, and it is presented as such in the park's official texts. Built at a scale of 1:5, only smaller children can get into the Regional Houses' interiors. Adults are left to watch from the outside, while the children go in and out of the different houses. The other sections were built at a scale of 1:2.5 (Matos 2010: 8). This difference in scale is particularly relevant in the Overseas Territories section, as it allows for adults to enter these houses effortlessly.

Big enough for older children and adults to get into, the houses of the Overseas Territories section were designed as more complex learning devices.[16] Inside each house representing a colonial possession (and now representing an independent nation), there were, and still are, objects of each "exotic" place on display. These range from musical instruments to ritual objects such as masks, but also basketry, household wares, and weapons. These objects are accompanied by small written texts (only in Portuguese). The latter made the ability to read central to the learning process itself, something not required in the Regional Houses, even when their interior was furnished. The inside of the "exotic" houses of the Overseas section is thus a place of Otherness, a strange place. What visitors come across inside these houses are strange objects made even more strange due to both their display in glass cases or mounted on walls (and thus away from children's prying hands) and to the little information available. All these characteristics of the world on display there produce and heighten an already existing sense of difference, and thus of cultural and social distance.[17] Young children do not find this section appealing, exiting the pavilions almost as soon as they go in, while adults take the time to go through the materials and respective information on display inside the pavilions.

Even though the material world (architecture and urban layout) has not changed after the 1974 revolution, major changes were effected in the park's written information, especially related to the Overseas Territories section (now the Portuguese-Speaking Countries section), found in leaflets and other official sources of description. So, the material world is the same, but is it the same "place" in Tuan's (2001) sense of the word? What are the imaginaries that the park objectifies to present-day visitors? Is this colonial space now a postcolonial space? If we attend to chronology alone, that is, to time elaps-

Figure 8.2. Original entrance (top) and present-day entrance (bottom) (Copyright: P. Santos).

ing, this is now a postcolonial space inasmuch as the Portuguese colonial era ended in 1975. However, can the changes in written discourse, from bluntly colonial (the empire) to postcolonial (a transnational globalization-induced Portuguese-speaking community) alter the colonial nature of the place?

THE INTRICACIES OF A COLONIAL PLACE IN POSTCOLONIAL TIMES

In the Portuguese-Speaking Countries section, by the entrance to each pavilion there was a miniature replica of a Padrão dos Descobrimentos stone on which a Portuguese text about the "discovery" of each territory is laid out.[18] Post-1974, the park's original stones were substituted by new ones, also placed by the entrance to each pavilion. Portuguese-proficient visitors always stop to read these stones' inscriptions on their way into the pavilions. In figure 8.3, Angola's former and current Padrão dos Descobrimentos stones are

Figure 8.3. Angola's original Padrão dos Descobrimentos (left) and present-day inscription (right) (Copyright: P. Santos).

shown. On the new stones, not only do we no longer find the miniaturized depiction of the stone pillar or the Portuguese royal coat of arms (which is substituted by a wind rose), but the written text has also been "cleansed" of all colonial undertones.

Angola's original Padrão dos Descobrimentos text reads as follows:

ANGOLA

In 1482, Diogo Cão sailed our ships to the Congo. Two years later he returned there to raise Portugal's Standard [*Padrão*]. He traveled up the Zaire River all the way to the Yelala Falls where he engraved his name and those of his companions in stone. He had dealings with the Congo's Negro king and brought to Portugal the latter's son, who King John II had baptized and educated. And so started, peacefully, the civilizing action of the Portuguese in Angola—our biggest Overseas Province.

The present-day stone reads:

POPULAR REPUBLIC OF ANGOLA

The first contacts of the Portuguese with Angola date from 1482 when the navigator Diogo Cão established friendly relations with the African civilizations south of the Equator. This navigator traveled beyond the mouth of the Zaire River and celebrated an alliance with the king of the Congo, to proceed with geographical surveys of the Angolan coastline. The presence of the Portuguese in Angola lasted over five centuries, and Portuguese sovereignty was held until 11 November 1975, when the new country became independent.

There are clear differences in the tone of each narrative. However, the stones of the colonial period, although no longer on display at the entrance to each pavilion/house, are actually not out of sight: while the new stones are in the entrance area, clearly visible, the old ones have been placed inside of the respective pavilion, although in an out-of-the-way corner. Nevertheless, a sufficiently inquisitive and Portuguese-proficient visitor can discover them and read the Estado Novo–produced text.

It is not only this material permanence of the Estado Novo–produced stones that might negate the complete absence of explicit colonial imaginary in today's experientiation of the theme park. Walking through the park, visitors very rarely come across depictions of human figures. If we exclude the statues located at the very rear of the park, in the gardened area beyond the Regional Houses section (an area that most visitors never get to, because it contains no miniature houses), the life-size bust of Bissaya-Barreto in the park's inner entrance area, and the larger-than-life-size full-body statue of Henry the Navigator by the Portuguese-led *mapa mundi*, located just before the Monumental Portugal section, all other human depictions are of scantily clad African men and women all located in the Overseas Territories/Portuguese-Speaking Countries section. In fact, as soon as one goes through the park's entrance, one is faced with a row of three larger-than-life-size African male statues (figure 8.4). These African male figures are represented only with head and muscled torso, with arms folded in front of the chest in a martial posture.[19] To this, one must add the background scenography of the vegetation: palm trees and dense foliage in an attempt to recreate a "savage nature" to match the "savage men."

This row of African torsos is one of the most frequent backgrounds for personal photographs by tourists, who take turns to pose in front of these statues, copying the figures' martial stance. A larger-than-life-size African female statue in "native" attire and baring her breasts is often used in a photographic composition in which, usually, young white male visitors climb over the woman in order to grasp her breasts and be photographed by their party.

However, perhaps these overtly racial and colonialist depictions were "invisible" to the untrained eye of the "average" visitor of Portuguese nationality. In fact, only a couple of my Portuguese students noted in their written reports the possible incorrectness of the presence of these African torsos, while the American students I accompanied during the visit were

Figure 8.4. Depiction of African male human figures (Copyright: P. Santos).

immediately struck by the colonial nature of this section of the park, an awareness often translated into referring to the historical relation Portugal had with the African slave trade to the Americas. However, the fact is that most of the reports handed in by the Portuguese students who visited the park throughout these years are marked by a strong identification with the Portuguese-speaking world depicted in Portugal dos Pequenitos. Sentences such as, "I felt proud to belong to the nation that had shown the world to the world" were not infrequent. What puzzled me when confronted with this emotional attachment was the fact that these students were young men and women who were born some fifteen years after the demise of the colonial empire and who were revisiting the park approximately thirty-five years after that same demise. As such, a nostalgia for formerly lived colonial times cannot really be an explanation for this emotional attachment to the colonial imaginary portrayed in Portugal dos Pequenitos, because those times were never directly part of these young people's lives. So, how can this emotional attachment be explained?

Apart from the role the use of the miniature plays in this identification with the park (see Santos 2014), the fact that kindergarten and primary schools organize field trips to Portugal dos Pequenitos, together with the often pleasurable experience of playing in the Regional Houses section, might predispose Portuguese individuals to develop a positive appreciation of the park when they go back to visit it as adults. But along with this socialization factor, one must also take into account that the students who wrote the visit reports were young men and women who were maturing in an epoch that is often referred to as high modernity, where playfulness and theming are recurrent factors, particularly in the tourist experience (Eco 1986; Urry 1990). However, this explanation is not sufficient when faced with the expressions of patriotic pride in my students' reports, and in the conversations I held with older Portuguese visitors during fieldwork. At play here is an element of Bourdieu's (2002) *field* and *habitus* and *doxa:* the schooling system. The Portuguese schooling system and the way the history of the nation has been taught in the last eighty years play a central role in this identification, namely the presentation of the period of the maritime voyages of discovery of the fifteenth and sixteenth centuries as the brightest time in Portuguese history, and the way colonial rule is addressed in the textbooks.

A study of present-day Portuguese history textbooks in schools, carried out by Araújo and Rodriguez Maeso (2013), identified a naturalization of the colonial system. This is achieved by never presenting sufficient historical contextualization of the Portuguese colonial rule and of the colonies' freedom movements "turning invisible the violent imposition of the colonial power" (Araújo and Rodriguez Maeso 2011: 3). Also, according to the same authors, the way slavery is treated in Portuguese history textbooks is tantamount to an institutionalization of social forgetting that denies the possibility of discussing its contemporary formations of race and racism in present-day Portuguese society (Araújo and Rodriguez Maeso 2011: 4).

The history taught in the Estado Novo schooling system was nationalist, "praising as good and dignified all the deeds that worked for the Nation" (Torgal 1988: 352). According to Mónica (1978), during the Estado Novo regime the history of Portugal was presented as constituted by alternating periods of "glory" and "darkness." The founding of the nation, the maritime voyages of discovery, the 1600s restoration of independent rule, and the "democratic" regime (i.e., Salazar's period) were the periods of Portuguese history portrayed as glorious, with the maritime expansion presented as "the acme of the history of the motherland" (Mónica 1978: 302). Although between 1968 and 1970 Portugal experienced an openness of the regime, there were really no major changes to be found in the way history was taught (L. Santos 1995: 1973). In fact, history textbooks still perpetuate many of the Estado Novo discourses (Viana 2011). Although presented in a more nuanced way, these discourses constitute a body of ideology that still marks the way nationalism, racism, and the history of the Other are present in today's Portugal. Thus, this absence of major changes in the way history has been taught in the last eighty years is a central factor when accounting for the emotional attachment to the reality on display in Portugal dos Pequenitos by both university students and older Portuguese visitors.

But there are still other elements in the postcolonial life of Portugal dos Pequenitos that appear even more puzzling than the presence of the original stone pillars' colonial texts, the colonial and racist imagery, and the emotional response of Portuguese visitors to the place. These other elements are two plaques, one in each pavilion, that testify to the visit of high officials of two African countries that were former Portuguese colonies, namely Guinea-Bissau and Mozambique . In the former, the visit was undertaken by the then prime minister and took place in 1998, while in the latter, the visit took place in 1999 and was undertaken by the then president of the republic.

The Guinea-Bissau plaque is very succinct in its information. It reads: "Visit of his Excellency the Prime Minister of the Republic of Guinea-Bissau in homage to the work of Bissaya-Barreto. Coimbra, 17 February 1998." The Mozambique plaque supplies a little more information. It reads: "Visit of his Excellency the President of the Republic of Mozambique Doctor Joaquim Chissano on occasion of the start of the campaign SUPPORTAFRICA-99 dedicated to the Republic of Mozambique. Coimbra, 23 April 1999." Two things immediately stand out in this last plaque. First, the reference to an aid campaign in favor of Mozambique, and second, the date. I have not yet been able to trace back and identify the aid campaign referred to, but its reference diverts the visit from just being a celebration of the world on display at Portugal dos Pequenitos. Concerning the date, the day of the visit is very close to 25 April, the day of the 1974 democratic revolution. Ever since 1975, that day is a public holiday during which national celebrations of the event take place. Looking at the year, 1999, we are taken back to the twenty-fifth anniversary of the 1974 revolution. President Chissano was thus in Portugal to take part in the celebrations of the twenty-fifth anniversary of the revolution that brought about the end of Portuguese colonial rule, and the independence of Mozambique. Further research is needed in order to contextualize these visits by high dignitaries. As this research stands, they are left as puzzling elements and a challenge to the attempts to reach an understanding of the postcolonial life of the park and the many layers of meaning it encompasses.

While I was awaiting an opportunity to undertake an ethnography of the park's visitors I carried out a brief survey of pictures of Portugal dos Pequenitos available on the Internet. I surveyed the comments on the images posted rather than the pictures themselves. I also looked for photos and comments on the park on web-based travel sites. What I found was a majority of positive comments on the park, namely, as a suitable place to take children, if you are traveling with any. But I also found an "immigration" link. These were cases of Brazilian or French citizens who obviously had a family and cultural connection to Portugal.[20] From all of the provinces on display in the Mainland/Regional Houses section, the Trás-os-Montes e Alto-Douro province seems to hold a particular place in relation to visitors. In the first half of the twentieth century, this Mainland province was a major source of Portuguese emigration to Brazil (Martins 2007). According to the park's director, not only is the park's staff often asked by Brazilian visitors where in the park the Trás-os-Montes regional house is located, but the park's shop also sells twice as many miniature replicas of houses from this region as any other.

The Internet photography survey also showed that for visitors with an emigration context, their holiday-time visit to Portugal and excursion to Portugal dos Pequenitos was a way to experience the whole of the country in a short period of time when they did not have time to experience the "whole of Portugal" for real, that is, by actually visiting the different regions and historical monuments. At least two of my students clearly stated in their reports that Portugal dos Pequenitos served this role in their life: born in another European country of Portuguese parents who had emigrated, the visit to the park as children with their family in their summer holidays assumed exactly that pedagogical role.

The ethnographic observations I carried out in the summer of 2012 allowed the delineation of types of visitors. One type is precisely constituted by a multigenerational extended family group of Portuguese descent. Usually clustered around an older couple (usually parents of the young adults and grandparents of the younger elements in the group), they are proficient in a foreign language (most frequently European French and American English), as well as in Portuguese. They are an extended family group of posttourists who are learning about Portugal through Eco's (1986: 16) the *real fake,* that is, learning about the real through their replicas.

All the cases referred to above display a mostly positive relationship to the reality on display in the park. However, concerning a more recent history of Portuguese colonial rule, namely, the strong presence of communities of African descent in Portugal today, the Internet photography survey supplied no postings from individuals of (identifiable) African descent. In all of my visits to the park, I rarely saw visitors of visually identifiable African descent. However, in the conversations I held with visitors to the park, I did come across individuals who had had direct experience of the places that are part of the Overseas Territories/Portuguese Speaking Countries section. Some acquired this experience through visiting such places as tourists, a few young adults through family origins, and older Portuguese visitors through military service during colonial rule. These individuals with direct knowledge of the places portrayed in this section were the only ones who commented on the inadequacy of the representation of those places as found inside the pavilions. However, their comments did not hinge on issues of the colonial imaginary per se, but on what they saw as a limited depiction of the actual cultural wealth and diversity that those places have. Like Egyptian visitors to the Egyptian exhibit of the 1889 Paris world's fair (Mitchell 1988: 1), for these visitors, the *real fake* was never consubstantiated in the representational devices created by the park's imagineers.

I finish this section with the only two instances (so far) of downright negative appreciation of the world represented in this theme park. One was a comment found through the photography Internet survey and posted on TripAdvisor by an obviously Portuguese-proficient French-speaking man. The photo was of one of the several Estado Novo ideology texts that one can find throughout the park celebrating Portugal's civilizing, that is, colonial, destiny. The comment was very critical of the colonial nature of the place. It ended by recommending that visiting the park should be avoided.[21]

The other case was the erasing of the name of the author of one of the several sentences that are printed on small tiles placed on the external walls of the Regional Houses. These short sentences or short rhymes are either popular sayings or sentences from well-known Portuguese writers. They all speak of morals and values closely associated with the Estado Novo ideology, such as the idea of the nation and the centrality of the family and Christianity. This particular tile is located in the inner part of the arched passage of a Regional House. The text reads as follows: "A vontade de obedecer, única escola para aprender a mandar" (The will to obey [is] the only school for learning how to command). At the bottom, completely erased, is the space that held the name of the author of that well-known sentence: António Oliveira Salazar.

CONCLUDING REMARKS

As a representational place, Portugal dos Pequenitos chose the rhetoric of realism. But how real is realism? In literature, the aesthetics of Realism lead the writer to an intentional mimicry of the real world in order to blur the division between fiction and reality (Lima, 1989). But any text, even when it is presented as realistic, is always a fictionalized construction filtered by the subjectivity of its creator, making it unadvisable to take such narratives as objective reproductions of the reality being described. Turn-of-the-century world's fairs, Disney's Anaheim park and the Las Vegas Strip all share that ambition "to really represent" and do it through the use of both the copy and the narrative, two elements also in use in Portugal dos Pequenitos.

To take Portugal dos Pequenitos as a text (a narrative) and as an artistic work (which it also is) is to examine an urban space that is the object of artistic figuration. It therefore assumes the quality of a double signifier: it is both the setting of the action and a symbolic and ideological construction of the nation and/or the Portuguese-speaking community. Portugal dos Pequenitos, being an urban space, with its faithful allocation of specific place sets for the actions being narrated, together with the value system that supports such allocation, becomes the producer of ideological and symbolic meanings that codify the creators' narrative as the work of the imagination (Appadurai 1996), even when it presents itself (as it does) as mimetic of the reality being narrated.

Portugal dos Pequenitos is a work of the imagination: of those who designed it in the first half of the twentieth century, and of those who visit it today. The crossing of these two imaginaries becomes objictified in the imaginary of the park as the concrete and lived experientiation by visitors of material worlds that are representational systems. Imaginaries are then realities that *become*.[22] The becoming takes place through the phenomenologically lived experientiation of Lefebvreian places (space as social product) by historically and socially produced Bourdieuian selves (the self as in relation to a *field,* a *habitus,* and a *doxa*). In Ricoeurian and Heideggerian terms, imaginaries are then *performed* and *dwelt in,* respectively. Portugal dos Pequenitos, as a tourist site that is a work of the imagination, assumes the quality of a text. Texts and narratives can be differentially perceived and emoted, that is, differentially performed by differentially located audiences, as the chapters by Bunten, Theodossopoulos, and Ferraris (this volume) show.

This diversity of relation to a single material world, that is, the ability to narrate differently, brings about the centrality of perspective in the sense of "situated agency." In this context "landscape" emerges as a useful concept for thinking about Portugal dos Pequenitos. This theme park is "a landscape of the nation" (or of the Portuguese-speaking community), in as much as the concept of landscape, as applied to the study of space, implies a cultural process, that is, a dynamic reality linked to differentially positioned knowledge or perspectives (Ingold 1994; Hirsch 1995). By taking Portugal dos Pequenitos as a landscape of the nation, we can see how the three theoretical strands outlined in the beginning of this chapter (identity, space, and narrative) meet and weave the complexity of the park's imaginary. Quoting Bender (1993: 3), "landscape is never inert, people engage with it, re-work it, appropriate, and contest it. It is part of the way in which identities are created and disputed, whether as an individual, group, or nation-state. Operating therefore at the juncture of history and politics, social relations and cultural perceptions, landscape has to be … a concept of 'high tension.'" The previous section of this chapter, with its ethnographically observed puzzling reality, highlighted the "high tension" quality of this theme park, that is, the junctures and disjunctures Portugal dos Pequenitos holds.

The high-tension quality of Portugal dos Pequenitos inevitably shows us an experientiation of this park, its imaginary, as being multiple and diverse. The most frequent form of conceptualizing diversity is through binary logic, with *dichotomy* and the *tap-root* (Deleuze and Guattari 1987) as, respectively, the actual processing of the reality and the working metaphor. However, the imaginary of Portugal dos Pequenitos, that is, the diversity of phenomenologically lived experientiation of this place, is better thought of as a *fascicular root* or as a *rhizome* (Deleuze and Guattari 1987). As I have come to realize, my difficulty in making sense of the imaginaries encountered through fieldwork at Portugal dos Pequenitos stems from the fact that I was approaching it from a tap-root conceptualization, while in fact the fascicular root or rhizome is probably the more adequate form to use to think about the park and the multiple levels of meaning and experientiations, that is, of the imaginaries it encapsulates.

According to Deleuze and Guattari, a rhizome

connects any point to any other point [and not necessarily within the same nature line] ... bring[ing] into play very different regimes of signs ... The rhizome is neither reducible to the One nor the multiple ... It is composed not of units but of dimensions, or rather directions in motion ... It constitutes linear multiplicities with *n* dimensions ... Unlike a structure, which is defined by a set of points and positions, with binary relations between the points and biunivocal relationships between the positions, the rhizome is made only of lines: lines of segmentarity and stratification as its dimensions. (1987: 21)

According to Hochbruck and Schlehe, "what is staged in themed environments is either the creation of a history of the nation ... as an offer to the visitor for imaginative identification, or the creation of a seemingly timeless exotic Other" (2010: 8). Portugal dos Pequenitos does not fit into this dichotomous model since, in fact, it does both. The self narrated and performed in Portugal dos Pequenitos, be it the colonial empire or the Portuguese-speaking community, is constituted by a diversity in unity.[23] The park's rhizomatic nature is what accounts for the park's multiple and coeval experiential dimensions, as expressed by its visitors' relations to the world on display there. Deceptively looking like a structure (its miniature streets, squares, and buildings), Portugal dos Pequenitos as experienced by its visitors is a set of lineaments that are set into a cartography by the very act of walking along the park's structures. According to Deleuze and Guattari (1987), these lineaments are not lineages of the arborescent type, because the rhizome is an antigenealogy. Unlike tracings, the rhizome pertains to a map that must be produced, constructed, a map that is always detachable, connectable, reversible, modifiable, and has multiple entryways and exits and its own lines of flight. "[T]he rhizome is ... non-hierarchical ... defined solely by a circulation of states. What is at question in the rhizome is ... all manner of '*becomings*'" (Deleuze and Guattari 1987: 21).

Portugal dos Pequenitos is a theme park that is a popular place among the majority of Portuguese visitors, not only because of its re-creation of a wonderland by the use of the miniature at a scale that allows the visiting of the buildings' interior (Santos 2014), its themed nature, and the attractiveness that such places have in today's posttourist world, but also due to the way that Portuguese history has been taught in the last eighty years. Constructivists consider that what tourists seek is not objective authenticity but symbolic authenticity resulting from social construction (Wang 1999). This notion of authenticity is thus relative, negotiable, contextually determined, and even ideological. The toured objects or "Others" are experienced as authentic not because they are originals or real, but because they are perceived as the symbols of authenticity. Portugal dos Pequenitos' material world and

the experientiation a visit there entails reinstate in an unquestioned manner, because phenomenologically experienced, the shared imaginary of the
greatness of the Portuguese identity (the colonial empire as the nation over-
blown and the global importance of the maritime voyages of discovery) and
of the benign nature of the Portuguese colonial regime (the *Luso-tropicalismo*
trope (Freyre 1998) objectified in the present-day existence of a brotherhood
of equal-status nations linked by the common Portuguese language). Thus,
while underlining the rhizomatic nature of the park, what is argued here is
that the reason why Portugal dos Pequenitos' imaginary is still so popular
with Portuguese national citizens is not because *it represents,* but because *it is.*

NOTES

1. Works such as Paulo (1990), Porto (1994), Babo (1997), Matos (2006), and Silva
   (2010).
2. In 2008, the number of visitors was as follows: Portugal dos Pequenitos: circa
   300,000 (number supplied by the director of the park); university grounds:
   190,000 (Universidade de Coimbra 2009). A comparison with the total number
   of visitors to Coimbra cannot be made because the only visitor statistics available for Coimbra are those of visitors who go to Coimbra's tourism office for
   information. In the year 2008, that number was 81,827 (numbers supplied by
   Entidade Regional Turismo Centro Portugal/Central Portugal Regional Tourism Board).
3. Number supplied by the park's director. The park only has visitor statistics
   based on types of tickets sold. It should be noted that Portugal dos Pequenitos
   is an expensive facility: a full-price ticket in 2013 is 8.95 euro (a full-price ticket
   for the university grounds is 7 euro).
4. In July 2012, I carried out a two-day intensive observation of the park's visitors..
   Apart from onsite observations, information was also obtained via conversations held with visitors and via a questionnaire answered by forty visitors.
5. I am thus indebted to my students, but also to the Portuguese Studies Program
   (PSP) of the University of California–Berkeley, and particularly to its executive director, Deolinda Adão, for accommodating my lectures on Portugal dos
   Pequenitos and thus giving me access to the view of non-Portuguese students. I
   am particularly indebted to Nelson Graburn for all his support.
6. "Experientiation" is used in Kant's sense of knowledge of place as genuinely
   local, knowledge that "is in itself experiential in the manner of *Erlebnis,* 'lived
   experience,' rather than of *Erfahrung,* the already elapsed experience" (Casey
   1996: 18).
7. Fantasyland is left out here.
8. The colonial empire was constituted as follows: the overseas territories consisted
   of Cape Verde, Guinea-Bissau, São Tomé and Principe, Angola, Mozambique,

Portuguese State of India (Goa, Daman, and Diu), Macau, and East Timor. The nation-empire was further constituted by continental Portugal (mainland) and insular Portugal (the Azores and Madeira archipelagos). Brazil, although an independent nation since 1822, is also part of the park, presented as *pátria irmã* (sister nation).

9. The posttourist is a tourist who has a lack of concern with authenticity and who knows that "[t]he world is a stage and [s/he] can delight in the multitude of games to be played" (Urry 1990: 91).

10. Matos (2010: 8) indicates the order of completion as follows: Mainland Portugal (1940); Coimbra Ensemble and the Overseas Portugal section (early 1940s); Monumental Portugal (1950–62). Silva (2010: 7) gives a slightly different account: Mainland Portugal and Coimbra ensemble (1938–40); Monumental Portugal (1941–49); Insular and Overseas Portugal (throughout the 1950s). The important element to retain here is that the park was built in stages over twenty-five years.

11. Today, the interiors of the miniature regional houses are empty, but originally they were furnished. The pedagogical role of the houses as a learning device was thus enhanced through the direct experience of the differences in material culture related to regional differences in modes of subsistence.

12. The "fall from grace" period of Portugal dos Pequenitos is seldom referred to. I have yet to find specific written references to it; I only have oral references from people who were adults at the time of the 1974 revolution about a (possible?) closure of the grounds.

13. See http://www.portugaldospequenitos.pt/index.php/Historia.html (accessed 1 July 2011).

14. See http://www.portugaldospequenitos.pt/ (accessed 1 July 2011).

15. For a detailed analysis of the visitors' perceived narrative of the place as they walk through the park, see Santos (2014).

16. The main imagineer of the park, Cassiano Branco, actually uses the word "lesson" to explain the two uses he makes of scale (see Matos 2010: 8). Mitchell, in his work on the Paris world's fair of 1889, refers to the use of the same word (1989: 220). This commonality of use addresses again the commonality of the nature of world's fairs and Portugal dos Pequenitos.

17. According to the park's director, the objects inside the Overseas Territories section were initially on display in the 1940 Lisbon Exposição do Mundo Português (Exhibition of the Portuguese World). This major propaganda event possessed an important colonial section. The relocation of some of its artifacts to Portugal dos Pequenitos establishes a real and direct connection between the nature of the park and the nature of colonial exhibitions argued for in this chapter.

18. The Padrão dos Descobrimentos (Discovery Standard) was a stone pillar headed by the Portuguese coat of arms that the navigators erected in each newly "discovered" territory so as to claim its possession for the Portuguese Crown.

19. According to the park's director, these gigantic African torsos had been on display in the 1940 Lisbon-based colonial exhibition.

20. Brazil was a strong Portuguese emigration destination in the late nineteenth and early twentieth centuries, while France became one in the 1960s and 1970s.

21. The comment in full: "Ce Portugal miniature est une honte pour l'image du pays, à au moins deux titres: (1) les attractions semblent dater essentiellement de 1940, date de l'inauguration. L'état des pavillons miniature est souvent déplorable, les expositions sous vitrine vont du minable à l'insultant pour l'intelligence de nos enfants, en tout cas ne reflètent pas du tout l'état de l'art de 2011 en matière d'activités culturelles pour les enfants; (2) le premier tiers du parc est dédié à la gloire de feu l'empire colonial, on a juste refait les panneaux pour dire PALOP (pays de langue officielle portugaise) à la place de 'colonies.' Mais ils restent quand même des panneaux d'origine [photo]. Et les pavillons de ces pays sont dénués d'objets ou d'expos pouvant intéresser des enfants. En un mot la révolution des œillets ne semble pas avoir atteint le Portugal dos Pequeninos, sans même parler du XXI° siècle. A éviter" http://www.tripadvisor.com/Tour ism-g189143-Coimbra_Coimbra_District_Central_Portugal-Vacations.html, photo number 936 (accessed 1 July 2011).

22. See Di Giovine's (this volume) imaginaire dialetic as an example of the processual and social-subject related nature of the realities observed in tourism sites.

23. Diversity in unity is a feature also found in Jakarta's Beautiful Indonesia in Miniature and in Dar es Salaam's Village Museum, as described by Salazar (2010), although both of these theme parks were built within a process of postcolonial nation building, which is not the case for Portugal dos Pequenitos.

REFERENCES

Appadurai, Arjun. 1996. *Modernity at Large: Cultural Dimensions of Globalization*. Minneapolis: University of Minnesota Press.

Anderson, Benedict. 1983. *Imagined Communities: Reflections on the Origins and Spread of Nationalism*. London: Verso.

Araújo, Marta, and Silvia Rodriguez Maeso. 2011. "A Institucionalização do Silêncio: A Escravatura nos Manuais de História Portugueses." *Revista Ensino Superior* 39 (January–March). http://www.snesup.pt/htmls/EFpkZAVVZZUCgtSUnj .shtml (accessed 1 May 2013).

———, eds. 2013. *Caderno de Discussão–"Ao Fim e ao Cabo Foi a Europa que Fez o Mundo Moderno": O Eurocentrismo na História e nos Seus Manuais*. Coimbra: CES.

Babo, M. Augusta. 1997. "A Naturalização da Cultura: Uma Representação Arquitectónica do Mundo: O Portugal dos Pequenitos." *Vértice*, 2nd ser. (May/June): 89–93.

Bender, Barbara, ed. 1993. *Landscape: Politics and Perspectives*. Oxford: Berg.

Bourdieu, Pierre. 2002. *Outline of a Theory of Practice*. Cambridge: Cambridge University Press.

Casey, Edward S. 1996. "How to Get from Space to Place in a Fairly Short Stretch of Time: Phenomenological Prolegomena." In *Senses of Place,* ed. Steven Feld and Keith Basso. Santa Fe, NM: School of American Research Press.

Clifford, James. 1997. *Routes: Travel and Translation in the Late Twentieth Century.* Cambridge, MA: Harvard University Press.

Deleuze, Gilles, and Felix Guattari. 1987. *A Thousand Plateaus: Capitalism and Schizophrenia.* Minneapolis: University of Minnesota Press.

Eco, Humberto. 1986. *Travels in Hyperreality.* San Diego: Harcourt Brace Jovanovich.

Eyssartel, Anne-Marie, and Bernard Rochette. 1992. *Des Mondes Inventés: Les parcs à theme.* Paris: Editions La Villette.

Freyre, Gilberto. (1933) 1998. *Casa Grande e Senzala,* Rio de Janeiro: Maya & Schmidt.

Hall, Stuart. 1997. "The Work of Representation." In *Representation: Cultural Representations and Signifying Practices,* ed. Stuart Hall. London: Sage.

Harvey, David. 1996. "From Space to Place and Back Again." In *Justice, Nature and the Geography of Difference.* Oxford: Blackwell.

Heidegger, Martin. 1997. *Basic Writings from "Being and Time" (1927) to "The Task of Thinking" (1964).* New York: Harper & Row.

Hirsch, Eric. 1995. "Introduction." In *The Anthropology of Landscape: Perspectives on Place and Space,* ed. Eric Hirsch and Michael O'Hanlon. Oxford: Oxford University Press.

Hochbruck, Wolfgang, and Judith Schlehe. 2010. "Introduction: Staging the Past." In *Staging the Past: Themed Environments in Transcultural Perspectives,* ed. Judith Schlehe, Michiko Uike-Bormann, Carolyn Oesterle, and Wolfgang Hochbruck. Bielefeld, Germany: Transcript.

Ingold, Tim. 1994. "Introduction to Social Life." In *Companion Encyclopedia of Anthropology: Humanity, Culture and Social Life,* ed. Tim Ingold. London: Routledge.

Lash, Scott. 1996. "Tradition and Limits of Difference." In *Detraditionalization,* ed. Paul Heelas, Scott Lash, and Paul Morris. Oxford: Blackwell.

Lefebvre, Henri. 1991. *The Production of Space.* Oxford: Blackwell.

Lima, Isabel P. 1989. *Trajectos – O Porto na Memória Naturalista.* Lisboa: Guimarães Editora.

Lukas, Scott A. 2007. "The Themed Space: Locating Culture, Nation, and Self." In *Themed Space,* ed. Scott A. Lukas. Lanham, MD: Lexington Books.

———. 2008. *Theme Park.* London: Reaktion Books.

Martins, da Graça L. F. 2007. "A Emigração do Nordeste Transmontano para o Brasil no Início do Século XX." *População e Sociedade* 14: 257–81.

Matos, Patrícia F. 2006. *As Côres do Império: Representações Raciais no Império Colonial Português.* Lisbon: ICS.

———. 2010. "A História e os Mitos: Manifestações da Ideologia Colonial na Construção do Portugal dos Pequenitos em Coimbra." *Guardianes de la Historia y de la Memoria: "Tradiciones"–Colecciones y Otras Manifestaciones (In)Materiales del Período Colonial,* 7th Congresso Internacional de Estudos Africanos no Mundo Ibérico, 1–28. http://repositorio-iul.iscte.pt/handle/10071/2194 (accessed 1 July 2011)

Merleau-Ponty, Maurice. 1989. *The Phenomenology of Perception.* London: Routledge.

Mitchell, Timothy. 1988. *Colonising Egypt.* Berkeley: University of California Press.

———. 1989. "The World as Exhibition." *Comparative Studies in Society and History* 31, no. 2: 217–36.

Mónica, M. Filomena. 1978. *Educação e Sociedade no Portugal de Salazar.* Lisbon: Editorial Presença.

Montês, António. 1939. "Assistência em Coimbra: Uma Demorada Visita ao Portugal dos Pequenitos". *Jornal Rádio Nacional,* Ano III, n° 124, 10 Dezembro.

Paulo, Heloísa. 1990. "Portugal dos Pequenitos: Uma Obra Ideológico-social de um Professor de Coimbra." *Revista de História da Ideias* 5, no. 12: 395–413.

Porto, Nuno. 1994. *Uma Introdução à Antropologia: Aula Teórica-prática no Âmbito das Provas de Aptidão Pedagógica e Capacidade Científica, Departamento de Antropologia. Faculdade de Ciências e Tecnologia. Universidade de Coimbra.* Coimbra: Universidade de Coimbra.

Ricoeur, Paul. 1991. *From Text to Action: Essays in Hermeneutics II.* Evanston, IL: Northwestern University Press.

———. 1992. *Oneself as Another.* Chicago: Chicago University Press.

Rydell, Robert W. 1993. *World of Fairs: The Century-of-Progress Expositions.* Chicago: University of Chicago Press.

Salazar, Noel B. 2010. "Imagineering Tailor-Made Pasts for Nation-Building and Tourism: A Comparative Perspective." In *Staging the Past: Themed Environments in Transcultural Perspectives,* ed. Judith Schlehe, Michiko Uike-Bormann, Carolyn Oesterle, and Wolfgang Hochbruck. Bielefeld, Germany: Transcript.

Santos, Luis F. 1995. "Os Programas de História do Ensino Secundário nas Duas Últimas Décadas (1974–94)." *Penélope–Fazer e Desfazer a História* 15: 171–88.

Santos, Paula M. 2003. "O Centro Histórico do Porto: Experienciação e Construção Identitária." In *Pluralidades Portuenses: Símbolos Locais, Relações Globais,* ed. Henrique G. Araújo, Paula M. Santos, and Paulo C. Seixas. Porto: Civilização Editora.

———. 2014. "Calling Upon the Empire: The Evocative Power of Miniatures in a Portuguese Nationalist Theme Park." In *Tourism and the Power of Otherness: The Seductions of Difference,* ed. David Picard and Michael di Giovine. Bristol: Channel View.

Silva, Cristina E. 2010. "Portugal Pequenino." *Resdomus:* 1–19. http://www.resdomus.blogspot.com (accessed 1 July 2011)

Sousa, Jorge P. 1999. *Bissaya-Barreto: Ordem e Progresso.* Coimbra: Livraria Minerva.

Thomas, Julian. 1996. *Time Culture and Identity: An Interpretative Archaeology.* London: Routledge.

Torgal, Luís R. 1988. "Estado, Ideologia e História de Portugal." *Revista de História* 8: 345–55.

———. 1989. *História e Ideologia.* Coimbra: Edições Minerva.

Tuan, Y-Fu. 2001. *Space and Place: The Perspective of Experience.* Minneapolis: University of Minnesota Press.

Universidade de Coimbra. 2009. "UC em Números." http://www.uc.pt/sobrenos/uc-numeros (accessed 1 July 2011)

Urry, John. 1990. *The Tourist Gaze: Leisure and Travel in Contemporary Societies.* London: Sage.

Viana, Clara. 2011. "Manuais de História ainda Contam o Mundo à Moda do Estado Novo." *O Público,* 27 March. http://www.publico.pt/educacao/noticia/manuais-de-historia-ainda-contam-o-mundo-a-moda-do-estado-novo-1486992 (accessed 1 May 2013)

Wang, Ning. 1999. "Rethinking Authenticity in Tourism Experience." *Annals of Tourism Research* 26, no. 2: 349–70.

Zukin, Sharon. 1991. *Landscapes of Power: From Detroit to Disney World.* Berkeley: University of California Press.

Chapter 9

Belize Ephemera, Affect, and Emergent Imaginaries

Kenneth Little

> Modern society [is] animated by new mythic powers located in the tactility of the commodity-image, the task is neither to resist nor admonish the fetish quality of modern culture, but rather to acknowledge, even submit to its fetish-powers, and attempt to channel them in revolutionary directions. Get with it! Get in touch with the fetish.
>
> —Michael Taussig, *The Nervous System*

FLASH/CHARGE

This is the story of a chance reencounter with an insignificant thing, a beer coaster, picked up at a beach party in Walliceville, Belize, and then found months later while working through the pages of my field notes.[1] The coaster, stuck between two blank pages of a notebook, and my reencounter with it, had an impact; it carried a charge that worked on me, as Marcel Proust (2003: 28) said things worked on him, "somewhere beyond the reach of the intellect." The sensations the object aroused in me organized as an unstable presence as they conjured a contact in the form of intense memory flashes. Imagine, a beer coaster, a disposable, functional object produced by the Belize Brewing Company to promote Lighthouse beer by way of the seductive image of three of the Belikin Beer Calendar Girls, having such an effect. It was a chance souvenir, a stubborn survivor of another time-place that brought its volatile contents to the present, disrupting the easy flow of things remembered and the smooth coherence of the moment. It agitated as

I began to recollect moments of its encounter against the logic of my field notes, working at the edges of the unthought, although vividly felt, as if I might slowly build a story in which to think it: a potentiality, an undecidability, a surprise complexity that adds to and augments a worlding.

The vivid sensory intensities of my encounter with a beer coaster were embodied and located where both verbal and visual archives were silent. Touching the beer coaster again, even such a ubiquitous materialization of the Belize everyday, though it is subject to the deracinating flow of transnational empire and the censoring process of official Belizean history of capital, commerce, labor, and the nation, sparked the power of a chance moment of possibility, both threatening and enabling. Attending to the beckoning luminosity of this fetish object is to feel a growth that narrative lacks: an incomposibility in the act of organizing itself, a sensuous excitement mixed with dread that made the fetish volatile as an incitement to an arresting pres-

Figure 9.1. Lighthouse beer coaster (Copyright: K. Little).

ence in the act of its becoming something, something bearing forth as a local
history of the present conditions of life, as an event, a moment generated out
of a lively cosmopolitics at the margins of empire.

Thus I turn to the affective charge of my beer coaster as ephemera,
as an emergent, nonsignifying quality of intention, an unqualified intensity, before it is systematized by narrative to become a named feeling in the
body, an emotion, a spoken vocabulary item in a codified language (Massumi 2002). In experience, affect accompanies narrative, but it is not governed by the same determinations. The force and intensity of an affective
charge of my beer coaster is not logically connected to its narrative/symbolic
content. There is, as Brian Massumi (2002: 8) explains, a disconnect of the
signifying order from intensity, which constitutes a different order of connection running parallel. But this intensity should not be mistaken for some
romantically raw experiential richness formed in the body. Intensities are
asocial because they have not been folded into a system that names them
as feelings, for they also bear the trace of past actions, including a trace of
their context organizing in the flesh. Such intensities, the affective qualities
of my beer coaster, conjured other imaginings, other effects that set off titil-
lating chains of felt associations not yet fully narrativized, but that still act
as sensations, as forces capable of exerting a deforming impulse on cultural
and linguistic codifications as tropicalizations.

The exciting danger of my beer coaster as ephemera is in realizing that
it could assemble histories of material-semiotic entanglements yet untold.
Such entanglements can agitate those histories we know and generate new
potentialities that affective intensities make possible, and thereby shake the
security of one's place in the world while conjuring "things to happen" out
of the intersections of flesh and object (cf. Haraway 2008: 18–19). Here the
materializations of my beer coaster act "as an abiding yet changeful presence, traversing distinctions between human and non-human, organic and
inorganic" (McLean 2011: 591; cf. Barad 2003). This is what Erin Manning
(2007: 134) calls "sensing beyond security" or what Lauren Berlant (2011)
calls a "cruel optimism," or how an object and its scenes of desire "matter"
not just because of their narrative content, or their representational power,
but because the thing encountered holds out potential and promise as it
becomes a seductive means of keeping clusters of affects attached to it, for
better or for worse. That's my beer coaster, and I began to track its affective charges through disparate scenes that gathered as stories, even as such
scenes also remained dispersed, floating, recombining, regardless of the signifying work they did.

The point is to slow the seductive urge to move to representational and
identity thinking and evaluative critique long enough to find a manner of

approaching the complexity and uncertainty of such stuff as it exerts a pull on us, as it tugs on us, in order to fashion some form of address adequate to its complexity. This means building an idiosyncratic figure of the material-semiotic connections that stuff produces as singularities; not representations, but "actual sites where forces gather to a point to instantiate something" in the flesh (Stewart 2003b: 1). It means attending to this figure of connectivity as an assembling, in this case a disparate beachfront party scene that pulled the course of writing about a beer coaster into a tangle of trajectories, contradictions, and disjunctures. Such a tangle included the impacts of "arresting images" (Stewart 2003a), like the day a mystery ship suddenly appeared in Walliceville Bay and the nervous euphoria it produced.

The mystery ship is equally ephemeral, and I track the way it conjured strange feelings of sudden appearances that made otherwise ordinary life in Walliceville nervous and haunting for locals, expats, and tourists alike. The haunting sensation that this event summoned, and the hopes and dreams of a tourist imaginary that grew as a cluster of impacts as such sensations became narrativized, are the result of a promise of vital connection as locals, expats, and tourists go with the intoxicating flow of tropical intensities: seductions, attachments, and impulses. Intensities like these make the social, whether good or bad, out of the ephemeral qualities of these arresting images and the incipient stories they inspire (Little 2013).

Anthropology's recent efforts to engage tourism imaginaries as a useful concept have shown a powerful predilection for recognizing their socially created representational qualities and their deployment in the act of cultural meaning making, in the way Leite, in her afterword to this volume, explains Bruner's thinking on the function of narratives. Imaginaries act to influence collective behavior as underlying interpretive maps and to transmit meaning more or less smoothly and in concert with personal imaginings and the global culture industries that act to circulate images of others, natures, cultures, artifacts, histories, adventures, and the like. It is to the significance of tourism imaginaries and their role in the transformations of tourist experience, the local lives of those "toured," and the political and economic effects and configurations of such operations that interests most of those working on such things. This is the overarching paradigm of this volume, as Salazar and Graburn usefully describe and map it in their introduction, the complications of which Leite enumerates as she takes up the work on tourist and tourism imaginaries, various models and concepts of which make up the majority of the chapters in this volume.

I want to ask another kind of question, one about the emergent qualities of tourism imaginaries, and about the generative forces of such emergence, about tourism imaginaries in the making. There is a danger in new approaches to tourism imaginaries taking their cue too exclusively from the socially relational logics of objects, images, dreams, technologies, flows of power and meaning, institutions, and capital that are already encoded into one story line or another, and so these approaches become calculation and definitional practices, matters of fact making that adhere to regimes of knowing organized under the "three pillars of anthropological representation" and insight: negation, identity, and being (Ochoa 2007: 479). To do so risks subordinating consideration of imaginaries in their incipient, sense uncertain, eccentric moments, as unstable and emergent vitalities, generative and activating forces that are not (yet) coded culturally, politically, or socially. Attending to imaginaries in the making, in this case the affective potentials found in a beer coaster and then in the appearance of a mystery ship and then finally in terms of expat ordinary life in Walliceville, means getting at the intersections of flesh and object and their lively and entangled couplings and assemblages. It means tracking intersectional coshaping potentials that incite as they instantiate and materialize things. Paradoxical and unfinished though these things may seem, lingering in the event of imaginaries in the making means lingering in the infinite event of becoming that seethes with uncodified potentials. Favoring an assemblage of affective forces approach rather than the political dialectics of representational strategies more familiar in tourism studies, and the dominant focus of the work in this volume, means sidestepping reason and drifting along through singular sites of collective excitation while becoming attuned to their affective atmospheres (Anderson 2009: 79; Stewart 2010).

This is a methodology more in the mode of "affirmative augmentation" (Massumi 2002: 17), as a composition of paradise imaginaries, in the way Leite defines them in her afterword. But I am trying to get at how these imaginaries throw themselves together in moments that are already present as potentialities—something waiting to happen in incommensurate objects (beer coasters), registers, circulations, and publics (a mystery ship's sudden appearance or the way an expat ordinary in Walliceville composes itself as an assemblage of discontinuous yet mapped elements), or what Leite usefully calls "the unpredictable forces that lurk around the edges of 'paradise.'" Such assemblages can be tracked through generative worldings of all sorts, like dreamworlds, ways of relating, impulses, encounters, distractions, and seductions of all kinds (Stewart 2008: 73).

This means thinking about tourism imaginaries in terms of their material affective intensity as "vibrant matter" (after Bennett 2010; McLean 2011), flesh and object attuning and attaching in an act of singular, materializing composition, before they are completely narrativized as cultural representations or as political-economic forces. This means that I am indebted to the history of compelling ethnographic work that Salazar and Graburn map out in their introduction. It also means that I sidestep a dialectical approach to imaginaries in the way that Di Giovine, in this volume and in his other work, has developed it as an "imaginaire dialectic" or the way Swain develops the concept of imaginariums as the "circulation of personal meanings and institutional imaginaries," while trying to retain something of Di Giovine's processual approach to production and reproduction and Swain's image of how the various strata of identity, history, politics, and storytelling pile up and rub against each other, producing new forces of connectivity.

It also means that I take one step back from Salazar's (2012: 864) notion that imaginaries are "socially transmitted representational assemblages that interact with people's personal imaginings and that are used as meaning-making and world-shaping devices," as the introduction explains, while still trying to suggest how an assemblage becomes a socially transmitted cultural representation in the making, but one lodged in the flesh as impulse, tension, sensation, connection. I am not interested in how a representational assemblage shapes emotional experience or where it comes from. What interests me instead is thinking about assemblages as discontinuous and incommensurate elements of image and flesh that throw themselves together as an affective intensity, as an eventfulness composed out of connection that expresses itself through a relay of sensations actualizing as a weak ontology of lived collective fictions made up of trajectories, differences, found affinities, and diacritical enjoinings (Stewart 2008: 72–73; cf. Saldanha 2007).

Walliceville, as a growing tourist destination in Belize, is a place of impacts, rapidly transforming into a tourist spectacle of some homogenized, global, dreamworld, adventure, pirate paradise, as if by some horrid and seductive magic, before everyone's very eyes, connecting locals up with the spasmodic effects and currents of global flows of images, capital, stuff, people, and culture. But I am not interested in debunking, with local objects and events, the several definitive structural features of global late liberal empire and capitalism and the meaning and effects of such things on local Belizean social life as they become taken up as the stuff of Caribbean tourism imaginaries. Rather, I want to begin to describe the forces of Caribbean imaginaries (see Feldman 2011; Sheller 2004), or tropicalizations (after Thompson 2006), as part of an "unfolding moment in which countless things are being actively generated as fugitive, shifting, indiscriminate, unsteady, and unfinished" (Stewart 2007: 1–2) in the rush and pitch toward some active realization yet uncaptured by what Deleuze and Guattari (1987) call "identity thinking."

This is akin to the way in which Benitez-Rojo (1992: 2–3) imagines the Caribbean. He describes it as a space of Chaos, as a discontinuous conjunc-

tion of unstable condensations, growths, decays, and half-told colonial and
subaltern stories that froth and surge together like a turbulent sea that conjures the eddies and pools of seething clumps of frayed seaweed, garbage,
flows of sunken drug boats and pirate stories, flying fish, mysterious strangers, tourists, downpours, and hurricanes that combine as networks of awk-
ward engagements. Such Chaos gestures toward things still unrecognized
and ungathered as concepts, and so they sidestep, shift, and drift uneasily as
singularities with unique textures, densities, and mixtures of intensities that
scuttle along the edges of events and experience, which suggests how force
becomes sensate as it becomes caught up in the "good life" tropicalizations
of paradise, or not (Stewart 2003b: 1–2). It means tracking the uncertain-
ties of what Stewart (2003b: 2–3) calls "rogue vitalities of bodily agitations,
modes of free-floating fascination, the secret life of the senses, and any other
site of collective excitation." It is about how a found beer coaster reignited
the affective dynamics of a time-place as a chronotope (after Bakhtin 1981),
lodged in the flesh, radiating force and new potentialities.

Combining Bakhtin (1981) and Bergson ([1912] 1991), the chronotope
can be considered a material assemblage of images with duration that contracts them into a spacialization and density, intensified but undifferentiated
as a logic of random disjunctions. The challenge here is to dwell in the event
of a tourism imaginary in the making, not as a reflection of power relations
or inequalities and how these are produced and reproduced or how exactly
they are troubled, contested, and transformed, but as affective intensities
that parallel imaginaries as representations as another mode of thought different in nature and constituting a space of potentiality where new forms of
life can emerge, what Povinelli (2011: 6–11) calls "spaces of otherwise."

EPHEMERA

Two Oxford English Dictionary definitions of ephemera are: (1) "of a fever
lasting only a day" and (2) "something which has a transitory existence."
Tourist contacts and encounters with stuff, which includes postcards, menus,
advertising brochures and pamphlets, magazines, napkins, ticket stubs to
events, places, and for travel, and, of course, beer coasters, evoke the sensations of the feverish and the transitory. This stuff is the clutter of travel. It
attracts, seduces, impresses instantly; it heats things up and flashes as a sensation with a transient impact, creating an affective charge as it assembles
flashes of feverish desire and potential before it piles up in the corners of
tourist attention, spent, exhausted. It is excessive stuff, the ruins of culture,
the stuff that once shouted its presence and function as it flashed by as

dreamworld enticement and wish image, even as it ends up scattered across hotel rooms or is found at the bottom of suitcases or in field notebooks, like fossils with a "radioactive" trace of life conjuring a history of some other time-place. The point is to dwell in such stuff and chance reencounters with it as found objects of another time-place and track its affective force, conjuring sensations that broadly circulate and give past events a continual motion of relation, contingency, and emergent potential.

Tracking the life of Belize ephemera means tracking its impacts, not so much as meaningful material culture but, rather, as commodity incantation, emergent forces of copy and contact, or what Walter Benjamin calls "profane illuminations." In his *The Arcades Project* (1999), Benjamin insisted on the nomadic tracing of dreams still resonant in discarded material things. His process of writing captions to found fragments and snapshots, gathered into loose assemblages, and the way his thought pressed close to commodity objects in order to be affected by them, illuminates the idea of copy and contact.

My beer coaster, for example, immediately brought me into agitated contact with an evening in paradise when members of the Belizean Jewels, a group of twelve calendar boys/strippers, entertained tourists at a beach bar. I want to track the free flow of Belikin beer coasters around which the shifting impulses of tourist imaginaries of the "good life" in "paradise" grew vibrant as desire and seductive promise. More generally, tracking tourist ephemera in Belize as arresting, affective forces—the contact zone of dreamworld enticements rubbing up against the transitory nature of a local world gone dreadfully wild for tourism—means holding my beer coaster close and following its felt impacts and half-realized effects (cf. Berlant 2011).

PARTY BOYS

The Sweet Sunsets Bar and Grill, once a popular lagoon-side watering hole just west of the public docks in Walliceville, used to pump out the "good life" with an intoxicating sensuousness that was eclipsed only by the excesses of its overstimulated patrons. On any given evening throughout most of the year, tourist and local bodies moved with the surge of the crowd, floated lazily on the pungent aroma of gunga around the bar and settled into dockside hammocks and loungers, taking in the vibe, swelling in intensity with the Rasta music, the flow of alcohol, the effects of the drugs, and the emergent rhythm of the scene. Walliceville and the Sweet Sunsets are places out of any dreamworld image of tropical paradise, places that realize the architecture, textures, and material culture of Caribbean pleasure. Relax.

Get with the image, with laid-back smiles all around, carried on a warm breeze. It all makes your body tingle as you melt into the groove, dizzy with anticipation. You can feel yourself losing control, "no shoes, no shirt, no problem." There is an intense attraction to this edgy ecstasy, a giddiness mixed with a touch of alarm at how good it all feels, and it acts as a contact high that seems tailor-made for a tropical night in paradise. This is a surge of the good life as paradise, and it fits with the image of Walliceville that is sold worldwide these days.

Flashback: the Sweet Sunsets was pumping out its version of the good life on a hot and sultry evening in mid-March 2004, when four male calendar models from the Belizean Jewels performed at the bar. The entertainment was sponsored by a local women's group and appropriately named by Audrey, one of the longtime expat owners of a popular beachside bar and grill, "Wild Things of Belize: Lady's Night Out." The Belizean Jewels were the Belize Brewing Company's male calendar models, the male parallel to the Belikin Beer Calendar Girls, but the men actually strip during performances, while the women, on the few occasions that they appear in public, stage bathing suit fashion shows. The event was a locally inspired ploy by the women's group meant to showcase local young men, and identify those with aspirations and bodies attractive and agile enough to become Belizean Jewels for the 2005 calendar, a sort of community women's group make-work project for male youth that hooked up with Belize's Dream's Come True Productions. Qualifications? To look hot enough to be able to fill out the demanding contours of a Melenie Matus-designed swimsuit while holding an infectious smile and an ability to dance and pose. Matus is a Belizean fashion designer with what an unnamed reporter for the San Pedro Sun described as "a knack for comfortable swimsuits and tanning-wear with sex appeal" (2004:22) who was making a splash in the global beachwear fashion market at the time.

The show started around nine, when the Jewels appeared on short bar tables provocatively stripping down to their swimsuits, showing their well-oiled and muscular bodies, beaded with sweat in the intense heat of the jam-packed barroom patio. This was all a tantalizing preview of what was to come later, when the Jewels put on a "for women only" strip show down at the Pelican Bar. When the Jewels arrived at the Sweet Sunsets the place went wild. Local and tourist women made riotous moves to get as close as they could to the four beefed-up models, the dreams of "drifting off with one of them," as Alice put it, carrying them along on waves of desire fed by the intensity of a mix of intoxicants, desire, and ear-splitting reggae music. Bodies surged forward toward the boys, limbs flying in every direction, struggling for attention while the Jewels moved their bodies seductively, grinding and smiling broadly to shrieks of delight. They threw calendars and beer coasters to the audience. Women, their bodies building intensity out of layer on layer of sensory impact, looked both shocked and thrilled to find themselves in the drivers' seat, grabbing for the men, the calendars, and the coasters all at once, while from the backseat the men in the audience became the noisy rumble of catcall hilarity and ridicule, picking up coasters and flinging them back at the men. The coasters flew everywhere.

Things looked like they were about to shift terribly out of control when Chas, a very large and local Creole man and the only self-identified gay person in Walliceville at the time, appeared from nowhere dressed in drag as a caricature of Aunt Jemima. Wearing a pair of revealing bright pink knickers under her trademark servant-girl dress along with her checkered head scarf, she was an arresting image, a force of menacing and jocular material contagion and potential. She couldn't have been happier with herself or with her imposing, heavyweight impact on the crowd. Chas's Aunt Jemima is what Stewart calls an "arresting image" (Stewart 2003a). She conjured a nervous moment when the pleasure of looking was retooled as all at once obtuse, erratic, pleasurable, and shocking, as the excited audience cut back and forth between global images of race and gender and some image of a local world caught awkwardly in its grips. Chas's image was a hilarious monstrosity that hit the senses with a mesmerizing, seductive, and repellent impact, a graphic mode of delirious fascination and laughter mixed with a hint of danger and aversion, a complex force, an assemblage of influences as some emergent vitality, in excess of any ideal representation of an ideological structure and way beyond the obvious meaning of a message.

Aunt Jemima's role as emcee was to sustain the excitement, prolong the ecstatic moment of beachfront pleasure. One of her strategies was to tell jokes about her seductive body with punch lines underlined by lifting her skirts, throwing out "sweet kisses" and beer coasters into the audience. Handfuls of beer coasters went flying everywhere. I caught one, but didn't think anything of it at the time and absent-mindedly stuck it in my pocket. Chas's image is a half-written sign of a discontinuous local social world crossing with the trajectories of a global, imperial one to become one of those sites where forces cluster into a nodal point of impacts that incite and instantiate something (Stewart 2003b), much like being right where you are, only more intensely (Massumi 2002: 10). It is how the shifts to a tourist-based neoliberal, postmodern capitalism have encouraged new affects and scenes of desire that are actively becoming tourism imaginaries, inspiring new narratives of race, gender, sexuality, and biopower that actively free new libidinal energies, new forces of becoming, and new examples of agency that are far from straightforward, but call on a jump and surge of affects when things resonate as both potential and degrading threat: a powerful force of the dreamworld good life in the making, contingent even if calculating, actualizing forces into something, some power.

In this contact zone, the body gorges itself on an excess of exotic pleasures and impulses metamorphosed into some monstrous "phantasmagorical enjoyment," outside the law of civilized life, in a state of exception, what I want to call a "duty-free" zone. This is life living up to the force of seductive tourist advertising, enough to be pulled into the loop of global, imperial forces that morph right along with it. But here life moves way beyond the advertised helter-skelter toward some threshold of vanishing, toward a death that will not die (Cazdyn 2012), an apocalypse eternally deferred: the good life as bare life, as desirously ephemeral as it is.

The shock and applause for Chas's Aunt Jemima image and performance focused everyone's attention on her as she introduced the local young men auditioning for the Jewels. As they were introduced individually, each performed a seductive dance, ripping their shirts and shorts off to reveal their new fashion swimsuits, to the music of Bob Marley. There was loud applause and laughter as family members, friends, and tourists alike screamed encouragement. But there was also a lot of teasing, mostly by local male friends, expats, and tourists. These faces read like an ambivalent mixture of embarrassment and delight, alarm and elation, agony and bliss as they grabbed at the coasters and sent them flying like Frisbees at the contestants and across the patio.

Afterward, Jimmy, one of the local guys trying out, could only say, "I nevah know that it was going to be that good man, because it actually came out well and I'm fine doing it. But I look foolish man, real foolish and nervous. I don't know what to do. I don't like it. But the girls like it, ya man! It was lovely. I feel good about it that way." Jimmy is what Sianne Ngai (2004) calls a "bad example." A bad example does not stand as a perfect representation of some idea or hegemonic image or some structure at work in Belize; rather, it is a line of potential, a trajectory of impulses that affective forces might take if left unchecked: a singularity or a matrix of forces actualizing as something (Stewart 2003b: 2).

Local men like Jimmy have been shocked and seduced into this new imperial edge-world of chronic, late liberal, capitalist blur in Belize, now almost completely fueled by the Belizean tourism industry, and touched by the threat and promise of a tourist culture of spectacle consumption frantically pumping out Caribbean representations as tropicalizations. Jimmy mixed drinks at the Sweet Sunsets and decided he had enough of "the stuff" to audition to become a Belizean Jewel. The Sweet Sunsets was built twelve years ago by two middle-aged English women after falling in love with Walliceville and the thought of a life in the tropics. Their tropicalization of the place included hiring young, good-looking local men like Jimmy to attract tourist attention, especially women's attention. In fact, the women owners hired and named the bar after another local, named Sweets, and they "shared their Sweets" between the two of them for years. "We have our Sweets every day," Alice chuckled one night while watching him eagerly mix up drinks and conversation with a group of tourists at the bar. Harriet jokingly calls Sweets her "love toy," but on that night in March Jimmy was their "crown jewel of the bar." Jimmy took an awful ribbing about his decision to audition from many of the local men who would have liked nothing better than to have replaced him, or find their own "sugar mommas" like Alice and Harriet, even as they are seduced and recoil in horror from the image of the sexy, carefree native that goes along with the performance. It's as if locals like Jimmy and Sweets are literally touched by the intimacy of the scene and make themselves its convulsive possession.

Stay in "tropical, happy-go-lucky, no worries" pleasure frame. Tourists love it. Like many of the locals I spent time with, Jimmy was eager to get out of Walliceville. Becoming a Belizean Jewel was his immediate image of freedom and his strategy of escape, this time into the seductive world of international modeling: "Just like on TV," Jimmy said. His public audition gestured toward a magical pleasure world beyond Belize; a world of success, high fashion, and money. If he could get the chance to show his body to others he could show everyone just how handsome and "gifted" he was. Impacts like these make up the plateaus of the social for Jimmy. And, in the space of tourism encounters, on a makeshift stage at a beach bar in Belize, ripping his clothes off while in "serious party mode," Jimmy gets high on an intoxicating pleasure and desire with a confidence that ricochets wildly between the raged extremes of a disquietingly hard life and the thrill of a reckless, seductive dream.

This is what Ann Cvetkovich (2003), in her work on public feelings, calls "traumatic realism." On the one hand, there is abjection. Jimmy sends handfuls of beer coasters into the crowd at the bar while dancing his version of seductive moves. Yet, on the other hand, there is a vital move to take on this force with intensity enough to capture it in the senses and make something of it. This is intensity disconnected from the signifying order. It is part of an assemblage of intoxications. For Jimmy, the impact of such a tropicalization of locals—wild, energized, savagely in rhythm—fails to represent the inflicting force of tourism as an object in the symbolic order of imperially inspired capitalism, so he feels compelled to live on and repeat those images. Yet, there is also Jimmy's confidence to take on the force of such images as a subject rushing to bear an affect toward some affirmative actualization, to make something out of an uncertain sense of circumstances: movement toward a sense of maneuverability and sense maneuverability. But this is no dialectical movement as much as it is an assemblage characterized by shifting configurations of flows and intensities in which things are constituted by a play of forces that take possession of them. In this sense, Jimmy's lack of fullness as a subject, his extreme vulnerability, comes not from a disconnection with reality, a slipping signifier, or from false consciousness, but from the promise of some vital connection as he goes with the nervous flow of such intoxicated moments of impact and new attachments: a bad example (cf. Berlant 2011).

In a couple of hours, the show was over and the excited crowd floated on a force field of ecstatic energy toward the women's show. An aching hush came over the bar patio. With the music turned down you could begin to hear the surf again and feel a faint sea breeze against the buzz of overstimulated bodies that faded as the crowd drifted down the beach.

THE MYSTERY SHIP

But the ephemeral agitates in other registers, too, like in the productive predicaments and augmentations of other arresting images of the tropical that have impacts. The day after the strip show, while walking along Walliceville's beachfront with Aiden toward our usual afternoon, after work, watering hole, the Drunken Pirate, he stopped to point out an impressive ship at anchor in Walliceville Bay. It was as if the ship had magically appeared. I said something to Aiden about how strange it was that at one moment the bay was clear of ship traffic but when I looked next there was a big boat suddenly at anchor. I thought it looked like a research vessel. Aiden laughed, "That's the magical mystery ship, at least that's what we call it here, because that boat always seems to appear, like 'poof'!" No one, including NGO officials, the village council leader, bar owners, tourist operators, village police officers, or the local head of the Belize Industry Tourism Association, who doubles as Walliceville's newspaper snoop, seemed to know why the mystery ship made these occasional ports of call, although everyone had a theory.

The silent appearance of the ship was a disquieting event. And while we drank our beers and talked about it, I found myself nervously playing with my beer coaster. The familiar image of the calendar girls, three of whom are the smiling, bikini clad bodies on my beer coaster, rubbing up against the mystery ship had an impact. It conjured an unsettling conjuncture of effects, a singularity, or what Massumi (2002: 17–18) calls a "disjunctive self-inclusion: a belonging to itself that is simultaneously an extendability to everything else with which [these things] might be connected." Four days later, "poof," the mystery ship disappeared just as mysteriously and suddenly as it had appeared. "It's still there you just can't see it," Julian insisted as he began a dreamy, laid-back conspiracy riff on the imponderables of space-age technologies he'd heard about from some tourist he knows who works for NASA.

Theories about the ship's appearance and disappearance became an elaborate set of stories. Some of these made more sense than others, but all of them were part of village-wide gossip that transformed in waves of free association as mystery ship stories moved from person to person and up and down the cayes. The ship was a drug boat operated by the Columbian drug cartel waiting on bales of cocaine. It was a National Geographic research (tourist) vessel counting whale sharks. It was a boat measuring channel depths in preparation for a dredging operation for the new megacruise ships that have now seduced local Belizean politicians and international tourism entrepreneurs further into the seamier sides of late liberalism and Caribbean capitalism. It was US Homeland Security, or the CIA or the FBI. It was a Russian-Cuban spy boat. It was a terrorist boat. It was an Italian millionaire's leisure boat. He sails to Walliceville every year at that time in March. It was an Australian's charter dive boat. Some said they knew of the Australian "skipper," apparently a drunk and a letch, but no one could remember his name and no one was sure they had ever actually seen him around.

The people of Walliceville, both longtime expats and locals, made sense of the ship through their stories, not by constructing explanations for its appearance and disappearance but by offering accounts of its nervous impacts and of its mysterious traces and effects. And as the stories piled up like shipwrecks on a reef, rocked by waves of telling and retelling, the event of the talk formed a tidal rush of dramatic and excessive images that overwhelmed the merely referential. These stories added a vivid intensity to things even if they never actually added up to any one reasonable explanation. And that is how they continued to spread.

Jimmy thought that the mystery ship might contain a film crew. He had heard that an international crew was supposed to film the strip show, that a film producer was searching for a new film star, or maybe it was a new fashion model. Jimmy was hardly interested in why they were there. More than most of the locals I spent time with, he desperately desired to "see the world in style" and he felt that finding work on the mystery ship might create for him a whole new international life of leisure, something modeled on his favorite reality TV show, *Survivor,* or some new life that felt like the adulatory exhilaration he experienced during his strip show dance performance.

He saw the boat as a sign of international pleasure, a sign of a seductive and magical world way beyond anything life in Belize could offer him. If he could only get on board he could show everybody how to party "Belizean style" and how sweet life could be with a "Creole Casanova." In this frame life could be sweet. The corollary: "locals" out of costume, out of focus, those who slip out of frame of the emergent tropicalizations of the place are a threat—another arresting image of impact that I will get to later.

This scene grows tactile and dense as it literally and nervously matters to Jimmy, and he in turn is possessed by it and the emergent cluster of sensations activated and actualized through it. And in the intersectional space of tourist encounters, Jimmy gets high on the lure of an enticing fantasy with an intoxicated confidence that bounces chaotically from the realities of village life to the tropical seductions of a globally circulating tourist imaginary. Here, it is the charge of nervous desires pulling into alignment and some visceral complicity of Jimmy laying claim to a composed tactility, literally into something that matters. The precariousness of Jimmy's life takes form as precarity pulls and aligns some contingent collection of forces, sensations, sensibilities, and materialities into something tentative and generative, "the transitional immediacy of a real relation ... coincident, but disjunct" (Massumi 2002: 5). Here an eventfulness is incited, and you can find its shimmering shapes in these scenes of attachment as things that matter cast an uncertain line along the hopeful edge an emergent imaginary (cf. Gregg and Seigworth 2010: 2–4).

But the mystery ship was a contagious image that flashed up uncontained by meaning or fact. Story subjects, objects, and events became performers in a spectacle that exceeded reason and the trajectories of cause and effect or truth and lie. The ship is yet another bad example, a singularity: an affective intensity, a force that suggests where a trajectory might lead if unchecked, which then becomes an event that literally "makes sense" of that force at the point of its affective and material emergence (Stewart 2003b: 2). The power of the storytelling that focused on the boat was that it drew listeners into a space of tense and lingering impacts and unseen forces, an affecting presence, a cultural poetics in the act of making something of itself as eventfulness. Mystery ship stories and all of the things associated with them became acts of creative contagion (Massumi 2002: 19).

As such, the mystery ship also became an arresting image. It served to focus anxieties and wild speculations about tourism encounters and about the dreamy seductions and nightmare chaos and contingencies of the world "out there." This was evident in the excessive exchange of conspiracy stories about US spies, drug dealers, strange tourists, terrorists, crazy locals, and corruption, a flow of narrative that conjured a nervous dread that agitated the smooth, tropical vibe of the place. As an arresting image, the ship supercharged a troubling state of suspense and suspension that haunted the place and its people, pulling them up short, and that lingered as a troubled impulse struggling to "make sense" and make something of things more generally.

It was the impulse to make something sensible of circumstances and events by fashioning stories about the mystery ship's appearance and disappearance that turned the sight of the ship into a tactile force. This arresting image of the mystery ship entered the local senses, lodging there, growing as an intensity, forming into a state of nervous suspense filled with resonance. The arresting image of the ship figures the force of what Deleuze (1988), after Spinoza, calls affect, the double sidedness of things where, as Massumi (2002: 12–18; cf. Zournazi 2003: 1–3, 11–12) explains, the virtual meets the actual, and where what "matters," as a materialization of local life in the making, is the permeable edge of potentiality itself.

As an arresting image, the boat is also a "tactile image." It is felt as a sudden, nervous interruption into the everyday world that then floods the senses with a proliferation of intense feelings, tinglings, images, and stories transforming matter into uncommon sensate affects that constantly exceed the requirements of reason and order. The tactile image assembles things not so much in an orderly or systematic fashion as in a manner that forcefully compels. The mystery ship's arrival and departure conjured an intense reverie mixed with dread that mimicked the dreamworld and nightmare that is now a constant in the continuous euphoric panic that haunts Walliceville's move into the big picture of world tourism these days. And then, poof, like a reverie, like a dream, like a trance and in a daze, it was gone.

JUST RELAX

In yet another frame that shocks the growing and nervous exhilaration of local, consumer, tourist tropicalization in Walliceville, new expat neighbors build their gated beach condos so that there is no public space or comportment left. Cozy holiday and retirement cocooning is where forms of paradise living have become tactile, and the bubble of fantasy life born of commoditized "local Caribbean culture" grows sensuously vibrant in the circulating impacts of a tropical dreamworld haven, still another arresting image. And it all places heavy demands on an image. The holiday/retirement house in paradise guards against the "outside world," with its wild scenes of crime, chaos, disease, and decay. It's good to escape to this hidden-away haven to revitalize and find renewal and a new purpose in life. Life's little pleasures hooked up to the big picture of paradise that settles into a dreamy connection with things, a resurgent image-affect of tourist pleasure mixed with a pension-retirement master plan.

Vitality and happiness unfold as if naturally and effortlessly, but anxiety and fear are the grounds over which it flows when the big-picture dreamworld implodes under the weight of its own embodiment and plays itself out to the point of nervous exhaustion. A dreamworld beyond the pale becomes a nightmare (Stewart 2007). That's when the dream is confronted with its own excessive strivings for pleasure, and you begin to ask yourself why you are trying so hard to relax. That is when the panic sets in. It is like rich, great-tasting food being the foretaste of heart disease. Your beach hideaway in paradise leads to a healthier life style and a chorus of new therapeutic routines that now set the controls for beachfront happiness. It is best to keep busy, so you put more effort into stabilizing the dream. You try to get involved in the community, to help build a cleaner village, and propose plans to deal with vermin, stray dogs, and the garbage. You build your beach dream home; maybe it is a time-share, with sophisticated surveillance technology, this time guaranteed to keep the local thieves out. You share information about community events and life at your next yoga class or massage at the spa. You play horseshoes with the locals on Saturday afternoons on the beach, making connections with them, and you feel good about positive contact; but it is a constant reminder that you find yourself surrounded by a nervous Otherness that is never quite assimilated or domesticated, no matter how strong your dreamworld image is of the pleasures of paradise.

But your involvement means you will never be able to escape the cruel world of corruption and fear just outside your gated or protected home. You cannot buy land or build without some Belizean ripping you off or stealing you blind. No local honors a commitment. Contracts are useless. The law does not work. Finally, all sorts of fears, of drugs, thieves, corruption, chaos, the sun, the strange weather, and unseen dangers swell and flex their muscles. And there you are, right back where you started, nervously weighing your life, as the future grows tense and tactile with an unanchored anxiety. It is at that moment that your attachment to this bit of paradise slips. No one told you about the downside, that it could be so tense or even downright dangerous. Your dreamworld image meets catastrophe with an impact that almost sends you nervously packing. Maybe you want out but cannot get out. Since 2008, the housing market for beach homes has almost dried up. You cannot get anyone to look after your place so that you can at least get away for a few weeks, knowing that if you leave it unattended that you will surely be robbed. Now you feel caught and you ask yourself, "Now what?"

And that is when the "mystery ship" mainlines into the flow of things at the Drunken Pirate, making an impact. At least that is what happened to "Captain Ted." Ted is a retired middle management auto executive in his midsixties, an expat from upstate Ohio, distinguished locally by his spurts of outlandish behavior. He has a nice retirement home, built up over the several years he has lived full time in Walliceville, a boat, property, and some business experience in Belize. He was at the Drunken Pirate the afternoon the mystery ship appeared. That is when he linked the mystery ship with cruise ships. This free association conjured dread and excitement as Ted and the rest of us turned the conversation to cruise ships potentially anchoring in Walliceville. If that happened, the only mystery left would be the one about who most stands to profit. Cruise ships could open business opportunities but they could destroy paradise, but property values will skyrocket or maybe not. But cruise ships would really put the place on the map. Who knows, there might be a Walmart involved or a major hotel chain. But it is all so "up in the air" and "there are such good points to be made pro and con cruise ships," and "it really is up to the Belizeans, you know. But then again their leaders are all corrupt and in politics for themselves and for the bribes from foreign business interests or the drug cartels." Ted's thinking about selling now, maybe moving on to Honduras or back to Ohio. Profit or no profit on his imagined property sale, Ted is tired of all the pressure, graft, and corruption and what it engenders materially, a smoldering random anger and sadness.

Maybe it is best to "lay low," Ted says to me. But he cannot help make the weird connection to the mystery ship when he thinks about his place in paradise and as he rides his own intense ups and downs of a strange happiness mixed with free-floating anxiety, like a pelican rides the air. Stick to conversations about the weather. Do not get involved. Remember the master plan. Do not panic. That is life. Take a deep breath. Have another snooze. Get drunk. Have a toke. But the specters of paradise keep reappearing to haunt the dream, like something out of the corner of your eye, some blot, something unassimilated, and not quite exhausted by what Lacan (1977) calls the Symbolic, something monstrous, something inhuman but breathing, an abject surge that points to a troubling vulnerability that haunts deep paradise. It is excessive and virtual, nothing you can put your hands on or completely figure out as, again, things nervously add to yet never add up, and it makes Ted nervous, angry, fearful, sad, and giddy about his image of a tropical paradise.

The rumors about big-time tourism development proliferated at a panic rate in Walliceville at the time of the mystery ship. And all of a sudden the image of paradise became indistinguishable from the sordid world of the international tourism industry. The point is how the virtual and the real collapse in on each other, their difference no longer relevant in the state of emergency that is rapidly forming as the generalized condition of the growth of a paradise on the margins of empire, teasing and encouraging new forms of life, new becomings as an emergent tourism cosmopolitics (cf. Stengers 2005).

AN EMERGENT TOURIST IMAGINARY
IN CHANCE REENCOUNTERS

What I am trying to accomplish here is something akin to what Isabelle Stengers (2005: 995) calls "cosmopolitics," where the cosmos instantiates itself as "the unknown constituted by multiple and divergent worlds, and to the articulations of which they could eventually be capable, as opposed to the temptation of a peace intended to be final." The practice of cosmopolitics is the opposite of finding a place of transcendent peace. It is a practice that Haraway (2008: 83) calls making "artful combinations" out of "speculative invention, and ontological risk," what she also calls figures. "Figures are not representations or didactic illustrations, but rather material-semiotic nodes or knots in which diverse bodies and meanings coshape one another" (Haraway 2008: 4).

Leite, in her afterword to this volume, puts the question about imaginaries nicely when she asks, "[H]ow do we capture an inchoate, fluid, dynamic phenomenon that is simultaneously demonstrably collective and yet necessarily ontologically particular?" Figures as knots, knotty nodes, like the speculative way in which this chapter is written, are in line with my notion of imaginaries as nonrepresentational assemblages, not (yet) representational, as Salazar (2012) usefully tracks them, but as a contingent and generative force on the way to a representation. My idea of an emergent imaginary starts there. Caribbean tropicalizations are creatively expressed materially in the flesh and used both materially and semiotically, but do not follow the demands of a dialectical expression, as Di Giovine, Swain, and several others in this volume have analyzed the imaginary. Their work deals with imaginaries in their representational modes, as fluid poetic and political contestations and as shifting fields of power and meaning. I am trying to gesture toward something that runs parallel to these processes as nonrepresentational, affective forces of intensity and potentiality, a sort of fluidity or flow not yet captured or contained, incommensurable incitements.

My chance reencounter with a beer coaster, the mystery ship, and the intensities of the tourist ordinary in Walliceville recall something of the generativity of a tourism imaginary as it instantiates itself in bad examples of the good life in paradise, on a beach, in Belize. I think this is what Taussig (in the epigraph) is getting at when he asks us to "get in touch with the fetish" (1998: 122). Mine is also an effort to track a moving object in order to evoke something of the entanglements of emergence and emergency that animate these bad examples as singularities (cf. Massumi 2002: 17–18). This means tracking things and events as conjunctures of force, as assemblages made lively through tourist imaginaries (tropicalizations, images of paradise) that incite seductive feelings of dreamworld relaxation and the affects of the good life to see what effects they have, what more they can do, and where they might lead if left unattended. The writing is meant to nomadically and mimetically track Caribbean tropicalizations of a dreamworld paradise resonant in the productive micropolitics of emergent structures of feeling that are generated through contact with my souvenir as it conjured the disparate scenes of a male model strip show competition at a beach bar, a mystery ship that appeared in Walliceville Bay, and the nervous intensities of ordinary expat and tourist life.

Seduction and shock are the affective forces that grow against the dreamworlds of tourism imaginaries of a Caribbean paradise and its nightmares. My Belikin beer coaster conjured arresting images, like the sudden appearance of Chas's Aunt Jemima in the middle of a public male strip show of Creole and mestizo male bodies. Bodies like Jimmy's interrupted the different stories of everyday life with an overpowering and contradictory sensibility that literally "makes matter" of a nervous encounter with, and an association that erupts out of, the order of tourist imaginaries Belizeans and tourists use to lay claim to paradise, whether it be spectacular or ordinary. When affect makes its jump between the visible thing, the idea, and the socially sensible, it leaves a vibrant and kinetic trace of uncanny connections that begins to mark otherwise disparate states of arrest. This is the nervous shock of an unassimilated trauma and the giddy euphoria that drifts like a catastrophic dream onto center stage in light of the magical and profound seductions of my reencounter with a beer coaster, in an uncanny place of encounters and becomings like Belize.

NOTES

1. All place and personal names have been changed. This is done as a sign of respect for my interlocutors and for the coastal village councils with whom I was in close consultation throughout the fieldwork and writing portions of my longterm research in Belize. It was their wish to remain anonymous, personally and

as a village. Some of the events are composites, but all direct quotes are actual speech acts of my interlocutors.

REFERENCES

Anderson, Ben. 2009. "Affective Atmospheres." *Emotion, Space and Society* 2: 77–81.
Bakhtin, Mikhail. 1981. "Forms of Time and Chronotope in the Novel." In *The Dialogical Imagination,* ed. Carly Emerson and Michael Holquist. Austin: University of Texas Press.
Barad, Karen. 2003. "Posthumanist Performativity: Toward an Understanding of How Matter Comes to Matter." *Signs: Journal of Women in Culture and Society* 28, no. 1: 801–31.
Benitez-Rojo, Antonio. 1992. *The Repeating Island: The Caribbean and the Postmodern Perspective.* Trans. James Maraniss. Durham, NC: Duke University Press.
———. 1999. *The Arcades Project.* Trans. H. Eiland and K. McLaughlin. Cambridge, MA: Harvard University Press.
Bennett, Jane. 2010. *Vibrant Matter: A Political Ecology of Things.* Durham, NC: Duke University Press.
Bergson, Henri. (1912) 1991. *Matter and Memory.* Trans. Nancy Margaret Paul and W. Scott Palmer. New York: Zone Books.
Berlant, Lauren. 2011. *Cruel Optimism.* Durham, NC: Duke University Press.
Cazdyn, Eric. 2012. *The Already Dead: The New Time of Politics, Culture and Illness.* Durham, NC: Duke University Press.
Cvetkovich, Anne. 2003. *An Archive of Feelings: Trauma, Sexuality, and Lesbian Public Cultures.* Durham, NC: Duke University Press.
Deleuze, Gilles, 1988. *Spinoza: Practical Philosophy.* Trans. Robert Hurley, San Francisco, CA: City Lights.
Deleuze, Gilles, and Felix Guattari. 1987. *A Thousand Plateaus: Capitalism and Schizophrenia.* Trans. B. Massumi. Minneapolis: University of Minnesota Press.
Feldman, Joseph. 2011. "Producing and Consuming 'Unspoilt' Tobago: Paradise Discourse and Cultural Tourism in the Caribbean." *Journal of Latin American and Caribbean Anthropology* 16, no. 1: 41–66.
Gregg, Mellisa, and Gregory J. Seigworth. 2010. "An Inventory of Shimmers." In *The Affect Theory Reader,* ed. Melissa Gregg and Gregory J. Seigworth. Durham, NC: Duke University Press.
Haraway, Donna. 2008. *When Species Meet.* Minneapolis: University of Minnesota Press.
Lacan, Jacques. 1977. *Écrits: A Selection.* New York: W.W. Norton.
Little, Kenneth. 2013. "Mr. Richie and the tourists." In *Emotion, Space and Society.* http://dx.doi.org/10.1016/j.emospa.2013.07.001 (accessed 27 January 2014).
Manning, Erin. 2007. *Politics of Touch: Sense, Movement, Sovereignty.* Minneapolis: University of Minnesota Press.
Massumi, Brian. 1995. "The Autonomy of Affect." *Cultural Critique* 31 (Fall): 83–109.

——. 2002. *Parables for the Virtual: Movement, Affect, Sensation.* Durham, NC: Duke University Press.

McLean, Stewart. 2011. "Black Goo: Forceful Encounters with Matter in Europe's Muddy Margins." *Cultural Anthropology* 26, no. 4: 589–619.

Ngai, Sianne. 2004. *Ugly Feelings.* Cambridge, MA: Harvard University Press.

Ochoa, Todd Ramon. 2007. "Versions of the Dead: Kalunga, Cuban-Kongo Materiality, and Ethnography." *Cultural Anthropology* 22, no. 4: 473–500.

Povinelli, Elizabeth. 2011. *Economies of Abandonment: Social Belonging and Endurance in Late Liberalism.* Durham, NC: Duke University Press.

Proust, Marcel. (1913) 2003. *Swann's Way.* New York: Viking Press.

Salazar, Noel. 2012. "Tourism Imaginaries: A Conceptual Approach." *Annals of Tourism Research* 39, no. 2: 863–82.

Saldanha, Arun. 2007. *Psychedelic White: Goa, Trance, and the Viscosity of Race.* Minneapolis: University of Minnesota Press.

Sheller, Mimi. 2004. "Demobilizng and Remobilizing Caribbean Paradise." In *Tourism Mobilities: Places to Play, Places in Play,* ed. Mimi Sheller and John Urry. London: Routledge.

Stengers, Isabelle. 2005. "The Cosmopolitical Proposal." In *Making Things Public: Atmospheres of Democracy,* ed. Bruno Latour and Peter Weibel. Cambridge, MA: MIT Press.

Stewart, Kathleen. 2003a. "Arresting Images." In *Aesthetic Subjects: Pleasures, Ideologies, and Ethics,* ed. Pamela Matthews and David McWhirter. Minneapolis: University of Minnesota Press.

——. 2003b. "A Perfectly Ordinary Life." In "Public Sentiments: Memory, Trauma, History, Action," ed. Ann Cvetkovich and Ann Pellegrini, *The Scholar and Feminist Online (S&F Online)* 2, no. 1 (Summer). http://www.barnard.edu/sfonline/, accessed 25 May 2009.

——. 2007. *Ordinary Affects.* Durham, NC: Duke University Press.

——. 2008. "Weak Theory in an Unfinished World." *Journal of Folklore Research* 45, no. 1: 71–82.

——. 2010. "Atmospheric Attunements." *Environment and Planning D: Society and Space* 29, no. 3: 445–53.

Taussig, Michael. 1998. *The Nervous System.* New York: Routledge.

The San Pedro Sun. 2004. "Matus fashion show dazzles the night," September 24 issue, page 22.

Thompson, Krista. 2006. *An Eye for the Tropics: Tourism, Photography, and Framing the Caribbean Picturesque.* Durham, NC: Duke University Press.

Zournazi, Mary. 2003. "An Interview with Brian Massumi." In *Hope: New Philosophies for Change,* ed. Mary Zournazi. New York: Routledge.

Chapter 10

Envisioning the Dutch Serengeti

An Exploration of Touristic Imaginings of the Wild in the Netherlands

Anke Tonnaer

The saying that "God created the world, but the Dutch created Holland" has ongoing appeal. Indeed, some regard the Dutch attitude toward the landscape in the light of a moral geography; the Dutch landscape in particular is seen as "the outcome of a series of dramatic interactions between man and nature" (Zwart 2003: 108). The question of how we relate to our environment is not merely a theoretical discussion; it has long been a passionate topic for public debate and geopolitical management by politicians, ecological conservationists, and project developers (Zwart 2003). The question gains particular pertinence through a paradoxical development: increasing globalization has sparked a growing interest worldwide in cultivation and revitalization of the regional and the local, and the particularities of place (Drenthen 2009: 205; see also Olwig and Jones 2008; Simon et al. 2010).

In this chapter, I discuss one particular development of place in the Netherlands, identified as the "new nature" or "rewilding project," seen through the prism of emerging and often competing tourism imaginaries. Tourism is, as Franklin and Crang (along with many others) have argued, "a significant modality through which transnational modern life is organized" (2001: 6–7). What people do, imagine, and experiment in tourism may prompt an expression of as well as a comment on sociopolitical processes outside the touristic "laboratory" (Franklin and Crang 2001: 7). Furthermore, as Moore has so cogently argued, both "the global" and "the local" as grounding tropes are not just concept-metaphors that academics use. She suggests that we look at how people themselves form the interconnections between the local and the global, and "to understand that process within specific contexts—economic, political, technological, symbolic" (Moore 2004: 81). Indeed, as Paasi argues, "people's awareness of being part of the global space of flows seems to have generated a search for new points of orientation, efforts to strengthen old boundaries and to create new ones, often based on identities of resistance" (2003: 475). Tourism offers a vital context for studying this dynamic, as "this form of consumption is a key part of identity formation ... and may be linked to other ideological commitments and activism in their home locale—political or religious" (Moore 2004: 82).

The Dutch are invited through the long-standing promotion campaign *Lekker Weg in Eigen Land*—roughly translated as "Out and about at home"—to enjoy the pleasures of their own country. The emphasis is on experiencing the unique character of the Netherlands, in other words, its "particularities." Given that the Dutch political climate, like in so many other European countries, is currently experiencing a nationalist and inward-facing turn, the question may arise of how national and regional identity and identification are linked to and expressed in tourism imaginaries of the Dutch landscape. In that light, it is striking that the largest nature conservation organization, Natuurmonumenten, in a recent membership drive rebranded itself using the tagline, "If you love the Netherlands," which has yielded some aggravated comments, not just because of a general Dutch dislike for all too overt declarations of patriotism, but more so because of its similarity to the slogans that certain populist political parties are using (e.g., a recent political party was named Trots op Nederland—"Proud of the Netherlands"). It illustrates that seemingly innocent leisure images are firmly entrenched in politically charged ground. Conservation and cultivation of the Dutch landscape offers another insight into how tourism imaginaries may come to take up a central position in processes of identity formation and place making.

In the Netherlands, there are several developments concurrently taking place that all reveal a particular reading of the nexus of landscape, identity, and land management. The most prominent and, until the recent government change, politically endorsed development is the so-called Ecologische Hoofdstructuur (EHS), the National Ecological Network, which refers to an effort in spatial planning to create ecological corridors between smaller and larger nature reserves across the Netherlands. The EHS is described as the backbone of Dutch nature.[1] There are also other, less mainstream initiatives that try to influence natural and cultural conservation, each spawned by a particular reading of what the Dutch landscape was "originally" like or what it should ideally look like, and how Dutch identity is coupled to this.

As an anthropologist, I may be skating on thin ice when entering this much-debated field, which is dominated by ecologists, nature administrators, and conservation activists. Put differently, my knowledge of the veracity of specific claims on the natural (pre)history of the Dutch lowlands is equal to that of the average citizen, whose interests in nature are expressed mainly through recreating in it. Indeed, the ability to talk in abstract terms such as "the natural environment" and "nature" puts those who cannot speak in social frames that transcend their particular places and times at a disadvantage in getting their perspective across (Carrier 2004a: 5, 7).

However, an anthropologist may enter the scene when considering that tourism is not only a developing sector economically, but, more importantly, that it is also for most Dutch the chief form for experiencing the landscape.[2] For instance, much of the Dutch agricultural area has been acquiring new functions, mainly by "returning lands to nature" and/or by developing them into recreational spaces, such as through farm camping. This chapter should therefore be seen as the sedimentation of an exploration in an evolving research project on heritage and identity in nature tourism practices in the Netherlands, set against the evolving political and cultural background of the European Union.[3]

The starting point is one very specific initiative for the redesign of relatively vast expanses of Dutch as well as European lands through an unconventional restoration strategy known, in rather oxymoronic terms, as "near-natural land management" or "nature development" (Neumann 1998: 28). It entails a hands-off approach that is "rooted in a radical reinterpretation of Europe's ecological history" (Schwartz 2005: 305). For one particular nature area in the Netherlands, this implies envisioning and striving to revive what is rather courageously labeled "the Dutch Serengeti." Nature development is a case study worthy of our attention, not just because notions of the "new wild" or new nature involve a very particular understanding of the landscape that has as its benchmark a natural state prior to a sedentary human presence and corresponding ideas for the right experience of the landscape. Unsurprisingly, these rewilding projects also meet diametrically opposed responses from cultural-historical proponents who regard the human presence and historically interwoven relation between man and nature as intrinsic to Dutch natural and cultural heritage.

The social support for the designing of the "new wild" depends on a conception of a viable imaginary[4] in which nature may prosper undisturbed, and the Dutch public can enjoy its spectacular scenery at the same time. Precisely this imaginary, however, is highly contested by others. In the view of the project's adversaries, the "new wild" largely amounts to a virtual concept in a man-made country like the Netherlands, and thus a manifest denial of a regionally developed attachment between man and nature.[5] Returning the land to nature would deprive the country of regional diversity, the cultural-historical legacy as well as "legibility" of the land, and, accordingly, a sense of place (Drenthen 2009: 212). Moreover, the opponents dispute the idea that the creation of a new wild leaves enough (hospitable) room for recreation.

The question is then what happens when different landscape discourses collide for gauging one's identity and one's sense of place (Hirsch 1995). In this chapter, I take up this question through an examination of what this divergence of perspectives means for assessing the tourist presence—that is, particular embodied practices and performances—in the natural environment. For, indeed, there is an "increasing demand for experiential tourism, often based on processes of temporal and spatial Othering" (see Salazar and Graburn, this volume; see also Fabian 2002). In this case, the starting point are two conflicting imaginaries in which nature emerges as Other. In thinking about nature development, the dichotomy rests ultimately on seeing nature as either a hospitable or a naturally hostile "host" for tourist "guests." The recurring question, then, is: what is the tourist's place in a "wild" space?

PERFORMATIVITY AND PLACE

The role of place in tourism is, clearly, much discussed in several studies (e.g., Bærenholdt et al. 2004; Coleman and Crang 2002b; Edensor 1998, 2000). Central to the understanding of the nexus of tourism and place is the notion of performativity.[6] Following Coleman and Crang, places are no longer viewed as "relatively fixed entities," but should be seen in a coproductive correlation with the "dynamic flows of tourists, images, and cultures" (2002a: 1; see also Salazar 2010). This fits the image of sand castles that Bærenholdt et al. invoke when characterizing tourism places as "tangible, yet fragile constructions, hybrids of mind and matter, imagination, and presence" (2004: 2).

This fragility and the ephemeral nature of tourism places is discussed sharply by Kirshenblatt-Gimblett (1998). When dealing with the heritage industry, and in particular the role of museums in creating tourism destinations, she points to the significance of the production of hereness that in the absence of actualities depends increasingly on virtualities (Kirshenblatt-Gimblett 1998: 169). I suggest that it is in the space that subsequently arises between production/creation and consumption/recreation that variable and contradictory imaginaries materialize (see Tonnaer 2008, 2010; Tonnaer et al. 2010; Tamisari 2010).

There are numerous examples and case studies that show this process at work (e.g., Bruner 2005; Stanley 1998). Bruner's case studies of New Salem, an Abraham Lincoln heritage site, show clearly how visitors are not so much concerned with authenticity in the sense of verisimilitude, even though this seems the main interest of the producers of the site. Rather, the consumers' experience appears much more to be about "a sense of identity, meaning, and attachment" through "learning about their past, playing with time frames, and enjoying the encounters, consuming nostalgia for a simpler bygone area," as well as buying into the idea of progress and celebrating America (Bruner 2005: 147). Indeed, as Bruner further argues, although the touristic border zone "is located in an actual place in the world, what is created is a cultural imaginary" (Bruner 2005: 18).

LANDSCAPE, NATURE, AND REGIONAL IDENTITY

The interpretive yet creative friction that is characteristic for touristic performance and place becomes especially visible when expanding the discussion to include ideas on nature, landscape, and regional identity (see Carrier 2004b; Hirsch and O'Hanlon 1995; Paasi 2003, 2008). Paasi provides a very lucid view on the current development of regional identity in relation to landscape. Landscape is, he notes, a complicated concept, as it connotes various aspects. It may be understood "as a kind of synthesis and expression of the meanings of physical surroundings and various material practices and their representations" (Paasi 2008: 513). Indeed, "landscapes structure social practices and the ways people organize their relations with their environment" (Paasi 2008: 511). Furthermore, images, practices, and identities connected to landscapes "are created in many different discourses," primarily in academic, administrative, and popular ones, which all produce different meanings for these categories (Paasi 2008: 518). In other words, Paasi states, "ideas of landscape are not developed *in vacuo*" (2008: 511, italics in original).

According to Paasi, regional identity is not "how the individual and the social are integrated in space," but the conceptualization of the sociospatial in the "production" of the individual/collective and vice versa (2003: 476). In this process, landscape becomes a relevant "*aide-mémoire* of a society's knowledge of itself," as Hastrup argues (2008: 54, italics in original). More particularly, "landscape becomes a *topos* of identity" (Hastrup 2008: 54, italics in original). As put by Hirsch, following Ingold (1993), "landscape is a cultural process," implying that an understanding of landscape is the outcome of the attempt to "realize in the foreground what can only be a potentiality and for the most part in the background" (Hirsch 1995: 22). There is thus a continuous dialectic between a "foreground" everyday social life ("us the way we are") and a "background" potential social existence ("us the way we might be"). The latter, Hirsch argues, can only be achieved fleetingly "in the human world of social relationships" (1995: 22). How this dialectic comes to pass in rewilding the Netherlands may be illuminated by taking a closer look at the case of "the Dutch Serengeti."

THE DUTCH SERENGETI

> Forester Jan Griekspoor informs me in great detail about the area and the foresters' tasks in it. In his all-terrain vehicle he drives me and my gear over to a hut near the cormorant colony. I have permission to call it my home for one week. During that time, it is likely that I will not meet anyone, as visitors are only allowed to enter the fringes of the reserve, and only if accompanied by foresters. While it is one of the few nature reserves that are not freely accessible for the general public, there simultaneously is hardly a spot in the country more in the focal point of attention—quite literally: the birding huts and the observation hills surrounding the reserve are virtually always occupied by enthusiasts on the lookout for birds, foxes and the hundreds of horses, deer, and cattle. Whenever someone is spotted tracking in the area who obviously is not a forester, phone calls will start pouring in, notifying the reserve's office that "someone is in the field illegally." Therefore, I will be wearing a forester's coat this week.
> —Bram Van der Klundert, *Expeditie wildernis*[7]

The Dutch Serengeti is the alternative name for a large nature reserve, officially called the Oostvaardersplassen, that it is being managed following the nature development principle.[8] The ecological theory behind this type of management is that the typical European landscape of alternating forests and open spaces was initially not created by human agricultural intervention but rather through grazing by wild herbivores in the preagricultural era (see Schwartz 2005: 305). The Oostvaardersplassen acts as a groundbreaking project in the Netherlands, and as an example to show that it is possible to revive a sort of primeval wilderness—in other words, a place where the dynamics of nature prior to human interference are being maximally restored.

The Oostvaardersplassen is a six-by-ten-kilometer nature reserve, about an hour's drive from Amsterdam. It is a vast, at least according to Dutch standards, marshland area, populated by large grazers, such as red deer, konik horses, and heck cows, as well as by tens of thousands of grey geese. These animals are said to play a key role in the natural dynamic of the area.

By grazing they create a mosaic of open water and specific marshland veg-etation, inviting other spectacular flora and fauna species such as the sea eagle and the raven to settle permanently in the area. The Oostvaardersplas-sen is, therefore, acclaimed as a gateway "to the Netherlands of thousands of years ago."[9]

Some pro-wilderness websites furthermore suggest that Europe too has a "big five"[10] that can match Africa's. In the European version, it consists of the red deer, the elk, the brown bear, the lynx, and the wolf. Such refer-encing implies subsequently that even in an overcultured country like the Netherlands, an experience of the wild can be adventurous, potentially dan-gerous, and hence "primitively" authentic.[11]

There is no doubt that the area's "unspoiled nature" character has great appeal. Indeed, in dubbing the reserve a Dutch equivalent of the Seren-geti, both the curiosity and the sympathy of the general public are being addressed. However, it should be noted that the reference to the wild nature of the African Serengeti is rather ironic in view of the colonial genesis of the famous park. Indeed, the historical development of national parks like the Serengeti National Park largely hinged on imaginaries in which Africa was seen "as earthly Eden—a romanticized wilderness in opposition to the decadent metropole" (Neumann 1998: 18). As Salazar (2006: 839) further explains, the emergence of tourism in that part of East Africa was "closely interwoven with the history of wildlife conservation" under German and British rule. Tourism was developed as "an industry catering to the needs of Westerners coming to observe and hunt 'exotic' animals," thus leading to the design of the park. Furthermore, whereas under colonial rule, Euro-pean administration "decided what was valuable heritage," nowadays this role has been taken over by global yet ultimately Western bodies, such as UNESCO and the World Conservation Union (Salazar 2006: 839).

Although further study is needed to find out how a notion such as the Serengeti has come to be used and circulated as a symbolic simile in the wilderness imaginary of the Netherlands, its resurfacing in Dutch land man-agement is a remarkable case in point of how imaginaries are moving glob-ally. The historically ingrained and sustained circulation of the image of the African savanna as a symbol of primal, Edenic nature has come to a point at which its colonial origins have become not only obfuscated, but now also feed back into a global ecological imaginary of contemporary environmen-talism (see Salazar and Graburn, this volume).[12]

Notwithstanding the imagined wild space, which is at least partially evoked by the wide horizons of the Serengeti, the actual area within the Oostvaardersplassen that is freely accessible to the public is relatively lim-ited, because of the terrain condition as well as the peace and quiet the herds need to prosper. The main ways of experiencing the area are through short, predetermined walks from the visitors' center or via excursions joining a forester. Robust nature is often very vulnerable, particularly in relation to its carrying capacity for human presence. And this is, as one senior spokesperson of Vogelbescherming Nederland, the Society for the Protection of Birds, puts it, the essential dilemma between creating public support for such nature development projects on the one hand, and safeguarding what you would like to achieve with that public support on the other. This issue becomes increasingly of general interest, since the number of Dutch nature reserves that are managed according to the nature development principle is growing. It affects not just visitors to the area, but even more so locals living in or close to those areas (Drenthen 2009).

Within the nature development "movement," for want of a better designation, there is no univocal agreement about the place of visitors/tourists in the wild landscape. Some of the stricter ecologists prefer to minimize human presence, urging to close rather than open nature reserves for recreation. There is, for example, a website that on the one hand asks visitors to share their future visions on Dutch wilderness and thus to create commitment. On the other hand, the browsing e-visitor is only allowed to see the contours and not the precise coordinates of the new wildernesses. These areas are there, it is stated, to remind us that we do not "own" nature.[13]

However, there are also ecologists that instead argue for a new type of experiencing nature, calling, among other things, for a radical "defencing" of former agricultural areas so as to allow for true wandering and hence a different awareness of place.[14] Indeed, a prominent restorationist who has been at the vanguard of rewilding Europe has used the phrase "insane oasis" (Drenthen 2009: 226) to characterize the possible meaning of new wildernesses. New wilderness emerges then as a place "where we can escape from the abundance of societal orders and regulations, and ... symbolizations of place" (Drenthen 2009: 226).

Here a parallel to Neumann's observations may be noted regarding what he terms the "national park ideal," a particular conceptualization of nature that since the foundation of the renowned Yellowstone National Park in the United States has served as a model for national parks worldwide (Neumann 1998: 9). According to Neumann, this model reflects the "landscape way of seeing: the removal of all evidence of human labor, the separation of the observer from the land, and the spatial division of production and consumption. *A national park is the quintessential landscape of consumption for modern society*" (Neumann 1998: 24, italics in original). In a similar vein, Carrier (2004a: 6) points out that in the environmentalist movement, nature and the environment are construed as a realm that is separate from social

practices and human experience. Accordingly, in the imaginary of the new
wild seen from a tourism perspective, the value of a touristic experience lies
in a kind of "placelessness," of being the Other in the landscape.

"INSANE OASIS" VERSUS LANDSCAPES OF MEMORY

> When visiting the Oostvaardersplassen Nature Reserve, we in fact do not enter
> "primeval nature" but instead very controlled parkland. In accordance with
> that assessment, the site should be judged on its recreational, educational, and
> aesthetic significance. Unfortunately, it is not the status of an educational rep-
> lica that is being aspired to. This place has to be a wilderness, with real nature.
> In reality, it is not so much "unspoiled, genuine nature" that is being main-
> tained here, but rather the idea of "unspoiled, genuine nature." The Oostvaard-
> ersplassen primarily underpin the myth of romantic environmental purity....
> Suddenly, we have become very far removed of the idea of "the wild." Access to
> the Oostvaardersplassen Nature Reserve, for one, is limited to a large degree:
> Man, as the great spoiler, has to be kept at bay as much as possible.
> —Patrick Van der Kroef, "Wat weerloos is, is niet per se van waarde"

It is precisely the emphasis on the value of estrangement as a visitor that
goes against the grain of initiatives that regard a traditional agricultural cultivation of the land as the basis of the Dutch landscape in its regional varieties, including its riverine landscapes, dikes, forests, and dunes. Roughly put,
the benchmark that these initiatives employ for determining their policy of
landscape development is the preindustrial, small-scale farming of the late
nineteenth century. There are numerous cultural-historical organizations as
well as associations that aim at the management, maintenance, and restoration of particular parts of the Dutch landscape according to an ethnographic
heritage and pastoral agrolandscape. Some of them are regionally oriented,
others nationally.[15] The starting point of all, however, is that "back in the
day," biodiversity, sustainability, legibility, or the beauty of the landscape
were not objectives in themselves, but rather the outcomes that arose more
or less organically through a symbiotic relationship between man and nature. Accordingly, they call for rural income support, to subsidize farmers
directly for their role as "stewards of the countryside" and "guardians of the
landscape" (Schwartz 2005: 296).

Clearly, the consequences of their underlying ecological assumptions
for a conception of tourism practices contrast fundamentally with that of the
rewilding program. Drenthen (2009: 221) puts forward that "seen from the
perspective of people who feel connected with the old landscape, the new nature reserves can at best lead to an impoverished (and probably perverted)

sense of place attachment." He suggests that this is caused by a considerable dependence on experts, such as ecologists, for the production of a narrative that "makes particular places legible" (Drenthen 2009: 221). An understanding of the place is thus no longer embodied but rather rationally attributed. Carrier (2004a: 7) notes this as a form of social power, that is, the ability to impose one's particular interpretation in preference over that of others.

A case study from Latvia by Katrina Schwartz (2005) is exemplary for the sentiments played out in competing discourses on sustainable rural development. In fact, her study provides an interesting report on the first international project by the same Dutch ecologists who are the devisers of many of the new nature initiatives in the Netherlands, and increasingly in wider Europe. Schwartz describes how one particular region in Latvia, which suffered from economic decline and population decrease, was selected by the Dutch conservationists for the creation of postagrarian wilderness. Incidentally, here is a remarkable similarity with the inception of the Oostvaardersplassen. Not only is the reserve situated in a man-made part of the Netherlands (in the province Flevoland, which is land reclaimed from the water), the area itself was originally destined as an industrial zone, but due to a lack of economic activity plans from the drawing board were never materialized.

In Schwartz's case study, developing concurrently with the project was a local initiative that "weighted the cultural landscape equally with the natural environment and celebrated the historically synergistic relationship between farming and ecology in the agrarian spirit of Latvianness-as-closeness-to-nature" (Schwartz 2005: 309). For these local heritage campaigners, expelling the farmer from his land was "fundamentally anti-national," as it went against the heart of what it means to be a Let (Schwartz 2005: 308). The way forward according to this vision was to protect and strengthen cultural heritage, and redevelop economically through forms of heritage tourism. Locals felt their view on the future and landscape was completely at odds with those of the Western foreigners and the rewilding project.

The situation in Latvia as described by Schwartz differs in many respects, if only because the distinction between local and visitor seems much more blurred in the Dutch context; that is, in a mobile and densely populated society like the Netherlands, visitor roles and local roles largely overlap (Van Koppen 2009: 231).[16] Appropriately, Salazar and Graburn (this volume) suggest viewing "locals" and "visitors" as "conglomerates of stakeholders," since they are both "by no means simple or solidary groups." Moreover, heritage enthusiasts in the Netherlands are often not tied to one place, but generally petition for their cause regionally or nationally. Even so, Schwartz's study does point to the emergence of different imaginaries as a result of different ways of dealing with our relation with place and history.

Furthermore, from her study we can gather how imaginaries may become, as Salazar and Graburn (this volume) note, "the symbolic objects of a significant contest over economic supremacy, territorial ownership, and identity." In the Netherlands, the majority of organizations and institutions taking an interest in natural conservation compete over state subsidies and public donations. Which imaginary is taken on as the predominant one in designing the landscape can have profound consequences for the access to political, financial, and sociocultural resources. In that light, it may be telling that the rewilding initiative gained significantly more funding over the past few years than the heritage campaigners have been able to procure in the same time span.

BETWEEN WILD SPACE AND PEASANTRY PLACE: SOME CONCLUDING REMARKS

"Thinking about Holland, I see broad rivers slowly moving through endless lowlands," is the first line of the poem that the Dutch people chose as the "Dutch Poem of the Century" in 2000.[17] Tellingly, it describes a riverine country, and the ongoing struggle of the Dutch against the water, which is the typical depiction of the moral geography of the Dutch landscape (Zwart 2003). It is this kind of imaginary, exemplified in the case of the Dutch Serengeti, that is being challenged in the current, growing type of development of place that imagines the Dutch landscape to be a new wilderness, having as its benchmark a natural state prior to a sedentary human presence.

The disagreement between the protagonists of the (new) wild and those who want a restoration of the preindustrial, nineteenth-century landscape suggests a world of difference in the perception of the environment. Yet, a closer study of both the wilderness imaginary and the opposing, idyllic cultured landscape imaginary shows that the underlying myths and stereotypes sprout from the same "imaginative reconstruction" (Leite 2005: 290, cited by Salazar and Graburn, this volume); that is, they can both be traced back to the same modernist imaginary of nature. The juxtaposition between the wild and the idyllic are "the inner tensions between two complementary stances to nature in modernity" (Van Koppen 2009: 232). Additionally, as Neumann (1998: 17) argues, the pastoral and the (wild) sublime are both part of the "cultural evolution of the idea of nature as a source of aesthetic value." Furthermore, both imaginaries are in fact part of a wider "global ecological imaginary of late twentieth-century environmentalism" (Salazar and Graburn, this volume), yet they diverge on the stance of which historical benchmark should be taken for current landscape management.

In the case of the Oostvaardersplassen, the recurrence of the Edenic myth of an unspoiled landscape through labeling the nature reserve as the Dutch version of the famous African national park underscores not only the idea's colonial origin, but implicitly also the evolutionary model that is governed by the principle that the greater the temporal distance between one's historical benchmark and the here and now, the more authentic one's acclaimed "natural landscape" is.[18] Indeed, the authenticity claim, and in its wake the decisive authority to intervene in the landscape, made by the rewilding protagonists rests on the idea that the time travel involved in seeing wilderness is larger and therefore more primitive and pure.

However, it is clear, as other studies have already shown (e.g., Schwartz 2005), that the lived sentiment cannot be satisfactorily explained through a mere philosophical or historical perspective. As Salazar has written elsewhere (2010: 46), "peoples and places are constructed in both the imaginative and material sense; destination making is as much about meaning or culture as it about hard cash and politics." Different narratives on the creation, legitimization, and contestation of the environment do translate into differently distributed access to land and its natural resources (Schwartz 2005: 294; Carrier 2004b). Leite (this volume, italics in original) rightly points out that "*tourism imaginaries* are those imaginaries ... that are not necessarily particular to tourism, but in one way or another *become culturally salient in* tourism settings." This seems to be the case for the discourses on Dutch nature. In describing and contextualizing the case of the Dutch Serengeti, I have thus far referred to conflicting "tourism imaginaries" as if these conceptions of the place and role of tourists in the landscape are commonplace in the discourses on the management of Dutch nature. Although both the rewilding development project and the cultural landscape restorationists ascribe part of a sustainable economic basis to an expansion of tourism—it is broadly recognized that the Netherlands has a great need for recreation sites (Drenthen 2009: 212)—very little attention has been given to the actual perceptions, performances, and practices of visitors to either wild spaces or peasantry places. In spite of this, the social basis of these projects is crucial to their success.

Debates are dominated by ambiguities surrounding notions such as sustainability and biodiversity—compound terms that have little imaginative weight for the lay public, and that, furthermore, deny "significance to our individual and local experiences" (Carrier 2004a: 8). This process of abstraction is, therefore, political (Carrier 2004a: 12). Moreover, the nature of the emplacement of tourists in the landscape is often assumed or prearranged. Indeed, regardless of their differences, a striking similarity between the organizations is the consistent accent on the importance of letting the

Dutch regain a sense of pride and ownership of their country. As the previously mentioned restorationist stated in a conversation: "That is the most important thing: they [Dutch locals] have to regain their pride of their local nature reserves." Yet, this is not achieved by a place constructed through a symbiosis with nature and human history and agency, but precisely through denying that symbiosis. Accordingly, the comparison to the African Serengeti is no coincidence in that regard; it suggests that "wild nature" is not un-Dutch at all.

Yet, as Veijola and Jokinen (1994: 136, italics in original) have reasoned, scholars "are so interested in *seeing* how the Western individual begins to 'frame landscapes,' 'to create closed spaces' and a panoramic view of things, while they fail to ask whether this *view,* this way of 'highlighting overviews,' leaves any place for meanings, experiences and knowledge created by, in and for the body." It is, seen from that perspective, likely that there is a significant gap between production and consumption. What are people seeking in joining excursions with a forester? How do long-distance walkers, a very popular activity among the Dutch, move through and experience the landscape? What is the relation between gathering knowledge, either cultural-historical or ecological, and just having a nice time with loved ones during a picnic, hike, or outdoor outing? What is people's emplacement in the landscape? Are we, as Augé (1995) suggests, decreasingly able to really connect to places as a result of overabundance of events, spatial overabundance, and the individualization of references?

Regional identity is, as Paasi (2003: 478) argues, "an interpretation of the process through which a region becomes institutionalized." However, an interpretation of people's connection to the landscape is not just a matter of experts, politicians, or bureaucrats, but rather comes about in a contingent dialectic between formal discourse, personal narratives, set rules and regulations, and idiosyncratic individual practices. Furthermore, in the case of imagining the wild in the Netherlands, it seems also a matter of a willingness to suspend disbelief. It is therefore important that we pay attention to "local, concrete orientations to the natural environment," so as to come to an understanding of "how people see the world around them" (Carrier 2004a: 14) and shape their actions and practices accordingly. Experience is personal and idiosyncratic, and may be reproducing or transforming abstract imaginaries.

A telling example of this are the mixed responses to the yearlong experiment of a Dutch senior government official who, following in the footsteps of writers like Roger Deakin (2008) and Robert McFarlane (2008), went on a solitary wilderness pilgrimage, contemplating the meaning of the wild in present-day society by camping for a week each month in one of the last or new wild places in the Netherlands. Throughout the year he kept a blog about his experiences, and he recently published those (Van de Klundert 2012). For him, there was no doubt about the presence of wild places, even in a densely populated country like the Netherlands. However, a journalist who was assigned to write about the project was not able to suspend his disbelief, and kept hearing water sport enthusiasts passing by, fifty meters away from the Dutch Thoreau's campsite (Janssen 2009).

It is this different, embodied awareness of nature—the way people themselves create meaning in a dialogic interplay with images, other tourists, experts, and place itself—that is the challenge for gaining insights into the interpretive process that occurs between production and consumption of imaginaries. Much more than in the strength of nature itself, it is in the vitality of modern-day tourists' imaginings that the successful emergence of a "Dutch Serengeti" is determined.

NOTES

1. Information on the EHS is taken from http://www.natuurbeheer.nu/Beleid/ Nederland/De_Ecologische_Hoofdstructuur_(EHS), accessed 4 November 2013. The former government (2010–12), based on a coalition of Liberals and Christian Democrats, ceased the financial support for the EHS, which essentially implied that the network will not reach its fulfillment, at least not in the near future. The rewilding initiatives referred to in this chapter prosper nonetheless, as these often operate on the basis of nongovernmental subsidies and seek financial liaisons within the business sector in order to develop their alternative ways of nature conservation.

2. At least 70 percent of the Dutch population experiences nature through different practices of recreation (Steenbekkers et al. 2008: 10). Foreign tourists are much less interested in Dutch nature; their main destinations are the central metropolitan areas of Amsterdam and, to a lesser degree, Rotterdam.

3. This chapter is based on preliminary fieldwork that I carried out between September and November 2010, including several interviews with key players in the field and literature review (both popular and scientific).

4. Important players in the creation of a wild imaginary are united in the organization Rewilding Europe, the foundation of which largely hinged on a Dutch initiative; see http://www.rewildingeurope.com, accessed 4 November 2013.

5. James Carrier argues that all terms, including "nature," landscape, and the built environment, are "implicated in the same human social and cultural processes." Following Kenneth Burke's notion of "second nature," he suggests that "cultural meanings and the social relations associated with them are 'first *ascribed* to nature, then "derived" from it'" (Burke 1965: 278, cited in: Carrier 2004a: 3, italics in original). In other words, the construction of the new wild is

as much a part of the same human dynamic—in spite of its suggestion of being a natural state prior to sedentary human presence—as the view that man and nature are intimately linked.

6. Performance is a central upcoming concept in tourism studies in general (see, e.g., Adler 1989; Bruner 2005; Tonnaer 2010; Tonnaer et al. 2010).

7   All translations are the author's own unless otherwise noted.

8. The term *Oostvaardersplassen* may need a short explication for non-Dutch speakers, as the word on the page could look rather lengthy in an English text. The name actually reveals the entanglement of the natural (geological) and cultural heritage of the area. Before the nature reserve was left to develop, and before the area was even "impoldered," that is, before the land was reclaimed from the sea, it was part of a large, shallow bay that was in direct contact with the North Sea. In this so-called Zuider Zee was a deep gully, which was used as fairway through which the seafarers left for the Far East in early colonial times, that is, in the days of the Dutch East Indies. The fairway was named Oostvaardersdiep. The current nature reserve borders on the Oostvaarders dyke, raised after the reclamation of the Zuider Zee. In short, *Oostvaarders* is thus a reference to the ships that sailed for the long-haul trade to the Dutch East Indies. The noun *plas* (plural: *plassen*) in this context means "large body of (still) water."

9. This quote was taken from the website of Staatsbosbeheer, the governmental organization that manages a large number of the nature reserves in the Netherlands see http://www.staatsbosbeheer.nl/Natuurgebieden/Oostvaardersplassen, accessed 4 November 2013.

10. See Salazar (2010) for a historical contextualization of this concept.

11. See, for example, http://www.ongerepte-natuur.nl, accessed 4 November 2013, a website that is run by a committed individual who aims to acquaint the wider public with the possibilities of wild nature in the Netherlands and the North Sea.

12. It would be valuable, furthermore, to study the interpretations that are given to the concept of the Serengeti by the environmentalists, politicians, and bureaucrats working on rewilding the Netherlands and Europe more broadly.

13. See, for example, http//www.wildernis.nu, accessed 4 November 2013.

14. "Defencing," *onthekking* in Dutch, is one of many neologisms that accompany the different quests and ecopolitical disputes in establishing "new wilderness" areas.

15. The organization Vereniging Nederlands Cultuurlandschap is a telling example. See their website at http://www.nederlandscultuurlandschap.nl/, accessed 4 November 2013.

16. Furthermore, for the purpose of this chapter, I present a particular reading of Schwartz's study. She contextualizes her analysis against the backdrop of Latvian nationalism and the complicated relation between Western and Eastern Europe, especially in the post–Soviet Union era.

17. The poem "Remembrance of Holland" is by Dutch poet Hendrik Marsman, who wrote it while being abroad in 1936.

18. In the chapters of Stasch, Theodossopolous, and Bunten (this volume) the same principle is at work, but in the spatial and temporal Othering of people (see also Tonnaer 2008, 2010).

REFERENCES

Adler, Judith. 1989. "Travel as Performed Art." *The American Journal of Sociology* 94, no. 6: 1366–91.

Augé, Marc. 1995. *Non-places: Introduction to an Anthropology of Supermodernity.* London: Verso.

Bærenholdt, Jørgen O., Michael Haldrup, Jonas Larsen, and John Urry. 2004. *Performing Tourist Places.* Aldershot, UK: Ashgate.

Bruner, Edward M. 2005. *Culture on Tour: Ethnographies of Travel.* Chicago: University of Chicago Press.

Carrier, James G., 2004a. "Introduction." In *Confronting Environments: Local Understandings in a Globalizing World,* ed. James G. Carrier. Walnut Creek, CA: Altamira Press.

———. ed. 2004b. *Confronting Environments: Local Understandings in a Globalizing World.* Walnut Creek, CA: Altamira Press.

Coleman, Simon, and Mike Crang. 2002a. "Grounded Tourists, Travelling Theory." In *Tourism: Between Place and Performance,* ed. Simon Coleman and Mike Crang. New York: Berghahn Books.

———, eds. 2002b. *Tourism: Between Place and Performance.* New York: Berghahn Books.

Deakin, Roger. 2008. *Wildwood: A Journey through Trees.* London: Penguin Books.

Drenthen, Martin. 2009. "Developing Nature Along Dutch Rivers: Place or Nonplace." In *New Visions of Nature: Complexity and Authenticity,* ed. Martin Drenthen, Jozef Keulartz, and James Proctor. Dordrecht: Springer.

Edensor, Tim. 1998. *Tourists at the Taj: Performance and Meaning at a Symbolic Site.* London: Routledge.

———. 2000. "Staging Tourism: Tourists as Performers." *Annals of Tourism Research* 27, no. 2: 322–44.

Fabian, Johannes. 2002. *Time and the Other: How Anthropology Makes Its Object.* 2nd ed. New York: Columbia University Press.

Franklin, Adrian, and Mike Crang. 2001. "The Trouble with Tourism and Travel Theory?" *Tourist Studies* 1, no. 1: 5–22.

Hastrup, Kirsten. 2008. "Icelandic Topography and the Sense of Identity." In *Nordic Landscapes: Region and Belonging on the Northern Edge of Europe,* ed. Michael Jones and Kenneth Olwig. Minneapolis: University of Minnesota Press.

Hirsch, Eric. 1995. "Landscape: Between Place and Space." In *The Anthropology of Landscape: Perspectives on Place and Space,* ed. Eric Hirsch and Michael O'Hanlon. Oxford: Clarendon Press.

Hirsch, Eric, and Michael O'Hanlon, eds. 1995. *The Anthropology of Landscape: Perspectives on Place and Space.* Oxford: Clarendon Press.

Ingold, Tim. 1993. "The Temporality of the Landscape." *World Archaeology* 25, no. 2: 152–74.

Janssen, Caspar. 2009. "Wildernis." *Volkskrant,* 25 November.

Kirshenblatt-Gimblett, Barbara. 1998. *Destination Culture: Tourism, Museums, and Heritage.* Berkeley: University of California Press.

Leite, Naomi. 2005. "Travels to an Ancestral Past: On Diasporic Tourism, Embodied Memory, and Identity." *Antropológicas,* no. 9: 273–302.

McFarlane, Robert. 2008. *The Wild Places.* London: Granta Books.

Moore, Henrietta. 2004. "Global Anxieties: Concept-Metaphors and Pre-theoretical Commitments in Anthropology." *Anthropological Theory* 4, no. 1: 71–88.

Neumann, Roderick P. 1998. *Imposing Wilderness: Struggles over Livelihood and Nature Preservation in Africa.* Berkeley: University of California Press.

Olwig, Kenneth, and Michael Jones. 2008. "Introduction: Thinking Landscape and Regional Belonging on the Northern Edge of Europe." In *Nordic Landscapes: Region and Belonging on the Northern Edge of Europe,* ed. Michael Jones and Kenneth Olwig. Minneapolis: University of Minnesota Press.

Paasi, Anssi. 2003. "Region and Place: Regional Identity in Question." *Progress in Human Geography* 27, no. 4: 475–85.

———. 2008. "Finnish Landscape as Social Practice: Mapping Identity and Scale." In *Nordic Landscapes: Region and Belonging on the Northern Edge of Europe,* ed. Michael Jones and Kenneth Olwig. Minneapolis: University of Minnesota Press.

Salazar, Noel B. 2006. "Touristifying Tanzania: Local Guides, Global Discourse." *Annals of Tourism Research* 33, no. 3: 833–52.

———. 2010. *Envisioning Eden: Mobilizing Imaginaries in Tourism and Beyond.* New York: Berghahn Books.

Schwartz, Katrina. 2005. "Wild Horses in a 'European Wilderness': Imagining Sustainable Development in the Post-communist Countryside." *Cultural Geographies* 12, no. 3: 292–320.

Simon, Carola, Paulus Huigen, and Peter Groote. 2010. "Analysing Regional Identities in the Netherlands." *Tijdschrift voor Economische en Sociale Geografie* 101, no. 4: 409–21.

Stanley, Nick. 1998. *Being Ourselves for You: The Global Display of Cultures.* London: Middlesex University Press.

Steenbekkers, Anja, Carola Simon, Lotte Vermeij, and Willem-Jan Spreeuwers. 2008. *Het Platteland van alle Nederlanders: Hoe Nederlanders het Platteland Zien en Gebruiken.* The Hague: Sociaal Cultureel Planbureau.

Tamisari, Franca. 2010. "Dancing for Strangers: Zorba the Greek Yolngu Style: A *Guillarata* by the Chooky Dancers of Elcho Island." In "Indigenous Tourism, Performance and Cross-Cultural Understanding in the Pacific," special issue, *La Ricerca Folklorica* 61: 61–72.

Tonnaer, Anke. 2008. "Tourism Dreaming: A Study of the Encounter Culture in Indigenous Cultural Tourism in Australia." PhD diss., University of Aarhus.

———. 2010. "A Ritual of Meeting: 'Sharing Culture' as a Shared Culture in Australian Indigenous Tourism." In "Indigenous Tourism, Performance and Cross-

Cultural Understanding in the Pacific," special issue, *La Ricerca Folkorica* 61: 21–31.

Tonnaer, Anke, Franca Tamisari, and Eric Venbrux. 2010. "Introduction: Performing Cross-Cultural Understanding in Pacific Tourism." In "Indigenous Tourism, Performance and Cross-Cultural Understanding in the Pacific," special issue, *La Ricerca Folklorica* 61: 3–10.

Van de Klundert, Bram. 2012. *Expeditie Wildernis: Ervaringen met het Sublieme in de Nederlandse Natuur.* Zeist: KNNV Uitgeverij.

Van der Kroef, Patrick. 2012. "Wat weerloos is, is niet per se van waarde: De schaduwzijde van het natuuridealisme." *De Groene Amsterdammer,* 9 February 2012.

Van Koppen, Kris. 2009. "Restoring Nature in a Mobile Society." In *New Visions of Nature: Complexity and Authenticity,* ed. Martin Drenthen, Jozef Keulartz, and James Proctor. Dordrecht: Springer.

Veijola, Soile, and Eeva Jokinen. 1994. "The Body in Tourism." *Theory, Culture & Society* 11, no. 1: 125–51.

Zwart, Hub. 2003. "Aquaphobia, Tulipmania, Biophilia: A Moral Geography of the Dutch Landscape." *Environmental Values* 12, no. 1: 107–28.

Afterword

Locating Imaginaries in the Anthropology of Tourism

Naomi Leite

We anthropologists seem to have a penchant for using our terms of art in idiosyncratic ways. Culture, power, religion, ethnicity, transnationalism, kinship, even tourism—core concepts like these take on subtly and sometimes dramatically different shades of meaning from one scholar's work to the next. Part of the variation is due to theoretical perspective, of course; in the writings of Lewis Henry Morgan and Clifford Geertz, for example, "culture" is scarcely the same concept (Kuper 2000). Other variations stem from the desire that our work reflect emic categories, and such divergent usages are typically prefaced with an explanation. But with some terms, I suspect, there is something a bit less intentional at work: a basic lack of conceptual unity, born of the recent importation of a term that carries multiple meanings in scholarship outside the discipline, such that no single definition has yet become the norm. Such appears to be the case with "imaginaries."

It is worth noting that "the imaginary" did not originate as an anthropological concept, though as this book indicates, it is fast becoming one. It has come to us from psychoanalysis, philosophy, and social theory, with Jacques Lacan, Cornelius Castoriadis, and Charles Taylor, each of whom developed a conceptually distinct use of the term, being the most commonly cited by anthropologists (Strauss 2006).[1] Cultural studies, too, has adopted the term, developing a robust if similarly conceptually murky literature on the (tourist) imaginary that goes back at least to the 1990s (e.g., O'Malley 1992; Desmond 1997). Hence, depending on the anthropologist and the intellectual lineage from which s/he draws the term, "the/an imaginary" might refer to what is distorted, repressed, or fantasized, driven by psychological needs (following Lacan); a composite image of a place or people drawn from pop culture representations (as in cultural studies); the self-image and values of a people (usually called *the social imaginary,* following Castoriadis); a broad assemblage of expectations and norms held by members of a society for how things should work (following Taylor); or something like the collective consciousness or imaginative capacity of an entire society or subgroup—which is how we get potentially reifying constructions like "the image of the primitive in the Western imaginary."

So what about this book? Is there a distinctly anthropological perspective on—or even common definition of—tourism imaginaries? Reading through these insightful, ethnographically grounded chapters, I am left with a sense of having traversed a landscape dotted with diverse clusters of tourism-related images, interactions, imagery, institutions, and imaginings, each cluster referred to as an imaginary but each involving different imaginative phenomena. To wit: both within and across the contributions to this volume, *the imaginary* and *imaginaries* are invoked variously in the sense of worldviews, discourses, images, fantasies, stereotypes, interpretive schemas, cultural frameworks for interaction with others (and Others), representational assemblages, the imaginings and expectations of the individual tourist, a globally disseminated touristic image of a particular place, the self-conscious collective identity of a "host" population, and the beliefs tourists hold about locals—and vice versa.[2] From these chapters we learn, too, that tourism imaginaries are at once collective, individual, global, intersubjective, ephemeral, tenacious, and emergent. They shape and reflect the assumptions of entire societies and yet "there are as many tourist imaginaries as there are tourists" (Di Giovine, this volume). Despite this conceptual heterogeneity, however, each chapter can readily be situated within a common overarching area of study: what cognitive anthropologist Claudia Strauss (2006: 322) calls "shared mental life," in this case specifically within the social field of tourism.

IMAGINING IMAGINARIES ANTHROPOLOGICALLY, OR MAPPING SHARED MENTAL LIFE IN TOURISM

If the idea of shared mental life seems to raise the specter of Carl Jung's collective unconscious, with its universal archetypes and narrative structures, it need not. What is meant here, as Arjun Appadurai explains in his articulation of imagination as a social practice, is something "no more and no less real than the collective representations of Émile Durkheim, now mediated through the complex prism of the modern media" (1996: 31). While Appadurai does not elaborate, let us pursue the analogy. For Durkheim, collective representations were ideational forms common to members of a society. In their collective aspect they existed as abstractions of shared ideas, "simplified and impoverished" relative to the fullness of the lived experiences in which they were used (Durkheim [1912] 2001: 327). The vision of imaginaries generated in this book is quite different, perhaps because of the accretive effect of the modern media Appadurai highlights: here, what is available is not an impoverished abstraction to be fleshed out in each instantiation, but a surfeit, an excess of imagery, discourse, narrative, and representation that spills over and colors individual travelers' perceptions of a toured landscape or people. As mental resources—in Noel Salazar's terms, "socially transmitted representational assemblages that interact with people's personal imaginings and are used as world-making and world-shaping devices" (Salazar 2011: 864)—imaginaries evidently contain far more fodder for the imagination than any individual experience can bring to light.

I want to say more about this idea of shared mental life, as it is the unspoken core of most anthropological uses of the imaginary, and particularly so in work on tourism. It is here that we may locate what a distinctively anthropological perspective entails. Like its conceptual predecessors, culture and ideology, the concept of imaginaries rests on the existence of ideas, beliefs, interpretive schemas, and imaginings that are potentially shared by large populations but, being products of the human mind, cannot be seen other than in their materializations or in the forms of encounter and interaction they motivate. Thus, because we can "see" them only through their effects, there is a danger of overestimating their consistency or reach, or hypostatizing them entirely as independent entities (Sneath et al. 2009; Rautenberg 2010; cf. Bruner 2005: 26). Strauss (2006: 326) poses the problem clearly: "What is the best way to understand compelling, widely shared, historically durable meanings without turning them into a ghostly abstraction … and without reifying societies as entities that can imagine?" Put another way, how do we capture an inchoate, fluid, dynamic phenomenon that is simultaneously demonstrably collective and yet necessarily ontologically particular? If we are to be true to anthropology's theoretical core, the answer can only be fine-grained, detailed, painstaking research, building on multiple lines of evidence and working from ethnographically telling moments on outward to the whole. We cannot presume the existence of an imaginary unless we have derived it from its material presences—representations, interactions, monumental forms—*and* verified our interpretations through careful attention to the commentary, assumptions, and behavior of individual people thinking and acting in the world-out-there. The contributions to this volume set a standard to be followed; Baptista, Swain, Stasch, and Di Giovine, with their fluid movement across multiple types and contexts of ethnographic evidence, are especially good examples.

The concept of shared mental life can and should be refined further, for the "imaginaries" described in these chapters vary tremendously in their relative abstraction and generalization.[3] At the most general level, we find Baptista's analysis of the imaginary of "community" in the modern moral order and its institutionalization in community-based tourism development projects in Mozambique. Because this imaginary exists in the abstract, embedded in a long tradition of critiques of modernity, it can potentially be mapped onto any location—and not necessarily only in relation to tourism. At the other end of the spectrum is Di Giovine's Pietrelcina, a single Italian town caught up in the process of creating and embodying a new imaginary of a single saint's early life there. This is an entirely specific, narrow use of the term "imaginary," here referring to something generated in and projected back onto a unique destination.[4] Somewhere in the middle lies Ferraris's tourist imaginary of Cambodia as past-in-the-present, with the destination being the great but long-vanished civilization of Angkor. While her analysis is particular to Cambodia, the imaginary is not; as is the case with Theodossopoulos's Emberá, Stasch's Korowai, and Bunten's indigenous tourism providers, there is a broader set of imagined relations at work, in which the touristic desire for cultural distance finds expression in temporal displacement, or "allotemporality" (Introduction, this volume). For Ferraris's Italian tourists, faced with the time-space compression of the global present, the only way to experience profound cultural difference is to locate the country of their destination in the past. In the chapters by Theodossopoulos, Stasch, and Bunten, many tourists carry an image of the "primitive" or "native" peoples they travel to see as still residing in the past themselves—maintaining traditional lifeways, untouched by the global cash economy or Western dress (Stasch, Theodossopoulos) or by cultural self-consciousness (Bunten).

So far, then, we have seen "imaginary" used in three related but distinct ways. The first is in the sense of a widely shared construct that could potentially become institutionalized in any number of settings, not limited to tourism. The second, and slightly less general, is in the sense of tourists' imaginings (imaginaries) of particular destinations or peoples, given shape by broader cultural conceptions (imaginaries in the most general sense) of the relationship between self and Other, commonality and difference, civilization and "the primitive," and so forth. Finally, the narrowest sense is as a continuously modified, constructed image of a unique place in relation to a particular history; in this case, "an imaginary" is defined as "the constantly deepening, individually instantiated mix of remembered narratives and images that serve to inform an object or place's meaning" (Di Giovine, this volume).

There are still more types of tourism imaginaries represented here. In Santos's study of Portugal dos Pequinitos and the Portuguese colonial imaginary, what is imagined is the Portuguese nation itself, by Portuguese nationals. The tourist destination is neither the origin nor the object of an imaginary, but rather a materialization of it. This is imaginary as self-image, a conception we also find mentioned in passing in the chapters by Bunten, Theodossopoulos, and Stasch, only in the latter cases it is the self-image of "hosts" in dialogue with the exoticizing imaginaries held by foreign tourists. Finally, there is the imaginary as a trace of something ephemeral, fleeting, felt as much as imagined. In Little's richly textured evocation of Walliceville, a tourist destination in Belize that has become caught up in globally circulating imaginaries of paradise, we move through a series of transient, contradictory, highly charged moments of tourist experience as they pile up into imaginaries-in-the-making. These "incipient, sense uncertain" imaginaries are not quite the assemblages we find described elsewhere. Indeed, in this treatment of the term, there is more than a hint of chaos and instability: these imaginaries may disappear before they are ever shared by anyone at all.

Having teased apart some of the many different uses of the term, I submit that a heuristic distinction should be made between the seemingly synonymous *tourism imaginaries* and *tourist imaginaries*. *Tourism imaginaries* are those imaginaries—conceptions, images, and imaginings of self or Other, place or people, abstract moral order or particular historical site, variously held by tourists, providers, local populations, development consultants, marketers, guides, etc.—that are not necessarily particular to tourism, but in one way or another *become culturally salient in* tourism settings. *Tourist imaginaries,* on the other hand, are more narrowly those *shared, composite images of* a place or people, whether as general types or as particular destinations, held by tourists, would-be tourists, and not-yet tourists as a result of widely circulating imagery and ideas. Both appear in this book. By way of illustration, consider the contrast between the chapters by Tonnaer and Little. Tonnaer elucidates tensions between Dutch rewilding development projects and the work of cultural landscape restorationists, where differing conceptions of nature and the environment lead to divergent attitudes about the place of tourists in a "natural" landscape. Little addresses objects as affective mnemonics for "eccentric" moments of tourist experience in a Caribbean tropical paradise, moments that give rise to new tourist imaginaries and new ways of being in a tourist destination. For Tonnaer, tourism is one part of a bigger picture involving identity, heritage constructs, and environmental restoration; for

Little, tourism—and, more specifically, emergent tourist imaginaries and the unpredictable forces that lurk around the edges of "paradise"—is the very context, setting, and heart of the study. This contrast suggests that while all *tourist* imaginaries could be included under the heading of *tourism* imaginaries, the reverse is not the case.

To study *tourism* imaginaries as defined here is, broadly speaking, to undertake an essentially anthropological project. Whatever the precise questions and location, the process of identifying and analyzing overarching ideologies, discourses, values, and systems of imagery (i.e., shared mental life) in relation to particular tourism-focused projects, interactions, strategies, commodities, and other material forms requires the trademark holism of sociocultural anthropology; designing such a study necessarily involves holding multiple domains of human life in the same frame, and thus calls for a full complement of ethnographic methods. The study of *tourist* imaginaries, on the other hand, and again as defined here, has been undertaken by scholars in any number of disciplines, among them history, comparative literature, cultural geography, performance studies, and of course cultural studies. A common approach is to interpret multiple representations of a particular (type of) destination or people—brochures, posters, postcards, advertisements, recordings, and so forth—to derive an understanding of "*the* tourist imaginary of [place/people]." Depending on the individual scholar, the resulting construct will be more or less monolithic and may or may not be corroborated with other cultural or historical evidence. The study of *tourist* imaginaries is thus not at all exclusive to anthropology, and indeed may in interdisciplinary settings be recognized first and foremost as a topic most commonly addressed in cultural studies.

It is by highlighting the flexibility and breadth of tourism imaginaries as an object of study, coupled with rigorous attention to ethnographically grounded argumentation, that this volume makes a particular contribution to interdisciplinary tourism studies. With its dual focus on ideational and material aspects of tourism imaginaries, it also builds on two earlier, highly influential concepts in the anthropological study of tourism that reflect the same bifocality: Tom Selwyn's "myths" and Edward Bruner's "narratives." For Selwyn (1996), tourist "myths"—widespread, idealized images or "stories" of types of places and people, drawn from a variety of sources and continuously reproduced by the tourism industry—serve to connect specific destinations with more general preoccupations and desires in the tourist's own society. These myths have both ideological and material dimensions, he argues, grounded in political-economic relations of core and periphery. Although he notes in the introduction to his 1996 edited volume that the essays therein "concentrate on … the construction in the internal world of the tourist imagination of ideas, images, myths, and fantasies about the Other" (1996: 10), among other topics, he and his contributors do not address the imagination in the sense of individual tourists' imaginative capacity, nor as an activity (i.e., *imagining*) to be studied processually.

For Bruner (2005: 19–27), tourists anticipate, experience, and make sense of their journey in terms of narrative, from the most abstract level ("metanarratives") to the most personal ("posttour stories"). Metanarratives are not specific to any one locality or tour, but instead function as conceptual schema for the journey. Touching on themes like the possibility of traveling to visit "authentic primitive cultures [that] are being eroded by the forces of modernization" (Bruner 2005: 21), they convey a framework of generic roles, dynamics, landscapes, relations, and outcomes that lend structure to tourists' otherwise inchoate experiences. "Pretour narratives," too, are quite general, but they take shape in the mind of the individual traveler in relation to the upcoming trip, based on metanarratives and "master narratives"— "the African primitive, the Balinese island paradise, Egypt as the land of the pharaohs" (2005: 22)—that are promulgated in pop culture media, tourism marketing, and other widely circulating systems of imagery. The total effect serves to shape tourists' imaginings and expectations (Bruner 2005: 22–23; see also Skinner and Theodossopoulos 2011). Here, too, the material is as important as the ideational, for it is through somatic experience of the physical destination that the imagined world of the pretour narrative comes to life (Bruner 2005: 24; Chronis 2012; Leite 2005).

Unlike Selwyn, Bruner does not explicitly elaborate his argument in relation to political economy; his primary focus is on the role of tourism narratives in relation to experience and meaning. Both approaches appear in the present volume, in some cases within a single chapter. In implicitly combining Bruner's processual analysis of the relationship between representation, imagination, and experience with Selwyn's (and his contributors') close attention to the political-economic contexts and effects of tourist myths and mythmaking, this volume offers an integrative perspective on imagination—and imaginaries—as both product and process.

PROCESS, FLUX, AND PLAY

Tourism imaginaries do not exist sui generis, nor are they static. However, as Salazar and Graburn note in the introduction to this volume, it can be difficult to trace their origins, particularly when they have been in circulation for a very long time. By looking at cases of tourist destinations that are just emerging, on the other hand, ethnographic research can shed revealing light on the macro- and microlevel processes through which imaginaries are (re)produced (cf. Adams 2004). For example, in Swain's wonderfully multilayered analysis of the efforts of two neighboring branches of an ethnic minority in Yunnan, China, to distinguish themselves as individual tourist destinations, we see how multiple strands of history, identity, culture, myth, and local and national politics come together in the making of locally self-determined "imaginariums"–Swain's term for "tourism sites where personal imaginings and institutional imaginaries dialectically circulate" (Swain, this volume). Di Giovine's study of Pietrelcina, too, documents an example of how (local) imaginaries develop and evolve, coining the phrase "imaginaire dialectic" to capture the continual process "whereby imaginaries based on tangible events and images are formed in the mind, materially manifested, and subsequently responded to, negotiated, and contested through the creation of tangible and intangible re-presentations" (Di Giovine, this volume). The chapters by Tonnaer, Bunten, Theodossopoulos, and Little each document the (re)production of imaginaries as well, though in quite different contexts and with likely divergent outcomes in terms of duration and degree to which they are popularly held.

The consumption and maintenance of imaginaries is in many ways easier to track. Participant observation among tourists at the destination, close reading of their posttour narratives, and fieldwork among guides and other "hosts" whose business it is to interact with them can all provide indications of the ways visitors draw upon both widely circulating and locally generated imaginaries to make sense of their experiences. In his study of Emberá indigenous tourism, for example, Theodossopoulos examines a series of questions tourists commonly ask of local people, and their interactions more generally, in order to identify the underlying imaginaries that shape their expectations and attitudes. His analysis reveals the widespread coexistence of inherently contradictory, but equally exoticizing, images of "the primitive"–romantic idealization and cultural denigration–that may or may not be disabused by the encounter, a similar situation to that revealed in Bunten's discussion of tourist responses to the Tjapukai Aboriginal Cultural Park. The chapters by Stasch and Baptista provide fruitful material for comparison on this topic, as does Ferraris's chapter.

An additional theme running through many of the chapters is the direct engagement of "toured" peoples with both tourist and tourism imaginaries (Bunten, Baptista, Theodossopoulos, Stasch, Swain, Little; cf. Fisher 1986; Selwyn 1996). To what extent do they consciously resist, appropriate, manipulate, or acquiesce to prevailing imaginaries? Under what conditions can counterimaginaries be mobilized by local populations, and with what likelihood of success? From Bunten's chapter on indigenous-run tourism venues, we learn that local providers respond to prevailing primitivist imaginaries by co-opting popular forms of cultural tourism display, including demonstrations of indigenous dance, crafts, and traditional practices. In "performing themselves" for tourists, meeting expectations for an exotic glimpse of difference, they harness a productive context in which to share alternative visions of their culture and history. In other settings, straightforward appropriation may be a more strategically advantageous move, as demonstrated by Baptista's chapter on the foreign imaginary of "community" and its role in NGO-based tourism development projects in Canhane, Mozambique. Swain's Sani Yi and Axi Yi provide yet another example, manipulating globally circulating imaginaries of indigenous "purity," Otherness, traditional culture, and rural life to market themselves as distinctive ethnic tourism destinations. Both groups also highlight different elements for different audiences, suggesting a sophisticated awareness of multiple imaginaries, cultural differences, and tourist desires. Their efforts reflect consciousness of their own position simultaneously as part of global humanity and as culturally distinct groups in relation to the world's peoples, a stance Swain refers to as "indigenous cosmopolitanism"—a phenomenon implicit in the descriptions of several other groups in this volume, as well. Notable, too, are contributors' analyses of how local populations fit foreign tourists into existing imaginaries or generate new ones to accommodate them (Theodossopoulos, Stasch; cf. Martinez 1996; Zarkia 1996).

As an aspect of human imagination, imaginaries are for all intents and purposes invisible. Yet, as nearly every chapter in this collection shows, they continuously crystallize in material form. Monuments, souvenirs, photographs, landscapes, maps, models, development projects, and patterned interactions between various actors in the social field of tourism all provide glimpses of shared mental life in operation. Some destinations are fairly direct objectifications of imaginaries prevalent at the time they were produced, whether as representations, reflections, or modes of organizing or utilizing space (Santos, Di Giovine, Tonnaer). When in the form of physical places, tourist sites may provide a point of embodied contact—as a mnemonic trigger, an imaginative prompt—with the imaginaries that motivated their original marking and marketing as destinations. Note, however, that the imaginaries tourists consciously or unconsciously recognize while visiting these destinations may well evolve over time, as Di Giovine and Santos take pains to stress. Paradoxically, as mnemonic nets, touchstones, and anchors, the ephemera of leisure travel—Little's beer coaster, for example—may provide a more durable point of contact, desired or not, with imaginaries both fleeting and tenacious. As Baptista argues, imaginaries also become materialized, or institutionalized, in the form of tourism development projects; and, perhaps most complexly of all, so too can they become momen-tarily concretized in interaction (Stasch, Theodossopoulos, Bunten). Stasch's analysis of the reciprocal imaginaries held by Korowai and their tourist visi-tors, and the ways in which they "amicably [talk] past each other," provides a particularly nuanced example.

In numerous and varied ways, the contributions to this volume illus-trate forcefully that the capacity for imagination itself is crucial to how tour-ists make sense of any engagement with the material realm, whether in the form of buildings, objects, landscapes, or other human beings. This is true not only of the role of imagination (and imaginaries) in creating pretour expectations, but also in the ongoing imaginative processes that shape the tourist's experience during the visit, as well as his or her understanding of it after the fact (cf. Bruner 2005; Chronis 2005, 2012; Leite 2007). More broadly, the chapters collected here all address processes, changes, ten-sions, and influences that take us beyond the tourist encounter and even the sphere of tourism in general. Not content with identifying and labeling tourism imaginaries as they arise in different ethnographic contexts, these chapters examine how they work in practice, on the ground, in the mutually constitutive realms of the ideational and the material.

OTHER IMAGINARIES, OTHER IMAGININGS

Whither the anthropological study of tourism imaginaries? Two promising research trajectories come to mind, the first ethnographically particular, the second theoretically integrative. Beginning with the ethnographically partic-ular, I am struck by the almost exclusive attention to imaginaries of *difference* in this volume. Of the three contributors who do not focus on some form of alterity, all address ethnographic situations where the imaginary is produced and consumed within a single nation (Santos, Di Giovine, Tonnaer). But what of tourism imaginaries of international or even global commonality, interconnection, solidarity, and kinship? Julia Harrison (2003) has convinc-ingly argued that many tourists hope for, and may actively seek out, mo-ments of connection *despite* cultural difference. Analyses of reader responses to photographs in *National Geographic,* that time-honored locus of "armchair tourism," similarly suggest an impulse to find indications of commonality even in the most exoticizing images of difference, for example, in the display of emotion or in depictions of mother-child relationships (Lutz and Col-lins 1993). At the most general level these are expressions of the humanist imaginary of "the family of man," according to which the common origin, and hence kinship, of the species supersedes our seemingly infinite cultural and phenotypic variety. With their emphasis on common life experiences and basic needs shared by all human beings, collections of international photographs like *The Family of Man* (1955) and *Material World: A Global Family Portrait* (1994) also source their visual rhetoric from this imaginary, which may account for their remarkable, lasting popularity (Edwards 1996).[5]

I am not suggesting that tourists' desire to find indications of global commonality, or to identify points of connection with local populations, makes it possible for them to "think away" all difference. On the contrary, it is precisely in the face of pronounced cultural difference that the vision of "a family of man" takes on such power. In her research on interactions between tourists and tourees in Turkey, for example, Hazel Tucker found that the local people most able to satisfy tourists' expectations are those who "develop knowledge and skill in being able to perform 'difference,' whilst simultaneously emerging from it in their developing of new forms of human connection" (2011: 37). A more limited imaginary of essential commonality or, more precisely, of a substrate of unifying ethnic kinship underlies the oft-noted desire of Jewish heritage tourists for informal contact with "exotic" local Jewish communities during their travels (e.g., Loeb 1989); it is this imaginary, with its attendant imagery of peoplehood, ancestral dispersal, and mutual dependence for survival that lends particular poignancy and force to the idea of meeting "lost" or "isolated" Jews in far-off lands (Leite 2011a).

The tension between imaginaries of commonality and imaginaries of difference is a ripe area for ethnographic research of the type exemplified in this volume. At the most general level, we might ask how and when an imaginary of humanity as global family surfaces in tourism, and to what extent that imaginary propagates through other representational channels. What more particular forms of tourism does it underpin and motivate? Consider "voluntourism" in the global South, which arguably rests on intertwined imaginaries of the exotic Native/Indigene/Other *and* the basic unity of humankind (cf. Baptista, this volume). Denominational volunteer tourism, which may be combined in practice with missionary work, presents additional layers of imagined interconnection, commonality, and difference: like the Jewish *Am Yisrael* (the Jewish people), global constructs like the Christian family (brothers and sisters in Christ) and the Muslim *ummah* (community of the faithful) may provide a potent interpretive schema for interactions between denominational tourists and their local, culturally distinct coreligionists. Whether participants engage in their efforts as solidary or altruism, privileging commonality or difference, are questions for ethnographic research (Fogarty 2009). What imaginaries lead participants to one perspective or another—or to hold both simultaneously? Similar questions could be asked of Global Exchange "reality tours" and other forms of tourism explicitly couched in terms of solidarity vis-à-vis shared struggle (e.g., feminist, religious, political, ethnic), a growing phenomenon that has thus far received relatively little attention (Higgins-Desbiolles and Russell-Mundine 2008; Spencer 2010). What imaginaries might we find in force there?

Tension between imaginaries of the known and the unknown, the foreign and the familiar, could also provide a fruitful framework for the study of "roots tourism," including both genealogical and diasporic tourism. What imaginaries of self and ancestry, kinship and displacement, homeland and return are invoked in tourism marketing by countries with historically high levels of emigration (Wulff 2007)? Are these congruent with imaginaries held by tourists themselves? Much work remains to be done on the representational assemblages, to use Salazar's phrase, that motivate and give shape to the emotional experiences tourists describe having as they interact with historical sites and local residents at the destination.[6] We would also gain significant insight from ethnographic analyses of meetings between genealogical tourists and their (presumed) relatives. Following the persuasive arguments laid out in this volume by Stasch and Theodossopoulos, attention to the reciprocal imaginaries that feed into and result from those encounters would be especially revealing (cf. Fisher 1986; Leite 2011a): might tourism itself be an instigating force in the creation of *new* imaginaries of homeland, ancestral/diasporic kinship, and belonging, with regard both to specific peoples and places and to broader cultural models?

Finally, the discourses and practices of heritage tourism seem to me a ripe arena for the study of tourism imaginaries. The very idea of "heritage" is based on the generative metaphor of family and familial inheritance (Graburn 2001; Leite 2011b); as such, the designation of a site as "world heritage" rhetorically positions the entire world as a (kinlike) community of heirs. Many national and world heritage sites are heavily visited by international tourists, and debates arise over who should be responsible for decisions about historical or cultural representation, preservation, and upkeep (Bruner 2005; cf. Tonnaer, this volume). As such, it would be productive to explore how sites designated as world (or national, or regional) heritage become touchstones for imaginaries of global interconnection, the human family, and mutual responsibility, or—on the other hand—of global inequality, dispossession, and disempowerment. More specifically, what imaginaries of ownership, belonging, and exclusion might be involved, and for whom? How does the international circulation of discourses and images of "heritage," whether material or immaterial, give rise to particular tourist experiences and local attitudes, and what experiences and attitudes does it foreclose?

These are fundamentally ethnographic questions, requiring ongoing participant observation in particular sites among tourists, local populations, planners, and so forth. Although they all involve forms of tourism currently studied by anthropologists, we have only just begun to address them in terms of imaginaries, in the mode of this volume. Following on the contributors' persuasive analyses of how imaginaries of difference reproduce relations of power and inequality, what if we were to examine equally pervasive, though perhaps more subtle, imaginaries of commonality as they take shape in particular ethnographic contexts? Around the world, voluntourism, "reality" and "solidarity" tourism, intercultural exchange, roots tourism, and heritage tourism are booming. Together with the ethnographic accounts of imaginaries of difference provided in this book, the study of coexisting imaginaries of commonality may help us understand why—and to what effect.

Another potential trajectory for future research would be theoretically integrative. Reading through this volume, I find myself puzzling over how collective imaginaries become personal imaginings, and vice versa. From an anthropological perspective, there can be no imaginaries without imagining subjects, people in the world-out-there. As a number of contributors point out, the relationship between the two is dialectical (Di Giovine, Swain, Tonnaer), and throughout the ten chapters we find clear indications, in a wide range of ethnographically particular settings, that imaginaries—as assemblages of imagery, discourse, narrative, and representation—profoundly influence individual imaginings, attitudes, and behaviors (Baptista, Bunten, Stasch, Theodossopoulos, Tonnaer). Yet for all their topical and ethnographic diversity, the chapters in this volume do not quite point the way to a collective, theoretical understanding of the imaginary-imagination relationship, nor even a unified formulation of the terms involved. As I noted above, this may partly be due to the breadth and relative immaturity of tourism imaginaries as an area of anthropological study; but I wonder how much richer our comprehension of tourism-related phenomena might become if we were to shift our focus to examine, for example, the extent to which tourists' individual imaginings and experiences are overdetermined by the totality of discourses and imagery they absorb prior to their travels.

This is a question already taken up by other observers of the relationship between tourism and shared mental life, most notably Bruner, who suggests that tourist experiences are underdetermined, in that "the tourist story is emergent in the enactment" (2005: 26). Bruner's constructivist account emphasizes the idiosyncrasy of each tourist's imaginings and experiences, even as they are given shape and significance by widely circulating narrative structures. The ethnographic cases presented in this volume point us in a different direction, toward the powerful influence of imaginaries as extraordinarily rich, collectively sourced resources for sense making and world shaping. To reiterate, these are not Durkheim's collective representations, "simplified and impoverished" abstractions that attain dimension only in the fullness of lived experience. Instead, inculcated and reinforced with layer upon layer of imagery, narrative, patterned interaction, logic, and practice, and propagated in a multitude of forms, the imaginaries of this book seem capable of flooding personal imaginings altogether.

Yet neither does this volume present a vision of tourism imaginaries as hegemonic forces that blot out all alternatives, for we have also learned that they are manipulated and resisted (Baptista, Bunten, Stasch), multiple and negotiated (Santos, Ferraris, Theodossopoulos, Tonnaer), and continuously in flux (Di Giovine, Swain, Little)—precisely as a result of the actions of *individual imagining subjects.* However, with few exceptions, here the acting subjects are members of local populations and those working in the tourism industry, whose awareness of imaginaries emerges out of repeated interaction with tourists (cf. Bunten 2008; Salazar 2010). Less clear is the relationship between widely circulating imaginaries and the tourists who are influenced by them. How is it that an individual comes to hold a given imaginary in the first place? Why one rather than another? Is it ever possible for tourists to experience an unfamiliar place or people without recourse to prevailing imaginaries?

One way to approach this line of questioning, following David Sneath, Martin Holbraad, and Morten Axel Pedersen, would be to undertake a comparative examination of "the specific 'technologies' through which imaginative capacities are moulded" (2009: 5) or, more precisely, the observable mechanisms by which collective imaginaries are invoked, influence, or surface in individual imaginings and in particular ethnographic contexts (e.g., as documented in Basu 2001, 2004; Brennan 2004; Bruner 2005; Causey 2003; Ebron 1999; Feldman 2008; Huberman 2012; Leite 2005, 2007, 2011a; Chronis 2012). Although only the most recent anthropological publications on this topic adopt the term "imaginaries," there is a substantial (and growing) ethnographic literature on the interrelationship of specific tourist sites, images and ideologies, tourist practices, and individual imagination and experience that awaits synthetic analysis. Much like the buildings, development programs, interactions, and other material forms examined in this book, social practices of imagining can be studied empirically. Greater attention to such practices, together with a rigorous theoretical distinction between practices observed and imaginaries inferred, may clarify the relationship between the two and help us avoid the rhetorical trap of tourism imaginaries that seemingly imagine themselves.

"IMAGINARIES" AS CONCEPT AND CATEGORY

Before concluding this volume on anthropological approaches to tourism imaginaries, it bears mention that the concept of imaginaries has not been universally embraced in our discipline. According to some critics, the imaginary is little more than "culture or cultural knowledge [or cultural models] in new clothes" (Strauss 2006: 322), a synonym for culture as "an overarching template of thought and action" (Sneath et al. 2009: 7) that is increasingly invoked as a stand-in solely because the older terms have been tarnished by their connotations of stasis and homogeneity. However, the contributions to this volume can hardly be accused of simply recycling the culture concept; instead, taken as a whole, they point to a novel theoretical construct, indeed a new category of analysis. As the term is used here, "imaginaries" span the material, representational, and ideational realms and readily transcend geographical and even cultural borders. As the chapters by Swain, Stasch, and Theodossopoulos make clear, toured populations need not be familiar with their visitors' cultural background in order to understand the imaginaries they hold; moreover, even the most processual, constructivist framings of the culture concept lack the fluidity and indeterminacy captured by the idea of the imaginary. The ultimate challenge presented by this volume, then, is not to refine or delimit what is meant by *tourism imaginaries,* but rather to embrace the entire range of imaginative phenomena it gathers under that heading as a single, useful category for anthropological analysis.

What does the concept/category of imaginaries offer anthropology that related terms—ideology, discourse, worldview, narrative, myth, representation, image, and so forth—do not? It should be apparent from the foregoing discussion that "imaginaries" encompasses all these terms and more; it is both more specific and more general than any of them; and it includes diverse imaginative phenomena at varying levels of abstraction and generalization. In its very lack of specificity, it allows simultaneous attention to process and product, the act of imagining and that which is imagined, commercial imagery and collective self-image, shared values and momentary transgressions. As the chapters included here demonstrate, at its best the anthropological study of tourism imaginaries combines processual analysis of the relationship between representation, practice, and experience with careful attention to political-economic conditions and effects. Fundamentally grounded in ethnographic practice, this approach tracks images, ideas, and individuals through diverse social fields that overlap and interpenetrate. Above all, it recognizes the centrality of the human capacity for imagination, both individually and collectively, in even the most disparate domains of life.

NOTES

1. The imagination, treated as a social phenomenon, has come into anthropological purview by a different route. Particularly influential formulations include the work of Benedict Anderson (1983) and Arjun Appadurai (1990, 1991, 1996).
2. This heterogeneous cluster of meanings may reflect the equally numerous range of referents of the term in the original French, *imaginaire*. As anthropologist Michel Rautenberg explains, "In French, 'imaginary' is often employed to express a large scope of significations, from fairy tales up to the [individual] imagination of an artist. But we also use 'social imaginary' in order to evoke a large part of social identity" (2010: 127).
3. It is noteworthy that although some contributors cite one or more theorists as the inspiration for their understanding of the imaginary (Baptista, Di Giovine, Little, Swain), the majority introduce the term without explanation or citation.
4. To be sure, Di Giovine addresses several levels of imaginaries about Padre Pio and his life—including those held by tourists drawn from other venues (films, books, the competing site of San Giovanni Rotondo)—all offering alternative representations that circulate far beyond the nation of the saint's birth.
5. *The Family of Man* began as an exhibition at the New York Museum of Modern Art and subsequently traveled to thirty-eight countries; it is said to have been "the most successful photographic exhibition of all time" (Edwards 1996: 216).
6. For accounts of roots tourism experiences in relation to narrative, expectation, and touristic practices on site, see, e.g., Bruner (1996), Ebron (1999), Basu (2004), Leite (2005), and Russell (2012).

REFERENCES

Adams, Kathleen M. 2004. "The Genesis of Touristic Imagery: Politics and Poetics in the Creation of a Remote Indonesian Island Destination." *Tourist Studies* 4, no. 2: 115–35.

Anderson, Benedict. 1983. *Imagined Communities: Reflections on the Origins and Spread of Nationalism.* London: Verso.

Appadurai, Arjun. 1990. "Disjuncture and Difference in the Global Cultural Economy." *Public Culture* 2, no. 2: 1–24.

——. 1991. "Global Ethnoscapes: Notes and Queries for a Transnational Anthropology." In *Recapturing Anthropology: Writing in the Present,* ed. Richard Fox. Santa Fe, NM: SAR Press.

——. 1996. *Modernity at Large: Cultural Dimensions of Globalization.* Minneapolis: University of Minnesota Press.

Basu, Paul. 2001. "Hunting Down Home: Reflections on Homeland and the Search for Identity in the Scottish Diaspora." In *Contested Landscapes: Movement, Exile, and Place,* ed. Barbara Bender and Margot Winer. Oxford: Berg.

———. 2004. "Route Metaphors of 'Roots Tourism.'" In *Reframing Pilgrimage*, ed. Simon Coleman and John Eade. London: Routledge.

Brennan, Denise. 2004. *What's Love Got To Do With It? Transnational Desires and Sex Tourism in the Dominican Republic*. Durham, NC: Duke University Press.

Bruner, Edward M. 1996. "Tourism in Ghana: The Representation of Slavery and the Return of the Black Diaspora." *American Anthropologist* 98, no. 2: 290–304.

———. 2005. *Culture on Tour: Ethnographies of Travel*. Chicago: University of Chicago Press.

Bunten, Alexis. 2008. "Sharing Culture or Selling Out? Developing the Commodi-fied Persona in the Heritage Industry." *American Ethnologist* 35, no. 3: 380–95.

Causey, Andrew. 2003. *Hard Bargaining in Sumatra: Western Travelers and Toba Bataks in the Marketplace of Souvenirs*. Honolulu: University of Hawaii Press.

Chronis, Athinodoros. 2005. "Co-constructing Heritage at the Gettysburg Story-scape." *Annals of Tourism Research* 32: 386–406.

———. 2012. "Between Place and Story: Gettysburg as Tourism Imaginary." *Annals of Tourism Research* 39: 1797–816.

Desmond, Jane C. 1997. "Invoking 'The Native': Body Politics in Contemporary Hawaiian Tourist Shows." *The Drama Review* 41, no. 4: 83–109.

Durkheim, Emile. (1912) 2001. *The Elementary Forms of the Religious Life*. Trans. Carol Cosman. Oxford: Oxford University Press.

Ebron, Paulla. 1999. "Tourists as Pilgrims: Commercial Fashioning of Transatlantic Politics." *American Ethnologist* 26: 910–32.

Edwards, Elizabeth. 1996. "Postcards—Greetings from Another World." In *The Tour-ist Image: Myths and Myth-Making in Tourism*, ed. Tom Selwyn. Chichester, UK: John Wiley.

Feldman, Jackie. 2008. *Above the Death Pits, Beneath the Flag: Youth Voyages to Poland and the Performance of Israeli National Identity*. Oxford: Berghahn Books.

Fisher, James F. 1986. "Tourists and Sherpas." *Contributions to Nepalese Studies* 14: 37–61.

Fogarty, Timothy. 2009. "Searching for Solidarity in Nicaragua: Faith-Based NGOs as Agents of Transcultural Voluntourism." In *Bridging the Gaps: Faith-Based Organizations, Neoliberalism, and Development in Latin America and the Caribbean*, ed. T. Hefferan, J. Adkins, and L. Occhipinti. Lanham, MD: Rowman and Littlefield.

Graburn, Nelson. 2001. "Learning to Consume: What Is Heritage and When Is It Traditional?" In *Consuming Tradition, Manufacturing Heritage*, ed. Nezar AlSayyad. New York: Routledge.

Harrison, Julia. 2003. *Being a Tourist: Finding Meaning in Pleasure Travel*. Vancouver: University of British Columbia Press.

Higgins-Desbiolles, Freya, and Gabrielle Russell-Mundine. 2008. "Absences in the Volunteer Tourism Phenomenon: The Right to Travel, Solidarity Tours and Transformation Beyond the One-Way." In *Journeys of Discovery in Volunteer Tour-ism: International Case Study Perspectives*, ed. Kevin Lyons and Stephen Wearing. Wallingford, UK: CABI.

Huberman, Jenny. 2012. *Ambivalent Encounters: Childhood, Tourism, and Social Change in Banaras, India.* New Brunswick, NJ: Rutgers University Press.

Kuper, Adam. 2000. *Culture: The Anthropologists' Account.* Cambridge, MA: Harvard University Press.

Leite, Naomi. 2005. "Journeys to an Ancestral Past: On Diasporic Tourism, Embodied Memory, and Identity." *Antropológicas* 9: 273–302.

———. 2007. "Materializing Absence: Tourists, Surrogates, and the Making of Jewish Portugal." In *Things That Move: Material Worlds of Tourism and Travel,* ed. Mike Robinson. Leeds, UK: Centre for Tourism and Cultural Change.

———. 2011a. "Global Affinities: Portuguese Marranos (*Anusim*), Traveling Jews, and Cultural Logics of Kinship." Ph.D. diss., University of California–Berkeley.

———. 2011b. "Speaking of Heritage, Thinking Through Kinship: Preservation, Ownership, and Questions of Commensurability." Paper presented at the annual meeting of the American Anthropological Association, Montreal, 16–20 November.

Loeb, Laurence. 1989. "Creating Antiques for Fun and Profit: Encounters Between Iranian Jewish Merchants and Touring Coreligionists." In *Hosts and Guests: The Anthropology of Tourism,* ed. Valene Smith, 2nd ed. Philadelphia: University of Pennsylvania Press.

Lutz, Catherine, and Jane Collins. 1993. *Reading National Geographic.* Chicago: University of Chicago Press.

Martinez, Dolores P. 1996. "The Tourist as Deity: Ancient Continuities in Modern Japan." In *The Tourist Image: Myths and Myth-Making in Tourism,* ed. Tom Selwyn. Chichester, UK: John Wiley.

O'Malley, Maureen. 1992. "Scenes From Cairo's Camel Market." *Inscriptions* 6: 134–52.

Rautenberg, Michel. 2010. "Stereotypes and Emblems in the Construction of Social Imagination." *Outlines: Critical Practice Studies* 2: 126–37.

Russell, Lynnette. 2012. "Remembering Places Never Visited: Connections and Context in Imagined and Imaginary Landscapes." *International Journal of Historical Archaeology* 16: 401–17.

Salazar, Noel B. 2010. *Envisioning Eden: Mobilizing Imaginaries in Tourism and Beyond.* Oxford: Berghahn Books.

———. 2011. "Tourism Imaginaries: A Conceptual Approach." *Annals of Tourism Research* 39, no. 2: 863–82.

Selwyn, Tom, ed. 1996. *The Tourist Image: Myths and Myth-Making in Tourism.* Chichester, UK: John Wiley.

Skinner, Jonathan, and Dimitrios Theodossopoulos, eds. 2011. *Great Expectations: Imagination and Anticipation in Tourism.* Oxford: Berghahn Books.

Sneath, David, Martin Holbraad, and Morten Axel Pedersen. 2009. "Technologies of the Imagination: An Introduction." *Ethnos* 74, no. 1: 5–30.

Spencer, Rochelle. 2010. *Development Tourism: Lessons from Cuba.* Farnham, UK: Ashgate.

Strauss, Claudia. 2006. "The Imaginary." *Anthropological Theory* 6, no. 3: 322–44.

Tucker, Hazel. 2011. "Success and Access to Knowledge in the Tourist-Local Encounter: Confrontations with the Unexpected in a Turkish Community." In *Great Expectations: Imagination and Anticipation in Tourism,* ed. Jonathan Skinner and Dimitrios Theodossopoulos. Oxford: Berghahn Books.

Wulff, Helena. 2007. "Longing for the Land: Emotions, Memory, and Nature in Irish Travel Advertisements." *Identities: Global Studies in Culture and Power* 14, no. 4: 527–44.

Zarkia, Cornélia. 1996. "Philoxenia: Receiving Tourists—But Not Guests—on a Greek Island." In *Coping with Tourists,* ed. Jeremy Boissevain. Oxford: Berghahn Books.

Contributors

João Afonso Baptista holds a PhD in social anthropology from the Martin Luther University, Germany. He is currently lecturer in the Department of Social and Cultural Anthropology at the University of Hamburg and involved as researcher in the interdisciplinary projects The Future Okavango (TFO) and Southern African Science Service Centre for Climate Change and Adaptive Land Management (SASSCAL). He is the author of, among others, "The Virtuous Tourist" (*American Anthropologist*, 2012).

Alexis Celeste Bunten is an Alaska Native scholar with a BA in art history from Dartmouth College and a PhD in anthropology from UCLA. She works as senior researcher for the FrameWorks Institute and as project ethnographer for Intellectual Property in Cultural Heritage (IPinCH) at Simon Fraser University, Canada.

Michael A. Di Giovine is assistant professor of anthropology at West Chester University of Pennsylvania, and honorary fellow in the Department of Anthropology at the University of Wisconsin–Madison. He is a founding member of the Tourism-Contact-Culture research network, a founding member and Program Chair of the American Anthropological Association's Anthropology of Tourism Interest Group, a member of the American Anthropological Association's Task Force on Cultural Heritage, and Book Reviews Editor of *Journeys: The International Journal of Travel and Travel Writing*.

Federica Ferraris received her PhD from the University of Milan–Bicocca. She was visiting research fellow at the Department of Anthropology, University of Sussex (2005–12). She has lectured on anthropology and ethnographic methods at the University of Bologna (2004–6) and at the Free University of Bozen (2005–6). Her research and teaching focus on sustainability and cultural tourism development in Cambodia and the Adriatic-

Ionian region and on Sikh migration. Her publications include various book chapters on pilgrimage and tourism.

Nelson H. H. Graburn was educated at Cambridge, McGill, and the University of Chicago (PhD 1963) and is professor of the Graduate School and professor emeritus of anthropology at the University of California–Berkeley. Among his books and edited volumes are: *Ethnic and Tourist Arts* (1976), *The Anthropology of Tourism* (1983), *To Pray, Pay and Play: the Cultural Structure of Japanese Domestic Tourism* (1983), *Tourism Social Sciences* (1991), 旅游人类学论文集 [Anthropology in the age of tourism] (2009), and *Tourism and Glocalization: Perspectives in East Asian Studies* (2010). He is a founding member of the International Academy for the Study of Tourism.

Naomi Leite received her PhD in anthropology from the University of California, Berkeley. She is curator of ethnography at the University of Nebraska State Museum and post-doctoral fellow in sociology at the University of Nebraska-Lincoln. Her research focuses on structures and experiences of global interconnection, with international tourism as a primary site for examining cross-cultural interaction, negotiation of identity, and imagination as a social practice. The co-founder of the Berkeley Tourism Studies Working Group, she has published on numerous topics in the anthropology of tourism. She is co-convener of the AAA Anthropology of Tourism Interest Group (2013–16).

Kenneth Little received his PhD in anthropology from the University of Virginia and is associate professor of anthropology at York University, Canada. He is the author of several articles and book chapters on tourism focusing on the rise of the "tourist state" in Belize. He is interested in new ways of thinking about and through flows, processes, impulses, and connections in touristic encounters, productions, and narratives as a means of tracking the enactments of precarity and hope under late liberal imaginaries and transformations in Belize.

Noel B. Salazar received his PhD from the University of Pennsylvania and is research professor in anthropology at the University of Leuven, Belgium. He is the author of *Envisioning Eden: Mobilizing Imaginaries in Tourism* (Berghahn Books, 2010) and numerous journal articles and book chapters on the anthropology of tourism. He is president of the European Association of Social Anthropologists (2013–14), founding member of the Young Academy of Belgium, chair of the IUAES Commission on the Anthropology of Tourism, and founding member of the AAA Anthropology of Tourism Interest Group.

Paula Mota Santos received her PhD in anthropology from University College London and is assistant professor at Fernando Pessoa University, Portugal. She has been visiting scholar in the Department of Landscape Architecture & Regional Planning, University of California–Berkeley. She has coedited "Ethnographies of Heritage and Power," a themed issue of the *International Journal of Heritage Studies* (2012), as well as books on heritage in Portugal and Spain. She has published several articles and book chapters on heritage, tourism, immigration, photography, and film/documentary, and has also directed two documentary films.

Rupert Stasch is associate professor of anthropology at University of California–San Diego. He is the author of *Society of Others: Kinship and Mourning in a West Papuan Place* (2009), and articles in journals such as *American Ethnologist, Annual Review of Anthropology,* and *The Australian Journal of Anthropology.* He edits the Berghahn Books series *ASAO Monographs in Pacific Anthropology* and is writing a book about relations between tourists and Korowai of West Papua.

Margaret Byrne Swain received her PhD in anthropology from the University of Washington, and is affiliated with the Women and Gender Studies Program at the University of California–Davis. She has carried out research primarily among the Kuna of San Blas, Panama, and the Sani of Shilin, Yunnan, China. Her research interests include feminist analysis of gender issues, critical tourism studies, and engagement of debates about the meanings and utility of cosmopolitanisms. She has edited the books *Gender/Tourism/Fun(?)* (2002) and *Explorers and Scientists in China's Borderlands* (2011). She is copresident of the ISA Tourism Research Cluster (2010–14) and has recently developed an online course on niche tourism.

Dimitrios Theodossopoulos is reader in social anthropology at the University of Kent, Canterbury. His research addresses the topics of exoticization, ethnic stereotypes, indigeneity, authenticity, resistance and protest, the economic crisis, and the politics of cultural representation in Panama and Greece. He is author of *Troubles with Turtles* (Berghahn Books, 2003), editor of *When Greeks Think about Turks* (Routledge, 2006), and coeditor of *United in Discontent: Local Responses to Cosmopolitanism and Globalization* (Berghahn Books, 2010) and *Great Expectations: Imagination, Anticipation and Enchantment in Tourism* (Berghahn Books, 2011).

Anke Tonnaer holds a PhD in anthropology from Aarhus University, Denmark. At present, she is assistant professor in anthropology at Radboud University Nijmegen, the Netherlands. Her research focuses predominantly on indigenous tourism, performance, and cross-cultural encounters, with a special focus on Aboriginal Australia, about which she has published several articles. Her recent research is taking her closer to home, including natural and cultural heritage and new wilderness in Europe.

Index

Page numbers in bold refer to figures and tables.

Aboriginal, 19, 37, 80–102, 106, 267
advertising, 7, 63, 65, 87–88, 161, 176,
    226, 230, 265. *See also* branding;
    brochures
affect, 21, 220–41, 264
Africa, 3, 9, 22n5, 42, 126, 134, 136,
    137, 139, 142n2, 149, 164–65, **204,**
    205–8, 210, 215n19, 253–54, 266
    East Africa, 9, 194, 248 (*see also*
        Mozambique)
    South Africa, 127, 131, 134
    West Africa, 164, 194, 208, 214n8 (*see*
        also Angola)
agency, 5, 13, 17, 50, 57, 71, 73, 92, 103,
    108, 118, 120, 133–34, 136, 142,
    165, 196, 212, 229, 254
ambivalence, 8–9, 19, 40, 42, 57–79
American West, the, 9. *See also*
    Americas, the; North America;
    South America; United States
Americas, the, 162, 207
Anderson, Benedict, 126, 148, 201,
    275n1
Angkor, 175–190n11, 263
Angola, 141, 204–5, 214n8
anthropologist, 5–7, 13, 15, 19, 46, 49,
    52, 61, 67, 86–87, 119, 148, 180–82,
    190n8, 244, 260–61, 272
    gaze, 180

anthropology, 1–2, 8, 13, 22, 50, 58,
    118, 141–42, 148, 166, 173–74,
    180–85, 188, 223–24, 260–62, 265,
    272, 274, 275n1
    of space, 195
    symbolic, 185
    of tourism, 1, 6, 32, 50–52, 58–59,
        166, 173, 180, 190n8, 223, 260,
        265, 269, 272, 274
Appadurai, Arjun, 8, 96n4, 261–62,
    275n1
archaeology, 2, 8, 10, 147, 149, 162,
    175–77, 183, 187–88
architecture, 10, 13, 21, 33, 81, 150, 155,
    157–58, 163, 176, 183, 187, 189,
    190n3, 194–95, 197–99, 202, 227
Ashima, 103, 110–15, **113,** 118–20,
    122n8
Asia, 191n15. *See also* Cambodia;
    China; India; Japan; Korea;
    Southeast Asia
assemblage, 1, 21–22, 81, 103, 151, 195,
    224–27, 229, 231–32, 238–39,
    261–62, 264, 271–72
Australia, 80–102, 178
authenticity, 4, 6, 8–9, 12–13, 19,
    38, 51, 53n5, 59–62, 67, 72–73,
    74–75n4, 81, 84, 86–92, 97n12,
    98n19, 104, 108, 116, 118–19, 132,
    148, 151, 162, 180, 213, 215n9, 246,
    248, 253, 266
Axi Yi, 19, 103–4, 108–10, 116–21, 268

backstage, 38, 48, 51, 67, 70, 91
Bali, **20**, 35, 185, 266
Belize, 220–41, **221**, 264
blogs, 7, 117–19, 167, 178, 184, 188, 189n1, 190n3, 193, 255
Boorstin, Daniel, 148
Bourdieu, Pierre, 207, 211
branding, 103–4, 110, 121n4, 161, 243
Brazil, 201, 209, 215n8, 216n20
brochure, 7, 172, 178–80, 184, 186–88, 189n1, 191n13, 193, 226, 265. *See also* advertising; guidebook
Bruner, Edward, 7, 37, 148–49, 223, 246, 265–66, 272

Cambodia, 149, 172–93, 263
   genocide in, 175, 186–87, 191n14
Canada, 22n4, 95, 164
Cannibal Tours, 37, 148
capital, 221, 224–25
   symbolic, 4, 16, 18, 105, 120, 130
Caribbean, 4, 21, 220–41, 264. *See also* Belize
Carrier, James, 249, 251, 255–56n5
Castoriadis, Cornelius, 19, 129, 133, 151, 260
Catholicism, 20, 108–11, 116, 147, 158–59, 166
Chagres National Park, Panama, 57, 62, 65, 74n1, 75n5
China, 5, 9, **14**, 103–24, 188, 267. *See also* Yunnan
Christianity. *See under* religion
chronotope, 197, 201, 226
clothing, 11, 31–49, 64, 66, 68, 70, 73, 75n7, 88, 110, **113**, 114, 117, 119, 205–6, 263. *See also* nudity
colonialism, 6, 8–9, 18, 22n5, 35, 38, 74, 86–87, 92–95, 96n1, 97n14, 107–8, 172–73, 185, 205, 208, 248, 253
   British, 3, 8
   in Cambodia, 184, 189
   in Caribbean, 226
   Dutch, 185, 197, 256n8

exhibitions, fairs and themed places, 197–99, 215n17, 215n19
   French, 19, 104, 110–11, 116, 184
   and imaginaries, 21, 23, 74, 87, 149, 194–219
   Portuguese, 194–214, 214–15n8, 215n18
   travel literature, 21, 173, 175, 185
   See also, postcolonialism; precolonialism
commoditization, 18, 48, 51, 58, 68, 84, 87–89, 93, 97n12, 103, 105–6, 108, 110–12, 117, 136, 158, 220, 235
commonality, 17, 121, 121n1, 133, 215n16, 263, 269–70, 272
community, 4–7, 15, 19, 57, 60–73, 74n1, 75n5, 75n7, 75n8, 75n9, 83, 88, 93–96, 97n6, 97n8, 105, 107–10, 112, 114–15, 117, 119–21, 122n6, 125–42, 142n1, 148, 199, 201–2, 204, 210–13, 228, 236, 263, 268, 270–71
computer, 61, 70. *See also* blogs; Internet; technology; websites
conservation, 137, 149, 155, 162, 242–44, 248, 251–52, 255n1. *See also* ecology
consumption, 5, 16, 81, 86, 105–6, 122n7, 128, 131–33, 136–37, 140, 149, 150, 154, 230, 243, 245, 249, 254–55, 267
contact. *See under* culture
cosmopolitanism, 18–19, 103–24
   Chinese concepts, 105–6, 121
   and indigeneity, 19, 104–6, 108, 118, 121
   indigenous, 111, 114, 117, 119, 268
   of tourists, 119
   Western concepts, 105
   See also metropolitanism
cosmopolitics, 222, 238
culture
   contact, 8, 12, 16, 18, 22n4, 47, 49, 61, 65, 70–71, 89, 98n20, 180, 183, 205, 226, 236, 268, 270

contact zone, 12, 93, 108, 149, 227, 230
indigenous, 81, 83, 11, 118

Deleuze, Gilles, 3, 212–13, 225, 235
rhizome, 195, 212–14
destination, 5, 7, 11, 16, 21, 51, 83, 85–103, 105, 121, 136, 148, 165, 172–91, 216n20, 245, 253, 263–68, 271
dialectic, 5, 13, 15, 19–20, 22, 103–105, 147–71, 224–25, 232, 238, 247, 254, 267, 272
difference, 4, 8, 10–11, 16–17, 32, 46, 50–52, 58, 61, 65, 69, 83, 89–91, 94, 105–6, 121, 136, 186, 198, 225, 263, 268–70, 272
Di Giovine, Michael, 5, 10, 20, 22, 176, 216n22, 225, 238, 261–64, 267–69, 272–73, 275n3, 275n5
Disney, 88, 199, 211
Disneyland, 88, 195, 198
documentary, 7, 37, 81, 92–93, 98n21, 156, 176
dream, 1, 4, 8, 10, 17, 21, 48, 92, 98n21, 136, 185, 223–24, 227–28, 231, 233–37, 239
dreamtime, 80–82, 87
dreamworlds, 224–39

ecology, 8, 17, 37, 49, 62, 95, 104–21, 242–55, 255n1
and farming, 251
See also conservation
economy, 40, 43–44, 53n4, 61–62, 73, 82–84, 94–95, 97n8, 98n18, 104, 108, 111, 115, 130, 156, 176, 189, 223–24, 243–44, 252–53, 263, 265–66, 274
Center for Aboriginal Economic Policy (Australia), 95
Indigenous Economic Development Agency (Australia), 83
ecotourism. *See under* tourism
egalitarianism: among the Korowai of Papua, 46–47

Emberá, 6, 18–19, 57–79, **59**, **61**, **69**, 263, 267
embodiment, 39–40, 112, 132, 134, 162, 185, 195–97, 221, 236, 245, 251, 255, 263, 268
ephemera, 21, 220–41, 264, 268
ethnography
"counter-ethnography," 50
global, "indigenous ethnographies," 115
multi-sited, 166, 174
ethnographic present, the, 181–82
of tourism, 2, 5–6, 13, 20, 22, 47, 52, 64, 75n8, 142, 148–49, 166, 173–74, 177, 180–81, 183, 195, 209–10, 212, 225, 250, 261–74
Europe, 3, 9–10, 35, 38, 42, 49–50, 52n2, 58, 65, 97–98n15, 107–8, 117, 156, 194, 197–98, 209–10, 243–55, 255n4, 256n12, 256n16
European Community, 163
Belgium, 10, 22n5
Poland, 119
Switzerland, 10, 127, 129
See also France; Germany; Ireland; Italy; Netherlands; Portugal; United Kingdom
European Union, 244
exhibition, 37, 85–86, 88, 163, 195
colonial, 197–99, 215n17, 215n19
exoticization, 1, 18–19, 31, 36, 38, 57–79, 264, 267, 269
self-exoticization, 91
expats, 15, 173, 187, 223–24, 228, 230, 233, 235, 237, 239
expectation, 3, 16–17, 42, 57–74, 80, 84–91, 97n12, 98n18, 105, 108, 131–32, 134, 151, 157, 159, 261, 266–70, 275n6

Fabian, Johannes, 172, 183–85
fantasies, 1–4, 8–11, 17, 22n1, 41, 84, 89, 105, 126, 136, 151, 214n7, 234–35, 260–61, 266

"fantasmatics," 4
fetish, 220, 221, 239
fieldwork (ethnographic), 6, 50, 52,
    57, 67, 74n1, 82, 127, 141–42,
    175, 180–81, 190n8, 207, 212,
    220–21, 239n1, 255n3, 267. *See also*
    ethnography
film, 1, 7, 22n5, 37, 74, 88, 103–4, 114,
    176. *See also* documentary
France, 6, 22–23n5, 37, 70, 104, 108–
    11, 116–17, 184, 209–10, 216n20
frontstage, 38, 70

gaze. *See under* anthropologist; host;
    tourist
Geertz, Clifford, 174, 181, 260
geography, 5, 7, 71, 106, 108, 119, 147,
    150, 161, 166, 173, 177, 183, 186,
    265
    moral, 242, 252
Germany, 34–35, 70–71, 75n6, 248
globalization, 64, 73, 84, 105–8, 139–
    40, 148, 173, 179, 181, 204, 242
    Giddens, 179
Graburn, Nelson, 6, 9, 22n4–5, 39–40,
    50, 52, 58, 74, 84–86, 103, 133,
    136, 165–66, 172, 177, 190n8, 197,
    223, 225, 245, 248, 251–52, 266
guidebook, 1, 7–8, 12–13, 107, 110,
    112–14, 173, 175–77, 179–80, 184,
    190n4

happiness, 75n7, 115, 119, 231, 236–37
Hawaii, 88, 97–98n15
Hegel, Georg, 149, 151
Heidegger, Martin, 3, 196, 212
heritage
    cultural, 6, 19, 81, 85–86, 88, 93, 96,
        108, 111, 115, 116, 119–21, 149,
        183, 189, 195, 244–46, 251, 256n8,
        270–71
    intangible, 5, 110, 115–17, 119
    natural, 110–11, 189, 244, 248, 250–
        52, 256n8, 264

politics, 96n4
world, 271
history, 8, 10, 13, 15, 20, 42, 50–51,
    60, 65, 68, 74, 81, 86–88, 97n9,
    104, 107–11, 128–31, 154, 162,
    172–90n4, 194, 199–201, 207–8,
    212, 222, 225, 244, 248, 251, 263,
    265, 267–68
host
    accounts, 52, 90, 189n1, 230
    gaze, **14**, 38–39, 98n18
    imaginaries, 13, 16, 31–53, 57–58,
        73–74, 86, 91, 93, 128, 231–34,
        264, 267
    role, 15, 71, 149, 229, 251

identity, 6, 13, 16, 19, 57–58, 64, 67, 84,
    91–93, 97n10, 105–8, 110, 117–18,
    130–31, 142, 195–201, 212, 214,
    222, 224–25, 243–46, 252, 254,
    261, 264, 267, 275n2
    global citizen, 106
    and marketing, 58, 87, 91, 108
    and space, 196, 201
image, 1, 2, 4, 5, 7–8, 10–13, 15–21,
    22n5, 36, 42, 51
    "destination image," "place image,"
        58, 62, 72, 74, 87, 106, 108–9, 114,
        117, 132, 134, 137–38, 147–67,
        172, 174–76, 184–85, 190n10, 209,
        223–37, 239, 243, 245–46, 255,
        261, 263–67, 269, 271, 272–74
    image-maker, 4
    imagery, 5, 8, 37–39, 208, 227, 228,
        261–62, 266, 270, 272, 273–74
    self-image, 5, 261, 264, 274
imaginaire dialectic, 20, 147, 150–52,
    164–67n2, 225, 267
imaginaries, 167, 197, 202, 275n3
    allotemporal, 10, 12, 21, 172,
        183–85
    anthropological, 2, 5, 13, 15, 18–19,
        22, 32, 37, 49, 58, 104, 114, 118–19,
        142, 212, 265, 269, 272–74, 275n1

and arts, 8, 12, 37, 82, 85–86, 88–89, 92, 110, 157–58, 163–64, 202, 211, 268, 270

circulation of, 1–3, 5, 7–13, 17–18, 22, 22n5, 37–38, 40, 58, 74, 103, 114, 149, 153, 165, 172, 207, 225, 248, 261–62, 264, 266, 268, 273–74, 275n4

collective, 3–4, 7–8, 15, 20, 31, 38, 87, 162, 201, 238, 261, 264, 270–73

construction of, 2, 5–8, 12–13, 15–19, 22n2, 37, 46, 80–81, 86–89, 92, 108, 112, 153, 226, 255, 267–68

counterimaginary, 267

and discourses, 1–3, 8, 10, 16, 18, 21, 22n5, 36, 131, 225, 261–62, 265, 271–72, 274

double bind, 19, 86, 90, 93, 97n12

global, 8, 11, 16, 58, 103, 105, 119, 261, 270

and images, 1–2, 7–8, 10–13, 15–21, 38, 41–42, 44, 49, 51, 74, 87, 106, 108, 114, 151–54, 156, 158, 165, 208–9, 224, 227, 239, 261–62, 264, 267–68, 270–4

individual, 1, 3–4, 12, 18–19, 165, 167, 176, 201, 225, 254, 261–62, 267, 272–73

institutional, 2–3, 7, 11, 13, 17, 19, 103, 105, 107–8, 112, 119, 133, 158, 165, 207–8, 225, 263, 267–68

and media, 7–12, 15, 21, 22n5, 27n4, 37, 41–42, 74, 85, 87–88, 110, 113–14, 158, 163–64, 207

and morality, 125–44

and narratives, 1, 7–12, 19, 21, 39, 42, 44, 81, 86, 104, 110, 112, 114, 151–54, 158, 176, 197, 211–12, 223, 229, 262–63, 271–72, 274, 275n2, 275n4

and practices, 4, 7, 12, 17, 39–42, 44, 81, 106, 110, 131, 268, 271, 273–74

self-imaginary, 12, 16

and space, 1–4, 6–12, 15–22, 36, 39, 42, 51, 60, 83, 86–87, 104, 107, 121, 148, 165, 172–73, 176–77, 184, 188, 195, 197, 199, 211, 235, 244, 248, 251, 263–64, 268, 271, 273, 275n4; "paracity," 198

and time, 8–12, 15, 18, 20–21, 36, 39, 49, 81, 83, 85–87, 104, 130–31, 165, 172–93, 197, 267–68

tourism vs. tourist, 264–65

tourist vs. host, 2, 7, 9–10, 13, 15–16, 18–19, 21, 31–32, 36, 38–39, 41, 46, 73, 82, 84, 87, 89, 92, 97n14, 136, 223, 239, 255, 261, 263–64, 268–71

See also Internet, the: cyber tourism

imaginarium, 19, 22, 103–21, 225, 267

imaginative reconstruction, 8, 252

India, 8–9, 182, 188, 194, 214n8

indigeneity, 19, 60, 67, 73, 97n10, 104–8, 118, 121, 121n2

interaction, 7, 13, 17–18, 32, 35, 37, 41, 45–46, 53n5, 71, 84–85, 97n18, 132, 148, 155, 167, 184, 242, 261–62, 265, 267–71, 273

Internet, the, 72, 75n8, 114, 117–19
  imaginariums, 118
  cyber tourism, 118, 155, 209–10
  See also blogs; computer; technology; websites

Ireland, 153, 155, 157–59, 167

Italy, 5–6, 20–21, 70–71, 75n6, 147–71, 172–73, 176–77, 180, 187–88, 189n2, 233, 263
  Florence, 10
  See also Italian Americans; Pietrelcina

Italian Americans, 153, 156, 164, 167, 198, 206, 210, 246

Japan, 10, 65, 112–13
  Kyoto and Nara, 10

Kirshenblatt-Gimblett, Barbara, 37, 88–89, 148–49, 245

Korea, 112, 119

Korowai, 18, 31–53n5, **33**, **34**, **43**, 263, 269

Lacan, Jacques, 45, 126, 151, 237, 260–61
landscape, 4, 16, 21, 32, 39, 41, 83, 91,104, 105, 107, 110–14, 118, 161, 179, 186–87, 197, 212, 242–55n5, 261–62, 266, 268–69
    cultural, 105, 251, 253, 264
    and identity, 246–47
language, 7, 11, 23–24n5, 35, 41, 64, 67, 70, 75n6, 81, 83, 86, 88, 98n20, 106–7, 109–13, 116, 118, 121n4, 122n8, 127, 139–40, 147, 199, 202, 204, 207, 210–14
Las Vegas, 195, 198–99, 211
Latour, Bruno, 3, 50, 52
Leite, Naomi, 8, 21–22, 53n3, 58, 121, 132–33, 166, 223–24, 238, 253
liminality, 86, 90, 149, 151, 177
literature, 1, 7–8, 21, 74, 103–5, 111, 113–14, 118, 158, 173, 175, 179–80, 210–11, 252, 256n17, 265, 275n4
local, the, 1–2, 6, 11–13, 15–20, 35, 49, 51, 58–60, 66, 71–73, 83, 87, 90–91, 93, 103, 105, 107–8, 115–16, 119–21, 126–29, 131, 137–40, 149–50, 152, 154–55, 161–64, 174, 179–80, 183, 187, 214n6, 222–36, 242–43, 249, 251, 254, 261, 264, 267–68

MacCannell, Dean, 38, 41, 51, 70, 148
magazine, 7, 37, 155, 163, 177, 226. *See also* National Geographic
materiality, 150, 152
media, 2, 4, 6–8, 10, 15, 33, 35, 37, 41–42, 51, 81, 85, 150, 155, 157, 163, 201, 261–62, 266
    mass, 11, 62, 85, 155 (*see also* film; television)
    print (*see* magazine; newspaper)
    See also blogs; websites
mediation theory, 149

methodology, 18, 22, 141, 147, 166, 173, 183, 224
metropolitanism, 42
migration, 104
    emigration, 209, 216n20, 271
    immigration, 209
    See also expats
missionary, 32, 75n9, 108–9, 111, 117, 165, 270
modernity, 4, 9–10, 13, 15, 20, 37, 50–51, 53n4, 60–62, 64, 66–68, 72, 87, 105–6, 109, 121, 125–26, 130–33, 135–36, 141–42, 157, 183–84, 207, 220, 242, 249, 252, 263, 266
    post-, 9, 13, 21, 181, 197, 199, 229
    pre-, 21, 60, 68, 72, 185
morality. *See under* imaginaries
Mozambique, 19, 125–43n4, **138**, 208–9, 214n8, 263, 268
museum, 7, 81, 85, 88–89, 103, 115, 175, 216n23, 245
    and imaginaries, 2, 13, 103
    "museumizing," 96n4
    tourist destinations as museums of themselves, 10, 12–13, 81
    Family of Man, 275
myth, 1, 3–4, 8, 10, 15, 19, 103–24, 130, 176, 220, 233, 250–55, 265–67, 274

narrative, 7, 11, 19–20, 86–87, 94, 106, 109, 127–28, 147, 149, 151–55, 157–59, 162–65, 172, 176–77, 181–84, 189, 195–97, 205, 211–12, 215n5, 221–23, 229, 234, 251, 253–54, 261–63, 265–67, 272–74, 275n6
    Heidegger and Ricoeur's concepts of, 195
    metanarrative, 266
National Geographic, 7, 37, 42, 82, 86, 233, 269
nature, 1, 4, 9–12, 15, 17, 21, 39–42, 60, 62, 80–81, 84, 111, 118, 140, 179, 206, 223, 242–59

development, 244, 247, 249, 253
  as "host," 245
  management, 243, 247–50, 252–53
  reserve, 44, 247–50, 253–54,
    256n8–9
  tourism, 244, 249, 255n2 (*see also*
    recreation)
  See also conservation; ecology; wild;
    wilderness
Netherlands, the, 21, 197, 242–44,
  247–48, 251–56. *See also* Serengeti,
  the: "Dutch Serengeti, the"
newspaper, 22n5, 37, 152, 200, 232
New World, the, 42
nongovernmental organization (NGO),
  15, 63, 75n9, 115, 126–34, 137–42,
  179, 232, 255n1, 268
non-West, 9, 17, 198
non-Western imaginaries, 17, 38
"North," the, 20, 125–26, 134, 136,
  138, 140, 142
North America, 9, 65, 70–71, 82, 165
nostalgia, 6, 8, 51, 57, 65, 67, 72, 87,
  104, 107, 110–11, 135, 185, 207,
  246
  "imperialist nostalgia," 6, 8, 72, 87
nudity, 18, 41–50, 53n4–5, 67, 116,
  205–6

Orientalism, 8, 18, 84, 149, 183, 186,
  188
Other, the/Otherness, 1, 8–9, 12,
  16–18, 35–36, 38–48, 54, 55, 58,
  60, 71, 73–74, 80, 83–88, 90, 93,
  97n14, 104, 106, 109, 120, 134,
  149, 151, 172, 178, 180, 182–84,
  187–88, 198, 202, 208, 213, 227,
  236, 245, 250, 261, 263–64, 266,
  268, 270
Othering, 2, 74, 245, 250, 257, 261,
  263–64, 268, 270

Panama, 57–79
  Embera of, 6, 18, 63

Papua, 18, 31–56
  Korowai lands in, **33**
  politics in, 34–35
paradise, 4, 21, 40, 53n4, 104, 185,
  224–28, 235–39, 264–66
payment, 18, 31, 41, 43–46, 48, 63–64,
  71, 89, 91, 128, 143n4
performance, 35, 46–48, 52, 68, 72, 81,
  85–90, 92–93, 97n8, 97–98n15,
  110, 112, 114–15, 119, 127, 134,
  149, 163, 181, 196, 212–13, 228,
  230–31, 233–34, 245, 265, 268, 270
photography, 7, 12, 34, 37, 39, 41, 44,
  48, 50, 66, 70–72, 109, 114, 116–17,
  119, 148–49, 185, 191n14, 206,
  209, 227, 268
  Family of Man, 275n5
  Internet survey, 209–210
Pietrelcina, Italy, 147–67, **160**, 263
pilgrim, 152–53, 155, 157–59, 162, 167
pilgrimage, 20, 153–54, 161, 165, 167,
  184
  pseudo-religious, 87
Pio of Pietrelcina, St., 150, 152–67,
  160, 275n4
place, 4, 6, 16–18, 20–21, 39, 51, 53n3,
  92, 103, 105–7, 121, 147–48,
  151–53, 165, 174, 177, 179, 183–84,
  195–99, 202, 204, 210–12, 214n6,
  215n15, 242–43, 245, 249–51
  performativity and, 245
  space as, 196
pleasure, 37, 51, 227, 229–31, 234–36,
  243
politics, 2, 3, 15–17, 21, 34, 63, 89, 104–
  6, 111–12, 119–20, 122n6, 126–27,
  130, 132, 154, 163, 166, 174, 189,
  190n3, 194, 201, 208–9, 212,
  223–25, 237–39, 242–44, 252–54,
  256n12, 256n14, 265–66, 271
  heritage, 96n4
  identity, 201
Portugal, 21, 194–219, 264
  Coimbra, 194

Salazar Estado Novo regime, 194,
199–201, 205, 208, 210–11
Portugal dos Pequenitos, 194–219,
200, 203, 206
Internet photography survey of, 209
world's fairs and, 215n16, 215n17
postcolonialism, 6, 21, 104–6
in Africa, 149
Cambodia, 149
and colonial imaginary, 194–216
in Sani and Axi tourism, 114–20
postmodernity. *See under* modernity
power, 2, 13, 17, 22, 37, 49, 64, 73, 83–
84, 87, 89, 91, 93–96, 106, 108, 118,
120–21, 130, 134, 137, 139, 142,
156, 165, 197, 207, 220, 222, 224,
226, 230, 238, 251, 260, 271–72
practice, 4, 17, 32, 47, 53n5, 59, 62–64,
70–71, 74–75n4, 90, 92, 106, 128,
131–32, 149–50, 156, 164, 173,
184, 244–46, 250, 253–54, 255n2,
261, 268, 271, 273–74, 275n6
Pratt, Mary Louise, 148–49
pre-colonialism, 88, 97n10
preservation
cultural, 119, 271
ecological, 95
historical, 162–63, 271
primitivism, 9–10, 19, 33, 35–43, 52n2,
53n4–5, 58, 60, 64–65, 67, 72–73,
104, 118, 248, 253, 261, 263,
266–68

realism, 198, 211, 231
recreation, 21, 135, 244–45, 249–50,
253, 255n2
religion, 3, 7, 15, 20, 35, 110, 112, 147,
150, 152, 165, 243, 260
Christianity, 42, 184, 211, 270
pseudo-religious pilgrimage, 87
tourists and coreligionists, 270–71
See also Catholicism; missionary
representation, 3–8, 19–20, 22n2, 31,
35, 38, 42, 52–53n2, 58, 62, 65,

73, 88–89, 91, 93, 98n18, 103,
117–18, 128, 134, 149–51, 174, 179,
181, 188, 195, 197, 210–11, 222–30,
246, 261–62, 275n4
cultural, 5, 65, 73, 81, 94, 98n18, 261,
265–74
Ricoeur, Paul, 3, 196, 212
romanticism, 8, 11, 52–53n2, 62, 67,
87, 148, 159, 175, 184–85, 222,
248, 250
and cultural denigration, 267
Rosaldo, Renato, 6, 8, 72, 177

Said, Edward, 4, 38, 149, 186
Salazar, Noel, 5, 22n5, 39–40, 50, 52,
58, 74, 84–85, 103, 133, 149, 151,
165–66, 172, 177, 197, 216n23, 223,
225, 238, 245, 248, 251–53, 262,
266, 271
San Giovanni Rotondo, 20, 150, 152–
59, 161–67, 275n4
Sani Yi, 19, 103, 108–20, **113, 120,**
121n4, 268
seduction, 1, 21, 148, 220, 222–27,
229–31, 234–35, 239
self, 42, 47, 58, 60, 71, 91, 151, 183–84,
196, 199, 186, 211, 213, 263–64, 271
Bourdieuian, 210–11
Heideggerian, 196
Ricoeurian, 196
Selwyn, Tom, 104, 265–67
Serengeti, the, 248, 253–54, 256n12
"Dutch Serengeti, the," 21,
242–56n8
sexuality, 9, 109, 206, 229, 231
eroticism, 18, 43, 228–29
Shilin (Stone Forest), 103–24, **113, 120**
Smith, Valene, 148
Sociology, 6, 135
"South," the, 128, 134, 136, 140, 270
South America, 194. *See* Brazil
Southeast Asia, 173, 175–76, 178, 184,
186–87
Indochina, 185, 190n9, 191n15

souvenir, 12, 81, 87, 109, 111–112, 114, 148, 180, 220, 226–27, 239, 265, 268

stereotype, 38–41, 45–46, 52–53n2, 58, 60–61, 64–66, 71, 73–74, 84, 87, 93–94, 104, 184, 186, 252
   challenge of by tour guides, 92
   rainforest life, 65

Strauss, Claudia, 3, 261–62

Swain, Margaret Byrne, 13, 19, 22, 225, 238, 262, 267–68, 272–74, 275n3

symmetry,18, 31–57

Taylor, Charles, 19, 132–33, 260–61

technology, 60–61, 67, 70, 73, 85, 109, 189, 236

television, 37, 42, 62, 67, 90, 115–17, 155–56, 158, 163–64, 191n15, 231, 233

textbooks, 7, 23n5, 207–8

Theodossopoulos, Dimitrios, 6, 13, 18–19, 40, 176, 212, 263–64, 267, 269, 271–74

Tibet, 9, 108, 110, 118, 121n2, 175

time, 10–11, 18–21, 36, 39, 62, 81, 86, 92, 104, 150–51, 165, 172–89, 197, 202, 204, 213, 220, 226, 246, 253, 268
   secularization of, 184

time-place, 197, 220, 226–27

time-space, compression and distantiation, 173, 177–78, 183, 188, 263

Tjapukai Aboriginal Cultural Park, 19, 80–98n19, 267

tour guide, 5, 7, 35, 45–46, 53n5, 64–66, 68–71, 75n6, 81–82, 91–92, 116, 139, 149, 155, 173, 177–78, 187–89n2, 264, 267

touree. *See* host

tourism
   community-based, 95, 97n8, 125–29, 133, 136–38, 263
   cultural, 9, 16, 31, 37, 51–52, 62–64,

66, 74n1, 80–93, 97n15, 103–24, 180, 185, 268

development, 19, 57, 63, 82–83, 94–95, 104–5, 108–12, 114–15, 117–18, **120**, 120, 126, 130–32, 149, 153–54, 174, 237, 263, 268

discourse, 8, 11, 118, 121, 148, 173, 180, 186

domestic, 65, 67, 72, 80, 103, 107, 111, 115–16, 119, 121, 149, 195, 214, 243–55n2, 269

eco-, 8–9, 95, 104, 116, 120, 125

ethical, 125–26, 132–33, 136, 139, 141

ethnic, 9, 19, 52, 103–24, 180, 185, 188, 268

heritage, 103–24, 251, 270–72

indigenous, 37, 57–58, 60, 62–63, 74n1, 75n5, 82–98n22, 103–24, 263, 167

mythical, 103–24

reality, 271–72

roots, 209–10, 271–72, 275n6

stakeholder, 15, 115, 121, 149, 166, 251

sustainable, 179

"voluntourism," 270, 272

tourist
   accounts, 8, 20, 81–82, 84–91, 96n2, 157–59, 172–74, 176, 179–80, 182, 184, 187–88, 189n2, 207, 210, 216n21, 247
   gaze, 7, 13, 19, 50, 72, 81–82, 84, 87, 91, 95, 98n18, 166, 180, 186 (*see also* anthropologist: gaze)
   as Other, 250
   posttourist, 199, 210, 213, 215n9
   role, 16, 32, 251, 253, 266
   TripAdvisor, 82, 96n2, 97n11, 98n19, 210, 216n21

tropicalization, 21, 222–39

UNESCO, 111, 149, 248
   world heritage site, 111, 271

unintentional primitivization, 19, 58, 72

United Kingdom, 22–23n5
  England, 6, 10, 70, 230
  Oxford, 10
United States, 87, 97–98n15, 112, 119,
    148, 158, 167, 198–99, 210–11, 246,
    249
  Alaska, 97n15
  See also American West; Hawaii; Las
    Vegas; North America
United States Agency for International
    Development (USAID), 127
urban, 48, 60, 66, 115, 120, 155–56,
    163, 190n4, 198–99, 202, 211

video games, 7, 176
virtual, the, 235–38, 244–45

websites, 7, 36, 82, 96n1, 96n2, 96n3,
    97n7, 97n9, 97n1, 98n16–17,
    98n22, 111, 116, 118, 167, 173, 188.
    See also blogs; computer; Internet;
    technology

West, the, 7–10, 17, 38, 50, 52, 53n4,
    58, 60, 62, 64–65, 71–73, 81,
    83, 86–87, 89–91, 93, 97n14–15,
    105–6, 109, 111, 121, 133–34, 149,
    183–85, 189, 248, 251, 254, 261
  clothing, 26, 73, 263
  See also American West, the;
    non-West
wild, the, 103, 242–59
  rewilding, 21, 242, 244, 247, 249–53,
    255n1, 255n4, 256n12, 264
  performance of, 245–46, 253
wilderness, 10, 21, 134, 247–49, 251,
    253
  tourism (*see under* nature)
  new (*see* wild, the: rewilding)

Yunnan, 103–129, 267, 269. *See also*
  China

Zomia, 103, 107–9, 118